IMPORTANT

ETS sends free test preparation material to each individual who registers for the GRE General Test. A CD-ROM containing *GRE POWERPREP Software – Test Preparation for the GRE General Test* is sent to individuals who register for the computer-based GRE General Test. The *GRE Practice General Test* book is sent to individuals who register for the paper-based GRE General Test. A free downloadable version of each is also available to anyone who visits the GRE Web site at **www.gre.org/pracmats.html.**

This publication contains the same information about how to prepare for the General Test, test-taking strategies, question strategies, etc., that is included in the free test preparation materials mentioned above. It also provides you with additional practice. It contains the verbal and quantitative sections from seven full-length paper-based GRE General Test editions, including two sections of each that are complete with explanations. It also contains two sample analytical writing topics and two analytical writing sections complete with scored sample essays at selected score points.

The verbal and quantitative sections in the GRE General Tests in this book contain questions written and administered prior to 1995. For this reason, some of the material covered in the questions may be dated. For example, a question may refer to a rapidly changing technology in a way that was correct in the 1980s and early 1990s, but not now. In addition, ETS has revised and updated its standards and guidelines for test questions so some questions may not meet current standards. Questions that do not meet current ETS standards, and would not appear in GRE tests administered today, are marked with an asterisk.

**For the latest information about the GRE General Test
and other GRE products and services,
visit the GRE Web site at
www.gre.org.**

Table of Contents

Table of Contents continued

Purpose of the GRE General Test

The GRE General Test is designed to help graduate school admission committees and fellowship sponsors assess the qualifications of applicants to their programs. It measures verbal, quantitative, and analytical writing skills that you have acquired over a long period of time.

Any accredited graduate or professional school, or any department or division within a school, may require or recommend that its applicants take the GRE General Test. The scores can be used by admissions or fellowship panels to supplement undergraduate records and other qualifications for graduate study. The scores provide common measures for comparing the qualifications of applicants and aid in the evaluation of grades and recommendations.

Structure of the General Test

Computer-Based General Test

The computer-based General Test contains four sections, one of which is an unidentified pretest section that can appear in any position in the test after the analytical writing section. Questions in the pretest section are being pretested for possible use in future tests and answers will not count toward your score. An identified research section that is not scored may also be included and this section would always appear at the end of the test. Questions in the research section are included for the purpose of ETS research and answers will not count toward your score.

Total testing time is up to 3 1/4 hours, not including the research section. The directions at the beginning of each section specify the total number of questions in the section and the time allowed for the section. The analytical writing section will always be first. For the Issue task, two essay topics will be presented and you will choose one. The Argument task does not present a choice of topics; instead, one topic will be presented. The verbal and quantitative sections may appear in any order, including an unidentified verbal or quantitative pretest section. Treat each section presented during your test as if it counts.

Typical Computer-Based General Test

Section	Number of Questions	Time
Analytical Writing	1 Issue task*	45 min.
	1 Argument task*	30 min.
Verbal	30	30 min.
Quantitative	28	45 min.
Pretest**	Varies	Varies
Research***	Varies	Varies

*   For the Issue task, two essay topics will be presented and you will choose one. The Argument task does not present a choice of topics; instead, one topic will be presented.
** An unidentified verbal or quantitative pretest section may be included and may appear in any order. It is not counted as part of your score.
*** An identified research section that is not scored may be included and it will always be at the end of the test.

Paper-Based General Test

In certain areas of the world, where computer-based testing is not available, the General Test is offered at paper-based administrations. The paper-based GRE General Test contains five sections. In addition, one unidentified pretest section may be included and this section can appear in any position in the test after the analytical writing section. Questions in the pretest section are being tested for possible use in future tests and answers will not count toward your score.

Total testing time is up to 3 3/4 hours. The directions at the beginning of each section specify the total number of questions in the section and the time allowed for the section. The analytical writing section will always be first. For the Issue task, two topics will be presented and you will choose one. The Argument task does not present a choice of topics; instead, one topic will be presented. The verbal and quantitative sections may appear in any order, including an unidentified verbal or quantitative pretest section. Treat each section presented during your test as if it counts.

Typical Paper-Based General Test

Section	Number of Questions	Time
Analytical Writing	1 Issue task*	45 min.
	1 Argument task*	30 min.
Verbal (2 sections)	38 per section	30 min. per section
Quantitative (2 sections)	30 per section	30 min. per section
Pretest**	Varies	30 min.

* For the Issue task, two essay topics will be presented and you will choose one. The Argument task does not present a choice of topics; instead, one topic will be presented.

** An unidentified verbal or quantitative pretest section may be included and may appear in any order after the analytical writing section. It is not counted as part of your score.

Scores Reported

Three scores are reported on the General Test:

1. a verbal score reported on a 200-800 score scale, in 10-point increments,
2. a quantitative score reported on a 200-800 score scale, in 10-point increments, and
3. an analytical writing score reported on a 0-6 score scale, in half-point increments.

If you answer no questions at all in a section (verbal, quantitative, or analytical writing), that section will be reported as a No Score (NS).

Descriptions of the analytical writing abilities characteristic of particular score levels are available in this publication on page 400, in the interpretive leaflet enclosed with your score report, in the *Guide to the Use of GRE Scores*, and on the GRE Web site at **www.gre.org**.

If you take the computer-based General Test, you will receive your unofficial verbal and quantitative scores at the test center; however, because of the essay scoring process, you will not receive your analytical writing score at that time. Official verbal, quantitative, and analytical writing scores will be sent to you and score recipients within 10 to 15 days after you take the test. However, the score reporting timeframe for test takers who choose to handwrite essay responses is up to six weeks.

If you take the paper-based General Test, scores will be sent to you and score recipients within six weeks after you take the test.

Beginning in July 2003, essay responses on the analytical writing section of the General Test will be sent to designated score recipients. If you test on or after July 1, 2003, your essay responses from your current and previous General Test administrations will be sent as part of your cumulative score record.

Preparing for the GRE General Test

Preparation for the test will depend upon the amount of time you have available and your personal preferences for how to prepare. At a minimum, before you take the GRE General Test, you should know what to expect from the test, including the administrative procedures, types of questions and directions, the approximate number of questions, and the amount of time for each section.

   The administrative procedures include registration and appointment scheduling, date, time, test center location, cost, score-reporting procedures, and availability of special testing arrangements. You can find out about the administrative procedures for the computer-based General Test in the *GRE Information and Registration Bulletin*. You can find out about the administrative procedures for the paper-based General Test in the *Supplement to the Bulletin*. Information is also available online at **www.gre.org**, or by calling Educational Testing Service (see the *GRE Information and Registration Bulletin* for telephone information).

   Before taking the GRE General Test, it is important to become familiar with the content of each of the sections of the test. You can become familiar with the verbal and quantitative sections by reading about the skills the sections measure, how the sections are scored, reviewing the strategies for each of the question types, and reviewing the sample questions with explanations. Determine which strategies work best for you. Remember — you can do very well on the test without answering every question in each section correctly.

   Everyone — even the most practiced and confident of writers — should spend some time preparing for the analytical writing section before arriving at the test center. It is important to review the skills measured, how the section is scored, scoring guides and score level descriptions, sample topics, scored sample essay responses, and reader commentary.

   To help you prepare for the analytical writing section of the GRE General Test, the GRE Program has published the entire pool of topics from which your test topics will be selected. You might find it helpful to review the entire Issue and Argument pools and to discuss some of the topics with a friend or teacher. You can view the published pools on the GRE Web site at **www.gre.org/pracmats.html** or you can obtain a copy by writing to GRE Program, PO Box 6000, Princeton, NJ 08541-6000.

   The topics in the analytical writing section relate to a broad range of subjects — from the fine arts and humanities to the social and physical sciences — but no topic requires specific content knowledge. In fact, each topic has been field-tested to ensure that it possesses several important characteristics, including the following:

- GRE test takers, regardless of their field of study or special interests, understood the topic and could easily discuss it.
- The topic elicited the kinds of complex thinking and persuasive writing that university faculty consider important for success in graduate school.
- The responses were varied in content and in the way the writers developed their ideas.

Test-Taking Strategies for the Computer-Based GRE General Test

IMPORTANT NOTE: Test-taking strategies appropriate for the verbal and quantitative sections of the computer-based GRE General Test are different from those that are appropriate for the verbal and quantitative sections of the paper-based GRE General Test. Be sure to follow the appropriate strategies for the testing format in which you will be testing. Computer-based testing strategies should not be used if you take the paper-based test.

Tutorials

The computer tutorial is included in the *GRE POWERPREP* software that will be sent to you when you register for the computer-based General Test. The tutorial teaches you how to use the features of the computer system to your advantage. You will find the system very easy to use, even if you have no prior computer experience. The ability to type is not necessary to the computer-based General Test. The tutorial shows you how to use a mouse to click on the appropriate area of your screen.

When you arrive at the test center on the test day, you will have the opportunity to complete an untimed computer tutorial before the actual test begins. Take all the time you need with the tutorial *before* you begin the test — even if you feel quite comfortable using computers; there might be differences between the testing software and software you normally use. You may return to any part of the tutorial, even after you begin work on the test sections, by clicking on the "Help" box at the bottom of your screen. However, any time you spend on the tutorial *after* you begin a test section will reduce the amount of time available for work on that section.

Some questions, graphs, or passages are too large to appear completely on the computer screen. In that case a "scroll bar" appears to the right of the material and the word "Beginning" appears on the information line at the top of the screen. These are your cues to scroll for more information. During the tutorial, make sure you learn how to scroll both slowly (line by line) and quickly (page by page) so that you can move to areas of text at the speed you desire.

If you choose to type your responses in the analytical writing section, pay attention to the tutorials for that section. It describes the question area, the typing box, and word processing tools.

Verbal and Quantitative Sections

In the computer-based GRE General Test, the verbal and quantitative sections are adaptive. At the start of each section, you will be presented with a test question of medium difficulty. If you answer that question correctly, the next question typically will be one of greater difficulty. If you answer the first question incorrectly, the next question typically will be one of lesser difficulty. As you answer each question, the computer scores the question and uses that information, as well as your responses to any preceding questions and information about the test design, to determine which question will be presented next. The computer does not always select a harder question when you answer a question correctly or an easier question when you answer incorrectly. This is because the test design includes several factors in addition to the difficulty level of the questions. The computer-adaptive sections are designed so that the questions you see are influenced by three factors:

- the difficulty level of the questions already answered (correctly and incorrectly)
- the required variety of question types
- the coverage of specific content

After answering any question, your next question will be the one that best reflects both your previous performance and the requirements of the test design. This means that different test takers will be given different questions.

Answering a question is a three-step process. First click on the oval next to your answer choice or click on any part of the text of that answer choice. Finish answering the question by clicking on "Next" and, then, "Answer Confirm." You can change your answer by clicking on a different answer choice any time before clicking on "Answer Confirm."

Because each question the computer selects for you is determined by your answers to previous questions, you cannot move on to the next question before you answer the question that appears on your screen. If you do not know the answer to a question, the only way to continue your test is to eliminate as many answer choices as possible and then select the answer you think is best. Remember — do not spend too much time on any one question.

Also, once you answer a question and confirm your response, you cannot return to that question and change your answer. The computer has already scored that answer and used it as a factor in selecting succeeding questions.

Budget enough time for each question so you can complete the test without having to rush at the end of each section. Some question types, such as reading comprehension, may take more time than others. The practice tests in the *GRE POWERPREP* software should help you determine the average amount of time you may want to spend per question as well as how much time to spend on each type of question.

Use your time wisely; don't rush. Remind yourself that answering one question correctly is better than hurrying to answer three questions and answering them incorrectly.

Read each question carefully to determine exactly what is being asked. Eliminate the wrong answers and select the best choice. Don't spend too much time on any one question. The last thing you want to do is waste valuable time on any one question. If, after you've given a question a reasonable amount of thought, you don't know the answer, eliminate as many answer choices as possible and then select and confirm the answer you think is best.

If you are running out of time at the end of a section, make every effort to complete the test. Data indicate that most test takers get higher scores if they finish the test. In fact, based on analyses of test takers, a majority will score higher if they finish the test than if they do not attempt to answer all of the questions. There is a chance that guessing at the end of the test can seriously lower your score. The best strategy is to pace yourself so you have time to consider each test question, and won't have to guess.

Analytical Writing Section

On the computer-based GRE General Test the two issue topics from which you will choose to write your response will appear on the computer screen. You will be given the option to type or handwrite your essay responses. In deciding whether to type or handwrite your responses, be aware that it may take significantly longer (up to six weeks) to report scores for handwritten responses. In the testing session, once you have confirmed your choice of whether to handwrite or type, you cannot change your response mode and you will utilize that mode for both the Issue and the Argument tasks.

It is important to budget your time. Within the 45-minute time limit for the Issue task, you will need to allow sufficient time to choose one of the two topics, think about the issue you've chosen, plan a response, and compose your essay. Within the 30-minute time limit for the Argument task, you will need to allow sufficient time to analyze the argument, plan a critique, and compose your response. Although GRE readers understand the time constraints under which you write and will consider your response a "first draft," you still want it to be the best possible example of your writing that you can produce under the testing circumstances.

Save a few minutes at the end of each timed section to check for obvious errors. Although an occasional typographical, spelling, or grammatical error will not affect your score, severe and persistent errors will detract from the overall effectiveness of your writing and thus lower your score.

Following the analytical writing section, an on-screen message will inform you of the opportunity to take a 10-minute break. There is a one-minute break between the other test sections. You might want to replenish your supply of scratch paper during each scheduled break. Section timing will not stop if you take an unscheduled break, so you should proceed with your test without interruption once it begins.

Test-Taking Strategies for the Paper-Based GRE General Test

Verbal and Quantitative Sections

When taking a verbal or quantitative section of the paper-based GRE General Test, you are free, within any section, to skip questions that you might have difficulty answering and to come back to them later during the time provided to work on that section. You may also change the answer to any question you recorded on the answer sheet by erasing it completely and filling in the oval corresponding to your desired answer for that question.

Each of your scores will be determined by the number of questions for which you select the best answer from the choices given. Questions for which you mark no answer or more than one answer are not counted in scoring. Nothing is subtracted from a score if you answer a question incorrectly. Therefore, to maximize your scores on the verbal and quantitative sections of the paper-based test, it is better for you to answer each and every question and not to leave any questions unanswered.

Work as rapidly as you can without being careless. This includes checking frequently to make sure you are marking your answers in the appropriate rows on your answer sheet. Since no question carries greater weight than any other, do not waste time pondering individual questions you find extremely difficult or unfamiliar.

You may want to work through a verbal or quantitative section of the GRE General Test quite rapidly, first answering only the questions about which you feel confident, then going back and answering questions that require more thought, and concluding with the most difficult.

During the actual administration of the GRE General Test, you may work only on the section the test center supervisor designates and only for the time allowed. You may not go back to an earlier section of the test after the supervisor announces, "Please stop work" for that section. The supervisor is authorized to dismiss you from the center for doing so. All answers must be recorded on your answer sheet. Answers recorded in your test booklet will not be counted. Given the time constraints, you should avoid waiting until the last five minutes of a test administration to record answers on your answer sheet.

Some questions on the GRE General Test have only four response options (A through D). All GRE answer sheets for the paper-based test contain response positions for five responses (A through E). Therefore, if an E response is marked for a four-option question, it will be ignored. An E response for a four-option question is treated the same as no response (omitted).

Analytical Writing Section

In the paper-based GRE General Test, the topics in the analytical writing section will be presented in the test book and you will handwrite your essay responses on the answer sheets provided. Make sure you use the correct answer sheet for each task.

It is important to budget your time. Within the 45-minute time limit for the Issue task, you will need to allow sufficient time to choose one of the two topics, think about the issue you've chosen, plan a response, and compose your essay. Within the 30-minute time limit for the Argument task, you will need to allow sufficient time to analyze the argument, plan a critique, and compose your response. Although GRE readers understand the time constraints under which you write and will consider your response a "first draft," you still want it to be the best possible example of your writing that you can produce under the testing circumstances.

Save a few minutes at the end of each timed task to check for obvious errors. Although an occasional spelling or grammatical error will not affect your score, severe and persistent errors will detract from the overall effectiveness of your writing and thus lower your score.

During the actual administration of the GRE General Test, you may work only on the particular writing task the test center supervisor designates and only for the time allowed. You may not go back to an earlier section of the test after the supervisor announces, "Please stop work" for that task. The supervisor is authorized to dismiss you from the center for doing so.

Following the analytical writing section, you will have the opportunity to take a 10-minute break. There is a one-minute break between the other test sections.

Review of the Verbal Section

Overview

The verbal section measures your ability to analyze and evaluate written material and synthesize information obtained from it, to analyze relationships among component parts of sentences, to recognize relationships between words and concepts, and to reason with words in solving problems. There is a balance of passages across different subject matter areas: humanities, social sciences, and natural sciences.

The verbal section contains the following question types:

- Antonyms
- Analogies
- Sentence Completions
- Reading Comprehension Questions

How the Verbal Section is Scored

Computer-Based General Test

On the computer-based General Test your score on the verbal section will depend on your performance on the questions presented and on the number of questions you answer in the time allotted. Because this section is computer adaptive, the questions are selected to reflect your performance on preceding questions and the requirements of the test design. Test design factors that influence which questions are presented include (1) the statistical characteristics (including difficulty level) of the questions already answered, (2) the required variety of question types, and (3) the appropriate coverage of content. Additional scoring information is provided in the *GRE POWERPREP* software and in the interpretive leaflet enclosed with your score report.

Paper-Based General Test

On the paper-based test scoring of the verbal section is essentially a two-step process. First, a raw score is computed. The raw score is the number of questions for which the best answer choice was given. The raw score is then converted to a scaled score through a process known as equating. The equating process accounts for differences in difficulty among the different test editions; thus, a given scaled score reflects approximately the same level of ability regardless of the edition of the test that was taken.

ANTONYMS

Antonyms measure your

- vocabulary
- ability to reason from a given concept to its opposite

Strategies for Answering

- Remember that antonyms are generally confined to nouns, verbs, and adjectives.
- Look for the word that is most nearly opposite to the given word.
- Try to define words precisely.
- Make up a sentence using the given word to help establish its meaning.
- Look for possible second meanings before choosing an answer.
- Use your knowledge of prefixes and suffixes to help define words you don't know.

Directions: Each question below consists of a word printed in capital letters followed by five lettered words or phrases. Choose the lettered word or phrase that is most nearly *opposite* in meaning to the word in capital letters. Since some of the questions require you to distinguish fine shades of meaning, be sure to consider all the choices before deciding which one is best.

1. DIFFUSE: (A) concentrate (B) contend
   (C) imply (D) pretend (E) rebel

2. MULTIFARIOUS:
   (A) deprived of freedom
   (B) deprived of comfort
   (C) lacking space
   (D) lacking stability
   (E) lacking diversity

Answer to Question 1

The best answer is (A). *Diffuse* means to permit or cause to spread out; only (A) presents an idea that is in any way opposite to *diffuse*.

Answer to Question 2

Multifarious means having or occurring in great variety, so the best answer is (E). Even if you are not entirely familiar with the meaning of *multifarious*, it is possible to use the clue provided by "multi-" to help find the right answer to this question.

ANALOGIES

Analogies measure your ability to recognize

- relationships among words and concepts they represent
- parallel relationships

Strategies for Answering

- Establish a relationship between the given pair before reading the answer choices.
- Consider relationships of kind, size, spatial contiguity, or degree.
- Read all of the options. If more than one seems correct, try to state the relationship more precisely.
- Check to see that you haven't overlooked a possible second meaning for one of the words.
- *Never* decide on the best answer without reading *all* of the answer choices.

Directions: In each of the following questions, a related pair of words or phrases is followed by five lettered pairs of words or phrases. Select the lettered pair that best expresses a relationship similar to that expressed in the original pair.

3. COLOR : SPECTRUM : : (A) tone : scale
   (B) sound : waves (C) verse : poem
   (D) dimension : space (E) cell : organism

4. HEADLONG : FORETHOUGHT : :
   (A) barefaced : shame
   (B) mealymouthed : talent
   (C) heartbroken : emotion
   (D) levelheaded : resolve
   (E) singlehanded : ambition

Answer to Question 3

The relationship between *color* and *spectrum* is not merely that of part to whole, in which case (E) or even (C) might be defended as correct. A *spectrum* is made up of a progressive, graduated series of *colors*, as a *scale* is of a progressive, graduated sequence of *tones*. Thus, (A) is the correct answer choice. In this instance, the best answer must be selected from a group of fairly close choices.

Answer to Question 4

The difficulty of this question probably derives primarily from the complexity of the relationship between headlong and forethought rather than from any inherent difficulty in the words. Analysis of the relationship between headlong and forethought reveals the following: an action or behavior that is headlong is one that lacks forethought. Only answer choice (A) displays the same relationship between its two terms.

——SENTENCE COMPLETIONS——

Sentence completions measure your ability to recognize words or phrases that both logically and stylistically complete the meaning of a sentence.

Strategies for Answering

- Read the incomplete sentence carefully.
- Look for key words or phrases.
- Complete the blank(s) with your own words; see if any options are like yours.
- Pay attention to grammatical cues.
- If there are two blanks, be sure that both parts of your answer choice fit logically and stylistically into the sentence.
- After choosing an answer, read the sentence through again to see if it makes sense.

Directions: Each sentence below has one or two blanks, each blank indicating that something has been omitted. Beneath the sentence are five lettered words or sets of words. Choose the word or set of words for each blank that *best* fits the meaning of the sentence as a whole.

5. **Early ------ of hearing loss is ------ by the fact that the other senses are able to compensate for moderate amounts of loss, so that people frequently do not know that their hearing is imperfect.**
   (A) discovery . . indicated
   (B) development . . prevented
   (C) detection . . complicated
   (D) treatment . . facilitated
   (E) incidence . . corrected

6. **The ------ science of seismology has grown just enough so that the first overly bold theories have been ------.**
   (A) magnetic . . accepted
   (B) fledgling . . refuted
   (C) tentative . . analyzed
   (D) predictive . . protected
   (E) exploratory . . recalled

Answer to Question 5

The statement that the other senses compensate for partial loss of hearing indicates that the hearing loss is not *prevented* or *corrected*; therefore, choices (B) and (E) can be eliminated. Furthermore, the ability to compensate for hearing loss certainly does not facilitate the early *treatment* (D) or the early *discovery* (A) of hearing loss. It is reasonable, however, that early *detection* of hearing loss is *complicated* by the ability to compensate for it. The best answer is (C).

Answer to Question 6

At first reading, there may appear to be more than one answer choice that "makes sense" when substituted in the blanks of the sentence. (A), (C), and (D) can be dismissed fairly readily when it is seen that *accepted*, *tentative*, and *protected* are not compatible with overly bold in the sentence. Of the two remaining choices, (B) is superior on stylistic grounds: theories are not *recalled* (E), and *fledgling* (B) reflects the idea of growth present in the sentence.

——READING COMPREHENSION——

Reading comprehension questions measure your ability to

- read with understanding, insight, and discrimination
- analyze a written passage from several perspectives

Passages are taken from the humanities, social sciences, and natural sciences.

Strategies for Answering

- Read the passage closely, then proceed to the questions.
  or

Skim the passage, then reread the passage closely as you answer the questions. You may want to try it both ways with sample questions to see what works best for you.

- Answer questions based on the content of the passage.
- Separate main ideas from supporting ideas.
- Separate the author's own ideas from information being presented.
- Ask yourself...
  — What is this about?
  — What are the key points?
  — How does the main idea relate to other ideas in the passage?
  — What words define relationships among ideas?

Directions: The passage is followed by questions based on its content. After reading the passage, choose the best answer to each question. Answer all questions following the passage on the basis of what is *stated* or *implied* in the passage.

Picture-taking is a technique both for annexing the objective world and for expressing the singular self. Photographs depict objective realities that already exist, though only the camera can disclose them. And they
(5) depict an individual photographer's temperament, discovering itself through the camera's cropping of reality. That is, photography has two antithetical ideals: in the first, photography is about the world and the photographer is a mere observer who counts for little; but in the
(10) second, photography is the instrument of intrepid, questing subjectivity and the photographer is all.

These conflicting ideals arise from a fundamental uneasiness on the part of both photographers and viewers of photographs toward the aggressive component in
(15) "taking" a picture. Accordingly, the ideal of a photographer as observer is attractive because it implicitly denies that picture-taking is an aggressive act. The issue, of course, is not so clear-cut. What photographers do cannot be characterized as simply predatory or as simply,
(20) and essentially, benevolent. As a consequence, one ideal of picture-taking or the other is always being rediscovered and championed.

An important result of the coexistence of these two ideals is a recurrent ambivalence toward photography's
(25) means. Whatever the claims that photography might make to be a form of personal expression on a par with painting, its originality is inextricably linked to the powers of a machine. The steady growth of these powers has made possible the extraordinary informativeness and
(30) imaginative formal beauty of many photographs, like Harold Edgerton's high-speed photographs of a bullet hitting its target or of the swirls and eddies of a tennis stroke. But as cameras become more sophisticated, more

automated, some photographers are tempted to disarm
(35) themselves or to suggest that they are not really armed, preferring to submit themselves to the limits imposed by premodern camera technology because a cruder, less high-powered machine is thought to give more interesting or emotive results, to leave more room for creative
(40) accident. For example, it has been virtually a point of honor for many photographers, including Walker Evans and Cartier-Bresson, to refuse to use modern equipment. These photographers have come to doubt the value of the camera as an instrument of "fast seeing." Cartier-Bresson,
(45) in fact, claims that the modern camera may see too fast.

This ambivalence toward photographic means determines trends in taste. The cult of the future (of faster and faster seeing) alternates over time with the wish to return to a purer past — when images had a handmade quality.
(50) This nostalgia for some pristine state of the photographic enterprise is currently widespread and underlies the present-day enthusiasm for daguerreotypes and the work of forgotten nineteenth-century provincial photographers. Photographers and viewers of photographs, it seems, need
(55) periodically to resist their own knowingness.

7. According to the passage, the two antithetical ideals of photography differ primarily in the
   (A) value that each places on the beauty of the finished product
   (B) emphasis that each places on the emotional impact of the finished product
   (C) degree of technical knowledge that each requires of the photographer
   (D) extent of the power that each requires of the photographer's equipment
   (E) way in which each defines the role of the photographer

8. According to the passage, interest among photographers in each of photography's two ideals can best be described as
   (A) rapidly changing
   (B) cyclically recurring
   (C) steadily growing
   (D) unimportant to the viewers of photographs
   (E) unrelated to changes in technology

Answer to Question 7

The best answer to this question is (E). Photography's two ideals are presented in lines 7-11. The main emphasis in the description of these two ideals is on the relationship of the photographer to the enterprise of photography, with the photographer described in the one as a passive observer and in the other as an active

18

questioner. Answer (E) identifies this key feature in the description of the two ideals – the way in which each ideal conceives or defines the role of the photographer in photography. Answers (A) through (D) present aspects of photography that are mentioned in the passage, but none of these choices represents a primary difference between the two ideals of photography.

Answer to Question 8

This question requires one to look for comments in the passage about the nature of photographers' interest in the two ideals of photography. While the whole passage is, in a sense, about the response of photographers to these ideals, there are elements in the passage that comment specifically on this issue. Lines 20-22 tell us that the two ideals alternate in terms of their perceived relevance and value, that each ideal has periods of popularity and of neglect. These lines support (B).

Lines 23-25 tell us that the two ideals affect attitudes toward "photography's means," that is, the technology of the camera; (E), therefore, cannot be the best answer. In lines 46-49, attitudes toward photographic means (which result from the two ideals) are said to alternate over time; these lines provide further support for (B). (A) can be eliminated because, although the passage tells us that the interest of photographers in each of the ideals fluctuates over time, it nowhere indicates that this fluctuation or change is rapid. Nor does the passage say anywhere that interest in these ideals is growing; the passage *does* state that the powers of the camera are steadily growing (line 28), but this does not mean that interest in the two ideals is growing. Thus (C) can be eliminated. (D) can be eliminated because the passage nowhere states that reactions to the ideals are either important or unimportant to viewers' concerns. Thus (B) is the best answer.

Review of the Quantitative Section

Overview

The quantitative section measures your basic mathematical skills, your understanding of elementary mathematical concepts, and your ability to reason quantitatively and solve problems in a quantitative setting. There is a balance of questions requiring arithmetic, algebra, geometry, and data analysis. These are content areas usually studied in high school.

Arithmetic questions may involve arithmetic operations, powers, operations on radical expressions, estimation, percent, absolute value, properties of integers (e.g., divisibility, factoring, prime numbers, odd and even integers), and the number line.

Algebra questions may involve rules of exponents, factoring and simplifying algebraic expressions, understanding concepts of relations and functions, equations and inequalities, solving linear and quadratic equations and inequalities, solving simultaneous equations, setting up equations to solve word problems, coordinate geometry, including slope, intercepts, and graphs of equations and inequalities, and applying basic algebra skills to solve problems.

Geometry questions may involve parallel lines, circles, triangles (including isosceles, equilateral, and 30°-60°-90° triangles), rectangles, other polygons, area, perimeter, volume, the Pythagorean Theorem, and angle measure in degrees. The ability to construct proofs is not measured.

Data Analysis questions may involve elementary probability, basic descriptive statistics (mean, median, mode, range, standard deviation, percentiles), and interpretation of data in graphs and tables (line graphs, bar graphs, circle graphs, frequency distributions).

Math Symbols and Other Information

The following information applies to all questions in the quantitative sections.

- These common math symbols may be used:

    $x < y$ (x is less than y)

    $x \neq y$ (x is not equal to y)

    $\sqrt{x}$ (the nonnegative square root of x, where $x \geq 0$)

    $|x|$ (the absolute value of x, where x is a real number)

    $n!$ (n factorial: the product of the first n positive integers)

    $m \parallel n$ (line m is parallel to line n)

    $m \perp n$ (line m is perpendicular to line n)

    A
    $B \quad C$ ($\angle ABC$ is a right angle)

- Numbers: all numbers used are real numbers.
- Figures:
    - the positions of points, angles, regions, etc., can be assumed to be in the order shown; angle measures are positive
    - a line shown as straight can be assumed to be straight
    - figures lie in a plane unless otherwise indicated
    - do not assume figures are drawn to scale unless stated

It is important to familiarize yourself with the basic mathematical concepts in the GRE General Test. The *Math Review* at the end of this section provides detailed information on the content of the quantitative section. You may also refer to *Preparing for the Verbal and Quantitative Sections of the GRE General Test* at **www.gre.org/codelst.html** and/or the Interactive General Test Sample Questions at **www.gre.org/practice_test**.

The quantitative section contains the following question types:

- Quantitative Comparison questions
- Problem Solving – Discrete Quantitative questions
- Problem Solving – Data Interpretation questions

Questions emphasize understanding basic principles and reasoning within the context of given information.

How the Quantitative Section is Scored

Computer-Based General Test

Your score on the quantitative section of the computer-based General Test will depend on your performance on the questions presented and on the number of questions you answer in the time allotted. Because the section is computer adaptive, the questions are selected to reflect your performance on preceding questions and the requirements of the test design. Test design factors that influence which questions are presented include (1) the statistical characteristics (including difficulty level) of the questions already answered, (2) the required variety of question types, and (3) the appropriate coverage of content. Additional scoring information is provided in the *GRE POWERPREP* software and in the interpretive leaflet enclosed with your score report.

Paper-Based General Test

The quantitative section of the paper-based GRE General Test is scored the same way as the verbal section. First, a raw score is computed. The raw score is the number of questions for which the best answer choice was given. The raw score is then converted to a scaled score through a process known as equating. The equating process accounts for differences in difficulty among the different test editions; thus, a given scaled score reflects approximately the same level of ability regardless of the edition of the test that was taken.

QUANTITATIVE COMPARISON
QUESTIONS

Quantitative comparison questions measure your ability to

- reason quickly and accurately about the relative sizes of two quantities
- perceive that not enough information is provided to make such a decision

Directions: Each of the following questions consists of two quantities, one in Column A and one in Column B. There may be additional information, centered above the two columns, that concerns one or both of the quantities. A symbol that appears in both columns represents the same thing in Column A as it does in Column B.

   You are to compare the quantity in Column A with the quantity in Column B and decide whether:

(A) The quantity in Column A is greater.
(B) The quantity in Column B is greater.
(C) The two quantities are equal.
(D) The relationship cannot be determined from the information given.

Note for individuals taking the paper-based GRE General Test: Since there are only four choices, NEVER MARK (E).*

Sample Questions

	Column A	Column B
1.	9.8	$\sqrt{100}$
2.	$(-6)^4$	$(-6)^5$
3.	The area of an equilateral triangle with side 6	The area of a right triangle with legs $\sqrt{3}$ and 9

$$x^2 = y^2 + 1$$

4.	x	y

Class	Class Size	Mean Score
1	50	89
2	30	81
3	20	85

Three classes took the same psychology test. The class sizes and (arithmetic) mean scores are shown.

5.	The overall (arithmetic) mean score for the 3 classes	85

---

* The answer sheet contains five choices for the verbal and quantitative sections.

Strategies for Answering

- Avoid extensive computation if possible. Try to estimate the answer.
- Consider all kinds of numbers before deciding. If under some conditions Column A is greater than Column B and for others, Column B is greater than Column A, choose "the relationship cannot be determined from the information given," without any further computation.
- Geometric figures may not be drawn to scale. Comparisons should be made based on the given information, together with your knowledge of mathematics, rather than on exact appearance.

Answer to Question 1

$\sqrt{100}$ denotes 10, the positive square root of 100. (For any positive number x, $\sqrt{x}$ denotes the *positive* number whose square is x.) Since 10 is greater than 9.8, the best answer is (B). It is important not to confuse this question with a comparison of 9.8 and x where $x^2 = 100$. The latter comparison would yield (D) as the correct answer because $x^2 = 100$ implies that either $x = 10$ or $x = -10$, and there would be no way to determine which value x would actually have.

Answer to Question 2

Since $(-6)^4$ is the product of four negative factors, and the product of an even number of negative numbers is positive, $(-6)^4$ is positive. Since the product of an odd number of negative numbers is negative, $(-6)^5$ is negative. Therefore, $(-6)^4$ is greater than $(-6)^5$ since any positive number is greater than any negative number. The best answer is (A). It is not necessary to calculate that $(-6)^4 = 1,296$ and that $(-6)^5 = -7,776$ in order to make the comparison.

Answer to Question 3

The area of a triangle is one half the product of the lengths of the base and the altitude. In Column A, the length of the altitude must first be determined. A sketch of the triangle may be helpful.

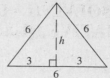

The altitude h divides the base of an equilateral triangle into two equal parts. From the Pythagorean Theorem, $h^2 + 3^2 = 6^2$, or $h = \sqrt{3}$. Therefore, the area of the triangle in Column A is $\left(\frac{1}{2}\right)(6)(3\sqrt{3}) = 9\sqrt{3}$. In Column B, the base and the altitude of the right triangle are the two legs; therefore, the area is $\left(\frac{1}{2}\right)(9)(\sqrt{3}) = \frac{9\sqrt{3}}{2}$. Since $9\sqrt{3}$ is greater than $\frac{9\sqrt{3}}{2}$, the best answer is (A).

Answer to Question 4

From the given equation, it can be determined that $x^2 > y^2$; however, the relative sizes of x and y cannot be determined. For example, if $y = 0$, then x could be 1 or -1 and, since there is no way to tell which number x is, the best answer is (D).

Answer to Question 5

The overall mean score could be found by weighting each mean score by the class size and dividing the result by 100, the total of all the class sizes, as follows.

$$\frac{(50)(89) + (30)(81) + (20)(85)}{100} = 85.8$$

Therefore, the best answer is (A). However, the calculations are unnecessary; classes 1 and 2 must have a mean greater than 85 since the mean of 89 and 81 is 85 and there are 20 more students in class 1 than in class 2. Since class 3 has a mean of 85, it must be true that the overall mean for the 3 classes is greater than 85.

PROBLEM SOLVING – DISCRETE
——QUANTITATIVE QUESTIONS——

Discrete quantitative questions measure

- basic mathematical knowledge
- your ability to read, understand, and solve a problem that involves either an actual or an abstract situation

Directions: Each of the following questions has five answer choices. For each of these questions, select the best of the answer choices given.

6. When walking, a certain person takes 16 complete steps in 10 seconds. At this rate, how many complete steps does the person take in 72 seconds?
   (A) 45
   (B) 78
   (C) 86
   (D) 90
   (E) 115

7. The average (arithmetic mean) of x and y is 20.
   If $z = 5$, what is the average of x, y, and z ?
   (A) $8\frac{1}{3}$ (B) 10 (C) $12\frac{1}{2}$ (D) 15 (E) $17\frac{1}{2}$

8. In a certain year, Minnesota produced $\frac{2}{3}$ and Michigan produced $\frac{1}{6}$ of all the iron ore produced in the United States. If all the other states combined produced 18 million tons that year, how many million tons did Minnesota produce that year?
   (A) 27   (B) 36   (C) 54   (D) 72   (E) 162

9. If $\frac{x}{3} - \frac{x}{6} + \frac{x}{9} - \frac{x}{12} = 1 - \frac{1}{2} + \frac{1}{3} - \frac{1}{4}$, then $x =$
   (A) 3   (B) 1   (C) $\frac{1}{3}$ (D) $-\frac{1}{3}$ (E) -3

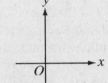

10. If the equation $y = 3x - 18$ were graphed on the coordinate axes above, then the graph would cross the y-axis at the point (x, y) where
    (A) $x = 0$ and $y = 18$
    (B) $x = 0$ and $y = -18$
    (C) $x = 0$ and $y = 6$
    (D) $x = 6$ and $y = 0$
    (E) $x = -6$ and $y = 0$

11. The operation denoted by the symbol ◆ is defined for all real numbers p and r as follows.

    $$p ◆ r = pr - p + r$$

    What is the value of $(-4) ◆ 5$?
    (A) -9
    (B) -11
    (C) -19
    (D) 19
    (E) 21

Strategies for Answering

- Determine what is given and what is being asked.
- Scan all answer choices before answering a question.
- When approximation is required, scan answer choices to determine the degree of approximation.
- Avoid long computations. Use reasoning instead, when possible.

23

Answer to Question 6

72 seconds represents 7 ten-second intervals plus 2/10 of such an interval. Therefore, the person who takes 16 steps in 10 seconds will take (7.2)(16) steps in 72 seconds.

$$(7.2)(16) = (7)(16) + (0.2)(16)$$
$$= 112 + 3.2$$
$$= 115.2$$

Since the question asks for the number of complete steps, the best answer is (E).

Answer to Question 7

Since the average of x and y is 20, $\frac{x+y}{2} = 20$, or $x + y = 40$. Thus $x + y + z = x + y + 5 = 40 + 5 = 45$, and therefore $\frac{x+y+z}{3} = \frac{45}{3} = 15$. The best answer is (D).

Answer to Question 8

Since Minnesota produced $\frac{2}{3}$ and Michigan produced $\frac{1}{6}$ of all the iron ore produced in the United States, the two states together produced $\frac{5}{6}$ of the iron ore. Therefore, the 18 million tons produced by the rest of the United States was $\frac{1}{6}$ of the total production. Thus the total United States production was (6)(18) = 108 million tons, and Minnesota produced $\frac{2}{3}(108) = 72$ million tons. The best answer is (D).

Answer to Question 9

This problem can be solved without a lot of computation by factoring $\frac{x}{3}$ out of the expression on the left side of the equation, i.e., $\frac{x}{3} - \frac{x}{6} + \frac{x}{9} - \frac{x}{12} = \frac{x}{3}\left(1 - \frac{1}{2} + \frac{1}{3} - \frac{1}{4}\right)$, and substituting the factored expression into the equation, obtaining $\frac{x}{3}\left(1 - \frac{1}{2} + \frac{1}{3} - \frac{1}{4}\right) = 1 - \frac{1}{2} + \frac{1}{3} - \frac{1}{4}$. Dividing both sides of the equation by $1 - \frac{1}{2} + \frac{1}{3} - \frac{1}{4}$ (which is not zero) gives the resulting equation $\frac{x}{3} = 1$. Thus $x = 3$ and the best answer is (A).

Answer to Question 10

A graph crosses the y-axis at a point (x, y) where $x = 0$. In the given equation, when $x = 0$, $y = 3(0) - 18 = -18$. Therefore, the graph would cross the y-axis at the point $(0, -18)$, and the best answer is (B).

Answer to Question 11

By the definition,
$$(-4) \blacklozenge 5 = (-4)(5) - (-4) + 5 = -20 + 4 + 5 = -11,$$
and therefore the best answer is (B).

PROBLEM SOLVING – DATA ─INTERPRETATION QUESTIONS─

Data interpretation questions measure your ability to

■ synthesize information and select appropriate data for answering a question
■ determine that sufficient information for answering a question is not provided

The data interpretation questions usually appear in sets and are based on data presented in tables, graphs, or other diagrams.

Directions: Each of the following questions has five answer choices. For each of these questions, select the best of the answer choices given.

Questions 12-14 refer to the following table.

PERCENT CHANGE IN DOLLAR AMOUNT OF SALES IN CERTAIN RETAIL STORES FROM 1977 TO 1979

| | Percent Change | |
Store	From 1977 to 1978	From 1978 to 1979
P	+ 10	− 10
Q	− 20	+ 9
R	+ 5	+ 12
S	− 7	− 15
T	+ 17	− 8

12. In 1979, for which of the stores was the dollar amount of sales greater than that of any of the others shown?
(A) P (B) Q (C) R (D) S
(E) It cannot be determined from the information given.

13. In store T, the dollar amount of sales for 1978 was approximately what percent of the dollar amount of sales for 1979?
(A) 86% (B) 92% (C) 109% (D) 117% (E) 122%

14. If the dollar amount of sales in store P was $800,000 in 1977, what was the dollar amount of sales in that store in 1979?
(A) $727,200 (B) $792,000 (C) $800,000
(D) $880,000 (E) $968,000

Questions 15-16 refer to the following graph.

NUMBER OF GRADUATE STUDENT APPLICANTS AT UNIVERSITY X, 1982-1991

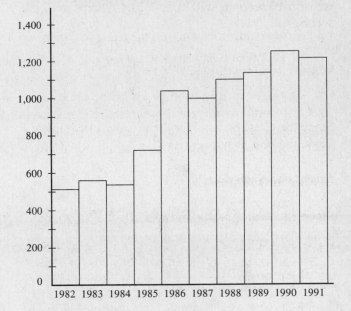

15. In which of the following years did the number of graduate student applicants increase the most from that of the previous year?
(A) 1985
(B) 1986
(C) 1988
(D) 1990
(E) 1991

16. Which of the following statements can be inferred from the graph?

I. The number of graduate student applicants more than doubled from 1982 to 1991.

II. For each of the years 1983 to 1991, inclusive, the number of graduate student applicants was greater than that of the previous year.

III. The greatest number of graduate students attended University X in 1990.

(A) I only
(B) II only
(C) III only
(D) I and III only
(E) I, II, and III

25

Strategies for Answering

- Scan the set of data to see what it is about.
- Try to make visual comparisons and estimate products and quotients rather than perform computations.
- Answer questions only on the basis of data given.

Answer to Question 12

Since the only information given in the table is the percent change from year to year, there is no way to compare the dollar amount of sales for the stores in 1979 or in any other year. The best answer is (E).

Answer to Question 13

If A is the amount of sales for store T in 1978,

then $0.08A$ is the amount of decrease and

$A - 0.08A = 0.92A$ is the amount of sales for 1979.

Therefore, the desired result can be obtained by dividing A by $0.92A$, which equals $\frac{1}{0.92}$, or approximately 109%. The best answer is (C).

Answer to Question 14

If sales in store P were $800,000 in 1977, then in 1978 they were 110 percent of that, i.e., $880,000. In 1979 sales were 90 percent of $880,000, i.e., $792,000.

Note that an increase of 10 percent in one year and a decrease of 10 percent in the following year does not result in the same dollar amount as the original dollar amount of sales because the base used in computing the percents changes from $800,000 to $880,000. The best answer is (B).

Answer to Question 15

This question can be answered directly by visually comparing the heights of the bars in the graph. The greatest increase in height between two adjacent bars occurs for the years 1985 and 1986. The best answer is (B).

Answer to Question 16

For this type of question, it is helpful to consider each statement separately. Statement I is true because, as shown in the graph, the number of applicants in 1982 was below 600 and the number in 1991 was above 1,200. Statement II is false because there are three years in which the number of applicants decreased from that of the previous year, namely 1984, 1987, and 1991. Statement III cannot be inferred from the graph because the graph shows only the number of applicants and gives no information about the number of students attending University X. Therefore, statement I only can be inferred from the graph, and the best answer is (A).

MATH REVIEW

The Math Review is designed to familiarize you with the mathematical skills and concepts likely to be tested on the Graduate Record Examinations General Test. This material, which is divided into the four basic content areas of arithmetic, algebra, geometry, and data analysis, includes many definitions and examples with solutions, and there is a set of exercises (with answers) at the end of each of these four sections. Note, however, this review is not intended to be comprehensive. It is assumed that certain basic concepts are common knowledge to all examinees. Emphasis is, therefore, placed on the more important skills, concepts, and definitions, and on those particular areas that are frequently confused or misunderstood. If any of the topics seem especially unfamiliar, we encourage you to consult appropriate mathematics texts for a more detailed treatment of those topics.

ARITHMETIC

1.1 Integers

The set of *integers*, *I*, is composed of all the counting numbers (i.e., 1, 2, 3, . . .), zero, and the negative of each counting number; that is,

$$I = \{\ldots, -3, -2, -1, 0, 1, 2, 3, \ldots\}.$$

Therefore, some integers are *positive*, some are *negative*, and the integer 0 is neither positive nor negative. Integers that are multiples of 2 are called *even integers*, namely $\{\ldots, -6, -4, -2, 0, 2, 4, 6, \ldots\}$. All other integers are called *odd integers*; therefore $\{\ldots, -5, -3, -1, 1, 3, 5, \ldots\}$ represents the set of all odd integers. Integers in a sequence such as 57, 58, 59, 60, or −14, −13, −12, −11 are called *consecutive* integers.

The rules for performing basic arithmetic operations with integers should be familiar to you. Some rules that are occasionally forgotten include:

(i) Multiplication by 0 always results in 0; e.g., $(0)(15) = 0$.

(ii) Division by 0 is not defined; e.g., $5 \div 0$ has no meaning.

(iii) Multiplication (or division) of two integers with different signs yields a negative result; e.g., $(-7)(8) = -56$ and $(-12) \div (4) = -3$.

(iv) Multiplication (or division) of two *negative* integers yields a positive result; e.g., $(-5)(-12) = 60$ and $(-24) \div (-3) = 8$.

The division of one integer by another yields either a zero remainder, sometimes called "dividing evenly," or a positive-integer remainder. For example, 215 divided by 5 yields a zero remainder, but 153 divided by 7 yields a remainder of 6.

$$
\begin{array}{r}
43 \\
5\overline{)215} \\
20 \\
\hline
15 \\
15 \\
\hline
0 = \text{Remainder}
\end{array}
\qquad
\begin{array}{r}
21 \\
7\overline{)153} \\
14 \\
\hline
13 \\
7 \\
\hline
6 = \text{Remainder}
\end{array}
$$

When we say that an integer *N* is *divisible by* an integer *x*, we mean that *N* divided by *x* yields a zero remainder.

The multiplication of two integers yields a third integer. The first two integers are called *factors*, and the third integer is called the *product*. The product is said to be a *multiple* of both factors, and it is also *divisible* by both factors. Therefore, since $(2)(7) = 14$, we can say that

> 2 and 7 are factors and 14 is the product,
> 14 is a multiple of both 2 and 7,
> and 14 is divisible by both 2 and 7.

Whenever an integer *N* is divisible by an integer *x*, we say that *x* is a *divisor* of *N*. For the set of positive integers, any integer *N* that has exactly two distinct positive divisors, 1 and *N*, is said to be a *prime number*. The first ten prime numbers are

$$2, 3, 5, 7, 11, 13, 17, 19, 23, \text{ and } 29.$$

The integer 14 is not a prime number because it has four divisors: 1, 2, 7, and 14. The integer 1 is not a prime number because it has only one positive divisor.

1.2 Fractions

A *fraction* is a number of the form $\frac{a}{b}$, where a and b are integers and $b \neq 0$. The a is called the *numerator* of the fraction, and b is called the *denominator*. For example, $\frac{-7}{5}$ is a fraction that has -7 as its numerator and 5 as its denominator. Since the fraction $\frac{a}{b}$ means $a \div b$, b cannot be zero. If the numerator and denominator of the fraction $\frac{a}{b}$ are both multiplied by the same integer, the resulting fraction will be equivalent to $\frac{a}{b}$. For example,

$$\frac{-7}{5} = \frac{(-7)(4)}{(5)(4)} = \frac{-28}{20}.$$

This technique comes in handy when you wish to add or subtract fractions.

To add two fractions with the same denominator, you simply add the numerators and keep the denominator the same.

$$\frac{-8}{11} + \frac{5}{11} = \frac{-8+5}{11} = \frac{-3}{11}$$

If the denominators are *not* the same, you may apply the technique mentioned above to make them the same before doing the addition.

$$\frac{5}{12} + \frac{2}{3} = \frac{5}{12} + \frac{(2)(4)}{(3)(4)} = \frac{5}{12} + \frac{8}{12} = \frac{5+8}{12} = \frac{13}{12}$$

The same method applies for subtraction.

To multiply two fractions, multiply the two numerators and multiply the two denominators (the denominators need not be the same).

$$\left(\frac{10}{7}\right)\left(\frac{-1}{3}\right) = \frac{(10)(-1)}{(7)(3)} = \frac{-10}{21}$$

To divide one fraction by another, first *invert* the fraction you are dividing by, and then proceed as in multiplication.

$$\frac{17}{8} \div \frac{3}{5} = \left(\frac{17}{8}\right)\left(\frac{5}{3}\right) = \frac{(17)(5)}{(8)(3)} = \frac{85}{24}$$

An expression such as $4\frac{3}{8}$ is called a *mixed fraction*; it means $4 + \frac{3}{8}$. Therefore,

$$4\frac{3}{8} = 4 + \frac{3}{8} = \frac{32}{8} + \frac{3}{8} = \frac{35}{8}.$$

In our number system, all numbers can be expressed in decimal form using base 10. A decimal point is used, and the place value for each digit corresponds to a power of 10, depending on its position relative to the decimal point. For example, the number 82.537 has 5 digits, where

"8" is the "tens" digit; the place value for "8" is 10.

"2" is the "units" digit; the place value for "2" is 1.

"5" is the "tenths" digit; the place value for "5" is $\frac{1}{10}$.

"3" is the "hundredths" digit; the place value for "3" is $\frac{1}{100}$.

"7" is the "thousandths" digit; the place value for "7" is $\frac{1}{1000}$.

Therefore, 82.537 is a short way of writing

$$(8)(10) + (2)(1) + (5)\left(\frac{1}{10}\right) + (3)\left(\frac{1}{100}\right) + (7)\left(\frac{1}{1000}\right), \text{ or}$$

$$80 + 2 + 0.5 + 0.03 + 0.007.$$

This numeration system has implications for the basic operations. For addition and subtraction, you must always remember to line up the decimal points:

$$\begin{array}{r} 126.5 \\ +\ \ 68.231 \\ \hline 194.731 \end{array} \qquad \begin{array}{r} 126.5 \\ -\ \ 68.231 \\ \hline 58.269 \end{array}$$

To multiply decimals, it is not necessary to align the decimal points. To determine the correct position for the decimal point in the product, you simply add the number of digits to the right of the decimal points in the decimals being multiplied. This sum is the number of decimal places required in the product.

$$\begin{array}{rl} 15.381 & \text{(3 decimal places)} \\ \times\ \ \ \ .14 & \text{(2 decimal places)} \\ \hline 61524 & \\ 15381\ \ \ & \\ \hline 2.15334 & \text{(5 decimal places)} \end{array}$$

To divide a decimal by another, such as $62.744 \div 1.24$, or

$$1.24\overline{)62.744}\,,$$

first move the decimal point in the divisor to the right until the divisor becomes an integer, then move the decimal point in the dividend the same number of places;

$$124\overline{)6274.4}$$

This procedure determines the correct position of the decimal point in the quotient (as shown). The division can then proceed as follows:

$$
\begin{array}{r}
50.6 \\
124\overline{)6274.4} \\
\underline{620} \\
744 \\
\underline{744} \\
0
\end{array}
$$

Conversion from a given decimal to an equivalent fraction is straightforward. Since each place value is a power of ten, every decimal can be converted easily to an integer divided by a power of ten. For example,

$$84.1 = \frac{841}{10}$$

$$9.17 = \frac{917}{100}$$

$$0.612 = \frac{612}{1000}$$

The last example can be reduced to lowest terms by dividing the numerator and denominator by 4, which is their *greatest common factor*. Thus,

$$0.612 = \frac{612}{1000} = \frac{612 \div 4}{1000 \div 4} = \frac{153}{250} \text{ (in lowest terms)}.$$

Any fraction can be converted to an equivalent decimal. Since the fraction $\frac{a}{b}$ means $a \div b$, we can divide the numerator of a fraction by its denominator to convert the fraction to a decimal. For example, to convert $\frac{3}{8}$ to a decimal, divide 3 by 8 as follows.

$$
\begin{array}{r}
0.375 \\
8\overline{)3.000} \\
\underline{24} \\
60 \\
\underline{56} \\
40 \\
\underline{40} \\
0
\end{array}
$$

1.4 Exponents and Square Roots

Exponents provide a shortcut notation for repeated multiplication of a number by itself. For example, "3^4" means $(3)(3)(3)(3)$, which equals 81. So, we say that $3^4 = 81$; the "4" is called an *exponent* (or power). The exponent tells you how many factors are in the product. For example,

$$2^5 = (2)(2)(2)(2)(2) = 32$$

$$10^6 = (10)(10)(10)(10)(10)(10) = 1,000,000$$

$$(-4)^3 = (-4)(-4)(-4) = -64$$

$$\left(\frac{1}{2}\right)^4 = \left(\frac{1}{2}\right)\left(\frac{1}{2}\right)\left(\frac{1}{2}\right)\left(\frac{1}{2}\right) = \frac{1}{16}$$

When the exponent is 2, we call the process *squaring*. Therefore, "5^2" can be read "5 squared."

Exponents can be negative or zero, with the following rules for any nonzero number m.

$$m^0 = 1$$

$$m^{-1} = \frac{1}{m}$$

$$m^{-2} = \frac{1}{m^2}$$

$$m^{-3} = \frac{1}{m^3}$$

$$m^{-n} = \frac{1}{m^n} \text{ for all integers } n.$$

If $m = 0$, then these expressions are not defined.

A *square root* of a positive number N is a real number which, when squared, equals N. For example, a square root of 16 is 4 because $4^2 = 16$. Another square root of 16 is -4 because $(-4)^2 = 16$. In fact, all positive numbers have two square roots that differ only in sign. The square root of 0 is 0 because $0^2 = 0$. Negative numbers do *not* have square roots because the square of a real number cannot be negative. If $N > 0$, then the positive square root of N is represented by $\sqrt{N}$, read "radical N." The negative square root of N, therefore, is represented by $-\sqrt{N}$.

Two important rules regarding operations with radicals are:
If $a > 0$ and $b > 0$, then

(i) $(\sqrt{a})(\sqrt{b}) = \sqrt{ab}$; e.g., $(\sqrt{5})(\sqrt{20}) = \sqrt{100} = 10$

(ii) $\dfrac{\sqrt{a}}{\sqrt{b}} = \sqrt{\dfrac{a}{b}}$; e.g., $\dfrac{\sqrt{192}}{\sqrt{4}} = \sqrt{48} = \sqrt{(16)(3)} = (\sqrt{16})(\sqrt{3}) = 4\sqrt{3}$

1.5 Ordering and the Real Number Line

The set of all *real numbers*, which includes all integers and all numbers with values between them, such as 1.25, $\frac{2}{3}$, $\sqrt{2}$, etc., has a natural ordering, which can be represented by the *real number line*:

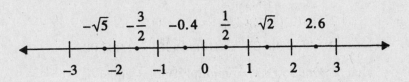

Every real number corresponds to a point on the real number line (see examples shown above). The real number line is infinitely long in both directions.

For any two numbers on the real number line, the number to the left is *less than* the number to the right. For example,

$$-\sqrt{5} < -\frac{3}{2}$$

$$-1.75 < \sqrt{2}$$

$$\frac{5}{2} < 7.1$$

Since $2 < 5$, it is also true that 5 is greater than 2, which is written "$5 > 2$." If a number N is *between* 1.5 and 2 on the real number line, you can express that fact as $1.5 < N < 2$.

The term *percent* means *per hundred* or *divided by one hundred*. Therefore,

$$43\% = \frac{43}{100} = 0.43$$

$$300\% = \frac{300}{100} = 3$$

$$0.5\% = \frac{0.5}{100} = 0.005$$

To find out what 30% of 350 is, you multiply 350 by either 0.30 or $\frac{30}{100}$,

$$30\% \text{ of } 350 = (350)(0.30) = 105$$

or

$$30\% \text{ of } 350 = (350)\left(\frac{30}{100}\right) = (350)\left(\frac{3}{10}\right) = \frac{1,050}{10} = 105.$$

To find out what percent of 80 is 5, you set up the following equation and solve for x:

$$\frac{5}{80} = \frac{x}{100}$$

$$x = \frac{500}{80} = 6.25$$

So 5 is 6.25% of 80. The number 80 is called the *base* of the percent. Another way to view this problem is to simply divide 5 by the base, 80, and then multiply the result by 100 to get the percent.

If a quantity *increases* from 600 to 750, then the *percent increase* is found by dividing the amount of increase, 150, by the base, 600, which is the first (or the smaller) of the two given numbers, and then multiplying by 100:

$$\left(\frac{150}{600}\right)(100)\% = 25\%.$$

If a quantity *decreases* from 500 to 400, then the *percent decrease* is found by dividing the amount of decrease, 100, by the base, 500, which is the first (or the larger) of the two given numbers, and then multiplying by 100:

$$\left(\frac{100}{500}\right)(100)\% = 20\%.$$

Other ways to state these two results are "750 is 25 *percent greater than* 600" and "400 is 20 *percent less than* 500."

In general, for any positive numbers x and y, where $x < y$,

$$y \text{ is } \left(\frac{y-x}{x}\right)(100) \text{ percent greater than } x$$

$$x \text{ is } \left(\frac{y-x}{y}\right)(100) \text{ percent less than } y$$

Note that in each of these statements, the base of the percent is in the denominator.

1.7 Ratio

The ratio of the number 9 to the number 21 can be expressed in several ways; for example,

$$9 \text{ to } 21$$
$$9:21$$
$$\frac{9}{21}$$

Since a ratio is in fact an implied division, it can be reduced to lowest terms. Therefore, the ratio above could also be written:

$$3 \text{ to } 7$$
$$3:7$$
$$\frac{3}{7}$$

1.8 Absolute Value

The *absolute value* of a number N, denoted by $|N|$, is defined to be N if N is positive or zero and $-N$ if N is negative. For example,

$$\left|\frac{1}{2}\right| = \frac{1}{2}, |0| = 0, \text{ and } |-2.6| = -(-2.6) = 2.6.$$

Note that the absolute value of a number cannot be negative.

ARITHMETIC EXERCISES

(Answers on pages 39 and 40)

1. Evaluate:

   (a) $15 - (6 - 4)(-2)$

   (b) $(2 - 17) \div 5$

   (c) $(60 \div 12) - (-7 + 4)$

   (d) $(3)^4 - (-2)^3$

   (e) $(-5)(-3) - 15$

   (f) $(-2)^4(15 - 18)^4$

   (g) $(20 \div 5)^2(-2 + 6)^3$

   (h) $(-85)(0) - (-17)(3)$

2. Evaluate:

   (a) $\dfrac{1}{2} - \dfrac{1}{3} + \dfrac{1}{12}$

   (b) $\left(\dfrac{3}{4} + \dfrac{1}{7}\right)\left(\dfrac{-2}{5}\right)$

   (c) $\left(\dfrac{7}{8} - \dfrac{4}{5}\right)^2$

   (d) $\left(\dfrac{3}{-8}\right) \div \left(\dfrac{27}{32}\right)$

3. Evaluate:

   (a) $12.837 + 1.65 - 0.9816$

   (b) $100.26 \div 1.2$

   (c) $(12.4)(3.67)$

   (d) $(0.087)(0.00021)$

4. State for each of the following whether the answer is an *even* integer or an *odd* integer.

   (a) The sum of two even integers

   (b) The sum of two odd integers

   (c) The sum of an even integer and an odd integer

   (d) The product of two even integers

   (e) The product of two odd integers

   (f) The product of an even integer and an odd integer

5. Which of the following integers are divisible by 8 ?

   (a) 312   (b) 98   (c) 112   (d) 144

6. List all of the positive divisors of 372.

7. Which of the divisors found in #6 are prime numbers?

8. Which of the following integers are prime numbers?
   19, 2, 49, 37, 51, 91, 1, 83, 29

9. Express 585 as a product of prime numbers.

10. Which of the following statements are true?

(a) $-5 < 3.1$

(g) $\sqrt{9} < 0$

(b) $\sqrt{16} = 4$

(h) $\dfrac{21}{28} = \dfrac{3}{4}$

(c) $7 \div 0 = 0$

(i) $-|-23| = 23$

(d) $0 < |-1.7|$

(j) $\dfrac{1}{2} > \dfrac{1}{17}$

(e) $0.3 < \dfrac{1}{3}$

(k) $(59)^3(59)^2 = (59)^6$

(f) $(-1)^{87} = -1$

(l) $-\sqrt{25} < -4$

11. Perform the indicated operations.

(a) $5\sqrt{3} + \sqrt{27}$

(b) $\left(\sqrt{6}\right)\left(\sqrt{30}\right)$

(c) $\left(\sqrt{300}\right) \div \left(\sqrt{12}\right)$

(d) $\left(\sqrt{5}\right)\left(\sqrt{2}\right) - \sqrt{90}$

12. Express the following percents in decimal form and in fraction form (in lowest terms).

(a) 15%   (b) 27.3%   (c) 131%   (d) 0.02%

13. Express each of the following as a percent.

(a) 0.8   (b) 0.197   (c) 5.2   (d) $\dfrac{3}{8}$ (e) $2\dfrac{1}{2}$ (f) $\dfrac{3}{50}$

14. Find:

(a) 40% of 15

(c) 0.6% of 800

(b) 150% of 48

(d) 8% of 5%

15. If a person's salary increases from $200 per week to $234 per week, what is the percent increase?

16. If an athlete's weight decreases from 160 pounds to 152 pounds, what is the percent decrease?

17. A particular stock is valued at $40 per share. If the value increases 20 percent and then decreases 25 percent, what is the value of the stock per share after the decrease?

18. Express the ratio of 16 to 6 three different ways in lowest terms.

19. If the ratio of men to women on a committee of 20 members is 3 to 2, how many members of the committee are women?

ANSWERS TO ARITHMETIC EXERCISES

1. (a) 19
   (b) −3
   (c) 8
   (d) 89
   (e) 0
   (f) 1,296
   (g) 1,024
   (h) 51

2. (a) $\frac{1}{4}$
   (b) $-\frac{5}{14}$
   (c) $\frac{9}{1,600}$
   (d) $-\frac{4}{9}$

3. (a) 13.5054
   (b) 83.55
   (c) 45.508
   (d) 0.00001827

4. (a) even
   (b) even
   (c) odd
   (d) even
   (e) odd
   (f) even

5. (a), (c), and (d)

6. 1, 2, 3, 4, 6, 12, 31, 62, 93, 124, 186, 372

7. 2, 3, 31

8. 19, 2, 37, 83, 29

9. (3)(3)(5)(13)

10. (a), (b), (d), (e), (f), (h), (j), (l)

11. (a) $8\sqrt{3}$
    (b) $6\sqrt{5}$
    (c) 5
    (d) $-2\sqrt{10}$

12. (a) 0.15, $\frac{3}{20}$
    (b) 0.273, $\frac{273}{1,000}$
    (c) 1.31, $\frac{131}{100}$
    (d) 0.0002, $\frac{1}{5,000}$

13. (a) 80%
    (b) 19.7%
    (c) 520%

    (d) 37.5%
    (e) 250%
    (f) 6%

14. (a) 6
    (b) 72

    (c) 4.8
    (d) 0.004

15. 17%

16. 5%

17. $36

18. 8 to 3, 8:3, $\frac{8}{3}$

19. 8

ALGEBRA

2.1 Translating Words into Algebraic Expressions

Basic algebra is essentially advanced arithmetic; therefore much of the terminology and many of the rules are common to both areas. The major difference is that in algebra variables are introduced, which allows us to solve problems using equations and inequalities.

If the square of the number x is multiplied by 3, and then 10 is added to that product, the result can be represented by $3x^2 + 10$. If John's present salary S is increased by 14 percent, then his new salary is $1.14S$. If y gallons of syrup are to be distributed among 5 people so that one particular person gets 1 gallon and the rest of the syrup is divided equally among the remaining 4, then each of these 4 people will get $\frac{y-1}{4}$ gallons of syrup. Combinations of letters (variables) and numbers such as $3x^2 + 10$, $1.14S$, and $\frac{y-1}{4}$ are called *algebraic expressions*.

One way to work with algebraic expressions is to think of them as *functions*, or "machines," that take an input, say a value of a variable x, and produce a corresponding output. For example, in the expression $\frac{2x}{x-6}$, the input $x = 1$ produces the corresponding output $\frac{2(1)}{1-6} = -\frac{2}{5}$. In function notation, the expression $\frac{2x}{x-6}$ is called a function and is denoted by a letter, often the letter f or g, as follows:

$$f(x) = \frac{2x}{x-6}.$$

We say that this equation *defines* the function f. For this example with input $x = 1$ and output $-\frac{2}{5}$, we write $f(1) = -\frac{2}{5}$. The output $-\frac{2}{5}$ is called the *value of the function* corresponding to the input $x = 1$. The value of the function corresponding to $x = 0$ is 0, since

$$f(0) = \frac{2(0)}{0-6} = -\frac{0}{6} = 0.$$

In fact, any real number x can be used as an input value for the function f, except for $x = 6$, as this substitution would result in a division by 0. Since $x = 6$ is not a valid input for f, we say that f is not defined for $x = 6$.

As another example, let h be the function defined by

$$h(z) = z^2 + \sqrt{z} + 3.$$

Note that $h(0) = 3$, $h(1) = 5$, $h(10) = 103 + \sqrt{10} \approx 106.2$, but $h(-10)$ is not defined since $\sqrt{-10}$ is not a real number.

2.2 Operations with Algebraic Expressions

Every algebraic expression can be written as a single term or a series of terms separated by plus or minus signs. The expression $3x^2 + 10$ has two terms; the expression $1.14S$ is a single term; the expression $\frac{y-1}{4}$, which can be written $\frac{y}{4} - \frac{1}{4}$, has two terms. In the expression $2x^2 + 7x - 5$, 2 is the *coefficient* of the x^2 term, 7 is the coefficient of the x term, and -5 is the *constant term*.

The same rules that govern operations with numbers apply to operations with algebraic expressions. One additional rule, which helps in simplifying algebraic expressions, is that terms with the same variable part can be combined. Examples are:

$$2x + 5x = (2 + 5)x = 7x$$
$$x^2 - 3x^2 + 6x^2 = (1 - 3 + 6)x^2 = 4x^2$$
$$3xy + 2x - xy - 3x = (3 - 1)xy + (2 - 3)x = 2xy - x$$

Any number or variable that is a factor of each term in an algebraic expression can be factored out. Examples are:

$$4x + 12 = 4(x + 3)$$
$$15y^2 - 9y = 3y(5y - 3)$$
$$\frac{7x^2 + 14x}{2x + 4} = \frac{7x(x + 2)}{2(x + 2)} = \frac{7x}{2} \ (\text{if } x \neq -2)$$

Another useful tool for factoring algebraic expressions is the fact that $a^2 - b^2 = (a + b)(a - b)$. For example,

$$\frac{x^2 - 9}{4x - 12} = \frac{(x + 3)(x - 3)}{4(x - 3)} = \frac{x + 3}{4} \ (\text{if } x \neq 3).$$

To multiply two algebraic expressions, each term of the first expression is multiplied by each term of the second, and the results are added. For example,

$$(x + 2)(3x - 7) = x(3x) + x(-7) + 2(3x) + 2(-7)$$
$$= 3x^2 - 7x + 6x - 14$$
$$= 3x^2 - x - 14$$

A statement that equates two algebraic expressions is called an *equation*. Examples of equations are:

$$3x + 5 = -2 \quad \text{(linear equation in one variable)}$$
$$x - 3y = 10 \quad \text{(linear equation in two variables)}$$
$$20y^2 + 6y - 17 = 0 \quad \text{(quadratic equation in one variable)}$$

2.3 Rules of Exponents

Some of the basic rules of exponents are:

(a) $x^{-a} = \dfrac{1}{x^a} \ (x \neq 0)$

Example: $4^{-3} = \dfrac{1}{4^3} = \dfrac{1}{64}$.

(b) $\left(x^a\right)\left(x^b\right) = x^{a+b}$

Example: $\left(3^2\right)\left(3^4\right) = 3^{2+4} = 3^6 = 729$.

(c) $\left(x^a\right)\left(y^a\right) = (xy)^a$

Example: $\left(2^3\right)\left(3^3\right) = 6^3 = 216$.

(d) $\dfrac{x^a}{x^b} = x^{a-b} = \dfrac{1}{x^{b-a}} \ (x \neq 0)$

Examples: $\dfrac{5^7}{5^4} = 5^{7-4} = 5^3 = 125$ and $\dfrac{4^3}{4^8} = \dfrac{1}{4^{8-3}} = \dfrac{1}{4^5} = \dfrac{1}{1,024}$.

(e) $\left(\dfrac{x}{y}\right)^a = \dfrac{x^a}{y^a} \ (y \neq 0)$

Example: $\left(\dfrac{3}{4}\right)^2 = \dfrac{3^2}{4^2} = \dfrac{9}{16}$.

(f) $\left(x^a\right)^b = x^{ab}$

Example: $\left(2^5\right)^2 = 2^{10} = 1,024$.

(g) If $x \neq 0$, then $x^0 = 1$.

Examples: $7^0 = 1$; $(-3)^0 = 1$; 0^0 is not defined.

2.4 Solving Linear Equations

(a) One variable.

To solve a linear equation in one variable means to find the value of the variable that makes the equation true. Two equations that have the same solution are said to be *equivalent*. For example, $x + 1 = 2$ and $2x + 2 = 4$ are equivalent equations; both are true when $x = 1$ and are false otherwise.

Two basic rules are important for solving linear equations.

(i) When the same constant is added to (or subtracted from) both sides of an equation, the equality is preserved, and the new equation is equivalent to the original.

(ii) When both sides of an equation are multiplied (or divided) by the same nonzero constant, the equality is preserved, and the new equation is equivalent to the original.

43

For example,

$$3x - 4 = 8$$
$$3x - 4 + 4 = 8 + 4 \quad \text{(4 added to both sides)}$$
$$3x = 12$$
$$\frac{3x}{3} = \frac{12}{3} \quad \text{(both sides divided by 3)}$$
$$x = 4$$

(b)   Two variables.

To solve linear equations in two variables, it is necessary to have two equations that are not equivalent. To solve such a "system" of simultaneous equations, e.g.,

$$4x + 3y = 13$$
$$x + 2y = 2$$

there are two basic methods. In the *first method*, you use either equation to express one variable in terms of the other. In the system above, you could express x in the second equation in terms of y (i.e., $x = 2 - 2y$), and then substitute $2 - 2y$ for x in the first equation to find the solution for y:

$$4(2 - 2y) + 3y = 13$$
$$8 - 8y + 3y = 13$$
$$-8y + 3y = 5 \quad \text{(8 subtracted from both sides)}$$
$$-5y = 5 \quad \text{(terms combined)}$$
$$y = -1 \quad \text{(both sides divided by } -5\text{)}$$

Then -1 can be substituted for y in the second equation to solve for x:

$$x + 2y = 2$$
$$x + 2(-1) = 2$$
$$x - 2 = 2$$
$$x = 4 \quad \text{(2 added to both sides)}$$

In the *second method*, the object is to make the coefficients of one variable the same in both equations so that one variable can be eliminated by either adding both equations together or subtracting one from the other. In the same example, both sides of the second equation could be multiplied by 4, yielding $4(x + 2y) = 4(2)$, or $4x + 8y = 8$. Now we have two equations with the same x coefficient:

$$4x + 3y = 13$$
$$4x + 8y = 8$$

If the second equation is subtracted from the first, the result is $-5y = 5$. Thus, $y = -1$, and substituting -1 for y in either one of the original equations yields $x = 4$.

2.5 Solving Quadratic Equations in One Variable

A *quadratic* equation is any equation that can be expressed as $ax^2 + bx + c = 0$, where a, b, and c are real numbers ($a \neq 0$). Such an equation can always be solved by the *formula*:

$$x = \frac{-b \pm \sqrt{b^2 - 4ac}}{2a}.$$

For example, in the quadratic equation $2x^2 - x - 6 = 0$, $a = 2$, $b = -1$, and $c = -6$. Therefore, the formula yields

$$x = \frac{-(-1) \pm \sqrt{(-1)^2 - 4(2)(-6)}}{2(2)}$$

$$= \frac{1 \pm \sqrt{49}}{4}$$

$$= \frac{1 \pm 7}{4}$$

So, the solutions are $x = \dfrac{1 + 7}{4} = 2$ and $x = \dfrac{1 - 7}{4} = -\dfrac{3}{2}$. Quadratic equations can have at most two real solutions, as in the example above. However, some quadratics have only one real solution (e.g., $x^2 + 4x + 4 = 0$; solution: $x = -2$), and some have no real solutions (e.g., $x^2 + x + 5 = 0$).

Some quadratics can be solved more quickly by *factoring*. In the original example,

$$2x^2 - x - 6 = (2x + 3)(x - 2) = 0.$$

Since $(2x + 3)(x - 2) = 0$, either $2x + 3 = 0$ or $x - 2 = 0$ must be true. Therefore,

$$
\begin{array}{ccc}
2x + 3 = 0 & & x - 2 = 0 \\
2x = -3 & \text{OR} & x = 2 \\
x = -\dfrac{3}{2} & &
\end{array}
$$

Other examples of factorable quadratic equations are:

(a)
$$x^2 + 8x + 15 = 0$$
$$(x + 3)(x + 5) = 0$$
$$\text{Therefore,} \quad x + 3 = 0; \ x = -3$$
$$\text{or} \quad x + 5 = 0; \ x = -5$$

(b)
$$4x^2 - 9 = 0$$
$$(2x + 3)(2x - 3) = 0$$

Therefore, $2x + 3 = 0; \; x = -\dfrac{3}{2}$

or $2x - 3 = 0; \; x = \dfrac{3}{2}$

2.6 Inequalities

Any mathematical statement that uses one of the following symbols is called an *inequality*.

$\neq$ "not equal to"
$<$ "less than"
$\leq$ "less than or equal to"
$>$ "greater than"
$\geq$ "greater than or equal to"

For example, the inequality $4x - 1 \leq 7$ states that "$4x - 1$ is less than or equal to 7." To *solve* an inequality means to find the values of the variable that make the inequality true. The approach used to solve an inequality is similar to that used to solve an equation. That is, by using basic operations, you try to isolate the variable on one side of the inequality. The basic rules for solving inequalities are similar to the rules for solving equations, namely:

(i) When the same constant is added to (or subtracted from) both sides of an inequality, the direction of inequality is preserved, and the new inequality is equivalent to the original.
(ii) When both sides of the inequality are multiplied (or divided) by the same constant, the direction of inequality is *preserved if the constant is positive*, but *reversed if the constant is negative*. In either case the new inequality is equivalent to the original.

For example, to solve the inequality $-3x + 5 \leq 17$,

$$-3x + 5 \leq 17$$
$$-3x \leq 12 \qquad \text{(5 subtracted from both sides)}$$
$$\frac{-3x}{-3} \geq \frac{12}{-3} \qquad \begin{array}{l}\text{(both sides divided by } -3\text{, which}\\ \text{reverses the direction of the inequality)}\end{array}$$
$$x \geq -4$$

Therefore, the solutions to $-3x + 5 \leq 17$ are all real numbers greater than or equal to -4. Another example follows:

$$\frac{4x + 9}{11} > 5$$
$$4x + 9 > 55 \qquad \text{(both sides multiplied by 11)}$$
$$4x > 46 \qquad \text{(9 subtracted from both sides)}$$
$$x > \frac{46}{4} \qquad \text{(both sides divided by 4)}$$
$$x > 11\frac{1}{2}$$

2.7 Applications

Since algebraic techniques allow for the creation and solution of equations and inequalities, algebra has many real-world applications. Below are a few examples. Additional examples are included in the exercises at the end of this section.

Example 1. Ellen has received the following scores on 3 exams: 82, 74, and 90. What score will Ellen need to attain on the next exam so that the average (arithmetic mean) for the 4 exams will be 85 ?

Solution: If x represents the score on the next exam, then the arithmetic mean of 85 will be equal to

$$\frac{82 + 74 + 90 + x}{4}.$$

So,

$$\frac{246 + x}{4} = 85$$
$$246 + x = 340$$
$$x = 94$$

Therefore, Ellen would need to attain a score of 94 on the next exam.

Example 2. A mixture of 12 ounces of vinegar and oil is 40 percent vinegar (by weight). How many ounces of oil must be added to the mixture to produce a new mixture that is only 25 percent vinegar?

Solution: Let x represent the number of ounces of oil to be added. Therefore, the total number of ounces of vinegar in the new mixture will be $(0.40)(12)$, and the total number of ounces of new mixture will be $12 + x$. Since the new mixture must be 25 percent vinegar,

$$\frac{(0.40)(12)}{12 + x} = 0.25.$$

Therefore,

$$(0.40)(12) = (12 + x)(0.25)$$
$$4.8 = 3 + 0.25x$$
$$1.8 = 0.25x$$
$$7.2 = x$$

Thus, 7.2 ounces of oil must be added to reduce the percent of vinegar in the mixture from 40 percent to 25 percent.

Example 3. In a driving competition, Jeff and Dennis drove the same course at average speeds of 51 miles per hour and 54 miles per hour, respectively. If it took Jeff 40 minutes to drive the course, how long did it take Dennis?

47

Solution: Let x equal the time, in minutes, that it took Dennis to drive the course. Since distance (d) equals rate (r) multiplied by time (t), i.e.,

$$d = (r)(t),$$

the distance traveled by Jeff can be represented by $(51)\left(\dfrac{40}{60}\right)$, and the distance traveled by Dennis, $(54)\left(\dfrac{x}{60}\right)$. Since the distances are equal,

$$(51)\left(\frac{40}{60}\right) = (54)\left(\frac{x}{60}\right)$$
$$34 = 0.9x$$
$$37.8 \approx x$$

Thus, it took Dennis approximately 37.8 minutes to drive the course. Note: since rates are given in miles per *hour*, it was necessary to express time in hours (i.e., 40 minutes equals $\dfrac{40}{60}$, or $\dfrac{2}{3}$, of an hour.)

Example 4. If it takes 3 hours for machine A to produce N identical computer parts, and it takes machine B only 2 hours to do the same job, how long would it take to do the job if both machines worked simultaneously?

Solution: Since machine A takes 3 hours to do the job, machine A can do $\dfrac{1}{3}$ of the job in 1 hour. Similarly, machine B can do $\dfrac{1}{2}$ of the job in 1 hour. And if we let x represent the number of hours it would take for the machines working simultaneously to do the job, the two machines would do $\dfrac{1}{x}$ of the job in 1 hour. Therefore,

$$\frac{1}{3} + \frac{1}{2} = \frac{1}{x}$$
$$\frac{2}{6} + \frac{3}{6} = \frac{1}{x}$$
$$\frac{5}{6} = \frac{1}{x}$$
$$\frac{6}{5} = x$$

Thus, working together, the machines take only $\dfrac{6}{5}$ hours, or 1 hour and 12 minutes, to produce the N computer parts.

Example 5. At a fruit stand, apples can be purchased for \$0.15 each and pears for \$0.20 each. At these rates, a bag of apples and pears was purchased for \$3.80. If the bag contained exactly 21 pieces of fruit, how many were pears?

Solution: If a represents the number of apples purchased and p represents the number of pears purchased, two equations can be written as follows:

$$0.15a + 0.20p = 3.80$$
$$a + p = 21$$

From the second equation, $a = 21 - p$. Substituting $21 - p$ into the first equation for a gives

$$0.15(21 - p) + 0.20p = 3.80$$
$$(0.15)(21) - 0.15p + 0.20p = 3.80$$
$$3.15 - 0.15p + 0.20p = 3.80$$
$$0.05p = 0.65$$
$$p = 13 \quad \text{(pears)}$$

Example 6. It costs a manufacturer \$30 each to produce a particular radio model, and it is assumed that if 500 radios are produced, all will be sold. What must be the selling price per radio to ensure that the *profit* (revenue from sales minus total cost to produce) on the 500 radios is greater than \$8,200 ?

Solution: If y represents the selling price per radio, then the profit must be $500(y - 30)$. Therefore,

$$500(y - 30) > 8,200$$
$$500y - 15,000 > 8,200$$
$$500y > 23,200$$
$$y > 46.40$$

Thus, the selling price must be greater than \$46.40 to make the profit greater than \$8,200.

2.8 Coordinate Geometry

Two real number lines (as described in Section 1.5) intersecting at right angles at the zero point on each number line define a *rectangular coordinate system*, often called the *xy-coordinate system* or *xy-plane*. The horizontal number line is called the *x*-axis, and the vertical number line is called the *y*-axis. The lines divide the plane into four regions called *quadrants* (I, II, III, and IV) as shown below.

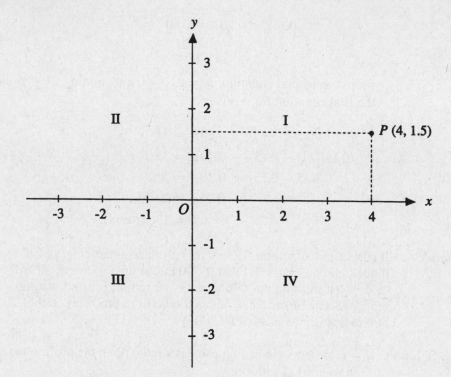

Each point in the system can be identified by an ordered pair of real numbers, (*x*, *y*), called *coordinates*. The *x*-coordinate expresses distance to the left (if negative) or right (if positive) of the *y*-axis, and the *y*-coordinate expresses distance below (if negative) or above (if positive) the *x*-axis. For example, since point *P*, shown above, is 4 units to the right of the *y*-axis and 1.5 units above the *x*-axis, it is identified by the ordered pair (4, 1.5). The *origin O* has coordinates (0, 0). Unless otherwise noted, the units used on the *x*-axis and the *y*-axis are the same.

To find the distance between two points, say $P(4, 1.5)$ and $Q(-2, -3)$, represented by the length of line segment PQ in the figure below, first construct a right triangle (see dotted lines) and then note that the two shorter sides of the triangle have lengths 6 and 4.5.

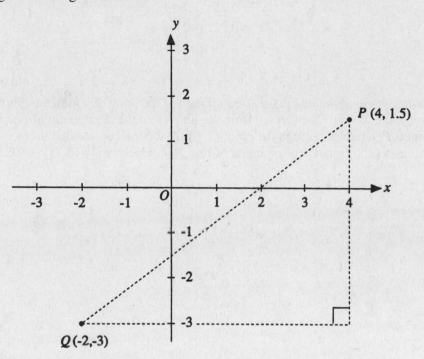

Since the distance between P and Q is the length of the hypotenuse, we can apply the Pythagorean Theorem, as follows:

$$PQ = \sqrt{(6)^2 + (4.5)^2} = \sqrt{56.25} = 7.5$$

(For a discussion of right triangles and the Pythagorean Theorem, see Section 3.3.)

A straight line in a coordinate system is a *graph* of a *linear equation* of the form $y = mx + b$, where m is called the *slope* of the line and b is called the *y-intercept*. The slope of a line passing through points $P(x_1, y_1)$ and $Q(x_2, y_2)$ is defined as

$$\text{slope} = \frac{y_1 - y_2}{x_1 - x_2} \quad (x_1 \neq x_2).$$

For example, in the coordinate system shown above, the slope of the line passing through points $P(4, 1.5)$ and $Q(-2, -3)$ is

$$\text{slope} = \frac{1.5 - (-3)}{4 - (-2)} = \frac{4.5}{6} = 0.75.$$

The *y-intercept* is the *y*-coordinate of the point at which the graph intersects the *y*-axis. The *y*-intercept of line PQ in the example above appears to be about -1.5, since line PQ intersects the *y*-axis close to the point $(0, -1.5)$. This can be confirmed by using the equation of the line, $y = 0.75x + b$, by substituting the coordinates of point Q (or any point that is known to be on the line) into the equation, and by solving for the y-intercept, b, as follows:

$$y = 0.75x + b$$
$$-3 = (0.75)(-2) + b$$
$$b = -3 + (0.75)(2)$$
$$b = -1.5$$

The *x-intercept* of the line is the x-coordinate of the point at which the graph intersects the x-axis. One can see from the graph that the x-intercept of line PQ is 2 since PQ passes through the point $(2, 0)$. Also, one can see that the coordinates $(2, 0)$ satisfy the equation of line PQ, which is $y = 0.75x - 1.5$.

ALGEBRA EXERCISES

(Answers on pages 56 and 57)

1. Find an algebraic expression to represent each of the following.

   (a) The square of y is subtracted from 5, and the result is multiplied by 37.
   (b) Three times x is squared, and the result is divided by 7.
   (c) The product of $(x + 4)$ and y is added to 18.

2. Simplify each of the following algebraic expressions by doing the indicated operations, factoring, or combining terms with the same variable part.

   (a) $3x^2 - 6 + x + 11 - x^2 + 5x$
   (b) $3(5x - 1) - x + 4$
   (c) $\dfrac{(x^2 + 9) - 25}{x - 4}$ $(x \neq 4)$
   (d) $(2x + 5)(3x - 1)$

3. What is the value of the function defined by $f(x) = 3x^2 - 7x + 23$ when $x = -2$?

4. If the function g is defined for all nonzero numbers y by $g(y) = \dfrac{y}{|y|}$, what is the value of $g(2) - g(-200)$?

5. Use the rules of exponents to simplify the following.

   (a) $(n^5)(n^{-3})$ (e) $(w^5)^{-3}$

   (b) $(s^7)(t^7)$ (f) $(5^0)(d^3)$

   (c) $\dfrac{r^{12}}{r^4}$ (g) $\dfrac{(x^{10})(y^{-1})}{(x^{-5})(y^5)}$

   (d) $\left(\dfrac{2a}{b}\right)^5$ (h) $\left(\dfrac{3x}{y}\right)^2 \div \left(\dfrac{1}{y}\right)^5$

6. Solve each of the following equations for x.

   (a) $5x - 7 = 28$
   (b) $12 - 5x = x + 30$
   (c) $5(x + 2) = 1 - 3x$
   (d) $(x + 6)(2x - 1) = 0$
   (e) $x^2 + 5x - 14 = 0$
   (f) $3x^2 + 10x - 8 = 0$

7. Solve each of the following systems of equations for x and y.

   (a) $x + y = 24$
        $x - y = 18$

   (b) $3x - y = 20$
        $x + 2y = 30$

   (c) $15x - 18 - 2y = -3x + y$
        $10x + 7y + 20 = 4x + 2$

8. Solve each of the following inequalities for x.

   (a) $-3x > 7 + x$
   (b) $25x + 16 \geq 10 - x$
   (c) $16 + x > 8x - 12$

9. Solve for x and y.

   $x = 2y$
   $5x < y + 7$

10. For a given two-digit positive integer, the tens digit is 5 greater than the units digit. The sum of the digits is 11. Find the integer.

11. If the ratio of $2x$ to $5y$ is 3 to 4, what is the ratio of x to y?

12. Kathleen's weekly salary was increased 8 percent to $237.60. What was her weekly salary before the increase?

13. A theater sells children's tickets for half the adult ticket price. If 5 adult tickets and 8 children's tickets cost a total of $27, what is the cost of an adult ticket?

14. Pat invested a total of $3,000. Part of the money yields 10 percent interest per year, and the rest yields 8 percent interest per year. If the total yearly interest from this investment is $256, how much did Pat invest at 10 percent and how much at 8 percent?

15. Two cars started from the same point and traveled on a straight course in opposite directions for exactly 2 hours, at which time they were 208 miles apart. If one car traveled, on average, 8 miles per hour faster than the other car, what was the average speed for each car for the 2-hour trip?

16. A group can charter a particular aircraft at a fixed total cost. If 36 people charter the aircraft rather than 40 people, the cost per person is greater by $12. What is the cost per person if 40 people charter the aircraft?

17. If 3 times Jane's age, in years, is equal to 8 times Beth's age, in years, and the difference between their ages is 15 years, how old are Jane and Beth?

18. In the coordinate system below, find the

    (a) coordinates of point Q

    (b) perimeter of $\triangle PQR$

    (c) area of $\triangle PQR$

    (d) slope, y-intercept, and equation of the line passing through points P and R

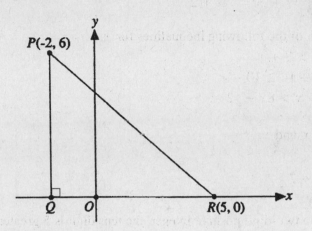

19. In the xy-plane, find the

    (a) slope and y-intercept of a graph with equation $2y + x = 6$

    (b) equation of the straight line passing through the point $(3, 2)$ with y-intercept 1

    (c) y-intercept of a straight line with slope 3 that passes through the point $(-2, 1)$

    (d) x-intercepts of the graphs in (a), (b), and (c)

ANSWERS TO ALGEBRA EXERCISES

1. (a) $37(5 - y^2)$, or $185 - 37y^2$

 (b) $\dfrac{(3x)^2}{7}$, or $\dfrac{9x^2}{7}$

 (c) $18 + (x + 4)(y)$, or $18 + xy + 4y$

2. (a) $2x^2 + 6x + 5$ (c) $x + 4$

 (b) $14x + 1$ (d) $6x^2 + 13x - 5$

3. 49

4. 2

5. (a) n^2 (e) $\dfrac{1}{w^{15}}$

 (b) $(st)^7$ (f) d^3

 (c) r^8 (g) $\dfrac{x^{15}}{y^6}$

 (d) $\dfrac{32a^5}{b^5}$ (h) $9x^2y^3$

6. (a) 7   (d) $-6, \dfrac{1}{2}$

 (b) -3 (e) $-7, 2$

 (c) $-\dfrac{9}{8}$ (f) $\dfrac{2}{3}, -4$

7. (a) $x = 21$ (c) $x = \dfrac{1}{2}$

      $y = 3$ $y = -3$

 (b) $x = 10$

      $y = 10$

8. (a) $x < -\dfrac{7}{4}$ (c) $x < 4$

 (b) $x \geq -\dfrac{3}{13}$

9. $x < \dfrac{14}{9}$, $y < \dfrac{7}{9}$

10. 83

11. 15 to 8

12. $220

13. $3

14. $800 at 10%; $2,200 at 8%

15. 48 mph and 56 mph

16. $108

17. Beth is 9; Jane is 24.

18. (a) (−2, 0)

 (b) $13 + \sqrt{85}$

 (c) 21

 (d) slope = $\dfrac{-6}{7}$, y-intercept = $\dfrac{30}{7}$,

  $y = \dfrac{-6}{7}x + \dfrac{30}{7}$, or $7y + 6x = 30$

19. (a) slope = $-\dfrac{1}{2}$, y-intercept = 3

 (b) $y = \dfrac{x}{3} + 1$

 (c) 7

 (d) 6, −3, $-\dfrac{7}{3}$

GEOMETRY

3.1 Lines and Angles

In geometry, a basic building block is the *line*, which is understood to be a "straight" line. It is also understood that lines are *infinite* in length. In the figure below, *A* and *B* are points on line *ℓ*.

That part of line *ℓ* from *A* to *B*, including the endpoints *A* and *B*, is called a *line segment*, which is *finite* in length. Sometimes the notation "*AB*" denotes line segment *AB* and sometimes it denotes the *length* of line segment *AB*. The exact meaning of the notation can be determined from the context.

Lines ℓ_1 and ℓ_2, shown below, intersect at point *P*. Whenever two lines intersect at a single point, they form four angles.

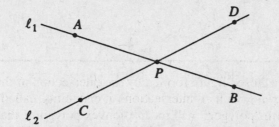

Opposite angles, called *vertical angles*, are the same size, i.e., have *equal measure*. Thus, $\angle APC$ and $\angle DPB$ have equal measure, and $\angle APD$ and $\angle CPB$ also have equal measure. The sum of the measures of the four angles is 360°.

If two lines, ℓ_1 and ℓ_2, intersect such that all four angles have equal measure (see figure below), we say that the lines are *perpendicular*, or $\ell_1 \perp \ell_2$, and each of the four angles has a measure of 90°. An angle that measures 90° is called a *right angle*, and an angle that measures 180° is called a *straight angle*.

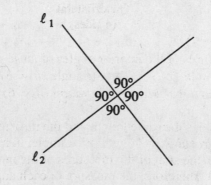

If two distinct lines in the same plane do not intersect, the lines are said to be *parallel*. The figure below shows two parallel lines, ℓ_1 and ℓ_2, which are intersected by a third line, ℓ_3, forming eight angles. Note that four of the angles have equal measure ($x°$) and the remaining four have equal measure ($y°$) where $x + y = 180$.

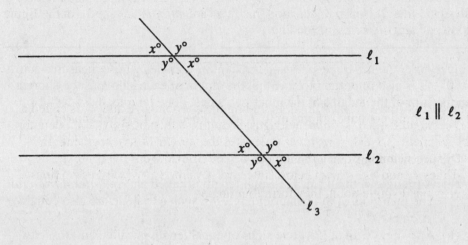

$\ell_1 \parallel \ell_2$

3.2 Polygons

A *polygon* is a closed figure formed by the intersection of three or more line segments, called *sides*, with all intersections at endpoints, called *vertices*. In this discussion, the term "polygon" will mean "convex polygon," that is, a polygon in which the measure of each interior angle is less than 180°. The figures below are examples of such polygons.

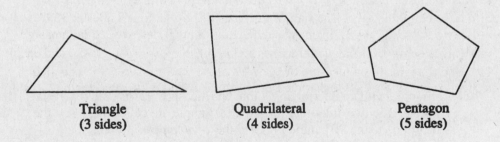

| Triangle | Quadrilateral | Pentagon |
| (3 sides) | (4 sides) | (5 sides) |

The sum of the measures of the interior angles of an *n*-sided polygon is $(n - 2)(180°)$. For example, the sum for a triangle ($n = 3$) is $(3 - 2)(180°) = 180°$, and the sum for a *hexagon* ($n = 6$) is $(6 - 2)(180°) = 720°$.

A polygon with all sides the same length and the measures of all interior angles equal is called a *regular polygon*. For example, in a *regular octagon* (8 sides of equal length), the sum of the measures of the interior angles is $(8 - 2)(180°) = 1,080°$. Therefore, the measure of each angle is $1,080° \div 8 = 135°$.

The *perimeter* of a polygon is defined as the sum of the lengths of its sides. The *area* of a polygon is the measure of the area of the region enclosed by the polygon.

In the next two sections, we look at some basic properties of the simplest polygons—triangles and quadrilaterals.

3.3 Triangles

Every triangle has three sides and three interior angles whose measures sum to $180°$. It is also important to note that the length of each side must be shorter than the sum of the lengths of the other two sides. For example, the sides of a triangle could not have lengths of 4, 7, and 12 because 12 is not shorter than $4 + 7$.

The following are special triangles.

(a) A triangle with all sides of equal length is called an *equilateral triangle*. The measures of three interior angles of such a triangle are also equal (each $60°$).

(b) A triangle with at least two sides of equal length is called an *isosceles triangle*. If a triangle has two sides of equal length, then the measures of the angles opposite the two sides are equal. The converse of the previous statement is also true. For example, in $\triangle ABC$ below, since both $\angle ABC$ and $\angle BCA$ have measure $50°$, it must be true that $BA = AC$. Also, since $50 + 50 + x = 180$, the measure of $\angle BAC$ must be $80°$.

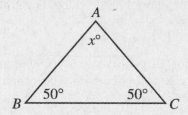

(c) A triangle with an interior angle that has measure $90°$ is called a *right triangle*. The two sides that form the $90°$ angle are called *legs* and the side opposite the $90°$ angle is called the *hypotenuse*.

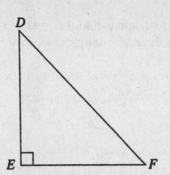

For right $\triangle DEF$ above, DE and EF are legs and DF is the hypotenuse. The *Pythagorean Theorem* states that for any right triangle, the square of the length of the hypotenuse equals the sum of the squares of the lengths of the legs. Thus, in right $\triangle DEF$

$$(DF)^2 = (DE)^2 + (EF)^2$$

This relationship can be used to find the length of one side of a right triangle if the lengths of the other two sides are known. For example, if one leg of a right triangle has length 5 and the hypotenuse has length 8, then the length of the other side can be calculated as follows:

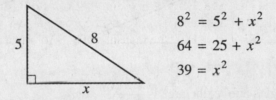

$$8^2 = 5^2 + x^2$$
$$64 = 25 + x^2$$
$$39 = x^2$$

Since $x^2 = 39$ and x must be positive, $x = \sqrt{39}$, or approximately 6.2.

The Pythagorean Theorem can be used to determine the ratios of the sides of two special right triangles:

An isosceles right triangle has angles measuring 45°, 45°, 90°. The Pythagorean Theorem applied to the triangle below shows that the lengths of its sides are in the ratio 1 to 1 to $\sqrt{2}$.

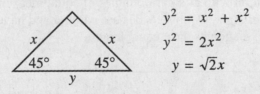

$$y^2 = x^2 + x^2$$
$$y^2 = 2x^2$$
$$y = \sqrt{2}x$$

A $30° - 60° - 90°$ right triangle is half of an equilateral triangle, as the following figure shows.

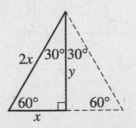

So the length of the shortest side is half the longest side, and by the Pythagorean Theorem, the ratio of all three side lengths is 1 to $\sqrt{3}$ to 2, since

$$x^2 + y^2 = (2x)^2$$
$$x^2 + y^2 = 4x^2$$
$$y^2 = 4x^2 - x^2$$
$$y^2 = 3x^2$$
$$y = \sqrt{3}x$$

The *area* of a triangle is defined as half the length of a base (b) multiplied by the corresponding height (h), that is,

$$\text{Area} = \frac{bh}{2}.$$

Any side of a triangle may be considered a base, and then the corresponding height is the perpendicular distance from the opposite vertex to the base (or an extension of the base). The examples below summarize three possible locations for measuring height with respect to a base.

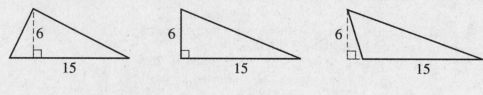

In all three triangles above, the area is $\frac{(15)(6)}{2}$, or 45.

3.4 Quadrilaterals

Every quadrilateral has four sides and four interior angles whose measures sum to $360°$. The following are special quadrilaterals.

(a) A quadrilateral with all interior angles of equal measure (each 90°) is called a *rectangle*. Opposite sides are parallel and have equal length, and the two diagonals have equal length.

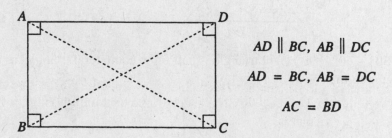

$AD \parallel BC,\ AB \parallel DC$

$AD = BC,\ AB = DC$

$AC = BD$

A rectangle with all sides of equal length is called a *square*.

(b) A quadrilateral with both pairs of opposite sides parallel is called a *parallelogram*. In a parallelogram, opposite sides have equal length, and opposite interior angles have equal measure.

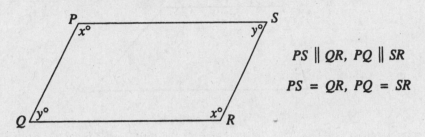

$$PS \parallel QR, \; PQ \parallel SR$$

$$PS = QR, \; PQ = SR$$

(c) A quadrilateral with one pair of opposite sides parallel is called a *trapezoid*.

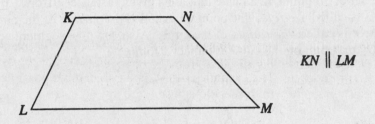

$$KN \parallel LM$$

For all rectangles and parallelograms the *area* is defined as the length of the base (b) multiplied by the height (h), that is

$$\text{Area} = bh$$

Any side may be considered a base, and then the height is either the length of an adjacent side (for a rectangle) or the length of a perpendicular line from the base to the opposite side (for a parallelogram). Here are examples of each:

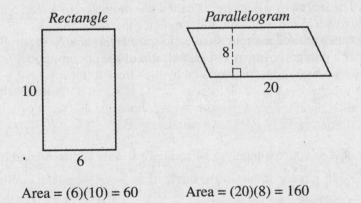

$$\text{Area} = (6)(10) = 60 \qquad \text{Area} = (20)(8) = 160$$

The area of a trapezoid may be calculated by finding half the sum of the lengths of the two parallel sides (b_1 and b_2) and then multiplying the result by the height (h), that is,

$$\text{Area} = \frac{1}{2}(b_1 + b_2)(h).$$

For example, for the trapezoid shown below with bases of length 10 and 18, and a height of 7.5,

63

$$\text{Area} = \frac{1}{2}(10 + 18)(7.5) = 105.$$

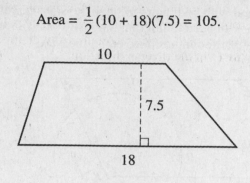

3.5 Circles

The set of all points in a plane that are a given distance r from a fixed point O is called a *circle*. The point O is called the *center* of the circle, and the distance r is called *the radius* of the circle. Also, any line segment connecting point O to a point on the circle is called *a radius*.

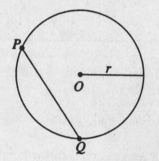

Any line segment that has its endpoints on a circle, such as PQ above, is called *a chord*. Any chord that passes through the center of a circle is called *a diameter*. The length of a diameter is called *the diameter* of a circle. Therefore, the diameter of a circle is always equal to twice its radius.

The distance around a circle is called its *circumference* (comparable to the perimeter of a polygon). In any circle, the ratio of the circumference c to the diameter d is a fixed constant, denoted by the Greek letter π:

$$\frac{c}{d} = \pi$$

The value of π is approximately 3.14 and may also be approximated by the fraction $\frac{22}{7}$. If r is the radius of the circle, then $\frac{c}{2r} = \pi$, so the circumference is related to the radius by the equation

$$c = 2\pi r.$$

Therefore, if a circle has a radius equal to 5.2, then its circumference is $(2)(\pi)(5.2) = (10.4)(\pi)$, which is approximately equal to 32.7.

On a circle, the set of all points between and including two given points is called an *arc*. It is customary to refer to an arc with three points to avoid ambiguity. In the figure below, arc *ABC* is the short arc from *A* to *C*, but arc *ADC* is the long arc from *A* to *C* in the reverse direction.

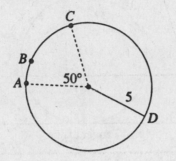

Arcs can be measured in degrees. The number of degrees of arc equals the number of degrees in the central angle formed by the two radii intersecting the arc's endpoints. The number of degrees of arc in the entire circle (one complete revolution) is 360. Thus, in the figure above, arc *ABC* is a 50° arc and arc *ADC* is a 310° arc.

To find the *length* of an arc, it is important to know that the ratio of arc length to circumference is equal to the ratio of arc measure (in degrees) to 360. In the figure above, the circumference is 10π. Therefore,

$$\frac{\text{length of arc } ABC}{10\pi} = \frac{50}{360}$$

$$\text{length of arc } ABC = \left(\frac{50}{360}\right)(10\pi) = \frac{25\pi}{18}$$

The *area* of a circle with radius r is equal to πr^2. For example, the area of the circle above is $\pi(5)^2 = 25\pi$. In this circle, the pie-shaped region bordered by arc *ABC* and the two dashed radii is called a *sector* of the circle, with central angle 50°. Just as in the case of arc length, the ratio of the area of the sector to the area of the entire circle is equal to the ratio of the arc measure (in degrees) to 360. So if S represents the area of the sector with central angle 50°, then

$$\frac{S}{25\pi} = \frac{50}{360}$$

$$S = \left(\frac{50}{360}\right)(25\pi) = \frac{125\pi}{36}$$

A *tangent* to a circle is a line that has exactly one point in common with the circle. A radius with its endpoint at the point of tangency is perpendicular to the tangent line. The converse is also true.

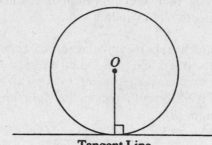

Tangent Line

If each vertex of a polygon lies on a circle, then the polygon is *inscribed* in the circle, or equivalently, the circle is *circumscribed* about the polygon. Triangle *RST* below is inscribed in the circle with center *O*.

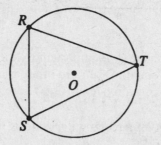

If each side of a polygon is tangent to a given circle, then the polygon is *circumscribed* about the circle, or equivalently, the circle is *inscribed* in the polygon. In the figure below, quadrilateral *ABCD* is circumscribed about the circle with center *O*.

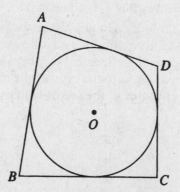

Two or more circles with the same center are called *concentric* circles.

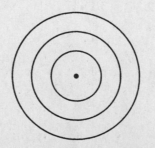

3.6 Three-Dimensional Figures

Basic three-dimensional figures include rectangular solids, cubes, cylinders, spheres, pyramids, and cones. In this section, we look at some properties of rectangular solids and right circular cylinders.

(a) A *rectangular solid* has six rectangular surfaces called *faces* (see figure below). Each line segment shown is called an *edge* (there are 12 edges), and each point at which the edges meet is called a *vertex* (there are 8 vertices). The dimensions of a rectangular solid are length (ℓ), width (w), and height (h).

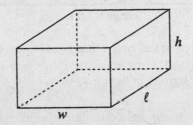

A rectangular solid with $\ell = w = h$ is called a *cube*. The *volume V* of a rectangular solid is the product of the three dimensions,

$$V = \ell wh$$

The *surface area A* of a rectangular solid is the sum of the areas of the six faces, or

$$A = 2(w\ell + \ell h + wh).$$

For example, if a rectangular solid has length 8.5, width 5, and height 10, then its volume is

$$V = (8.5)(5)(10) = 425,$$

and its surface area is

$$A = 2[(5)(8.5) + (8.5)(10) + (5)(10)] = 355.$$

(b) A *right circular cylinder* is shown in the figure below. Its bases are circles with equal radii and centers P and Q, respectively, and its height PQ is perpendicular to both bases.

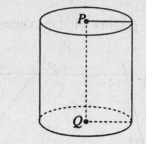

The *volume* V of a right circular cylinder with a base radius r and height h is the area of the base multiplied by the height, or

$$V = \pi r^2 h.$$

The *surface area* A of a right circular cylinder is the sum of the two base areas and the area of the curved surface, or

$$A = 2\left(\pi r^2\right) + 2\pi rh.$$

For example, if a right circular cylinder has a base radius of 3 and a height of 6.5, then its volume is

$$V = \pi(3)^2(6.5) = 58.5\pi,$$

and its surface area is

$$A = (2)(\pi)(3)^2 + (2)(\pi)(3)(6.5) = 57\pi.$$

GEOMETRY EXERCISES

(Answers on page 72)

1. Lines l and m below are parallel. Find the values of x and y.

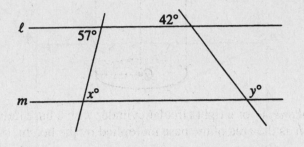

2. In the figure below, $AC = BC$. Find the values of x and y.

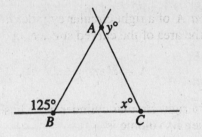

3. In the figure below, what relationship must hold among angle measures x, y, and z ?

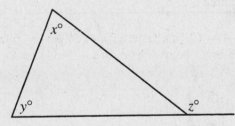

4. What is the sum of the measures of the interior angles of a decagon (10-sided polygon) ?

5. If the polygon in #4 is regular, what is the measure of each interior angle?

6. The lengths of two sides of an isosceles triangle are 15 and 22, respectively. What are the possible values of the perimeter?

7. In rectangle *ABDE* below, $AB = 5$, $BC = 7$, and $CD = 3$. Find the

   (a) area of *ABDE*

   (b) area of triangle *BCF*

   (c) length of *AD*

   (d) perimeter of *ABDE*

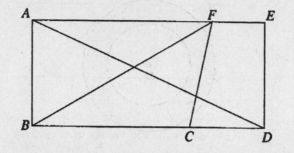

8. In parallelogram *ABCD* below, find the

   (a) area of *ABCD*

   (b) perimeter of *ABCD*

   (c) length of diagonal *AC*

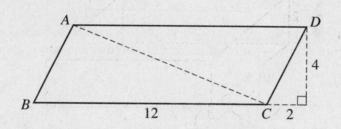

9. The circle with center *O* below has radius 4. Find the

   (a) circumference

   (b) length of arc *ABC*

   (c) area of the shaded region

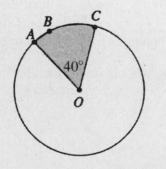

10. The figure below shows two concentric circles each with center O. If the larger circle has radius 12 and the smaller circle has radius 8, find the

    (a) circumference of the larger circle

    (b) area of the smaller circle

    (c) area of the shaded region

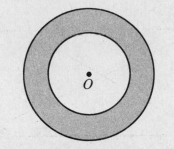

11. For the rectangular solid below, find the

    (a) surface area

    (b) length of diagonal AB

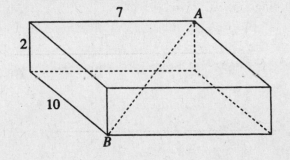

ANSWERS TO GEOMETRY EXERCISES

1. $x = 57$, $y = 138$

2. $x = 70$, $y = 125$

3. $z = x + y$

4. $1,440°$

5. $144°$

6. 52 or 59

7. (a) 50   (c) $5\sqrt{5}$
   (b) 17.5   (d) 30

8. (a) 48   (c) $2\sqrt{29}$
   (b) $24 + 4\sqrt{5}$

9. (a) 8π (c) $\dfrac{16\pi}{9}$
   (b) $\dfrac{8\pi}{9}$

10. (a) 24π (c) 80π
    (b) 64π

11. (a) 208
    (b) $3\sqrt{17}$

DATA ANALYSIS

4.1 Measures of Central Location

Two common measures of central location, often called "average," for a discrete set of numerical values or measurements are the *arithmetic mean* and the *median*.

The *average* (*arithmetic mean*) of n values is defined as the *sum of the n values divided by n*. For example, the arithmetic mean of the values 5, 8, 8, 14, 15, and 10 is $60 \div 6 = 10$.

If we order the n values from least to greatest, the *median* is defined as *the middle value if n is odd* and *the sum of the two middle values divided by 2 if n is even*. In the example above, $n = 6$, which is even. Ordered from least to greatest, the values are 5, 8, 8, 10, 14, and 15. Therefore, the median is

$$\frac{8 + 10}{2} = 9.$$

Note that for the same set of values, the arithmetic mean and the median need not be equal, although they could be. For example, the set of values 10, 20, 30, 40, and 50 has arithmetic mean = median = 30.

Another measure of central location is called the *mode*, which is defined as *the most frequently occurring value*. For the six measurements above, the mode is 8.

4.2 Measures of Dispersion

Measures of dispersion, or spread, for a discrete set of numerical values or measurements take many forms in data analyses. The simplest measure of dispersion is called the *range*, which is defined as the *greatest measurement minus the least measurement*. So, in the example in 4.1 above, the range for the six values is 15 minus 5, or 10.

Since the range is affected by only the two most extreme values in the set of measurements, other measures of dispersion have been developed that are affected by every measurement. The most commonly used of these other measures is called the *standard deviation*. The value of the standard deviation for a set of n measurements can be calculated by (1) first calculating the arithmetic mean, (2) finding the difference between that mean and each measurement, (3) squaring each of the differences, (4) summing the squared values, (5) dividing the sum by n, and finally (6) taking the nonnegative square root of the quotient. The following demonstrates this calculation for the example used in 4.1.

x	$x-10$	$(x-10)^2$
5	-5	25
8	-2	4
8	-2	4
10	0	0
14	4	16
15	5	25
		74

$$\text{standard deviation} = \sqrt{\frac{74}{6}} \approx 3.5$$

The standard deviation can be roughly interpreted as the average distance from the arithmetic mean for the n measurements. The standard deviation cannot be negative, and when two sets of measurements are compared, the one with the larger dispersion will have the larger standard deviation.

4.3 Frequency Distributions

For some sets of measurements, it is more convenient and informative to display the measurements in a *frequency distribution*. For example, the following values could represent the number of dependent children in each of 25 families living on a particular street.

$$1, 2, 0, 4, 1, 3, 3, 1, 2, 0, 4, 5, 2,$$
$$3, 2, 3, 2, 4, 1, 2, 3, 0, 2, 3, 1$$

These data can be grouped into a *frequency distribution* by listing each different value (x) and the frequency (f) of occurrence for each value.

Frequency Distribution

x	f
0	3
1	5
2	7
3	6
4	3
5	1
Total	25

The frequency distribution format not only provides a quick summary of the data, but it also simplifies the calculations of the central location and dispersion measures. For these data, the x's can be summed by multiplying each x by its frequency and then adding the products. So, the arithmetic mean is

$$\frac{(0)(3) + (1)(5) + (2)(7) + (3)(6) + (4)(3) + (5)(1)}{25} = 2.16$$

The median is the middle (13th) x value in order of size. The f values show that the 13th x value must be a 2. The range is 5 minus 0, or 5. The standard deviation can also be calculated more easily from a frequency distribution, although in practice it is likely that a programmable calculator would be used to calculate both the mean and the standard deviation directly from the 25 measurements.

4.4 Counting

Some definitions and principles basic to counting are:

(a) *If one task has* n *possible outcomes and a second task has* m *possible outcomes, then the joint occurrence of the two tasks has* (n)(m) *possible outcomes.* For example, if Town A and Town B are joined by 3 different roads, and Town B and Town C are joined by 4 different roads, then the number of different routes from Town A to Town C through B is (3)(4), or 12. Each time a coin is flipped, there are 2 possible outcomes: heads or tails. Therefore, if a coin is flipped 4 times, then the number of possible outcomes is (2)(2)(2)(2), or 16.

(b) *For any integer* n *greater than* 1, *the symbol* n!, *pronounced "n factorial," is defined as the product of all positive integers less than or equal to* n. *Also,* 0! = 1! = 1. Therefore,

$$0! = 1$$
$$1! = 1$$
$$2! = (2)(1) = 2$$
$$3! = (3)(2)(1) = 6$$
$$4! = (4)(3)(2)(1) = 24$$

and so on.

(c) *The number of ways that* n *objects can be ordered is* n!. For example, the number of ways that the letters A, B, and C can be ordered is 3!, or 6. The six orders are

$$ABC, \ ACB, \ BAC, \ BCA, \ CAB, \text{ and } CBA$$

(d) *The number different subsets of* r *objects that can be selected from* n *objects* (r ≤ n), *without regard to the order of selection, is*

$$\frac{n!}{(n-r)!\,r!}.$$

For example, the number of different committees of 3 people that can be selected from 5 people is

$$\frac{5!}{(5-3)!\,3!} = \frac{5!}{2!\,3!} = \frac{120}{(2)(6)} = 10.$$

These 10 subsets are called *combinations* of 5 objects selected 3 at a time.

4.5 Probability

Everyday there are occasions in which decisions must be made in the face of uncertainty. The decision-making process often involves the selection of a course of action based on an analysis of possible outcomes. For situations in which the possible outcomes are all equally likely, the *probability that an event E occurs*, represented by "$P(E)$", can be defined as

$$P(E) = \frac{\text{The number of outcomes involving the occurrence of } E}{\text{The total number of possible outcomes}}.$$

For example, if a committee of 11 students consists of 2 seniors, 5 juniors, and 4 sophomores, and one student is to be selected at random to chair the committee, then the probability that the student selected will be a senior is $\frac{2}{11}$.

In general, "$P(E)$" can be thought of as a number assigned to an event E which expresses the likelihood that E occurs. If E cannot occur, then $P(E) = 0$, and if E must occur, then $P(E) = 1$. If the occurrence of E is uncertain, then $0 < P(E) < 1$. The probability that event E does NOT occur is $1 - P(E)$. For example, if the probability is 0.75 that it will rain tomorrow, then the probability that it will not rain tomorrow is $1 - 0.75$, or 0.25.

The probability that events E and F both occur can be represented by $P(E \text{ and } F)$*, and the probability that at least one of the two events occurs can be represented by $P(E \text{ or } F)$**. One of the fundamental relationships among probabilities is called the *Addition Law*:

$$P(E \text{ or } F) = P(E) + P(F) - P(E \text{ and } F).$$

---

*Many texts use $P(E \cap F)$.

**Many texts use $P(E \cup F)$.

For example, if a card is to be selected randomly from a standard deck of 52 playing cards, E is the event that a heart is selected, and F is the event that a 9 is selected, then

$$P(E) = \frac{13}{52}, \; P(F) = \frac{4}{52}, \text{ and } P(E \text{ and } F) = \frac{1}{52}.$$

Therefore, $P(E \text{ or } F) = \frac{13}{52} + \frac{4}{52} - \frac{1}{52} = \frac{16}{52} = \frac{4}{13}$.

Two events are said to be *independent* if the occurrence or nonoccurrence of either one in no way affects the occurrence of the other. It follows that if events E and F are independent events, then $P(E \text{ and } F) = P(E) \cdot P(F)$. Two events are said to be *mutually exclusive* if the occurrence of either one precludes the occurrence of the other. In other words, if events E and F are mutually exclusive, then $P(E \text{ and } F) = 0$.

Example: If $P(A) = 0.45$ and $P(B) = 0.20$, and the two events are independent, what is $P(A \text{ or } B)$?

According to the Addition Law:

$$\begin{aligned} P(A \text{ or } B) &= P(A) + P(B) - P(A \text{ and } B) \\ &= P(A) + P(B) - P(A) \cdot P(B) \\ &= 0.45 + 0.20 - (0.45)(0.20) \\ &= 0.56 \end{aligned}$$

If the two events in the example above had been mutually exclusive, then $P(A \text{ or } B)$ would have been found as follows:

$$\begin{aligned} P(A \text{ or } B) &= P(A) + P(B) - P(A \text{ and } B) \\ &= 0.45 + 0.20 - 0 \\ &= 0.65 \end{aligned}$$

4.6 Data Representation and Interpretation

Data can be summarized and represented in various forms, including tables, bar graphs, circle graphs, line graphs, and other diagrams. The following are several examples of tables and graphs, each with questions that can be answered by selecting the appropriate information and applying mathematical techniques.

Example 1.

FOREIGN TRADE OF COUNTRY *X*, 1968-1980
(in United States dollars)

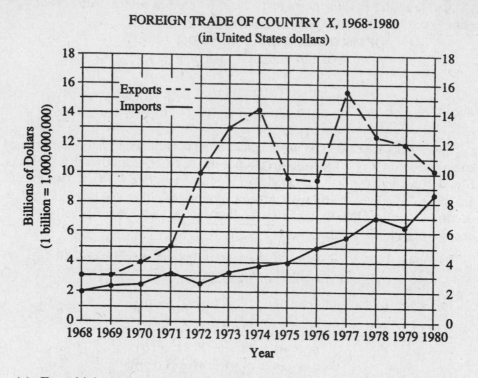

(a) For which year shown on the graph did exports exceed the previous year's exports by the greatest dollar amount?

(b) In 1973 the dollar value of imports was approximately what percent of the dollar value of exports?

(c) If it were discovered that the import dollar amount shown for 1978 was incorrect and should have been $3.1 billion instead, then the average (arithmetic mean) import dollar amount per year for the 13 years would be how much less?

Solutions:

(a) The greatest increase in exports form one year to the next is represented by the dotted line segment with the steepest positive slope, which is found between 1976 and 1977. The increase was approximately $6 billion. Thus, the answer is 1977.

(b) In 1973, the dollar value of imports was approximately $3.3 billion, and the dollar value of exports was $13 billion. Therefore, the answer is $\frac{3.3}{13}$, or approximately 25%.

(c) If the import dollar amount in 1978 were $3.1 billion, rather than the table amount, $7 billion, then the sum of the import amounts for the 13 years would be reduced by $3.9 billion. Therefore, the average per year would be reduced by $\frac{\$3.9}{13}$ billion, which is $0.3 billion, or $300 million.

Example 2.

**UNITED STATES PRODUCTION
OF PHOTOGRAPHIC EQUIPMENT
AND SUPPLIES IN 1971**

Total: $3,980 million

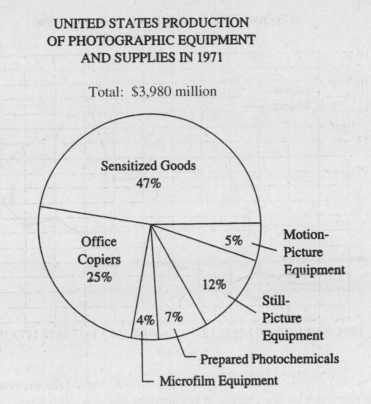

(a) In 1971 what was the ratio of the value of sensitized goods to the value of still-picture equipment produced in the United States?

(b) If the value of office copiers produced in 1971 was 30 percent higher than the corresponding value in 1970, what was the value of office copiers produced in 1970 ?

(c) If the areas of the sectors in the circle graph are drawn in proportion to the percents shown, what is the measure, in degrees, of the central angle of the sector representing the percent of prepared photochemicals produced?

Solutions:

(a) The ratio of the value of sensitized goods to the value of still-picture equipment is equal to the ratio of the corresponding percents shown. Therefore, the ratio is 47 to 12, or approximately 4 to 1.

(b) The value of office copiers produced in 1971 was (0.25)($3,980), or $995 million. Therefore, if the corresponding value in 1970 was x, then $x(1.30) = 995 million, or $x = 765 million.

(c) Since the sum of the central angles for the six sectors is 360°, the central angle for the sector representing prepared photochemicals is (0.07)(360)°, or 25.2°.

Example 3.

TOTAL STUDENT ENROLLMENT
(PART-TIME + FULL-TIME)
IN COLLEGE *R* : 1976-1980

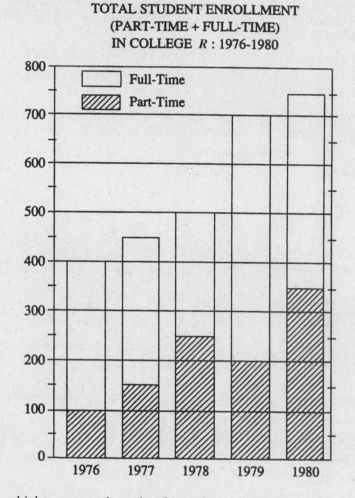

(a) For which year was the ratio of part-time enrollment to total enrollment the greatest?

(b) What was the full-time enrollment in 1977 ?

(c) What was the percent increase in total enrollment from 1976 to 1980 ?

Solutions:

(a) It is visually apparent that the height of the shaded bar compared to the total height of the bar is greatest in 1978 (about half the total height). No calculations are necessary.

(b) In 1977 the total enrollment was approximately 450 students, and the part-time enrollment was approximately 150 students. Thus, the full-time enrollment was 450 − 150, or 300 students.

(c) The total enrollments for 1976 and 1980 were approximately 400 and 750, respectively. Therefore, the percent increase from 1976 to 1980 was

$$\frac{750 - 400}{400} = \frac{350}{400} = 0.875 = 87.5\%.$$

Example 4.

CONSUMER COMPLAINTS RECEIVED BY THE CIVIL AERONAUTICS BOARD

Category	1980 (percent)	1981 (percent)
Flight Problems	20.0%	22.1%
Baggage	18.3	21.8
Customer service	13.1	11.3
Oversales of seats	10.5	11.8
Refund problems	10.1	8.1
Fares	6.4	6.0
Reservations and ticketing	5.8	5.6
Tours	3.3	2.3
Smoking	3.2	2.9
Advertising	1.2	1.1
Credit	1.0	0.8
Special passengers	0.9	0.9
Other	6.2	5.3
	100.0%	100.0%
Total Number of Complaints	22,998	13,278

(a) Approximately how many complaints concerning credit were received by the Civil Aeronautics Board in 1980 ?

(b) By approximately what percent did the total number of complaints decrease from 1980 to 1981 ?

(c) Which of the following statements can be inferred from the table?

I. In 1980 and in 1981, complaints about flight problems, baggage, and customer service together accounted for more than 50 percent of all consumer complaints received by the Civil Aeronautics Board.

II. The number of special passenger complaints was unchanged from 1980 to 1981.

III. From 1980 to 1981, the number of flight problem complaints increased by more than 2 percent.

Solutions:

(a) In 1980, 1 percent of the complaints concerned credit, so the number of complaints was approximately (0.01)(22,998), or 230.

(b) The decrease in total complaints from 1980 to 1981 was 22,998 − 13,278, or 9,720. Therefore, the percent decrease was 9,720 ÷ 22,998, or 42 percent.

(c) Since 20.0 + 18.3 + 13.1 and 22.1 + 21.8 + 11.3 are both greater than 50, statement I is true. The percent of special passenger complaints did remain the same for 1980 to 1981, but the *number* of special passenger complaints decreased because the total number of complaints decreased. Thus, statement II is false. The percents shown in the table for flight problems do in fact increase more than 2 percentage points. However, the *number* of flight problem complaints in 1980 was (0.2)(22,998), or 4,600, and the number in 1981 was (0.221)(13,278), or 2,934. So, the number of flight problem complaints actually decreased from 1980 to 1981. Therefore, statement I is the only statement that can be inferred from the table.

Example 5.

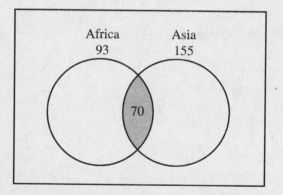

In a survey of 250 European travelers, 93 have traveled to Africa, 155 have traveled to Asia, and 70 have traveled to both of these continents, as illustrated in the *Venn diagram* above.

(a) How many of the travelers surveyed have traveled to Africa but <u>not</u> to Asia?

(b) How many of the travelers surveyed have traveled to <u>at least one</u> of the two continents Africa and Asia?

(c) How many of the travelers surveyed have traveled <u>neither</u> to Africa <u>nor</u> to Asia?

Solutions:

A Venn diagram is useful for sorting out various sets and subsets that may overlap. The rectangular region represents the set of all travelers surveyed; the two circular regions represent the two groups of travelers to Africa and Asia; and the shaded region represents the subset of those who have traveled to both continents.

(a) The set described here is represented by *that part of the left circle that is not shaded*. This description suggests that the answer can be found by taking the shaded part away from the first circle—in effect, subtracting the 70 from the 93, to get 23 travelers who have traveled to Africa but not to Asia.

(b) The set described here is represented by that part of the rectangle that is *in at least one of the two circles*. This description suggests adding the two numbers 93 and 155. But the 70 travelers who have traveled to both continents would be counted twice in the sum $93 + 155$. To correct the double counting, subtract 70 from the sum so that these 70 travelers are counted only once:
$$93 + 155 - 70 = 178.$$

(c) The set described here is represented by that part of the rectangle that is *not in either circle*. Let N be the number of these travelers. Note that the entire rectangular region has two main nonoverlapping parts: the part *outside* the circles and the part *inside* the circles. The first part represents N travelers and the second part represents $93 + 155 - 70 = 178$ travelers (from question (b)). Therefore,
$$250 = N + 178,$$

and solving for N yields
$$N = 250 - 178 = 72.$$

DATA ANALYSIS EXERCISES

(Answers on page 91)

1. The daily temperatures, in degrees Fahrenheit, for 10 days in May were 61, 62, 65, 65, 65, 68, 74, 74, 75, and 77.

    (a) Find the mean, median, and mode for the temperatures.

    (b) If each day had been 7 degrees warmer, what would have been the mean, median, and mode for those 10 measurements?

2. The ages, in years, of the employees in a small company are 22, 33, 21, 28, 22, 31, 44, and 19.

    (a) Find the mean, median, and mode for the 8 ages.

    (b) Find the range and standard deviation for the 8 ages.

    (c) If each of the employees had been 10 years older, what would have been the range and standard deviation of their ages?

3. A group of 20 values has mean 85 and median 80. A different group of 30 values has mean 75 and median 72.

    (a) What is the mean of the 50 values?

    (b) What is the median of the 50 values?

4. Find the mean, median, mode, range, and standard deviation for x, given the frequency distribution below.

x	f
0	2
1	6
2	3
3	2
4	4

5. In the frequency distribution below, y represents age on last birthday for 40 people. Find the mean, median, mode, and range for y.

y	f
17	2
18	7
19	19
20	9
21	2
22	0
23	1

6. How many different ways can the letters in the word STUDY be ordered?

7. Martha invited 4 friends to go with her to the movies. There are 120 different ways in which they can sit together in a row. In how many of those ways is Martha sitting in the middle?

8. How many 3-digit positive integers are odd and do not contain the digit "5"?

9. From a box of 10 light bulbs, 4 are to be removed. How many different sets of 4 bulbs could be removed?

10. A talent contest has 8 contestants. Judges must award prizes for first, second, and third places. If there are no ties, (a) in how many different ways can the 3 prizes be awarded, and (b) how many different groups of 3 people can get prizes?

11. If the probability is 0.78 that Marshall will be late for work at least once next week, what is the probability that he will not be late for work next week?

12. If an integer is randomly selected from all positive 2-digit integers (i.e., the integers 10, 11, 12, . . . , 99), find the probability that the integer chosen has

    (a) a "4" in the tens place

    (b) at least one "4"

    (c) no "4" in either place

13. In a box of 10 electrical parts, 2 are defective.

    (a) If one part is chosen randomly from the box, what is the probability that it is not defective?

    (b) If two parts are randomly chosen from the box, without replacement, what is the probability that both are defective?

14. The table shows the distribution of a group of 40 college students by gender and class.

	Sophomores	Juniors	Seniors
Males	6	10	2
Females	10	9	3

If one student is randomly selected from this group, find the probability that the student chosen is

    (a) not a junior

    (b) a female or a sophomore

    (c) a male sophomore or a female senior

15. $P(A \text{ or } B) = 0.60$ and $P(A) = 0.20$.

    (a) Find $P(B)$ given that events A and B are mutually exclusive.

    (b) Find $P(B)$ given that events A and B are independent.

16. Lin and Mark each attempt independently to decode a message. If the probability that Lin will decode the message is 0.80, and the probability that Mark will decode the message is 0.70, find the probability that

    (a) both will decode the message

    (b) at least one of them will decode the message

    (c) neither of them will decode the message

17.

AVERAGE AND HIGH WIND SPEED FOR SELECTED STATIONS OVER A 10-YEAR PERIOD (1971-80) (miles per hour)		
Station	Average	High
Atlanta, GA	9.1	71
Boston, MA	12.6	65
Buffalo, NY	12.3	91
Chicago, IL	10.4	60
Cincinnati, OH	7.1	49
Denver, CO	9.0	56
Miami, FL	9.2	132
Montgomery, AL	6.7	72
New York, NY	9.4	70
Omaha, NE	10.8	109
Pittsburgh, PA	9.3	58
San Diego, CA	6.7	51
Washington, DC	9.3	78

SPEED AND OFFICIAL DESIGNATIONS OF WINDS	
Designation	Miles per Hour
Calm	Less than 1
Light air	1 to 3
Light breeze	4 to 7
Gentle breeze	8 to 12
Moderate breeze	13 to 18
Fresh breeze	19 to 24
Strong breeze	25 to 31
Near gale	32 to 38
Gale	39 to 46
Strong gale	47 to 54
Storm	55 to 63
Violent storm	64 to 73
Hurricane	74 and above

(a) Which station has a high wind speed that is the median of the high wind speeds for all the stations listed?

(b) For those stations that have recorded hurricane winds at least once during the 10-year period, what is the arithmetic mean of their average wind speeds?

(c) For how many of the stations is the ratio of high wind speed to average wind speed greater than 10 to 1 ?

87

18.

PUBLIC AND PRIVATE SCHOOL EXPENDITURES
1965 – 1979
(in billions of dollars)

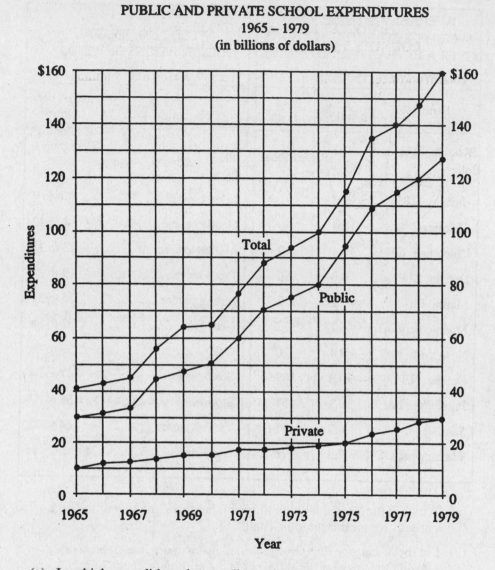

(a) In which year did total expenditures increase the most from the year before?

(b) In 1979 private school expenditures were approximately what percent of total expenditures?

19.

DISTRIBUTION OF WORKFORCE
BY OCCUPATIONAL CATEGORY FOR
COUNTRY X IN 1981 AND PROJECTED FOR 1995

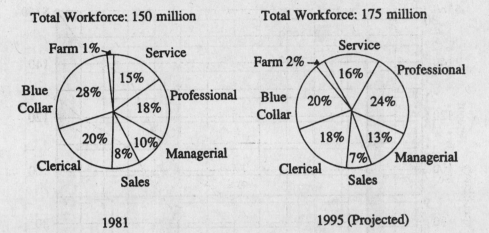

Total Workforce: 150 million   Total Workforce: 175 million

1981   1995 (Projected)

(a) In 1981, how many categories each comprised more than 25 million workers?

(b) What is the ratio of the number of workers in the Professional category in 1981 to the projected number of such workers in 1995 ?

(c) From 1981 to 1995, there is a projected increase in the number of workers in which of the following categories?

    I. Sales

    II. Service

    III. Clerical

20.

FAMILY *X*'S EXPENDITURES AS A PERCENT OF
ITS GROSS ANNUAL INCOME*

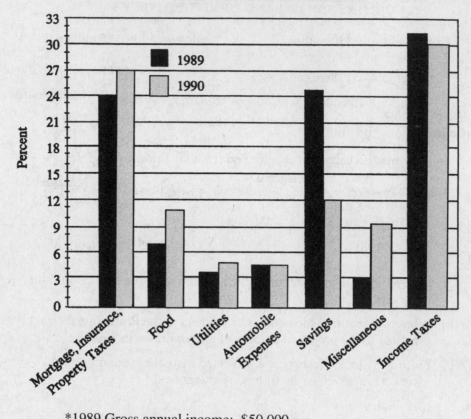

*1989 Gross annual income: $50,000
1990 Gross annual income: $45,000

(a) In 1989 Family *X* used a total of 49 percent of its gross annual income for two of the categories listed. What was the total amount of Family *X*'s income used for those same categories in 1990 ?

(b) Family *X*'s gross income is the sum of Mr. *X*'s income and Mrs. *X*'s income. In 1989 Mr. and Mrs. *X* each had an income of $25,000. If Mr. *X*'s income increased by 10 percent from 1989 to 1990, by what percent did Mrs. *X*'s income decrease for the same period?

ANSWERS TO DATA ANALYSIS EXERCISES

1. (a) mean = 68.6, median = 66.5, mode = 65

    (b) Each measure would have been 7 degrees greater.

2. (a) mean = 27.5, median = 25, mode = 22

    (b) range = 25, standard deviation ≈ 7.8

    (c) range = 25, standard deviation ≈ 7.8

3. (a) mean = 79

    (b) The median cannot be determined from the information given.

4. mean = 2, median = 2, mode = 1, range = 4, standard deviation ≈ 1.4

5. mean = 19.15, median = 19, mode = 19, range = 6

6. 120

7. 24

8. 288

9. 210

10. (a) 336   (b) 56

11. 0.22

12. (a) $\frac{1}{9}$ (b) $\frac{1}{5}$ (c) $\frac{4}{5}$

13. (a) $\frac{4}{5}$ (b) $\frac{1}{45}$

14. (a) $\frac{21}{40}$ (b) $\frac{7}{10}$ (c) $\frac{9}{40}$

15. (a) 0.40   (b) 0.50

16. (a) 0.56   (b) 0.94   (c) 0.06

17. (a) New York   (b) 10.4   (c) Three

18. (a) 1976   (b) 19%

19. (a) Three   (b) 9 to 14, or 9/14   (c) I, II, and III

20. (a) $17,550   (b) 30%

Review of the Analytical Writing Section

Overview

The analytical writing section is a new section of the GRE General Test, introduced in October 2002, that tests your critical thinking and analytical writing skills. It assesses your ability to articulate and support complex ideas, analyze an argument, and sustain a focused and coherent discussion. It does not assess specific content knowledge.

The analytical writing section consists of two separately-timed analytical writing tasks:

- a 45-minute "Present Your Perspective on an Issue" task
- a 30-minute "Analyze an Argument" task

You will be given a choice between two Issue topics. Each states an opinion on an issue of broad interest and asks you to discuss the issue from any perspective(s) you wish, so long as you provide relevant reasons and examples to explain and support your views.

You will not have a choice of Argument topics. The Argument task presents a different challenge from that of the Issue task: it requires you to critique a given argument by discussing how well reasoned you find it. You will need to consider the logical soundness of the argument rather than to agree or disagree with the position it presents.

The two tasks are complementary in that one requires you to construct your own argument by taking a position and providing evidence supporting your views on the issue, whereas the other requires you to critique someone else's argument by assessing its claims and evaluating the evidence it provides.

How the Analytical Writing Section is Scored

Each response is holistically scored on a 6-point scale according to the criteria published in the GRE analytical writing scoring guides on pages 396 and 398. Holistic scoring means that each response is judged as a whole: readers do not separate the response into component parts and award a certain number of points for a particular criterion or element such as ideas, organization, sentence structure, or language. Instead, readers assign scores based on the overall quality of the response, considering all of its characteristics in an integrated way. Excellent organization or poor organization, for example, will be part of the readers' overall impression of the response and will therefore contribute to the score, but organization, as a distinct feature, has no specific weight.

In general, GRE readers are college and university faculty experienced in teaching courses in which writing and critical thinking skills are important. All GRE readers have undergone careful training, passed stringent GRE qualifying tests, and demonstrated that they are able to maintain scoring accuracy.

To ensure fairness and objectivity in scoring

- responses are randomly distributed to the readers
- all identifying information about the test takers is concealed from the readers
- each response is scored by two readers
- readers do not know what other scores a response may have received
- the scoring procedure requires that each response receive identical or adjacent scores from two readers; any other score combination is adjudicated by a third GRE reader

The scores given for the two tasks are then averaged for a final reported score. The score level descriptions, presented on page 400, provide information on how to interpret the total score on the analytical writing section. The primary emphasis in scoring the analytical writing section is on critical thinking and analytical writing skills.

Present Your Perspective on an Issue Task

Understanding the Issue Task

The Issue task assesses your ability to think critically about a topic of general interest and to clearly express your thoughts about it in writing. Each topic, presented in quotation marks, makes a claim about an issue that test takers can discuss from various perspectives and apply to many different situations or conditions. Your task is to present a compelling case for your own position on the issue. Be sure to read the claim carefully and think about it from several points of view, considering the complexity of ideas associated with those perspectives. Then, make notes about the position you want to develop and list the main reasons and examples that you could use to support that position.

The Issue task allows considerable latitude in the way you respond to the claim. Although it is important that you address the central issue, you are free to take any approach you wish. For example, you might

- agree absolutely with the claim, disagree completely, or agree with some parts and not others
- question the assumptions the statement seems to be making
- qualify any of its terms, especially if the way you define or apply a term is important to developing your perspective on the issue
- point out why the claim is valid in some situations but not in others
- evaluate points of view that contrast with your own perspective
- develop your position with reasons that are supported by several relevant examples or by a single extended example

The GRE readers scoring your response are not looking for a "right" answer — in fact, there is no correct position to take. Instead, the readers are evaluating the skill with which you articulate and develop an argument to support your position on the issue.

Understanding the Context for Writing: Purpose and Audience

The Issue task is an exercise in critical thinking and persuasive writing. The purpose of this task is to determine how well you can develop a compelling argument supporting your own perspective on an issue and to effectively communicate that argument in writing to an academic audience. Your audience consists of college and university faculty who are trained as GRE readers to apply the scoring criteria identified in the scoring guide for the Issue task (see page 396).

To get a clearer idea of how GRE readers apply the issue scoring criteria to actual responses, you should review scored sample Issue essay responses and readers' commentaries. The sample responses, particularly at the 5 and 6 score levels, will show you a variety of successful strategies for organizing, developing, and communicating a persuasive argument. The readers' commentaries discuss specific aspects of analysis and writing, such as the use of examples, development and support, organization, language fluency, and word choice. For each response, the commentary points out aspects that are particularly persuasive as well as any that detract from the overall effectiveness of the essay.

Preparing for the Issue Task

Because the Issue task is meant to assess the persuasive writing skills that you have developed throughout your education, it has been designed neither to require any particular course of study nor to advantage students with a particular type of training.

Many college textbooks on composition offer advice on persuasive writing that you might find useful, but even this advice might be more technical and specialized than you need for the Issue task. You will not be expected to know specific critical thinking or writing terms or strategies; instead, you should be able to use reasons, evidence, and examples to support your position on an issue. Suppose, for instance, that an Issue topic asks you to consider whether it is important for government to provide financial support for art museums. If your position is that government should fund art museums, you might support your position by discussing the reasons art is important and explain that museums are public places where art is available to anyone. On the other hand, if your position is that government should not support museums, you might point out that, given limited governmental funds, art museums are not as deserving of governmental funding as are other, more socially important, institutions. Or, if you are in favor of government funding for art museums only under certain conditions, you might focus on the artistic criteria, cultural concerns, or political conditions that you think should determine how — or whether — art museums receive government funds. It is not your position that matters so much as the critical thinking skills you display in developing your position.

An excellent way to prepare for the Issue task is to practice writing on some of the published topics. There is no "best" approach: some people prefer to start practicing without regard to the 45-minute time limit; others prefer to take a "timed test" first and practice within the time limit. No matter which approach you take when you practice the Issue task, you should review the task directions, then

- carefully read the claim made in the topic and make sure you understand the issue involved; if it seems unclear, discuss it with a friend or teacher
- think about the issue in relation to your own ideas and experiences, to events you have read about or observed, and to people you have known; this is the knowledge base from which you will develop compelling reasons and examples in your argument that reinforce, negate, or qualify the claim in some way
- decide what position on the issue you want to take and defend — remember you are free to agree or disagree completely or to agree with some parts or some applications but not others
- decide what compelling evidence (reasons and examples) you can use to support your position

Remember that this is a task in critical thinking and persuasive writing. Therefore, you might find it helpful to explore the complexity of a claim in one of the topics by asking yourself the following questions:

- What, precisely, is the central issue?
- Do I agree with all or with any part of the claim? Why or why not?
- Does the claim make certain assumptions? If so, are they reasonable?
- Is the claim valid only under certain conditions? If so, what are they?
- Do I need to explain how I interpret certain terms or concepts used in the claim?
- If I take a certain position on the issue, what reasons support my position?
- What examples — either real or hypothetical — could I use to illustrate those reasons and advance my point of view? Which examples are most compelling?

Once you have decided on a position to defend, consider the perspective of others who might not agree with your position. Ask yourself:

- What reasons might someone use to refute or undermine my position?
- How should I acknowledge or defend against those views in my essay?

To plan your response, you might want to summarize your position and make brief notes about how you will support the position you're going to take. When you've done this, look over your notes and decide how you will organize your response. Then write a response developing your position on the issue. Even if you don't write a full response, you should find it helpful to practice with a few of the Issue topics and to sketch out your possible responses. After you have practiced with some of the topics, try writing responses to some of the topics within the 45-minute time limit so that you have a good idea of how to use your time in the actual test.

It would probably be helpful to get some feedback on your response from an instructor who teaches critical thinking or writing or to trade papers on the same topic with other students and discuss one another's responses in relation to the scoring guide. Try to determine how each paper meets or misses the criteria for each score point in the guide. Comparing your own response to the scoring guide will help you see how and where you might need to improve.

Deciding Which Issue Topic to Choose

Remember that the GRE General Test will contain two Issue topics from the published pool; you must choose one of these two. Because the 45-minute timing begins when you first see the two topics, you should not spend too much time making a decision. Instead, try to choose fairly quickly the issue that you feel better prepared to discuss.

Before making a choice, read each topic carefully. Then decide on which topic you could develop a more effective and well-reasoned argument. In making this decision, you might ask yourself:

- Which topic do I find more interesting or engaging?
- Which topic more closely relates to my own academic studies or other experiences?
- On which topic can I more clearly explain and defend my perspective?
- On which topic can I more readily think of strong reasons and examples to support my position?

Your answers to these questions should help you make your choice.

The Form of Your Response

You are free to organize and develop your response in any way that you think will effectively communicate your ideas about the issue. Your response may, but need not, incorporate particular writing strategies learned in English composition or writing-intensive college courses. GRE readers will not be looking for a particular developmental strategy or mode of writing; in fact, when GRE readers are trained, they review hundreds of issue responses that, although highly diverse in content and form, display similar levels of critical thinking and persuasive writing. Readers will see, for example, some issue responses at the 6 score level that begin by briefly summarizing the writer's position on the issue and then explicitly announcing the main points to be argued. They will see others that lead into the writer's position by making a prediction, asking a series of questions, describing a scenario, or defining critical terms in the quotation. The readers know that a writer can earn a high score by giving multiple examples or by presenting a single, extended example. Look at the sample Issue responses, particularly at the 5 and 6 score levels, to see how other writers have successfully developed and organized their arguments.

You should use as many or as few paragraphs as you consider appropriate for your argument — for example, you will probably need to create a new paragraph whenever your discussion shifts to a new cluster of ideas. What matters is not the number of examples, the number of paragraphs, or the form your argument takes but, rather, the cogency of your ideas about the issue and the clarity and skill with which you communicate those ideas to academic readers.

Directions: Present your perspective on the issue below, using relevant reasons and/or examples to support your views.

Sample Topic

"Unfortunately, the media tend to highlight what is sensational at the moment. Society would be better served if the media reported or focused more fully on events and trends that will ultimately have the most long-term significance."

Strategies for this Topic

You could take several positions in responding to this claim

- Yes, the media sensationalize events and society would benefit if they approached events differently.
- Yes, they sensationalize, but they serve societal needs in doing so.
- Whether society benefits from sensationalism may be dependant on various factors.
- There are some benefits to reporting sensational events, but also some drawbacks.
- You may also take positions that qualify the claim to make it applicable in some situations and not in others.

Your analysis might draw examples from a specific society, country, or situation, or it might draw them from multiple sources. Your analysis could also focus on one or more types of media, such as newspapers, television, radio, or the Internet.

Before you stake out a position, take a few moments to reread the claim. To analyze it, consider questions such as these:

- What are the causes of sensational journalism, i.e., Why do the media tend to sensationalize events?
- Who benefits from media sensationalism? In what ways?
- Are there instances when the media should highlight sensational events? If so, when?
- What is the role of the media in society? Does the public expect the media to sensationalize events?
- What are the effects of sensationalizing events or of focusing on issues with more long-term significance? Are these effects positive or negative for society?

Now you can organize your thoughts into two groups:

1. Reasons and examples to support the stated claim
2. Reasons and examples to support an opposing point of view

If you find one set of reasons clearly more persuasive than the other, consider developing an argument from that perspective. As you build your argument, keep in mind the opposing points that you can argue against.

If both groups have compelling points, consider developing a position supporting, not the stated claim, but a more limited, complex, or qualified claim. Then you can use reasons and examples from both sides to discuss the complexities and implication of the issue.

Essay Response* – Score 6

Media in the 21st Century is a complicated industry, with many forms and varying "standards", but the task of defining the appropriate role and/or primary purpose of media in general is as old as the very idea of communication itself. Is

---

* Essay responses are reproduced exactly as written, including errors, misspellings, etc., if any.

the role of media to serve the needs of society? If so, then in what way? Should media be used to serve in the sense of "deliver services", therefore presenting to whatever part of the public is identified as "audience" whatever that audience seems most to want? Are media simply in business, struggling as any business might to identify and exploit relevant markets? Conversely, is the role of media to serve society in the sense of focusing on the "greater good"; to serve as a sort of lighthouse, directing its audience toward "safer" or otherwise better shores? As difficult as it is to struggle with the balancing act required to manage these competing, and often conflicting interests, media as a whole can not avoid its inherently difficult, and possibly insurmountable challenges. Media provides a service by supplying consumers with information, access to other markets, and most recently through the internet, direct access to each other. It serves up whatever a focus group prescribes as most likely to make a target audience laugh, think, or stare in stunned silence – whatever has been shown to keep the T.V. turned on, the radio blaring, and the newspaper on the front porch. Media also serve the public in the sense that many forms of newspapers, magazines, and even television shows are designed to truly enlighten and uplift, sometimes even if no audience or advertiser will subsidize presenting this information. Some members of the media are so committed to this ideal that they make little money, or none at all. Some others are more known for sensational material, such as MTV's Jackass, or for sensationalizing events in people's real lives, such as Jerry Springer. However, it is not the level of sensation that dictates whether or not something is useful, nor whether it is significant in the short or long term.

The reality is that many consumers of media have grown up enmeshed in the cyclical pattern of passive consumption of visual media in larger and larger amounts, thus training the brain to create what a leading neuroscientist calls "neural grooves" that leave it less able to assimilate information presented in other ways. Part of our culture's fixation on the startling visual images that permeate most media is largely explained by this phenomenon, and has little to do with the significance of the message, or the sensational value of the presentation, which are two entirely different things. Sometimes very significant messages that are produced only for the greater good, rather than commercial benefit, are also sensational in the sense that they focus on the most extreme and/or most visually startling aspects of whatever topic is being addressed.

Even so, the lack of consideration of the long term consequences of one's behavior or of public policy as a whole is a major flaw of our society today. This is shown in the (mostly) losing battle of prevention programs which aim to reduce dangerous behaviors, such as AIDS prevention and teen smoking. It is also revealed in more public spheres, such as the often hostile transition from one President's policies to the next, rather than maintaining a course of action that may require more than 4-8 years to complete. Our society is mobile, restless and impatient, and while the media reinforce these characteristics, it is not certain that our society would be better served by a more long-term focus on the part of media, especially if we are bound as a culture to live from one neuron's fire to the next.

Finally, it is certain that whatever role media plays, it is a significant part of modern culture, and its impact will be both significant and long-term. Whether that impact makes us better or worse as human beings and as a society is, thankfully, left for future generations to discover.

Reader Commentary for Essay Response – Score 6

This outstanding essay not only analyzes the complexities of the issue, but it also recognizes the limitations inherent in the issue.

The argument presented in this essay is impressively complex and substantiated by clearly persuasive examples. Paragraph 1 begins with a series of pointed rhetorical questions and moves into an assessment of the various "inherently difficult and possibly insurmountable challenges" faced by various media. Paragraph 2 discusses the impact on the brain of the "consumption of visual media in larger and larger amounts." Paragraph 3 moves beyond analyzing the issue to claim that the flaws attributed to the media are, in fact, flaws inherent in society itself. The conclusion comments on the impact these mirror images — society and media — may have on the future.

The response contains a wide variety of examples from the generic to the specific, from the media to the work of a neuroscientist. Syntax and language are outstanding. There is a range of sentence variety and meaning is skillfully conveyed.

For these reasons, this response received a 6.

Essay Response – Score 5

Unfortunately, the media tend to highlight what is sensational at the moment. Society would be better served if the media reported or focused more fully on events and trends that will ultimately have the most long-term significance. There are several reasons why this statement is true.

Firstly, the trend over time is that history tends to repeat itself. Due to this idea, it is imperative for the media to focus on news items with long term significance since there is much to be learned in each generation that can affect and determine ones behavior in coming generations. Since history repeats itself, the successes and likewise the mistakes of our elders have ramifications for many years. Media is an important tool whereby the young are educated. The young must be given an opportunity to learn from the mistakes of their elders and thus avoid those same mistakes. Often identical issues arise in different eras. The young of today are the trendsetters of the next generation. If the media would focus on events with long term significance, then the young would have the opportunity to avoid certain pitfalls and make stronger advancements.

Secondly, sensational events do not remain long in a person's mind since they are often so fleeting. On the other hand, an intelligent and thinking person can stand to gain a lot if the media would focus on events and trends that will ultimately have the most long-term significance. This is because an intelligent person absorbs all the knowledge he or she can and applies it to his or her daily life. For example, a report in the media about a new breakthrough medicine or a new effective treatment for cancer may encourage people suffering from diseases to seek the appropriate intervention that they were previously unaware of.

Lastly, another reason why it is important for media to highlight events of long term significance is because sensational news items are often rubbish and consist of news items of questionable morality. Many sensational newspapers often exaggerate stories in order to create an impression of something that never really happened. Children may find it hard to diffrentiate between reality and exaggerations. As such, the stories often reported in the sensational media may not be appropriate for children and in fact are often not reality. If a parent worries enough in advance about his or her child's moral standards, they will realize that many sensational news stories are not appropriate for children to listen to, to see and to hear. News items that have long-term significance will hopefully be reported truthfully in the media. Of course children should be educated to absorb news items in order to stimulate their intellect. A caring and concerned parent knows that sensational stories which promote the wrong values do not serve to stimulate the mind; these stories help to erode values and confuse children.

Unfortunately, the media tend to highlight what is sensational at the moment. Society would be better served if the media reported or focused more fully on events or trends that will ultimately have the most long term signifcance. This is true because history tends to repeat itself and it is important to learn from the mistakes and successes of our elders. Also, sensational news items only tittilate; they do not instruct. Lastly, sensational news items are often exaggerated in the media and too often promote the wrong values. A concerned parent knows that only news items of significance will stimulate a child's intellect.

Reader Commentary for Essay Response – Score 5

This response presents a generally thoughtful analysis of the issue, evident in its carefully organized development of three major reasons why the media should highlight events of long-term significance. Each of the three main points is supported with well-chosen examples and analysis. In paragraph 4, the writer argues that sensational reporting tends to focus on "rubbish" and often exaggerates news stories. The writer then analyzes the effect of this practice on children and parenting.

   However, neither the analysis nor the organization is skillful enough to merit a score of 6. Many of the points are repetitive, and the conclusion merely restates the main points. Language use is not very precise, adding to the wordiness of the response (e.g., paragraph 4 "to listen to, to see and to hear.") However, overall, ideas are expressed clearly, the examples are well chosen, and the analysis investigates the complexities of the issue. Thus, the response is strong enough to have received a 5.

Essay Response – Score 4

The media has a huge influence on the way that our society views itself and how it will ultimately change. If the media reported on things that are positive and informative it may effect our society in a positive way. However, what if the media did take on this responsibility? They would have to use their discretion on what was positive and informative. They would also have to determine what bad news our society should hear and what to keep us in the dark about. It is my opinion that although it may not be helpful to our society, the media gives us the information that we want. If we give the media the power to only provide information that they see fit then it embarks upon the freedom of the press that we Americans hold so dear.

   It is true that the media tends to highlight what is sensational at the moment. That is because the moment is what so many of us are concerned about. We want to know what is going on here and now. For instance, people are intrigued when they look at the television set and see entertainers doing something that they think is not right. Parents want to know in a sense what is influencing their children. They want to be aware of the new trends. The media aides them in their search for information. Information that they may not be able to get from talking to their teens. It may give a better idea of why their teen has suddenly began to act or dress a certain way. The nature of teenagers is that they will usually act or dress in a way that emulates media stars that they admire even if it isn't appropriate for them to do so. It can certainly be argued that it would be helpful if the media pointed out that it is just a trend, just like the ones people have gone through in the past, but then again, how could they be sure?

   In essence, the media gives us what we want. We decide through our channel selections what we want to see and what information we want them to provide. It is true that the media tend to highlight what is sensational at the moment. However, I would rather have imput on what is being shown on televison. If we leave it up to the media we dont get our full say so in what we want to see. If we dont like what is being reported we would be out of luck.

Reader Commentary for Essay Response – Score 4

This essay presents a competent analysis of the issue and demonstrates adequate control of the elements of writing.

   The writer takes the position that the only viable way to prevent "media sensationalism" is censorship, and therefore sensationalism is the price we pay for a free media. Examples are thin; the only specific (hypothetical) example given is of teenagers imitating entertainers whom they admire. Most of the essay presents the writer's opinions with little support.

Ideas are expressed clearly for the most part, but occasionally there is a problematical statement: ". . . then it embarks upon the freedom . . ." (paragraph 1); ". . . it is just a trend, just like the ones people have gone through the past, but then again, how could they be sure?" (paragraph 2). Language and syntax are handled only adequately.

For these reasons, this response was scored a 4.

Essay Response – Score 3

Yes, the media do tend to hightlight issues that are sensational at the moment, but people would not benefit if the media tried to focus on topics that in there opinion would only have a long lasting impact on the public. Who has the right, to decide on what topic would best serve the needs of the public in the future? In other words, no one can tell what present situation will have that long-term significance. Lastly, the public has the right to know about present topics and this does include the sensational ones as well. One cannot assume a present topic which happens to be the sensational topic would not impact the world in the future.

The impact on the public because of world events, will have a variable outcome on many individuals. Take the terrorist attacks for example. Would the media have the right to assume the outcome of September 11th? The job of the media is to inform the public on important present events. An addition the present focus of the media is the terrorist attacks, and these events could possible affect the world for years to come. This world event played a different role in different countries whether is was the loss of loved ones, jobs, or financial stability. Others in the world may not have been significantly affected by the attacks and are probably wondering when the coverage will end. In short we will not know the outcome until later in life, so the news should be delivered by the media and continued.

Secondly, the media firmly believes the public has a right to know information and this includes the popular topics for most people. These are the topics that happen to be sensational, like September 11th. We cannot argue if present topics will be remembered in the future. Every one of us remembers events in which others have forgotten.

Let the media perform their job without censorship. This includes "sensational topics" which are revelant at the moment. We can predict but not assume the role present topics will play on a society at any given time. We can only inform the public, give the facts, and hope we learn from the past to better the future.

Reader Commentary for Essay Response – Score 3

This response addresses the issue by arguing that no one has "the right" to decide what to cover or "can tell" what will have long-term significance. The example of the terrorist attack provides relevant support for the writer's position. The second point ("Secondly"), that the media are committed to the public's "right to know," is relevant but poorly developed, concluding with the tangential claim that "Every one of us remembers events in which others have forgotten." Confusion arises with the final sentence: the writer abruptly introduces a new idea ("hope we learn from the past to better the future") that does not relate in any direct way to the preceeding argument.

Besides the occasional lack of clarity, the argument is limited by the writer's use of language, as in these examples:

- "in there opinion" paragraph 1 (Is it the public's opinion or that of the media?)
- "One cannot assume a present topic which happens to be the sensational topic would not impact the world in the future." paragraph 1 (This sentence is unnecessarily wordy and vague.)
- "We can predict but not assume" paragraph 4 (Assume, or know for certain?)

Analysis, development, and clarity are limited; thus this response was scored as a 3.

Essay Response – Score 2

The media of the United States is a powerful force which triggers emotion within people. It often propels action. The sensationalistic images on which it chooses to focus, stick in people's minds. People often react without pausing to think about and put into perspective what they have seen or heard. The media could actually be a service to society if it would direct it's focus toward events that in the long run would would have the most significance and positive effect.

This is a nice thought, but it would take a great deal of effort to change what people are used to wanting from the media. People in our country, in general enjoys sensationalism. We would much rather watch an exciting car chase ending in a spin out and an explotion of a gas station.

The media is a business like any other. It is selling the product that the general public, its comsumers, want. No one wants to hear about important news stories, for example, how to cure hunger in a third world country.

The situation with the media will not change because it is serving society's needs.

Reader Commentary for Essay Response – Score 2

This response takes a position on the issue, arguing that the media focus on sensationalism because that is what people want. However, the development and organization of that position are seriously flawed. Some ideas are not logically connected: the statement about "important news stories," (paragraph 3) for example, more logically belongs as a follow-up to the statement about watching a car chase (paragraph 2). The concluding statement seems to contradict the statement made at the end of the first paragraph. Thus it is unclear whether the statement made at the end of the first paragraph represents the writer's own opinion or is a paraphrase of the stated issue.

The response is further flawed with problems in sentence structure and with errors that frequently interfere with meaning: unclear pronoun reference ("It" in line 1); confusing contractions (paragraph 1 "it's" instead of "its"), and subject-verb problems (paragraph 2 "People . . . enjoys").

For all of these reasons, the response received a score of 2.

Essay Response – Score 1

The proposition is an interesting one: society would be better served if the media reported or focused more fully on events and trends that will ultimately have the most long-term significance. I will present three reasons to justify my position: culture, technology, and overall goals.

First, culture. The culture of a country is what contributes to priorities. This is observed in many countries and in many different situations over the world.

Second technology. Technology is the reason why it has a powerful impact on the way people live their life today.

Third, overall goals. It can be seen that the overall goal derives from what is the current status and the desirable future to make a difference.

In conclusion, these reasons show that society would be better served if the media reported or focused more fully on events and trends that will ultimately have the most long-term significance.

Reader Commentary for Essay Response – Score 1

Despite its very clear organizational pattern and, at times, its sentence-level coherence, this response displays no analysis or understanding of the issue. The opening and closing lines repeat the words given in the topic, but none of the statements about culture, technology, and goals relate to media and sensationalism. This lack of connection to the issue and the lack of overall coherence mark this response as seriously deficient, and so it was scored as a 1.

Understanding the Argument Task

The Argument task assesses your ability to understand, analyze, and evaluate arguments and to clearly convey your analysis in writing. The task consists of a brief passage in which the author makes a case for some course of action or interpretation of events by presenting claims backed by reasons and evidence. Your task is to discuss the logical soundness of the author's case by critically examining the line of reasoning and the use of evidence. This task requires you to read the argument very carefully. You might want to read it more than once and possibly make brief notes about points you want to develop more fully in your response. In reading the argument, you should pay special attention to

- what is offered as evidence, support, or proof
- what is explicitly stated, claimed, or concluded
- what is assumed or supposed, perhaps without justification or proof
- what is not stated, but necessarily follows from what is stated

In addition, you should consider the structure of the argument — the way in which these elements are linked together to form a line of reasoning; that is, you should recognize the separate, sometimes implicit steps in the thinking process and consider whether the movement from each one to the next is logically sound. In tracing this line, look for transition words and phrases that suggest that the author is attempting to make a logical connection (e.g., *however, thus, therefore, evidently, hence, in conclusion*).

An important part of performing well on the Argument task is remembering what you are not being asked to do. You are not being asked to discuss whether the statements in the argument are true or accurate; instead, you are being asked whether conclusions and inferences are validly drawn from the statements. You are not being asked to agree or disagree with the position stated; instead, you are being asked to comment on the thinking that underlies the position stated. You are not being asked to express your own views on the subject being discussed (as you were in the Issue task); instead, you are being asked to evaluate the logical soundness of an argument of another writer and, in doing so, to demonstrate the critical thinking, perceptive reading, and analytical writing skills that university faculty consider important for success in graduate school.

The Argument task is primarily a critical thinking task requiring a written response. Consequently, the analytical skills displayed in your critique carry great weight in determining your score.

Understanding the Context for Writing: Purpose and Audience

The purpose of the task is to see how well equipped you are to insightfully analyze an argument written by someone else and to effectively communicate your critique in writing to an academic audience. Your audience consists of college and university faculty who are trained as GRE readers to apply the scoring criteria identified in the scoring guide for the Argument task (see page 398).

To get a clearer idea of how GRE readers apply the Argument scoring criteria to actual essays, you should review scored sample Argument essay responses and readers' commentaries. The sample responses, particularly at the 5 and 6 score levels, will show you a variety of successful strategies for organizing and developing an insightful critique. You will also see many examples of particularly effective uses of language. The readers' commentaries discuss specific aspects of analytical writing, such as cogency of ideas, development and support, organization, syntactic variety, and facility with language. These commentaries will point out aspects that are particularly effective and insightful as well as any that detract from the overall effectiveness of the responses.

Preparing for the Argument Task

Because the Argument task is meant to assess analytical writing and informal reasoning skills that you have developed throughout your education, it has been designed so as not to require any specific course of study or to advantage students with a particular type of training. Many college textbooks on rhetoric and composition have sections on informal logic and critical thinking that might prove helpful, but even these might be more detailed and technical than the task requires. You will not be expected to know methods of analysis or technical terms. For instance, in one topic an elementary school principal might conclude that the new playground equipment has improved student attendance because absentee rates have declined since it was installed. You will not need to see that the principal has committed the *post hoc, ergo propter hoc* fallacy; you will simply need to see that there are other possible explanations for the improved attendance, to offer some common-sense examples, and perhaps to suggest what would be necessary to verify the conclusion. For instance, absentee rates might have decreased because the climate was mild. This would have to be ruled out in order for the principal's conclusion to be valid.

Although you do not need to know special analytical techniques and terminology, you should be familiar with the directions for the Argument task in the practice tests and with certain key concepts, including the following:

- **Alternative explanation** – a possible competing version of what might have caused the events in question; an alternative explanation undercuts or qualifies the original explanation because it too can account for the observed facts
- **Analysis** – the process of breaking something (e.g., an argument) down into its component parts in order to understand how they work together to make up the whole; also a presentation, usually in writing, of the results of this process
- **Argument** – a claim or a set of claims with reasons and evidence offered as support; a line of reasoning meant to demonstrate the truth or falsehood of something
- **Assumption** – a belief, often unstated or unexamined, that someone must hold in order to maintain a particular position; something that is taken for granted but that must be true in order for the *conclusion* to be true
- **Conclusion** – the end point reached by a line of reasoning, valid if the reasoning is sound; the resulting assertion
- **Counterexample** – an example, real or hypothetical, that refutes or disproves a statement in the *argument*

An excellent way to prepare for the Argument task is to practice writing on some of the published topics. There is no one way to practice that is best for everyone. Some prefer to start practicing without adhering to the 30-minute time limit. If you follow this approach, take all the time you need to analyze the argument. No matter which approach you take, you should

- carefully read the argument — you might want to read it over more than once
- identify as many of its claims, conclusions, and underlying assumptions as possible
- think of as many alternative explanations and counterexamples as you can
- think of what additional evidence might weaken or lend support to the claims
- ask yourself what changes in the argument would make the reasoning more sound

Jot down each of these thoughts as a brief note. When you've gone as far as you can with your analysis, look over the notes and put them in a good order for discussion (perhaps by numbering them). Then write a critique by fully developing each of your points in turn. Even if you choose not to write a full essay response, you should find it very helpful to practice analyzing a few of the arguments and sketching out your responses. When you become quicker and more confident, you should practice writing some Argument responses within the 30-minute time limit so that you will have a good sense of how to pace yourself in the actual test. For example, you will not want to discuss one point so exhaustively or to provide so many equivalent examples that you run out of time to make your other main points.

You might want to get feedback on your response(s) from a writing instructor, a philosophy teacher, or someone who emphasizes critical thinking in his or her course. It can also be very informative to trade papers on the same topic with fellow students and discuss one another's responses in terms of the scoring guide. Focus not so much on giving the "right scores" as on seeing how the papers meet or miss the performance standards for each score point and what you therefore need to do in order to improve.

How to Interpret Numbers, Percentages, and Statistics in Argument Topics

Some arguments contain numbers, percentages, or statistics that are offered as evidence in support of the argument's conclusion. For example, an argument might claim that a certain community event is less popular this year than it was last year because only 100 people attended this year in comparison with 150 last year, a 33 percent decline in attendance. *It is important to remember that you are not being asked to do a mathematical task with the numbers, percentages, or statistics.* Instead you should evaluate these as evidence that is intended to support the conclusion. In the example above, the conclusion is that a community event has become less popular. You should ask yourself: does the difference between 100 people and 150 people support that conclusion? Note that, in this case, there are other possible explanations; for example, the weather might have been much worse this year, this year's event might have been held at an inconvenient time, the cost of the event might have gone up this year, or there might have been another popular event this year at the same time. Each of these could explain the difference in attendance, and thus would weaken the conclusion that the event was "less popular." Similarly, percentages might support or weaken a conclusion depending on what actual numbers the percentages represent. Consider the claim that the drama club at a school deserves more funding because its membership has increased by 100 percent. This 100 percent increase could be significant if there had been 100 members and now there are 200 members, whereas the increase would be much less significant if there had been 5 members and now there are 10. Remember that any numbers, percentages, or statistics in Argument topics are used only as evidence in support of a conclusion, and you should always consider whether they actually support the conclusion.

The Form of Your Response

You are free to organize and develop your critique in any way that you think will effectively communicate your analysis of the argument. Your response may, but need not, incorporate particular writing strategies learned in English composition or writing-intensive college courses. GRE readers will not be looking for a particular developmental strategy or mode of writing. In fact, when GRE readers are trained, they review hundreds of Argument responses that, although highly diverse in content and form, display similar levels of critical thinking and analytical writing. Readers will see, for example, some essays at the 6 score level that begin by briefly summarizing the argument and then explicitly stating and developing the main points of the critique. The readers know that a writer can earn a high score by analyzing and developing several points in a critique or by identifying a central flaw in the argument and developing that critique extensively. Look at the sample Argument responses, particularly at the 5 and 6 score levels, to see how other writers have successfully developed and organized their critiques.

You should make choices about format and organization that you think support and enhance the overall effectiveness of your critique. This means using as many or as few paragraphs as you consider appropriate for your critique — for example, creating a new paragraph when your discussion shifts to a new point of analysis. You might want to organize your critique around the organization of the argument itself, discussing the argument line by line. Or you might want to first point out a central questionable assumption and then move on to discuss related flaws in the argument's line of reasoning. Similarly, you might want to use examples if they help illustrate an important point in your critique or move your discussion forward (remember, however, that, in terms of your ability to perform the Argument task effectively, it is your critical thinking and analytical writing, not your ability to come up with examples, that is being assessed). What matters is not the form the response takes, but how insightfully you analyze the argument and how articulately you communicate your analysis to academic readers within the context of the task.

Directions: Discuss how well reasoned you find this argument.

Sample Topic

The following appeared in a popular health and fitness magazine.

"A ten-year study of a group of 552 men from Elysia showed that long-term consumption of caffeinated black tea was associated with a much lower risk of stroke. Of these men, those who drank more than three cups of black tea a day had a 70 percent lower risk of stroke than those who drank no tea. These results suggest that health-conscious people should consume at least three cups of black tea a day, beginning early in life."

Strategies for this Topic

This argument cites the results of a ten-year study of men from Elysia to draw a very broad and general conclusion that all "health-conscious people" should drink at least three cups of black tea a day, beginning at an early age.

In developing your analysis of the argument, you should ask yourself whether the study results actually support the general conclusion. In particular, you might want to consider such questions as the following:

- Is the observed association between tea drinking and reduced stroke risk necessarily a causal relationship, as the argument assumes?
- Could there be other factors, such as diet and/or exercise that might account for the observed reduction in stroke risk?
- Were the men in the study at high risk of having a stroke to begin with?
- Had the men in the study drunk three cups of caffeinated black tea a day, beginning early in life?
- Would the results of a study of men from Elysia be necessarily applicable to a wider population — that is, to women and to people who are not from Elysia?
- Is a ten-year study of this kind long enough to yield an accurate measure of the reduction in stroke risk?
- Would drinking one or two cups of caffeinated black tea a day have the same presumed benefit as drinking three cups of the tea a day?
- Are there other health risks associated with drinking three cups of caffeinated black tea, especially for the young?

Considering possible answers to questions such as these will help you identify several weaknesses in the argument's line of reasoning. You can then develop each of these points in your critique of the argument.

Essay Response* – Score 6

Before prescribing large quantities of black tea to the general population, the evidence given in the argument should be examined from several other angles. The researchers who conducted the Elysia study seem to have assumed that drinking three cups of black tea a day has preserved the health of some of the Elysian men without examining any other factors which may have affected the results of the study.

First of all, for an experiment to be accurate, it must be controlled, with a balance between the experimental and the control groups. In the above study, though, we know nothing about the ages, backgrounds, and general health of the

---
* Responses are reproduced exactly as written, including errors, misspellings, etc., if any.

men involved. We also do not know if the tea drinkers were of the same age, background, and general health as those who did not drink tea. Further, if the tea drinking men in the study were all quite young when the study began, they might only be 35 years old today and thus be at small risk of stroke just because of their age. The same is true of their general health. If they exercised regularly, ate healthily and never smoked, then their decreased risk of stroke might have nothing to do with consumption of black tea and might simply be an indication of a healthy lifestyle.

We might also ask: How do the two groups of men break down in terms of ethnicity? Do all the men in one group belong to one ethnic group and all the men in the other belong to a different ethnic group? Perhaps the tea drinkers are from an ethnic group whose members have a low risk for stroke as compared with the ethnic group of those who drank no tea. If this were the case, the study's results would be questionable, at best.

Another element to consider is this: perhaps the group who have a higher risk of stroke have this higher risk not because they abstain from drinking tea but because they are heavy smokers, or are grossly overweight, or because they are all in their 70s and 80s and are in poor health and have circulatory problems. We just don't know.

Furthermore, even if Elysian tea in certain amounts is beneficial to men, what about women? The argument says nothing about tea's effect on women, so it therefore cannot make the recommendation that all people should drink the tea. Perhaps there is something in the tea which would adversely affect women. Perhaps there is something in the tea which, when drunk in prescribed amounts, will adversely affect a woman's ability to bear healthy children. The point is, a generalization about women cannot be made from studies done on men; studies done exclusively on men on the risk of heart attack have taught us that much. In addition, the argument fails to rule out possible side-effects that might make tea drinking inadvisable for some people.

What if we consider some important terminology in the argument? For example, what does "long term" mean? In the ten years of the study, does "long term" mean all ten years? Or does it mean several months at a time over a period of X number of years? And what does "lower risk of stroke" mean? Does it mean that the tea-drinking men will still probably suffer strokes, but not until their later years? Or that they absolutely will not have a stroke, no matter what? The problem is that key terms in the argument are too vague to be meaningful.

In conclusion, any legitimate experiment must be strictly controlled and include a broad cross-section of the population. The Elysian study fails to do that.

Reader Commentary for Essay Response – Score 6

This cogent and well-articulated response presents an insightful analysis of three central problems in the argument:

- apparent absence of necessary controls in the study of Elysian men (e.g., the study failed to consider variables such as subjects' age, diet, and general health, and did not necessarily have balanced experimental and control groups)
- unwarranted generalization (e.g., from Elysian men to Elysian women and children)
- use of vague terminology (e.g., "long-term" and "lower risk")

Development of each of these points is both thorough and cogent. The writer asks effective rhetorical questions and provides specific examples of the kinds of details that are missing from the argument. In addition, overall organization is exceptionally clear, and transitions both between and within paragraphs are smooth. Throughout the response, the writer clearly establishes logical connections with the use of phrases such as "Another element to consider," and "The same is true."

The writing is generally free of errors. Indeed, sentences are typically gracefully constructed with careful embedding and subordination that suit the complexity of the writer's analysis.

In summary, this response is outstanding; it offers a compelling critique of the argument's flaws and conveys meaning skillfully.

Essay Response – Score 5

This argument on the surface presents a reasonable conclusion which may be of interest to many people. However, looking deeper into the argument, I notice an inconsistency between the study and the conclusion. There is inconsistency between the study done on men and the suggestion made to all "health-concious people." The statistics did not give enough background on the men who were observed in drinking the tea. Finally, a ten year study does not necessarily indicate what long term effects would be for a person's entire life.

The study says that Elysian men were shown to have a lower risk of stroke after drinking three cups of black tea a day. Now, the argument suggests that ALL health-concious people should drink three cups of the tea a day. The particular men studied probably do not share the same characteristics as all health-concious people. What about women? There bodies are very different from men's and the effects of drinking black tea may be negative as opposed to the positive effects on these men.

Another important point overlooked is that the argument did not give enough background on these men. It did not indicate their ages, their original risk of stroke and in general any other health conditions that would differentiate these tea-drinking men from all other men in the world. Because the tea had this particular effect on these men from this particular part of the world does not mean it will provide the same benefits for all other people from all over the world.

Ten years is not a sufficient amount of time to conclude that people should drink tea from early on in their lives until they die. The study can not take into account the potential adverse effects of drinking tea for say 40 years or more. Also, the conclusion says people should begin drinking tea early on in life. How early is early? Two year old children should probably not be drinking three cups of black tea a day to prevent stroke 40 years down the road.

This study has many missing parts it needs to include before it can be conclusive. Giving people this information is not only possibly risking their health but also is essentially misleading them. Many people are unaccounted for in the study but are included in the conclusion which could present a danger to them. Though it would be nice to take this study at face value, it could be very dangerous to do so for many people.

Reader Commentary for Essay Response – Score 5

This generally thoughtful and well developed response identifies and analyzes three significant problems in the argument:

- the unsupported generalization of the study results from a sample of 552 men to "ALL health-conscious people"
- the apparent absence of demographic and medical data on the study participants
- the insufficient time-frame of the study (e.g., a ten year study cannot adequately predict the detrimental effects of very long-term tea drinking)

Development for each of these points is clear and sensible, and the organizational pattern is certainly logical. The writer addresses each of three questionable features of the argument, but the analysis lacks the fuller detail and precise reasoning of a 6 response. A more insightful and thoughly developed response, for instance, might specifically discuss several reasons why the study's lack of a representative sample fails to support the overly general conclusion about "all health conscious people."

This writer conveys meaning clearly despite the fact that some incidental errors are evident. Sentences are appropriately varied, but the response sometimes displays both unclear syntax (e.g., in paragraph one, "Finally, a ten year study does not necessarily indicate what long term effects would be for a person's entire life.") and errors in word choice (e.g., in paragraph two, "There bodies..."). However, the scoring guide allows these minor errors and meaning is generally clear. The critique is sufficiently thoughtful and well-developed for this response to merit a score of 5.

Essay Response – Score 4

The argument above is not sound or persuasive. The argument is that the consumption of more than 3 cups of black tea early in life is associated with lower risk of stroke. The independent variable which is the consumption of black tea is regarded as a positive cause for the less risk of stroke, which is the dependent variable.

First, the sampling procedure is unclear and the sample lacks validity. We don't know anything about those 552 men from Elysia except some of them consume more black tea than the others. Were they randomly selected? Do they represent a larger population? There maybe some association. But the conclusion shouldn't be drawn so quickly. The risk of stroke may be associated with many more independent variables.

Second, the sample is not reliable. Besides, only men were selected for the sampling size. Women were not included. Since male and female may present different results in the study, one certainly can't claim that the 552 men can represent all the population. The study time is also long. During the ten years, many things may happen to influence the result of the study.

Third, there are many spurious variables which may influence the result of the study. Whether one is born with poor health, whether one has regular exercise, and one's habit of eating may all contribute to the possibility of having a stroke in later life.

Therefore, the argument above is not persuasive. The conclusion can't be drawn from the sample population which lacks representativeness.

Reader Commentary for Essay Response – Score 4

This response identifies three flaws in the argument's logic, and correctly reasons that the argument is neither sound nor persuasive. The writer's critique finds fault with the unclear sampling procedure, the unrepresentative sample, and the study's unspecified extraneous variables.

Each of these points is sensibly supported and the response is organized satisfactorily. However, while the critique is competent, it never attains the degree of development of a 5 response since each of the points is only minimally examined.

The writing is reasonably clear and controlled, but incorrect wording, imprecise word choice, and occasional grammatical errors constitute distracting errors. The writer's fluency is no better than adequate, and, in fact, contributes to a competent but sometimes muddled analysis. For instance, the response criticizes the sample's reliability (paragraph 3), while apparently intending to question its representativeness, and complains about spurious variables (paragraph 4) instead of intervening, confounding, or extraneous variables. Even so, the writer appropriately critiques the argument and conveys ideas with sufficient clarity to warrant a score of 4.

Essay Response – Score 3

The reasoning behind this argument is flawed. First of all the argument is weak because of its bias results. Only males were included in this study which then clearly portrays its inability to generalize results. Obviously the researchers lacked knowledge for how to conduct a control- and- experimental group research design. One of the disadvantages of this kind of research is that it precludes the generalization of any of the results.

There is also misleading information regarding the given numbers. When conducting this kind of studies one must state rates and not numbers, since numbers do not yield overall population information unlike rates.

The study also assumed that by having seventy percent of the males who had continously drink tea with lower risk of stroke, that all healthy people should do the same.

This argument could be improve by avoiding generalizations and misleading information which strongly weakens the argument in this context.

Reader Commentary for Essay Response – Score 3

This abbreviated response offers three reasons to doubt the argument's bogus reasoning, but only one of these (e.g., paragraph 1 "Only males were included in this study which then clearly portrays its inability to generalize results") constitutes a competent analysis. A second reason (e.g., paragraph 2 "misleading information regarding the given numbers") suggests that study results should be expressed as "rates and not numbers," but this critique is irrelevant and unfounded. Finally, the writer also appears to take issue with the argument's recommendation for all people, but fails to provide any support for this point.

The writing is comprehensible, but exhibits frequent minor errors, including imprecise word choice, vague pronoun use, and grammatical problems. Thus, while the response displays some competence in critiquing the argument, it earns a score of 3 because it demonstrates limitations in both writing and analysis.

Essay Response – Score 2

Although I feel that this study was done in good conscience, I cannot condone the drinking of any form of caffienated drink. Drinking tea may indeed lower one's risk of having a stroke, but it could also increase a person's risk of heart disease, high blood pressure, and other health problems that are associated with the heavy and steady imbibing of caffienated beverages.

Furthermore, there are plenty of other viable and safe ways that people can reducer their chances of having a stroke. For example, if people were to exercise more, this would decrease the risk of heart disease and high blood pressure, two health conditions that are know to be associated with the risk of stroke. Also maintaining a proper diet and having regular checkups with a physician could contribute to a reduced risk of stroke. These strategies are much safer and are possibly even cheaper ways to avoid strokes or any other health problems that may occur in a persons' life.

In conclusion, I do not agree with the findings of this study or the recommendation based on it. I feel that the study was a waste of taxpayer's money and time. The argument is blatant and misleading in that it implies that if you want to be "health-conscious", you should drink black tea, regardless of the harmful side-effects that may occur as a result.

Reader Commentary for Essay Response – Score 2

Instead of providing logical analysis of the argument, this writer simply reacts against the notion of drinking caffeinated beverages. In essence, the response presents nothing more than the writer's own views on the subject. The conclusion disagrees with the study's findings, but offers no analytical support; instead it offers a personal belief that the study "was a waste of taxpayer's money and time."

It is worth noting that the response is clearly organized and that the writer displays competence and sometimes even sophistication in language use. These features prevent the score from falling below a score of 2, but the response cannot earn a higher score since the writer has failed to analyze the argument.

Essay Response – Score 1

Its a few mintues before the biggest family celebration is about to begin. It is the event of my grandparents' sixtieth anniversaries. They both have 85 old. As I sat there looking around the room my grandparents are the busy persons in the room making sure that every thing was in order to enjoy celebration. As a young girl growing up I can not recalled seeing my grandparents drinking any form of caffeine. As a result of the healthy that my grandparents live and contiunes to live I beg to differ from these finding in study. I strongly believed that a healthy life style is contribute by a combination of factors not just drinking tea.

Reader Commentary for Essay Response – Score 1

This response appears to attempt to critique the argument's recommendation with anecdotal evidence (e.g., the writer's grandparent's continued health despite avoidance of caffeine), but it provides no analysis of the argument. Furthermore, the response exhibits persistent errors in verb tense and agreement, and the final two sentences display garbled syntax. In sum, the response demonstrates fundamental deficiencies in both analysis and writing, and therefore merits a score of 1.

Taking the Practice Tests

After you have become familiar with the three sections of the General Test, it is time to take one or more of the practice tests in this book to see how well you do. This will help you become familiar with the directions and types of questions, and if you are planning to take the paper-based General Test, it will help you determine how to pace yourself during the actual test. The total time that should be allotted for each verbal section is 30 minutes. The total time that should be allotted to each quantitative section is 30 minutes. The total time that should be allotted to each Issue task is 45 minutes, and the total time that should be allotted to each Argument task is 30 minutes. The answer sheets are provided on pages 413-442.

Evaluating Your Performance

Verbal and Quantitative Sections

The two tables after each test edition contain information to help you evaluate your performance on the verbal and quantitative sections. The first table contains the correct answers to the questions in the verbal and quantitative sections. Compare your answer to each question to the correct answer given in the list, crossing out questions you answered incorrectly or omitted. This table also contains the P+. The P+ is the percent of examinees who answered the question correctly and is based on the examinees who took that edition of the test. This information enables you to see how other examinees performed on each question. It can also help identify content areas in which you need more practice and review.

Next, add the number of correct answers in the two verbal sections to obtain your raw verbal score. Add the number of correct answers in the two quantitative sections to obtain your raw quantitative score. The second table contains information that enables you to convert your raw scores to scaled scores (on a 200-800 scale). Look up each of your raw scores and determine the scaled score that corresponds to the raw scores you obtained. Once you determine your scaled scores, you can evaluate your performance by comparing your scaled scores with those of others who have taken the GRE General Test. The interpretive table on page 384 is based on those examinees who took the verbal and quantitative sections on the GRE General Test between October 1, 1998, and September 30, 2001 and provides for each scaled score, the percent of examinees who earned lower scores. For example, the column next to the verbal scaled score 460 indicates 45 percent. This means that 45 percent of the examinees tested between October 1998 and September 2001 earned verbal scores below 460. For each score you earned on each practice test, note the percent of GRE examinees who earned lower scores. This is a reasonable indication of your rank among GRE General Test examinees if you have taken the practice tests under standard timing conditions.

It may be helpful to compare your scores to scores of examinees whose intended graduate school major field is similar to your own. The table on page 384 shows you the average scores of people in various categories of intended graduate major fields who took the General Test between October 1998 and September 2001. You can evaluate your scores by finding the major field category most closely related to your career goals and see how your performance compares with others who are striving for similar goals.

Analytical Writing Section

One way to evaluate your performance on the Issue and Argument topics you answered on each of the practice tests is to compare your essay responses to the scored sample essay responses for these topics. Scored sample essay responses at selected score levels (score 6, score 4, and score 2) are presented on pages 401 to 411 for each of the Issue topics and Argument topics presented in the two analytical writing sections.

The final scores for each of the essays are averaged and rounded up to the nearest half-point interval. A single score is reported for the analytical writing section. You should review the score level descriptions on page 400 to better understand the analytical writing abilities characteristic of particular score levels.

Next Steps

Once you have evaluated your performance on the practice tests in this book, you can determine what type of additional preparation you might want to do for the test. Individuals interested in additional test preparation are advised to visit the GRE Web site at **www.gre.org/pracmats.html** for other preparation materials and suggestions.

IMPORTANT

The following seven practice tests contain only the verbal and quantitative sections of previously administered GRE General Tests*. The allotted time on the back cover of each practice test refers to the total time allowed when the test was administered in its original format. You should allow 30 minutes for each verbal and quantitative section. In an actual GRE General Test administered October 1, 2002 or later, the verbal and quantitative sections will be preceded by the Analytical Writing measure, which consists of one issue and one argument task.

---

* Certain questions do not meet ETS's current standards and would not appear in a GRE General Test administered today. They have been marked with an asterisk.

THE GRADUATE RECORD
EXAMINATIONS®

General Test
(with explanations)

<u>Directions:</u> Each sentence below has one or two blanks, each blank indicating that something has been omitted. Beneath the sentence are five lettered words or sets of words. Choose the word or set of words for each blank that <u>best</u> fits the meaning of the sentence as a whole.

1. Physicists rejected the innovative experimental technique because, although it ------- some problems, it also produced new -------.

   (A) clarified..data
   (B) eased..interpretations
   (C) resolved..complications
   (D) caused..hypotheses
   (E) revealed..inconsistencies

2. During a period of protracted illness, the sick can become infirm, ------- both the strength to work and many of the specific skills they once possessed.

   (A) regaining   (B) denying   (C) pursuing
   (D) insuring   (E) losing

3. The pressure of population on available resources is the key to understanding history; consequently, any historical writing that takes no cognizance of ------- facts is ------- flawed.

   (A) demographic..intrinsically
   (B) ecological..marginally
   (C) cultural..substantively
   (D) psychological..philosophically
   (E) political..demonstratively

4. It is puzzling to observe that Jones's novel has recently been criticized for its ------- structure, since commentators have traditionally argued that its most obvious ------- is its relentlessly rigid, indeed schematic, framework.

   (A) attention to..preoccupation
   (B) speculation about..characteristic
   (C) parody of..disparity
   (D) violation of..contradiction
   (E) lack of..flaw

5. It comes as no surprise that societies have codes of behavior; the character of the codes, on the other hand, can often be -------.

   (A) predictable   (B) unexpected
   (C) admirable   (D) explicit   (E) confusing

6. The characterization of historical analysis as a form of fiction is not likely to be received ------- by either historians or literary critics, who agree that history and fiction deal with ------- orders of experience.

   (A) quietly..significant
   (B) enthusiastically..shifting
   (C) passively..unusual
   (D) sympathetically..distinct
   (E) contentiously..realistic

7. For some time now, ------- has been presumed not to exist: the cynical conviction that everybody has an angle is considered wisdom.

   (A) rationality
   (B) flexibility
   (C) diffidence
   (D) disinterestedness
   (E) insincerity

GO ON TO THE NEXT PAGE.

Directions: In each of the following questions, a related pair of words or phrases is followed by five lettered pairs of words or phrases. Select the lettered pair that best expresses a relationship similar to that expressed in the original pair.

8. STUDY:LEARN :: (A) pervade:encompass (B) search:find   (C) gather:win   (D) agree:keep   (E) accumulate:raise

9. CORRAL:HORSES :: (A) den:lions (B) meadow:sheep   (C) herd:cattle (D) nest:birds   (E) coop:chickens

10. LULLABY:SONG ::
    (A) narrative:volume
    (B) lecture:tutor
    (C) paragraph:page
    (D) diatribe:discourse
    (E) invective:compliment

*11. DIE:SHAPING :: (A) glue:attaching (B) anchor:sailing   (C) drill:boring (D) pedal:propelling   (E) ink:printing

12. MERCENARY:MONEY ::
    (A) vindictive:revenge
    (B) scholarly:library
    (C) immaculate:cleanliness
    (D) thirsty:water
    (E) belligerent:invasion

13. AUTHORITATIVENESS:PUNDITS ::
    (A) dedication:signatories
    (B) sobriety:executors
    (C) sensitivity:literati
    (D) recklessness:warriors
    (E) allegiance:partisans

*14. STRUT:WING :: (A) lever:handle (B) axle:wheel   (C) buttress:wall (D) beam:rivet   (E) well:pipe

15. FAWN:IMPERIOUSNESS ::
    (A) equivocate:directness
    (B) elaborate:originality
    (C) boggle:imagination
    (D) manipulate:repression
    (E) coddle:permissiveness

16. TROUBLED:DISTRAUGHT ::
    (A) annoyed:disillusioned
    (B) disturbed:interrupted
    (C) covetous:rapacious
    (D) outmoded:ostentatious
    (E) tranquil:placid

GO ON TO THE NEXT PAGE.

The evolution of intelligence among early large mammals of the grasslands was due in great measure to the interaction between two ecologically synchronized groups of these ani-
(5) mals, the hunting carnivores and the herbivores that they hunted. The interaction resulting from the differences between predator and prey led to a general improvement in brain functions; however, certain components of intelligence were
(10) improved far more than others.

The kind of intelligence favored by the interplay of increasingly smarter catchers and increasingly keener escapers is defined by attention—that aspect of mind carrying con-
(15) sciousness forward from one moment to the next. It ranges from a passive, free-floating awareness to a highly focused, active fixation. The range through these states is mediated by the arousal system, a network of tracts converg-
(20) ing from sensory systems to integrating centers in the brain stem. From the more relaxed to the more vigorous levels, sensitivity to novelty is increased. The organism is more awake, more vigilant; this increased vigilance results in the
(25) apprehension of ever more subtle signals as the organism becomes more sensitive to its surroundings. The processes of arousal and concentration give attention its direction. Arousal is at first general, with a flooding of impulses in the
(30) brain stem; then gradually the activation is channeled. Thus begins concentration, the holding of consistent images. One meaning of intelligence is the way in which these images and other alertly searched information are used in the con-
(35) text of previous experience. Consciousness links past attention to the present and permits the integration of details with perceived ends and purposes.

The elements of intelligence and conscious-
(40) ness come together marvelously to produce different styles in predator and prey. Herbivores and carnivores develop different kinds of attention related to escaping or chasing. Although in both kinds of animal, arousal stimulates the
(45) production of adrenaline and norepinephrine by the adrenal glands, the effect in herbivores is primarily fear, whereas in carnivores the effect is primarily aggression. For both, arousal attunes the animal to what is ahead. Perhaps it does not
(50) experience forethought as we know it, but the animal does experience something like it. The predator is searchingly aggressive, innerdirected, tuned by the nervous system and the adrenal hormones, but aware in a sense closer to human

(55) consciousness than, say, a hungry lizard's instinctive snap at a passing beetle. Using past events as a framework, the large mammal predator is working out a relationship between movement and food, sensitive to possibilities in cold trails
(60) and distant sounds—and yesterday's unforgotten lessons. The herbivore prey is of a different mind. Its mood of wariness rather than searching and its attitude of general expectancy instead of anticipating are silk-thin veils of tranquility over an explosive endocrine system.

17. The author is primarily concerned with

(A) disproving the view that herbivores are less intelligent than carnivores
(B) describing a relationship between animals' intelligence and their ecological roles
(C) establishing a direct link between early large mammals and their modern counterparts
(D) analyzing the ecological basis for the dominance of some carnivores over other carnivores
(E) demonstrating the importance of hormones in mental activity

18. The author refers to a hungry lizard (line 55) primarily in order to

(A) demonstrate the similarity between the hunting methods of mammals and those of nonmammals
(B) broaden the application of his argument by including an insectivore as an example
(C) make a distinction between higher and lower levels of consciousness
(D) provide an additional illustration of the brutality characteristic of predators
(E) offer an objection to suggestions that all animals lack consciousness

GO ON TO THE NEXT PAGE.

118

19. It can be inferred from the passage that in animals less intelligent than the mammals discussed in the passage

(A) past experience is less helpful in ensuring survival
(B) attention is more highly focused
(C) muscular coordination is less highly developed
(D) there is less need for competition among species
(E) environment is more important in establishing the proper ratio of prey to predator

20. The sensitivity described in lines 56-61 is most clearly an example of

(A) "free-floating awareness" (lines 16-17)
(B) "flooding of impulses in the brain stem" (lines 29-30)
(C) "the holding of consistent images" (lines 31-32)
(D) "integration of details with perceived ends and purposes" (lines 37-38)
(E) "silk-thin veils of tranquility" (line 64)

21. The author's attitude toward the mammals discussed in the passage is best described as

(A) superior and condescending
(B) lighthearted and jocular
(C) apologetic and conciliatory
(D) wistful and tender
(E) respectful and admiring

22. The author provides information that would answer which of the following questions?

I. Why is an aroused herbivore usually fearful?
II. What are some of the degrees of attention in large mammals?
III. What occurs when the stimulus that causes arousal of a mammal is removed?

(A) I only   (B) III only   (C) I and II only
(D) II and III only   (E) I, II, and III

23. According to the passage, improvement in brain function among early large mammals resulted primarily from which of the following?

(A) Interplay of predator and prey
(B) Persistence of free-floating awareness in animals of the grasslands
(C) Gradual dominance of warm-blooded mammals over cold-blooded reptiles
(D) Interaction of early large mammals with less intelligent species
(E) Improvement of the capacity for memory among herbivores and carnivores

24. According to the passage, as the process of arousal in an organism continues, all of the following may occur EXCEPT

(A) the production of adrenaline
(B) the production of norepinephrine
(C) a heightening of sensitivity to stimuli
(D) an increase in selectivity with respect to stimuli
(E) an expansion of the range of states mediated by the brain stem

GO ON TO THE NEXT PAGE.

Tocqueville, apparently, was wrong. Jacksonian America was not a fluid, egalitarian society where individual wealth and poverty were ephemeral conditions. At least so argues E. Pessen in his iconoclastic study of the very rich in the United States between 1825 and 1850.

Pessen does present a quantity of examples, together with some refreshingly intelligible statistics, to establish the existence of an inordinately wealthy class. Though active in commerce or the professions, most of the wealthy were not self-made, but had inherited family fortunes. In no sense mercurial, these great fortunes survived the financial panics that destroyed lesser ones. Indeed, in several cities the wealthiest one percent constantly increased its share until by 1850 it owned half of the community's wealth. Although these observations are true, Pessen overestimates their importance by concluding from them that the undoubted progress toward inequality in the late eighteenth century continued in the Jacksonian period and that the United States was a class-ridden, plutocratic society even before industrialization.

25. According to the passage, Pessen indicates that all of the following were true of the very wealthy in the United States between 1825 and 1850 EXCEPT:

(A) They formed a distinct upper class.
(B) Many of them were able to increase their holdings.
(C) Some of them worked as professionals or in business.
(D) Most of them accumulated their own fortunes.
(E) Many of them retained their wealth in spite of financial upheavals.

26. The author's attitude toward Pessen's presentation of statistics can be best described as

(A) disapproving
(B) shocked
(C) suspicious
(D) amused
(E) laudatory

27. Which of the following best states the author's main point?

(A) Pessen's study has overturned the previously established view of the social and economic structure of early nineteenth-century America.
(B) Tocqueville's analysis of the United States in the Jacksonian era remains the definitive account of this period.
(C) Pessen's study is valuable primarily because it shows the continuity of the social system in the United States throughout the nineteenth century.
(D) The social patterns and political power of the extremely wealthy in the United States between 1825 and 1850 are well documented.
(E) Pessen challenges a view of the social and economic system in the United States from 1825 to 1850, but he draws conclusions that are incorrect.

GO ON TO THE NEXT PAGE.

28. BOISTEROUS: (A) grateful (B) angry
(C) clever (D) frightened (E) quiet

29. EMIT: (A) absorb (B) demand
(C) mistake (D) prevent (E) require

30. METAMORPHOSE: (A) move ahead
(B) remain unaltered (C) descend slowly
(D) examine in haste (E) prepare in advance

31. ALLY: (A) mediator (B) felon
(C) adversary (D) inventor
(E) conspirator

32. OFFHAND:
(A) accurate
(B) universal
(C) appropriate
(D) premeditated
(E) disputatious

33. BROACH: (A) keep track of
(B) lay claim to (C) close off (D) soothe
(E) simplify

34. GIST: (A) artificial manner
(B) trivial point (C) informal procedure
(D) eccentric method (E) singular event

35. DIVESTITURE: (A) acquisition
(B) promotion (C) subsidization
(D) consultation (E) monopolization

36. EXTANT: (A) extensive (B) extraneous
(C) extricable (D) extinct (E) extra

37. TRACTABILITY: (A) infertility
(B) implausibility (C) incorrigibility
(D) impenetrability (E) indefatigability

38. NOISOME:
(A) attractively fragrant
(B) subtly flattering
(C) consistently patient
(D) softly glowing
(E) gradually diminishing

S T O P

Numbers: All numbers used are real numbers.

Figures: Position of points, angles, regions, etc. can be assumed to be in the order shown; and angle measures can be assumed to be positive.

Lines shown as straight can be assumed to be straight.

Figures can be assumed to lie in a plane unless otherwise indicated.

Figures that accompany questions are intended to provide information useful in answering the questions. However, unless a note states that a figure is drawn to scale, you should solve these problems NOT by estimating sizes by sight or by measurement, but by using your knowledge of mathematics (see Example 2 below).

Directions: Each of the Questions 1-15 consists of two quantities, one in Column A and one in Column B. You are to compare the two quantities and choose

A if the quantity in Column A is greater;
B if the quantity in Column B is greater;
C if the two quantities are equal;
D if the relationship cannot be determined from the information given.

Note: Since there are only four choices, NEVER MARK (E).

Common
Information: In a question, information concerning one or both of the quantities to be compared is centered above the two columns. A symbol that appears in both columns represents the same thing in Column A as it does in Column B.

	Column A	Column B	Sample Answers
Example 1:	2×6	$2 + 6$	● Ⓑ Ⓒ Ⓓ Ⓔ

Examples 2-4 refer to $\triangle PQR$.

Example 2:	PN	NQ	Ⓐ Ⓑ Ⓒ ● Ⓔ

(since equal measures cannot be assumed, even though PN and NQ appear equal)

Example 3:	x	y	Ⓐ ● Ⓒ Ⓓ Ⓔ

(since N is between P and Q)

Example 4:	$w + z$	180	Ⓐ Ⓑ ● Ⓓ Ⓔ

(since PQ is a straight line)

GO ON TO THE NEXT PAGE.

A if the quantity in Column A is greater;
B if the quantity in Column B is greater;
C if the two quantities are equal;
D if the relationship cannot be determined from the information given.

	Column A	Column B
1.	(40% of 50) + 60	(60% of 50) + 40

	Column A	Column B
2.	$\frac{1}{12}$ of 17	$\frac{1}{17}$ of 12

$$x + y = -1$$

	Column A	Column B
3.	x	y

	Column A	Column B
4.	23(784)	24(783)

$$0 < r < t$$

	Column A	Column B
5.	$\frac{r}{t}$	$\frac{t}{r}$

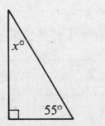

	Column A	Column B
6.	x	35

For each home in Town X, the amount of property tax is p percent of the value of the home. The property tax on a home whose value is $45,000 is $1,200.

	Column A	Column B
7.	The property tax on a home in Town X whose value is $54,000	$1,300

The area of square region S is 36.

	Column A	Column B
8.	The perimeter of S	24

A printer numbered consecutively the pages of a book, beginning with 1 on the first page. In numbering the pages, he printed a total of 189 digits.

	Column A	Column B
9.	The number of pages in the book	100

The average (arithmetic mean) of x, y, and 6 is 3.

	Column A	Column B
10.	$\frac{x + y}{2}$	$\frac{3}{2}$

GO ON TO THE NEXT PAGE.

A   if the quantity in Column A is greater;
B   if the quantity in Column B is greater;
C   if the two quantities are equal;
D   if the relationship cannot be determined from the information given.

<u>Column A</u>   <u>Column B</u>   <u>Column A</u>   <u>Column B</u>

Triangular regions T_1 and T_2 have equal m, p, and x are positive integers and $mp = x$.
areas and have heights h_1 and h_2, respectively.

                                            14. m x
11. $\dfrac{\text{The area of } T_1}{h_1}$ $\dfrac{\text{The area of } T_2}{h_2}$

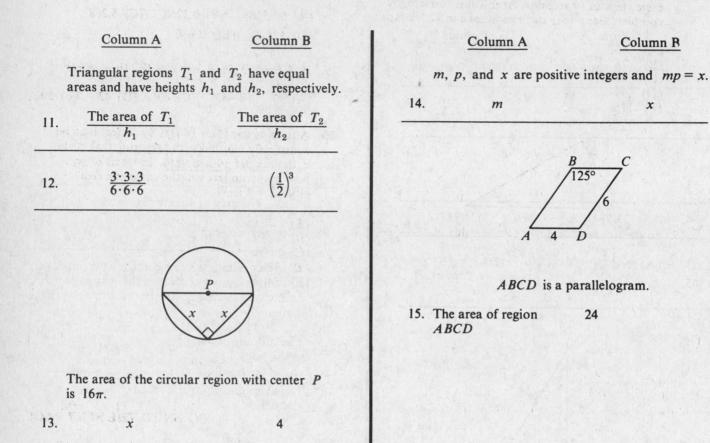

12. $\dfrac{3 \cdot 3 \cdot 3}{6 \cdot 6 \cdot 6}$ $\left(\dfrac{1}{2}\right)^3$

$ABCD$ is a parallelogram.

15.   The area of region   24
      $ABCD$

The area of the circular region with center P
is 16π.

13. x 4

GO ON TO THE NEXT PAGE.

124

16. When walking, a certain person takes 16 complete steps in 10 seconds. At this rate, how many complete steps does the person take in 72 seconds?

(A) 45
(B) 78
(C) 86
(D) 99
(E) 115

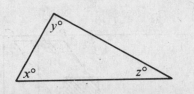

17. In the figure above, what is the value of $\dfrac{x+y+z}{45}$?

(A) 2   (B) 3   (C) 4   (D) 5   (E) 6

18. $52.68 \times \dfrac{1}{100} =$

(A) 0.05268   (B) 0.5268   (C) 5.268
(D) 526.8   (E) 52,680

19. If $b-c=3$, and $a+c=32$, then $a+b=$

(A) 30   (B) 35   (C) 40   (D) 42   (E) 50

20. A rectangular floor 18 feet by 10 feet is to be completely covered with carpeting that costs x dollars per square yard. In terms of x, how many dollars will the carpeting cost? (1 yard = 3 feet)

(A)   20x
(B)   28x
(C)   60x
(D)   180x
(E)   540x

GO ON TO THE NEXT PAGE.

125

Questions 21-25 refer to the following graphs.

COLLEGE *R*: ENROLLMENT AND CONTRIBUTIONS
1976-1980

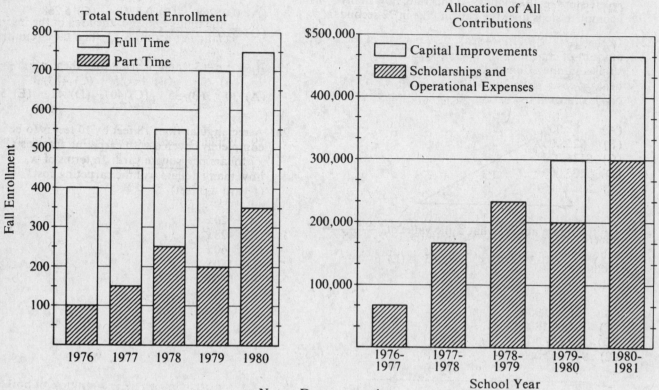

Note: Drawn to scale.

21. What was the total number of students enrolled at College *R* in the fall of 1979 ?

    (A) 200
    (B) 250
    (C) 500
    (D) 650
    (E) 700

22. By what percent did the number of part-time students enrolled increase from the fall of 1979 to the fall of 1980 ?

    (A) 7%

    (B) 42%

    (C) $66\frac{2}{3}\%$

    (D) 75%

    (E) 80%

GO ON TO THE NEXT PAGE.

23. What was the increase, if any, in the number of full-time students enrolled at College R from the fall of 1976 to the fall of 1977 ?

    (A) 0   (B) 50   (C) 100
    (D) 150   (E) 200

24. In the 1978-1979 school year, if 12 percent of the amount of contributions allocated to scholarships and operational expenses was allocated to heating costs, approximately how much was NOT allocated to heating costs?

    (A) $2,000
    (B) $25,000
    (C) $176,000
    (D) $205,000
    (E) $250,000

25. Approximately what was the total amount of contributions to College R from the 1978-1979 school year through the 1980-1981 school year, inclusive?

    (A) $967,000
    (B) $1,000,000
    (C) $9,000,000
    (D) $9,667,000
    (E) $10,000,000

---

26. If $x \neq 0$, then $\dfrac{x(x^2)^3}{x^2} =$

    (A) x^2 (B) x^3 (C) x^4 (D) x^5 (E) x^6

27. Seven is equal to how many thirds of seven?

    (A) $\dfrac{1}{3}$

    (B)   1

    (C)   3

    (D)   7

    (E)   21

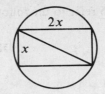

28. In the figure above, if the area of the inscribed rectangular region is 32, then the circumference of the circle is

    (A) 20π (B) $4\pi\sqrt{5}$ (C) $4\pi\sqrt{3}$
    (D) $2\pi\sqrt{5}$ (E) $2\pi\sqrt{3}$

29. Which of the following equals the reciprocal of $x - \dfrac{1}{y}$, where $x - \dfrac{1}{y} \neq 0$?

    (A) $\dfrac{1}{x} - y$

    (B) $- \dfrac{y}{x}$

    (C) $\dfrac{y}{x-1}$

    (D) $\dfrac{x}{xy-1}$

    (E) $\dfrac{y}{xy-1}$

30. A certain integer n is a multiple of both 5 and 9. Which of the following must be true?

    I. n is an odd integer.
    II. n is equal to 45.
    III. n is a multiple of 15.

    (A) III only
    (B) I and II only
    (C) I and III only
    (D) II and III only
    (E) I, II, and III

S T O P

IF YOU FINISH BEFORE TIME IS CALLED, YOU MAY CHECK YOUR WORK ON THIS SECTION ONLY.
DO NOT WORK ON ANY OTHER SECTION IN THE TEST.

Time—30 minutes
38 Questions

Directions: Each sentence below has one or two blanks, each blank indicating that something has been omitted. Beneath the sentence are five lettered words or sets of words. Choose the word or set of words for each blank that best fits the meaning of the sentence as a whole.

1. The ------- of mass literacy coincided with the first industrial revolution; in turn, the new expansion in literacy, as well as cheaper printing, helped to nurture the ------- of popular literature.

   (A) building..mistrust
   (B) reappearance..display
   (C) receipt..source
   (D) selection..influence
   (E) emergence..rise

2. Although ancient tools were ------- preserved, enough have survived to allow us to demonstrate an occasionally interrupted but generally ------- progress through prehistory.

   (A) partially..noticeable
   (B) superficially..necessary
   (C) unwittingly..documented
   (D) rarely..continual
   (E) needlessly..incessant

3. In parts of the Arctic, the land grades into the landfast ice so ------- that you can walk off the coast and not know you are over the hidden sea.

   (A) permanently   (B) imperceptibly
   (C) irregularly   (D) precariously
   (E) slightly

4. Kagan maintains that an infant's reactions to its first stressful experiences are part of a natural process of development, not harbingers of childhood unhappiness or ------- signs of adolescent anxiety.

   (A) prophetic   (B) normal
   (C) monotonous   (D) virtual
   (E) typical

5. An investigation that is ------- can occasionally yield new facts, even notable ones, but typically the appearance of such facts is the result of a search in a definite direction.

   (A) timely   (B) unguided   (C) consistent
   (D) uncomplicated   (E) subjective

6. Like many eighteenth-century scholars who lived by cultivating those in power, Winckelmann neglected to neutralize, by some ------- gesture of comradeship, the resentment his peers were bound to feel because of his ------- the high and mighty.

   (A) quixotic..intrigue with
   (B) enigmatic..familiarity with
   (C) propitiatory..involvement with
   (D) salutary..questioning of
   (E) unfeigned..sympathy for

7. In a ------- society that worships efficiency, it is difficult for a sensitive and idealistic person to make the kinds of ------- decisions that alone spell success as it is defined by such a society.

   (A) bureaucratic..edifying
   (B) pragmatic..hardheaded
   (C) rational..well-intentioned
   (D) competitive..evenhanded
   (E) modern..dysfunctional

GO ON TO THE NEXT PAGE.

8. TABLECLOTH:TABLE :: (A) tent:ground
    (B) shirt:hanger   (C) window:sill
    (D) sheet:mattress   (E) cloud:earth

9. CANVAS:PAINTER :: (A) leather:shoe
    (B) brush:palette   (C) chisel:wood
    (D) marble:sculptor   (E) hammer:carpenter

10. MANSION:RESIDENCE ::
    (A) limousine:automobile
    (B) chandelier:candle
    (C) tuxedo:wardrobe
    (D) diamond:rhinestone
    (E) yacht:harbor

*11. DOOR:ROOM :: (A) rudder:anchor
    (B) boat:ship   (C) patio:terrace
    (D) hatch:hold   (E) basement:attic

12. CHOREOGRAPHY:DANCE ::
    (A) ceremony:sermon
    (B) agenda:advertisement
    (C) poetry:recitation
    (D) instrumentation:conductor
    (E) plot:story

13. EVAPORATE:VAPOR ::
    (A) petrify:stone   (B) centrifuge:liquid
    (C) saturate:fluid   (D) corrode:acid
    (E) incinerate:fire

14. ASSUAGE:SORROW ::
    (A) retaliate:antipathy
    (B) dampen:ardor
    (C) entrust:reliability
    (D) counsel:reluctance
    (E) withhold:appreciation

15. NUMB:INSENSIBLE :: (A) reflect:luminous
    (B) burnish:lustrous   (C) heckle:raucous
    (D) repulse:odious   (E) braid:sinuous

16. AUDACIOUS:TREPIDATION ::
    (A) refractory:intransigence
    (B) laconic:volubility
    (C) sordid:aspiration
    (D) cursory:accumulation
    (E) derisive:subordination

GO ON TO THE NEXT PAGE.

"I want to criticize the social system, and to show it at work, at its most intense." Virginia Woolf's provocative statement about her intentions in writing *Mrs. Dalloway* has regularly

(5) been ignored by the critics, since it highlights an aspect of her literary interests very different from the traditional picture of the "poetic" novelist concerned with examining states of reverie and vision and with following the intricate pathways

(10) of individual consciousness. But Virginia Woolf was a realistic as well as a poetic novelist, a satirist and social critic as well as a visionary: literary critics' cavalier dismissal of Woolf's social vision will not withstand scrutiny.

(15)   In her novels, Woolf is deeply engaged by the questions of how individuals are shaped (or deformed) by their social environments, how historical forces impinge on people's lives, how class, wealth, and gender help to determine

(20) people's fates. Most of her novels are rooted in a realistically rendered social setting and in a precise historical time.

    Woolf's focus on society has not been generally recognized because of her intense antipathy

(25) to propaganda in art. The pictures of reformers in her novels are usually satiric or sharply critical. Even when Woolf is fundamentally sympathetic to their causes, she portrays people anxious to reform their society and possessed of

(30) a message or program as arrogant or dishonest, unaware of how their political ideas serve their own psychological needs. (Her *Writer's Diary* notes: "the only honest people are the artists," whereas "these social reformers and philan-

(35) thropists . . . harbor . . . discreditable desires under the disguise of loving their kind. . . .") Woolf detested what she called "preaching" in fiction, too, and criticized novelist D. H. Lawrence (among others) for working by

(40) this method.

    Woolf's own social criticism is expressed in the language of observation rather than in direct commentary, since for her, fiction is a contemplative, not an active art. She describes phenom-

(45) ena and provides materials for a judgment about society and social issues; it is the reader's work to put the observations together and understand the coherent point of view behind them. As a moralist, Woolf works by indirection, subtly

(50) undermining officially accepted mores, mocking, suggesting, calling into question, rather than asserting, advocating, bearing witness: hers is the satirist's art.

    Woolf's literary models were acute social ob-

(55) servers like Chekhov and Chaucer. As she put it in *The Common Reader*, "It is safe to say that not a single law has been framed or one stone set upon another because of anything Chaucer said or wrote; and yet, as we read him, we are absorb-

(60) ing morality at every pore." Like Chaucer, Woolf chose to understand as well as to judge, to know her society root and branch—a decision crucial in order to produce art rather than polemic.

17. Which of the following would be the most appropriate title for the passage?

(A) Poetry and Satire as Influences on the Novels of Virginia Woolf

(B) Virginia Woolf: Critic and Commentator on the Twentieth-Century Novel

(C) Trends in Contemporary Reform Movements as a Key to Understanding Virginia Woolf's Novels

(D) Society as Allegory for the Individual in the Novels of Virginia Woolf

(E) Virginia Woolf's Novels: Critical Reflections on the Individual and on Society

18. In the first paragraph of the passage, the author's attitude toward the literary critics mentioned can best be described as

(A) disparaging
(B) ironic
(C) facetious
(D) skeptical but resigned
(E) disappointed but hopeful

19. It can be inferred from the passage that Woolf chose Chaucer as a literary model because she believed that

(A) Chaucer was the first English author to focus on society as a whole as well as on individual characters

(B) Chaucer was an honest and forthright author, whereas novelists like D. H. Lawrence did not sincerely wish to change society

(C) Chaucer was more concerned with understanding his society than with calling its accepted mores into question

(D) Chaucer's writing was greatly, if subtly, effective in influencing the moral attitudes of his readers

(E) her own novels would be more widely read if, like Chaucer, she did not overtly and vehemently criticize contemporary society

GO ON TO THE NEXT PAGE.

20. It can be inferred from the passage that the most probable reason Woolf realistically described the social setting in the majority of her novels was that she

(A) was aware that contemporary literary critics considered the novel to be the most realistic of literary genres
(B) was interested in the effect of a person's social milieu on his or her character and actions
(C) needed to be as attentive to detail as possible in her novels in order to support the arguments she advanced in them
(D) wanted to show that a painstaking fidelity in the representation of reality did not in any way hamper the artist
(E) wished to prevent critics from charging that her novels were written in an ambiguous and inexact style

21. Which of the following phrases best expresses the sense of the word "contemplative" as it is used in lines 43-44 of the passage?

(A) Gradually elucidating the rational structures underlying accepted mores
(B) Reflecting on issues in society without prejudice or emotional commitment
(C) Avoiding the aggressive assertion of the author's perspective to the exclusion of the reader's judgment
(D) Conveying a broad view of society as a whole rather than focusing on an isolated individual consciousness
(E) Appreciating the world as the artist sees it rather than judging it in moral terms

22. The author implies that a major element of the satirist's art is the satirist's

(A) consistent adherence to a position of lofty disdain when viewing the foibles of humanity
(B) insistence on the helplessness of individuals against the social forces that seek to determine an individual's fate
(C) cynical disbelief that visionaries can either enlighten or improve their societies
(D) fundamental assumption that some ambiguity must remain in a work of art in order for it to reflect society and social mores accurately
(E) refusal to indulge in polemic when presenting social mores to readers for their scrutiny

23. The passage supplies information for answering which of the following questions?

(A) Have literary critics ignored the social criticism inherent in the works of Chekhov and Chaucer?
(B) Does the author believe that Woolf is solely an introspective and visionary novelist?
(C) What are the social causes with which Woolf shows herself to be sympathetic in her writings?
(D) Was D. H. Lawrence as concerned as Woolf was with creating realistic settings for his novels?
(E) Does Woolf attribute more power to social environment or to historical forces as shapers of a person's life?

GO ON TO THE NEXT PAGE.

It is a popular misconception that nuclear fusion power is free of radioactivity; in fact, the deuterium-tritium reaction that nuclear scientists are currently exploring with such zeal produces both alpha particles and neutrons. (The neutrons are used to produce tritium from a lithium blanket surrounding the reactor.) Another common misconception is that nuclear fusion power is a virtually unlimited source of energy because of the enormous quantity of deuterium in the sea. Actually, its limits are set by the amount of available lithium, which is about as plentiful as uranium in the Earth's crust. Research should certainly continue on controlled nuclear fusion, but no energy program should be premised on its existence until it has proven practical. For the immediate future, we must continue to use hydroelectric power, nuclear fission, and fossil fuels to meet our energy needs. The energy sources already in major use are in major use for good reason.

24. The primary purpose of the passage is to

    (A) criticize scientists who believe that the deuterium-tritium fusion reaction can be made feasible as an energy source
    (B) admonish scientists who have failed to correctly calculate the amount of lithium available for use in nuclear fusion reactors
    (C) defend the continued short-term use of fossil fuels as a major energy source
    (D) caution against uncritical embrace of nuclear fusion power as a major energy source
    (E) correct the misconception that nuclear fusion power is entirely free of radioactivity

25. It can be inferred from the passage that the author believes which of the following about the current state of public awareness concerning nuclear fusion power?

    (A) The public has been deliberately misinformed about the advantages and disadvantages of nuclear fusion power.
    (B) The public is unaware of the principal advantage of nuclear fusion over nuclear fission as an energy source.
    (C) The public's awareness of the scientific facts concerning nuclear fusion power is somewhat distorted and incomplete.
    (D) The public is not interested in increasing its awareness of the advantages and disadvantages of nuclear fusion power.
    (E) The public is aware of the disadvantages of nuclear fusion power but not of its advantages.

26. The passage provides information that would answer which of the following questions?

    (A) What is likely to be the principal source of deuterium for nuclear fusion power?
    (B) How much incidental radiation is produced in the deuterium-tritium fusion reaction?
    (C) Why are scientists exploring the deuterium-tritium fusion reaction with such zeal?
    (D) Why must the tritium for nuclear fusion be synthesized from lithium?
    (E) Why does the deuterium-tritium reaction yield both alpha particles and neutrons?

27. Which of the following statements concerning nuclear scientists is most directly suggested in the passage?

    (A) Nuclear scientists are not themselves aware of all of the facts surrounding the deuterium-tritium fusion reaction.
    (B) Nuclear scientists exploring the deuterium-tritium reaction have overlooked key facts in their eagerness to prove nuclear fusion practical.
    (C) Nuclear scientists may have overestimated the amount of lithium actually available in the Earth's crust.
    (D) Nuclear scientists have not been entirely dispassionate in their investigation of the deuterium-tritium reaction.
    (E) Nuclear scientists have insufficiently investigated the lithium-to-tritium reaction in nuclear fusion.

GO ON TO THE NEXT PAGE.

28. PERSEVERE: (A) put into   (B) send out
    (C) take away   (D) give up
     (E) bring forward

29. WATERPROOF: (A) soggy   (B) natural
    (C) unglazed   (D) viscous   (E) permeable

30. AMALGAMATE: (A) separate   (B) fixate
    (C) terminate   (D) calibrate   (E) correlate

31. PUNGENCY: (A) boredom   (B) redundancy
    (C) unresponsiveness   (D) blandness
     (E) insignificance

32. ANARCHY: (A) courtesy   (B) hope
    (C) order   (D) neutrality   (E) importance

33. INCURSION: (A) loss of respect
    (B) lack of resolve   (C) reparation
     (D) relapse   (E) retreat

34. ABROGATE: (A) uphold   (B) defer
    (C) discuss secretly   (D) admit willingly
     (E) read thoroughly

35. HAPLESS: (A) excited   (B) elated
    (C) fortunate   (D) completely self-reliant
     (E) assured of success

36. AVER: (A) collect   (B) augment
    (C) placate   (D) deny   (E) encourage

37. SEDULOUS: (A) presumptuous
    (B) ponderous   (C) treacherous
     (D) careless   (E) useless

38. INSULARITY:
    (A) overzealousness
    (B) cosmopolitanism
    (C) susceptibility
    (D) willing hospitality
    (E) knowledgeable consideration

S T O P

**IF YOU FINISH BEFORE TIME IS CALLED, YOU MAY CHECK YOUR WORK ON THIS SECTION ONLY.
DO NOT WORK ON ANY OTHER SECTION IN THE TEST.**

SECTION 4

Time—30 minutes
30 Questions

<u>Numbers:</u>   All numbers used are real numbers.

<u>Figures:</u>   Position of points, angles, regions, etc. can be assumed to be in the order shown; and angle measures can be assumed to be positive.

Lines shown as straight can be assumed to be straight.

Figures can be assumed to lie in a plane unless otherwise indicated.

Figures that accompany questions are intended to provide information useful in answering the questions. However, unless a note states that a figure is drawn to scale, you should solve these problems NOT by estimating sizes by sight or by measurement, but by using your knowledge of mathematics (see Example 2 below).

<u>Directions:</u>   Each of the <u>Questions 1-15</u> consists of two quantities, one in Column A and one in Column B. You are to compare the two quantities and choose

    A   if the quantity in Column A is greater;
    B   if the quantity in Column B is greater;
    C   if the two quantities are equal;
    D   if the relationship cannot be determined from the information given.

<u>Note:</u>   Since there are only four choices, NEVER MARK (E).

<u>Common Information:</u>   In a question, information concerning one or both of the quantities to be compared is centered above the two columns. A symbol that appears in both columns represents the same thing in Column A as it does in Column B.

	Column A	Column B	Sample Answers
Example 1:	2×6	$2 + 6$	● Ⓑ Ⓒ Ⓓ Ⓔ

Examples 2-4 refer to $\triangle PQR$.

	Column A	Column B	Sample Answers
Example 2:	PN	NQ	Ⓐ Ⓑ Ⓒ ● Ⓔ

(since equal measures cannot be assumed, even though PN and NQ appear equal)

Example 3:	x	y	Ⓐ ● Ⓒ Ⓓ Ⓔ

(since N is between P and Q)

Example 4:	$w + z$	180	Ⓐ Ⓑ ● Ⓓ Ⓔ

(since PQ is a straight line)

GO ON TO THE NEXT PAGE.

134

A if the quantity in Column A is greater;
B if the quantity in Column B is greater;
C if the two quantities are equal;
D if the relationship cannot be determined from the information given.

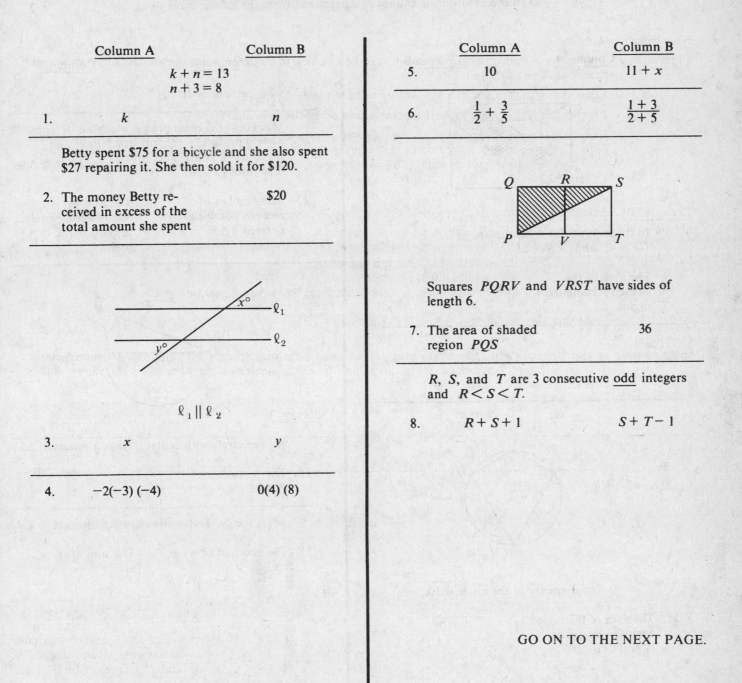

	Column A	Column B
	$k + n = 13$	
	$n + 3 = 8$	
1.	k	n

Betty spent $75 for a bicycle and she also spent $27 repairing it. She then sold it for $120.

	Column A	Column B
2.	The money Betty received in excess of the total amount she spent	$20

$\ell_1 \parallel \ell_2$

	Column A	Column B
3.	x	y
4.	$-2(-3)(-4)$	$0(4)(8)$

	Column A	Column B
5.	10	$11 + x$
6.	$\frac{1}{2} + \frac{3}{5}$	$\frac{1+3}{2+5}$

Squares $PQRV$ and $VRST$ have sides of length 6.

	Column A	Column B
7.	The area of shaded region PQS	36

R, S, and T are 3 consecutive <u>odd</u> integers and $R < S < T$.

	Column A	Column B
8.	$R + S + 1$	$S + T - 1$

GO ON TO THE NEXT PAGE.

A   if the quantity in Column A is greater;
B   if the quantity in Column B is greater;
C   if the two quantities are equal;
D   if the relationship cannot be determined from the information given.

Column A	Column B

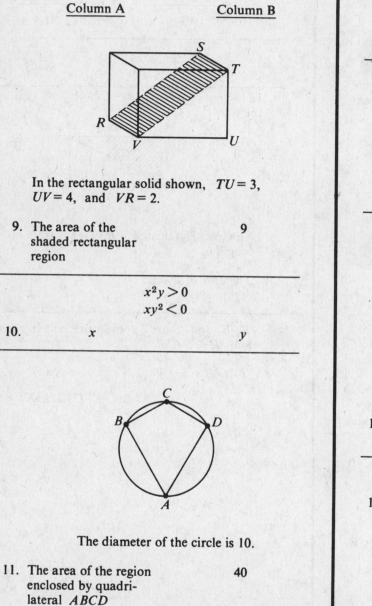

In the rectangular solid shown, $TU = 3$, $UV = 4$, and $VR = 2$.

9. The area of the shaded rectangular region

    9

$$x^2 y > 0$$
$$xy^2 < 0$$

10. x y

The diameter of the circle is 10.

11. The area of the region enclosed by quadrilateral $ABCD$

    40

Column A	Column B

12. $2\frac{1}{2}$ percent of 1,120 $2^2 \cdot 7$

Working at constant rates, machine R completely presses x records in 0.5 hour and machine S completely presses x records in 0.75 hour ($x > 0$).

13. The number of records completely pressed by R in 3 hours

    The number of records completely pressed by S in 4 hours

The circle with center O has a radius of 5.

14. The perimeter of $\triangle ABC$

    24

---

x, y, and z are negative integers.

15. The product of x, y, and z

    The sum of x, y, and z

GO ON TO THE NEXT PAGE.

16. $\sqrt{(42-6)(25+11)}$

    (A) 6   (B) 18   (C) 36

    (D) 120   (E) 1,296

17. The price per pair of brand X socks is \$2 and the price per pair of brand Y socks is \$3. If there is no sales tax and a customer chooses only from among these two brands, what is the greatest number of pairs of socks that he can buy with exactly \$25 ?

    (A) 9
    (B) 10
    (C) 11
    (D) 12
    (E) 20

18. What is the remainder when 6^3 is divided by 8 ?

    (A) 5
    (B) 3
    (C) 2
    (D) 1
    (E) 0

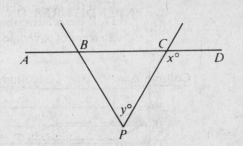

19. In the figure above, $BP = CP$. IF $x = 120$, then $y =$

    (A) 30   (B) 60   (C) 75   (D) 90   (E) 120

20. If $y = 3x$ and $z = 2y$, then in terms of x, $x + y + z =$

    (A) $10x$ (B) $9x$ (C) $8x$

    (D) $6x$ (E) $5x$

GO ON TO THE NEXT PAGE.

Questions 21-25 refer to the following data.

EXPENDITURES ON FOOD AND SELECTED NONFOOD ITEMS, 1973

Percent of Average Annual Income (before taxes) Spent by Families on
Food and Selected Nonfood Items

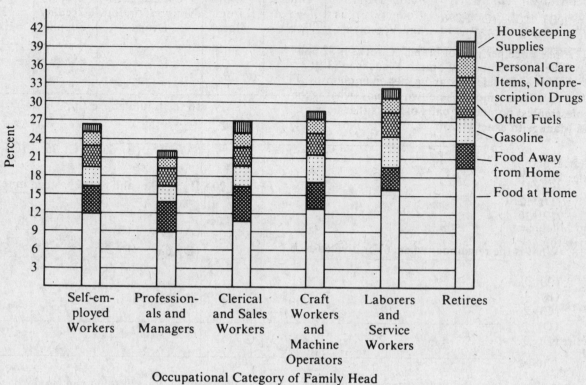

Occupational Category of Family Head

Note: Drawn to scale.

GO ON TO THE NEXT PAGE.

Average Weekly Food and Household Expenditures

Occupational Category of Family Head	Percent of Food and Household Expenditures						Average Weekly Food and Household Expenditures
	Food at Home			Food Away from Home	Personal Care Items, Nonprescription Drugs	House-keeping Supplies	
	Meats, Poultry, Seafood	Cereals, Bakery and Dairy Products, Fruits and Vegetables	Other Food at Home				
Self-employed Workers	22	25	14	22	10	7	$35.88
Professionals and Managers	19	23	11	29	11	7	$38.77
Clerical and Sales Workers	21	22	11	28	11	7	$32.07
Craft Workers and Machine Operators	23	25	15	21	9	7	$35.44
Laborers and Service Workers	24	27	14	19	9	7	$28.86
Retirees	23	29	14	16	11	7	$19.83

21. For which of the following categories was the percent of the average annual income (before taxes) spent on food at home the least?

    (A) Self-employed workers
    (B) Professionals and managers
    (C) Clerical and sales workers
    (D) Craft workers and machine operators
    (E) Laborers and service workers

22. Approximately what average amount per week did the families of professionals and managers spend on food away from home?

    (A) $2
    (B) $8
    (C) $11
    (D) $29
    (E) $38

23. Approximately what percent of the average weekly food and household expenditures of clerical and sales workers was spent on fruits and vegetables?

    (A) 4% (B) 7% (C) 22% (D) 25%
    (E) It cannot be determined from the information given.

24. Approximately what percent of the total average annual income (before taxes) of retirees was spent on meats, poultry, and seafood (consumed at home) ?

    (A) 7% (B) 10% (C) 20%
    (D) 23% (E) 31%

25. Which of the following statements can be inferred from the information given?

    I. Of the categories shown, retirees had the greatest average annual incomes (before taxes).
    II. For all the categories shown, the average amount spent per week on housekeeping supplies was the same.
    III. Of the categories shown, the average amount spent per week on meats, poultry, and seafood (consumed at home) was greatest for craft workers and machine operators.

    (A) I only (B) II only (C) III only
    (D) I and II (E) II and III

GO ON TO THE NEXT PAGE.

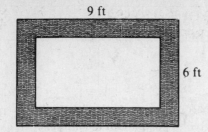

9 ft

6 ft

26. The rectangular rug shown in the figure above has a floral border 1 foot wide on all sides. What is the area, in square feet, of that portion of the rug that excludes the border?

(A) 28
(B) 40
(C) 45
(D) 48
(E) 53

27. If $\frac{d-3n}{7n-d} = 1$, which of the following must be true about the relationship between d and n?

(A) n is 4 more than d.

(B) d is 4 more than n.

(C) n is $\frac{7}{3}$ of d.

(D) d is 5 times n.

(E) d is 2 times n.

28. How many positive whole numbers less than 81 are NOT equal to squares of whole numbers?

(A) 9   (B) 70   (C) 71   (D) 72   (E) 73

29. Of the following, which could be the graph of $2 - 5x \leq \frac{6x-5}{-3}$?

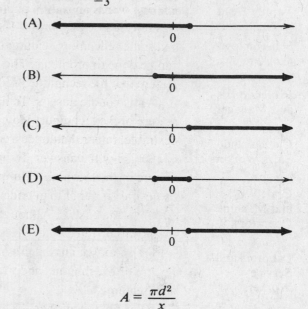

(A)

(B)

(C)

(D)

(E)

$$A = \frac{\pi d^2}{x}$$

30. If the formula above gives the area A of a circular region in terms of its diameter d, then $x =$

(A) $\frac{1}{4}$ (B) $\frac{1}{2}$ (C) 1   (D) 2   (E) 4

S T O P

IF YOU FINISH BEFORE TIME IS CALLED, YOU MAY CHECK YOUR WORK ON THIS SECTION ONLY. DO NOT WORK ON ANY OTHER SECTION IN THE TEST.

SECTION 1

1. The word "because" indicates that the second part of the sentence, where the missing words appear, explains why an innovative experimental technique was rejected by physicists. The word "although" indicates that the technique had some redeeming feature; the first missing word is something positive that can be done to problems. The second missing word is some undesirable feature that the technique produced.

    (A) is not the answer. To have "clarified" problems would be a redeeming feature of the technique. However, producing new "data" is also probably desirable, rather than undesirable.

    (B) is not the answer. To have "eased" problems would be a redeeming feature of the technique. But producing new "interpretations" is also likely to be desirable, rather than undesirable.

    (C) is the answer. Although a technique "resolved" some problems, it might still be rejected because it produced new "complications."

    (D) is not the answer. To have "caused" problems is not a redeeming feature of a technique, and to produce new "hypotheses" is not an undesirable feature.

    (E) is not the answer. To have "revealed" some problems may or may not be a redeeming feature of a technique. Producing "inconsistencies" may in some circumstances be undesirable. However, there is not enough information in the sentence to allow you to determine whether producing "inconsistencies" and revealing problems are desirable or undesirable.

2. The last part of the sentence explains what happens when the sick become infirm. To become infirm means to experience diminished vigor.

    (A) is not the answer. Becoming infirm does not mean "regaining" strength and skills; it means the opposite.

    (B) is not the answer. A person who has become infirm may be said to be denied strength and skills, rather than to be "denying" them.

    (C) is not the answer. A person who has become infirm may at the same time be "pursuing" strength and skills, but the condition of infirmity is not defined in this way.

    (D) is not the answer. To become infirm does not imply "insuring" strength and skills.

    (E) is the answer. To experience diminished vigor implies "losing" strength and skills.

3. The first part of the sentence emphasizes that, in order to understand history, it is important to take into account the great importance of the pressure of population on available resources. The word "consequently" indicates that the second part of the sentence describes a conclusion that follows from the statement made in the first part. In this case, what follows is a judgment

141

about any historical writing that does not show recognition of the correctness of the statement. The first missing word will provide a one-word description of the type of fact suggested by the first part of the sentence. The second missing word describes in what way writing that fails to take this type of fact into account is flawed.

(A) is the answer. "Demographic" facts are derived from the study of human populations. The "pressure of population" mentioned in the first clause is a "demographic" consideration. Because the sentence indicates that these facts are very important, you can conclude that the author believes that writing that fails to take them into account is "intrinsically" (essentially) flawed.

(B) is not the answer. The statement made in the first part of the sentence could be described as a statement about "ecological" facts (loosely, facts about the relationship of organisms to their environment). However, in view of the great importance ascribed to the information in the statement, it would be inappropriate to call work that ignores facts relating to the statement "marginally" flawed.

(C) is not the answer. The pressure of population on resources is not primarily a "cultural" fact. There is no information in the passage that suggests a relationship between culture, or a particular culture, and the pressure of population on resources.

(D) is not the answer. The pressure of population on resources is not primarily a "psychological" fact. There is no information in the sentence that suggests a relationship between psychology and the pressure of population on resources.

(E) is not the answer. The word "political" does not adequately describe the type of fact suggested by the information in the first part of the sentence.

4. The word "since" indicates that the second part of the sentence explains why recent criticism of the structure of Jones' novel is puzzling. The first missing word helps to explain why the novel has been recently criticized. The second part of the sentence gives the characteristic of the novel that has traditionally been criticized, and the second missing word is a general name for such a characteristic.

(A) is not the answer. If critics have traditionally argued that the novel's "preoccupation" is with structure, then it is not puzzling that it has been recently criticized for its "attention to" structure.

(B) is not the answer. Having a rigid framework as an obvious "characteristic" does not make "speculation about" structure puzzling.

(C) is not the answer. A "disparity" implies a difference among two or more elements, rather than a characteristic of a single entity.

(D) is not the answer. There is no information in the sentence that would lead one to regard a rigid framework as a "contradiction."

(E) is the answer. One might well be puzzled that a novel is criticized for "lack of" structure, when its rigid framework is often seen as an obvious "flaw."

5. The words "on the other hand" indicate that people's reactions to the character of societies' codes of behavior are not like their reactions to the fact of the codes' existence. Reaction to the existence of codes is likely to be the opposite of reaction to the character of codes.

   (A) is not the answer. To be "predictable" means to come as no surprise.

   (B) is the answer. To be "unexpected" means to be surprising.

   (C) is not the answer. Being "admirable" is not the opposite of being unsurprising.

   (D) is not the answer. To be "explicit" is not the opposite of being unsurprising.

   (E) is not the answer. To be thought "confusing" is not the opposite of being thought unsurprising.

6. The first missing word describes a way in which historians and literary critics are not likely to react to the suggestion that historical analysis is a form of fiction. The second missing word will depend on how the first missing word characterizes this way of reacting.

   (A) is not the answer. The agreement that history and fiction deal with "significant" orders of experience does not explain why neither historians nor literary critics will react "quietly."

   (B) is not the answer. The agreement that history and fiction deal with "shifting" orders of experience does not explain why neither historians nor literary critics will react "enthusiastically."

   (C) is not the answer. The agreement that history and fiction deal with "unusual" orders of experience does not explain why neither historians nor literary critics will react "passively."

   (D) is the answer. If historians and literary critics agree that history and fiction are "distinct" orders of experience, then they are unlikely to react "sympathetically" to the idea that historical analysis is a form of fiction.

   (E) is not the answer. The agreement that history and fiction deal with "realistic" orders of experience does not explain why neither historians nor literary critics will react "contentiously."

7. The colon (:) indicates that the second part of the sentence will explain the first part. The missing word will describe the opposite of the cynical conviction that "everybody has an angle," that is, that each person is concerned primarily with his or her own interests.

   (A) is not the answer. "Rationality," or reasonableness, is not the opposite of self-interest.

   (B) is not the answer. "Flexibility," which can mean a tendency to yield to influence or ability to respond to change, is not the opposite of self-interest.

   (C) is not the answer. "Diffidence" (reserve, timidity, or lack of confidence) is not the opposite of self-interest.

   (D) is the answer. "Disinterestedness" means lack of self-interest.

   (E) is not the answer. "Insincerity," or lack of honesty, is not the opposite of self-interest.

8. People "study" in order to "learn." Therefore, a rationale for this analogy could be "People X (study) in order to Y (learn)," or "One way to Y (learn) is to X (study)."

(A) is not the answer. To "pervade" (spread through every part of something) is not a way to "encompass" (surround the outside of something).

(B) is the answer. People "search" in order to "find"; one way to "find" something is to "search" for it.

(C) is not the answer. There is no necessary connection between "gather" and "win"; winning is not implied in the definition of gathering.

(D) is not the answer. There is no necessary connection between "agree" and "keep"; keeping is not implied in the definition of agreeing.

(E) is not the answer. Without more specific information, one cannot conclude that people "accumulate" in order to "raise."

9. "Horses" are kept in a "corral." A rationale for this analogy could be "X is an enclosure where people keep Y."

(A) is not the answer. "Lions" may live in a "den," but a "den" is not an enclosure where they are kept by people.

(B) is not the answer. "Sheep" may live in a "meadow," but a "meadow" is not an enclosure.

(C) is not the answer. A "herd" is a group of "cattle," not an enclosure.

(D) is not the answer. "Birds" may live in a "nest," but a "nest" is not an enclosure where they are kept by people.

(E) is the answer. A "coop" is an enclosure where people keep "chickens."

10. A "lullaby" is a "song" sung to put children to sleep. Therefore, a rationale for this analogy could be "X is a particular kind of Y."

(A) is not the answer. A "narrative" is a story, which could appear in a "volume," or the telling of a story, which might have "volume" (loudness). A "narrative" is not a kind of "volume."

(B) is not the answer. A "lecture" may be given by a "tutor"; it is not a kind of "tutor."

(C) is not the answer. A "paragraph" may appear on a "page" and thus be part of a "page," but is is not a kind of "page."

(D) is the answer. A "diatribe" is a bitter or abusive kind of "discourse" (an extended expression of thought).

(E) is not the answer. "Invective" is verbal abuse, and not a kind of "compliment."

11. "Die" has several meanings, but its use with "shaping" suggests that here it should be taken to mean a tool used to form an object. This definition suggests that a rationale for this analogy could be "X is a tool used for Y, where Y is done to something else."

(A) is not the answer. "Glue" can be used for "attaching" things, but

144

"glue" is a substance rather than a tool.

(B) is not the answer. An "anchor" is used in "sailing," but "sailing" is not done by the "anchor."

(C) is the answer. A "drill" is a tool used for "boring" (making holes by piercing).

(D) is not the answer. A "pedal," e.g., the gas pedal in an automobile, may be a part of a mechanism that propels something. However, a "pedal" cannot propel alone, but only as part of a more complex mechanism.

(E) is not the answer. "Ink" is used in "printing," but it is a substance rather than a tool.

12. "Mercenary" means having a strong desire for "money" or serving as a soldier for pay rather than for a cause. You can tell that "mercenary" is used as an adjective, not as a noun, because "vindictive," the first word in choice (A), can be used only as an adjective, and not as a noun. A rationale for this analogy could be "X is an attribute of human character that means to seek or desire Y."

(A) is the answer. "Vindictive" means disposed to seek "revenge", to be "vindictive" means to desire "revenge."

(B) is not the answer. A "library" may be desired by one who is "scholarly," but this desire is not a part of the definition of scholarliness.

(C) is not the answer. One who is "immaculate" may desire "cleanliness," but "immaculate," which means being clean, is not necessarily a human attribute, as is "mercenary." In addition, to be "immaculate" is not usually thought of as an undesirable quality, as is being "mercenary."

(D) is not the answer. One who is "thirsty" may desire "water," but to be "thirsty" is not usually thought of as an undesirable quality, as is being "mercenary." Thirst is not an attribute of human character.

(E) is not the answer. One who is "belligerent" (combative) may wish to invade another's territory, but "invasion" is only one of many ways to show belligerence, and is not implied in the definition of belligerence.

13. "Pundits" are persons who are learned, or who are or act authoritative. Therefore, a rationale for this analogy could be "X is by definition a personal characteristic of persons called Y."

(A) is not the answer. "Signatories" are people who sign. In various situations, they may have many characteristics, including "dedication," but this specific characteristic is not necessarily implied in the word "signatories."

(B) is not the answer. One hopes that "executors" (for instance, people who execute wills) will be characterized by "sobriety," but "sobriety" is not necessarily a characteristic of "executors."

(C) is not the answer. "Literati" (people who are educated or intellectual) are not necessarily characterized by "sensitivity."

(D) is not the answer. "Recklessness" is not necessarily a characteristic of "warriors."

(E) is the answer. "Partisans" are people who support a particular person or cause and are therefore characterized by "allegiance."

14. A stationary structural element that is designed to support an airplane's "wing" is called a "strut." Therefore, a rationale for this analogy could be "X is a stationary structural element that can support a Y."

(A) is not the answer. A "lever" may have a "handle" or it may be a "handle," but a "lever" does not provide strengthening support for a "handle."

(B) is not the answer. An "axle" is a shaft on which a "wheel" revolves, and might be said to provide some support to the "wheel." However, a "wing" does not turn about a "strut" as a "wheel" turns about an "axle."

(C) is the answer. A "buttress" is a stationary structure whose primary purpose is to support a "wall."

(D) is not the answer. A "beam" may be fastened to something else by a "rivet," but the "rivet" does not support the "beam."

(E) is not the answer. A "pipe" might be considered part of a "well," or it might bring water from a "well," but a "pipe" is not designed to support a "well."

15. To "fawn" means to court favor in a cringing or flattering manner. One who fawns is not characterized by "imperiousness" (arrogance, or a commanding presence). A rationale for this analogy could be "To X is to show a lack of Y."

(A) is the answer. To "equivocate" means to lie or deceive, and shows a lack of "directness."

(B) is not the answer. To "elaborate" means to provide more detail; it does not imply anything about "originality."

(C) is not the answer. To "boggle" means to hesitate or to be startled; it does not indicate a lack of "imagination."

(D) is not the answer. To "manipulate" can mean to operate or to use deceitfully for one's own ends. To "manipulate" does not necessarily show a lack of "repression."

(E) is not the answer. To "coddle" means to pamper; it implies "permissiveness" rather than a lack of it.

16. To be "distraught" means to be greatly "troubled" or to show that one is "troubled." Therefore, a rationale for this analogy could be "To be Y is to be very X."

(A) is not the answer. To be "disillusioned" (shown an unpleasant truth) could cause one to become "annoyed," but "disillusioned" does not mean to be very "annoyed" or to show annoyance.

(B) is not the answer. To be "interrupted" means to be "disturbed" by a particular occurrence rather than to be "disturbed" to an extreme degree.

(C) is the answer. To be "covetous" means to desire the possessions of others. To be "rapacious" means to be excessively "covetous," or to be insatiable in desiring things.

(D) is not the answer. To be "ostentatious" means to make an excessive display of oneself or one's possessions. To be "outmoded" means to be unfashionable. The two cannot be directly related to one another without more information.

(E) is not the answer. "Tranquil" and "placid" both mean calm; neither implies an intensification of the other.

17. This question asks you to identify the author's primary concern. The author makes a number of different points, but all of them are focused on a single main concern.

(A) is not the answer. The author makes the point that herbivores and carnivores are both intelligent groups of animals but does not compare their intelligence.

(B) is the answer. The primary concern of the passage is introduced in the first paragraph, and the rest of the passage presents additional information about the relationship described in that paragraph.

(C) is not the answer. No direct comparison is made in the passage between early animals and their later counterparts. The author's emphasis is on gradual evolution of certain traits.

(D) is not the answer. There is no indication in the passage that some carnivores dominate others.

(E) is not the answer. Hormones are mentioned in the last paragraph as an important element in animal awareness, but to demonstrate their importance is not the author's primary concern.

18. This question refers you to a specific element in the passage. You are to identify the role this element plays in the passage, specifically its role in furthering the author's argument.

(A) is not the answer. The example of the hungry lizard provides a contrast to the hunting behavior of the large mammal predators discussed in the passage; it does not demonstrate a similarity.

(B) is not the answer. The example of the hungry lizard presents a contrast to the hunting behavior of large animal predators, rather than an extension of the author's argument.

(C) is the answer. The "hungry lizard's instinctive snap" is contrasted with the mammal's awareness. The purpose of the contrast is to make a distinction between higher and lower levels of consciousness.

(D) is not the answer. The lizard's behavior illustrates a particular form of consciousness, not a form of brutality. Brutality is not mentioned as a characteristic of predators.

(E) is not the answer. The hungry lizard is presented as an animal that lacks higher consciousness, not as an "objection" to the suggestion that all animals lack consciousness.

19. This question asks you to draw a conclusion from the information in the

passage about animals, not discussed in the passage, that are less intelligent than the animals that are discussed.

(A) is the answer. In lines 32-35, the author defines intelligence in terms of an animal's use of past experience. In the context of the entire passage, it can be inferred that more intelligent animals, such as the grassland mammals discussed, are better able to use past experience to help them survive than are less intelligent animals.

(B) is not the answer. The second paragraph of the passage indicates that attention is more highly focused in animals of greater, rather than less, intelligence.

(C) is not the answer. The author does not discuss muscular coordination as an element in intelligence.

(D) is not the answer. The passage discusses the role played by competition in the development of intelligence in certain species but gives no indication that in less intelligent species there is less need for competition.

(E) is not the answer. There is no discussion in the passage of how a proper ratio of prey to predator is established.

20. To answer this question, you must determine the meaning of the words quoted from the passage in each option, and then determine which quotation is most clearly illustrated by the words quoted in lines 56-61.

(A) is not the answer. The "free-floating awareness" mentioned in lines 16-17 is described as passive, whereas the sensitivity described in lines 56-61 implies activity on the part of the predator.

(B) is not the answer. Lines 29-30 describe the general arousal that precedes the focusing of an animal's attention, whereas the sensitivity described in lines 56-61 illustrates more focused activity.

(C) is not the answer. Lines 56-61 describe an animal's use of consistent images not just its ability to hold these images.

(D) is the answer. In lines 56-61, the animal's sensitivity connects "details" such as cold trails and distant sounds with food, the perceived end.

(E) is not the answer. Line 64 is part of a description of prey. Lines 56-61 describe the sensitivity of predators.

21. This question asks you to use information in the passage to judge the author's attitude toward the main subject, intelligent mammals.

(A) is not the answer. Even though the author suggests in lines 49-56 that human consciousness is higher than that of other animals, the way in which this superiority is described does not indicate contempt, as "condescending" suggests.

(B) is not the answer. The author discusses mammals in terms of scientific theory, and not in a spirit of fun.

(C) is not the answer. There is no reason to believe that the author considers the mammals' feelings as he discusses them. There is no suggestion of apology or conciliation.

(D) is not the answer. There is no indication in the passage that the author wishes that the mammals or their situation were different, as "wistful" suggests, or that the author feels tenderness for them.

(E) is the answer. The author's description of the animals' intelligence and ability to focus attention, as well as the statement that these elements come together "marvelously" (line 40), suggests that the author respects and admires at least some of their characteristics.

22. To answer this question, you must first determine which of the three questions (I, II, and III) can be answered using the information in the passage. Then you must determine which of the given answer choices includes the Roman numerals of those questions.

 I. can be answered. An aroused herbivore is fearful because it must be ready for what is ahead, including escaping from a predator.
 II. can be answered. Lines 16-17 describe two degrees of attention in large mammals, the highest degree and the lowest.
 III. cannot be answered. The author discusses only animals' reactions to the presence of stimuli, not their reaction to the removal of a stimulus.

(A) is not the answer. I can be answered using information provided in the passage, but II can also be answered.

(B) is not the answer. III cannot be answered using information provided in the passage.

(C) is the answer. Both I and II can be answered using information provided in the passage.

(D) is not the answer. II can be answered using information provided in the passage, but III cannot be answered.

(E) is not the answer. I and II can be answered using information provided in the passage, but III cannot be answered.

23. This question asks you to identify a reason given in the passage for improved brain function among early large mammals.

(A) is the answer. It directly paraphrases the statement in lines 6-8, which describes the author's view of the development of improved brain function in early mammals.

(B) is not the answer. It is likely that the persistence of "free-floating awareness" played a part in the animals' survival, but there is no indication in the passage that brain function improved because of it.

(C) is not the answer. The passage does not discuss the relationship between mammals and reptiles in general.

(D) is not the answer. There is no discussion in the passage of the interaction between large mammals and less intelligent species.

(E) is not the answer. Improved capacity for memory is an improvement in brain function, rather than a reason for improved brain function.

24. This question asks you what does NOT occur during arousal. To answer the question, you must first determine what does occur.

(A) is not the answer. According to lines 43-46, arousal does stimulate the production of adrenaline.

(B) is not the answer. According to lines 43-46, arousal does stimulate the production of norepinephrine.

(C) is not the answer. Lines 22-27 indicate that as arousal increases, sensitivity to stimuli increases.

(D) is not the answer. Lines 27-32 suggest that the animal becomes increasingly focused on certain stimuli as arousal increases.

(E) is the answer. There is no indication in the passage that the range of states mediated by the brain stem expands during arousal.

25. The author of the passage discusses the work of another author, Pessen. This question asks what statements the author of the passage attributes to Pessen concerning the very wealthy in the United States between 1825 and 1850. You are to identify the one statement that CANNOT be correctly attributed to Pessen. Therefore, you must first determine which of the statements given can be attributed to Pessen.

(A) is not the answer. According to the passage, Pessen presents examples to show the existence of a wealthy, or upper, class in Jacksonian America. Therefore, the statement in (A) can be attributed to Pessen.

(B) is not the answer. In the second paragraph, the author indicates that, according to Pessen, the wealthiest one percent in several cities "constantly increased its share." Therefore, the statement in (B) can be attributed to Pessen.

(C) is not the answer. In the second paragraph, the author indicates that, according to Pessen, some of the wealthy were "active in commerce (business) or the professions." Therefore, the statement in (C) can be attributed to Pessen.

(D) is the answer. According to the second paragraph, "most of the wealthy were not self-made, but had inherited family fortunes." Therefore, they did NOT accumulate their own fortunes.

(E) is not the answer. According to the passage, the fortunes of the most wealthy survived financial crises that destroyed lesser fortunes. Therefore, the statement in (E) can be attributed to Pessen.

26. To answer this question, you must determine the attitude of the author of the passage toward Pessen's presentation of statistics. The author of the passage discusses Pessen's statistics near the beginning of the second paragraph. He calls Pessen's statistics "refreshingly intelligible."

(A) is not the answer. At the end of the second paragraph, the author of the passage indicates disapproval of the conclusions Pessen draws from statistics. However, he is not "disapproving" of Pessen's presentation of those statistics.

(B) is not the answer. The author of the passage does not indicate that he is surprised or repulsed by Pessen's presentation of statistics.

(C) is not the answer. Though the author of the passage does not agree with the conclusions that Pessen draws from his statistics, he does not indicate that he is "suspicious" of Pessen's presentation of statistics.

(D) is not the answer. Though the author of the passage does not agree with the conclusions that Pessen draws from his statistics, he does not indicate that he is "amused" by Pessen's presentation of statistics.

(E) is the answer. The words "refreshingly intelligible" can be taken as praise, so "laudatory" describes the author's attitude toward Pessen's presentation of statistics.

27. This question asks you to identify the main point that the author of the passage makes. To do this, you must separate the author's description of Pessen's work and views from the author's evaluation of Pessen's work.

(A) is not the answer. According to the first paragraph, Pessen's argument, if it were true, would overturn a previously established view. However, in the rest of the passage, the author argues that Pessen has not succeeded in making a convincing case for the new view.

(B) is not the answer. The author seems to accept the idea that Pessen's views, which contrast with Toqueville's, have some merit, even though Pessen's conclusions are not entirely correct. The passage does not indicate that Toqueville's analysis is definitive.

(C) is not the answer. The author does not mention a primary reason why Pessen's study is valuable; in addition, only the first half of the nineteenth century is discussed.

(D) is not the answer. Pessen's study contributed to the documentation about the extremely wealthy, but the passage is about Pessen's study rather than about general documentation. In addition, the passage does not discuss explicitly the political power of the extremely wealthy.

(E) is the answer. According to the first paragraph, Pessen challenges Tocqueville's view. According to the second paragraph, Pessen's conclusions are incorrect.

28. "Boisterous" means noisy and high-spirited. It implies activity as well as noise.

(A) is not the answer. To be "grateful" means to appreciate something. The means of expressing appreciation is not necessarily associated with particular levels of noise or activity.

(B) is not the answer. One who is "angry" might be, but is not necessarily, quiet.

(C) is not the answer. To be "clever" means to be quick-witted or resourceful. It does not imply a level of activity or of feeling.

(D) is not the answer. A "frightened" person might not behave boisterously, but there is not, by definition, a connection between the two.

(E) is the answer. "Quiet" can imply low levels of both noise and activity.

29. To "emit" means to give out or send out.

(A) is the answer. To "absorb" means to take in.

(B) is not the answer. To "demand" means to ask for. It may imply a desire to take in, but it is not the opposite of sending out.

(C) is not the answer. To "mistake" means to make an error of an unspecified kind.

(D) is not the answer. To "prevent" means to keep from occurring. Emission might be prevented, but the preventing itself is not the opposite of emitting.

(E) is not the answer. To "require" means to have a compelling need. To need something does not mean the same thing as to receive it, so "require" is not the opposite of "emit."

30. To "metamorphose" means to change or be transformed into something else.

(A) is not the answer. Metamorphosis might be part of a process of moving ahead, but to "metamorphose" is not the opposite of moving ahead.

(B) is the answer. To "remain unaltered" is the opposite of changing or being transformed into something else.

(C) is not the answer. To "descend slowly" means to come down without speed. Coming down is not the opposite of transformation.

(D) is not the answer. Examining in haste has no clear relationship to metamorphosis.

(E) is not the answer. Preparing in advance is a preliminary step, not the opposite of transforming.

31. An "ally" is a helper or supporter. To be an "ally" has to do with a person's relationships with others, rather than with a particular quality a person has.

   (A) is not the answer. A "mediator" is one who reconciles differences among other parties without taking sides.

   (B) is the not answer. A "felon" is one who has committed a crime.

   (C) is the answer. An "adversary" is an enemy, one who operates against another rather than helping or supporting.

   (D) is not the answer. An "inventor" is one who comes up with new ideas. Inventiveness does not imply anything about a person's relationships with others.

   (E) is not the answer. A "conspirator" is one who plots with others as an "ally." A conspiracy may involve a plot against another person, but to be a "conspirator" is not necessarily to be an enemy.

32. "Offhand" means done without preparation or much prior thought. It refers to a person's actions or statements.

   (A) is not the answer. To be "accurate" means to be correct or free from error. An "offhand" statement is not necessarily an inaccurate one.

   (B) is not the answer. To be "universal" means to be applicable everywhere. It does not imply anything about prior thought or preparation.

   (C) is not the answer. Something "offhand" is not by definition the opposite of "appropriate."

   (D) is the answer. "Premeditated" means thought about or prepared for ahead of time.

   (E) is not the answer. To be "disputatious" means to be likely to argue. This quality does not imply anthing about either preparation or lack of preparation.

33. To "broach" means to open up. It can mean opening or breaking into an actual thing, such as a container or building, or it can refer to opening a topic for discussion.

   (A) is not the answer. To "keep track of" means to follow the progress of something. It does not necessarily suggest opening or closing.

   (B) is not the answer. To "lay claim to" means to call one's own. It raises questions of ownership but it is not the opposite of opening up or introducing.

   (C) is the answer. To "close off" is to end discussion, or to end access to something.

   (D) is not the answer. To "soothe" means to comfort or placate. In some situations, broaching could cause the opposite of comforting or placating, but "soothe" is not the opposite of "broach."

   (E) is not the answer. To "simplify" means to lessen complication. To "broach" is not necessarily to complicate.

34. The "gist" (of an argument, for instance,) is the main, or most important, point.

(A) is not the answer. An "artificial manner" is an affected or unnatural way of behaving, rather than a part of an argument or discussion.

(B) is the answer. A "trivial point" is an unimportant one.

(C) is not the answer. An "informal procedure" is a method of operation that is not rigidly specified. There is no reason to suppose that it is unrelated to the main point.

(D) is not the answer. An "eccentric method" is a way of operating that is peculiar to a person or group. There is no reason to suppose that it is unrelated to the main point.

(E) is not the answer. A "singular event" is an occurrence that is individual or unusual. There is no reason to suppose that it is unrelated to the main point.

35. "Divestiture" is a taking away of something, presumably desirable, that was formerly possessed or owned. One can divest oneself, or one can be divested of something during "divestiture."

(A) is the answer. "Acquisition" means coming into possession of something desired.

(B) is not the answer. "Promotion" means the act of advancing or raising to a new, better position. One could be divested of a new position, but the idea of a position is not included in the definition of "divestiture" as it is in the definition of "promotion."

(C) is not the answer. "Subsidization" means the act of giving money or aid in any of several possible situations. "Subsidization" refers to a continuing process of being granted something rather than to the point at which something is attained.

(D) is not the answer. "Consultation" means a conferring among people. It does not have to do with giving or taking.

(E) is not the answer. "Monopolization" implies having all of something, whereas "divestiture" does not imply amount or degree of investing.

36. "Extant" means still existing. It may refer to living things, or to documents or other inanimate objects.

(A) is not the answer. To be "extensive" means to cover a large area. Something that is "extensive" must still exist.

(B) is not the answer. "Extraneous" means inessential, but it does not imply nonexistence.

(C) is not the answer. Something "extricable" can be removed or disentangled. Such a thing is not nonexistent.

(D) is the answer. "Extinct" means, in the case of an animal or kind of animal, no longer existing or living.

(E) is not the answer. "Extra" means additional. It may imply unimportance, but it does not imply nonexistence.

37. "Tractability" can be a characteristic of either persons or materials. When applied to materials, it suggests that something is easily changed or molded. When "tractability" refers to a person, it implies obedience or a tendency to be easily influenced by others.

(A) is not the answer. "Infertility" means inability to produce or reproduce. It does not imply anything about character when it is used to describe persons.

(B) is not the answer. "Implausibility" means unbelievability.

(C) is the answer. One who is incorrigible cannot be changed. "Incorrigibility" implies an unwillingness to be influenced by others.

(D) is not the answer. "Impenetrability" may, in some circumstances, suggest unwillingness to be influenced by others, but it goes further in that it implies an obliviousness to efforts to influence. An impenetrable person is unaware that influence is being exerted.

(E) is not the answer. "Indefatigability" means tirelessness. It does not, by itself, imply resistance to influence.

38. "Noisome" means bad-smelling. It suggests not only unpleasant smell, but also harmful nature or unwholesomeness.

(A) is the answer. To be "attractively fragrant" means to have a pleasant smell.

(B) is not the answer. To be "subtly flattering" means to pay a possibly undeserved compliment without seeming to do so. It docs not necessarily suggest anything about smell or wholesomeness.

(C) is not the answer. To be "consistently patient" means to constantly carry on without complaint. It does not necessarily suggest anything about smell or wholesomeness.

(D) is not the answer. "Softly glowing" means giving off a non-glaring light. It does not imply anything about smell.

(E) is not the answer. "Gradually diminishing" means slowly becoming smaller. It does not necessarily suggest anything about how something smells or about its wholesomeness.

SECTION 2

1. One way to compare these quantities is to note that

$$40\% \text{ is } \frac{40}{100} \text{ or } \frac{4}{10} \text{ or } \frac{2}{5} \text{ or } 0.4$$

and that

$$60\% \text{ is } \frac{60}{100} \text{ or } \frac{6}{10} \text{ or } \frac{3}{5} \text{ or } 0.6.$$

The following may be easiest:

(40% of 50) + 60
= (2/5 × 50) + 60 = 20 + 60
= 80
(60% of 50) + 40
= (3/5 × 50) + 40 = 30 + 40
= 70

Answer is A

2. $\frac{1}{12}$ of 17 is $\frac{17}{12}$ whereas

$\frac{1}{17}$ of 12 is $\frac{12}{17}$.

Since $\frac{17}{12} > 1$ and $1 > \frac{12}{17}$,

then $\frac{17}{12} > \frac{12}{17}$.

Answer is A

3. There are infinitely many pairs of values for x and y that will make the sentence true. Here are three examples:

$$\left(-\frac{1}{2}\right) + \left(-\frac{1}{2}\right) = -1$$
$$2 + (-3) = -1$$
$$-3 + 2 = -1$$

In the first example, $x = y$; in the second, $x > y$; and in the third, $x < y$. Therefore, the relationship between x and y cannot be determined.

Answer is D

4. You could multiply the given numbers to determine which (if either) is larger. However, you can avoid this by rewriting each product as follows:

(A)   23(784)
    = 23(783 + 1)
    = (23)(783) + (23)(1)

(B)   24(783)
    = (23 + 1)(783)
    = (23)(783) + (1)(783)

The underlined parts are equal, and 23 < 783, so (B) is greater.

Answer is B

5. You are given that $0 < r < t$. This means that both t and r are positive numbers, and r is the smaller of the two. Since both numbers are positive, $\frac{r}{t}$ must be less than 1 whereas $\frac{t}{r}$ is greater than 1. (For example, $0 < 2 < 5$ and $\frac{2}{5}$ is less than 1 but $\frac{5}{2}$ is greater than 1.)

Answer is B

6. The sum of the measures of the three angles of any triangle is 180°. In the figure, one angle is designated as a right angle, or 90°. Therefore, $x + 55$ must also equal 90, so $x = 35$.

Answer is C

7. There are a number of ways to solve the problem posed here. One of the simplest is to notice that the home valued at $54,000 has $1\frac{1}{5}$ the value of the $45,000 home. Since the one valued at $45,000 is taxed at $1,200, the tax on the $54,000 home should be $1\frac{1}{5} \times \$1,200$, or $\$1,200 + \frac{1}{5}(\$1,200)$, which is $\$1,200 + \$240 = \$1,440$.

Answer is A

For another solution, see the next page.

Since the tax rate is the same for each home in city X, you can set up a proportion as follows, comparing amount of tax to the value of the house:

$$\frac{x}{54,000} = \frac{1,200}{45,000}. \text{ Then}$$

$$45,000x = (54,000)(1,200)$$

$$\text{or} \quad 45x = (54)(1,200)$$

$$\text{so} \quad x = \frac{(54)(1,200)}{45}$$

$$= 1,440$$

Answer is A

8. You are given information about the area of a square region, and asked about its perimeter. If the area of the region is 36, then each side of the square must be 6, so the perimeter is $4 \times 6 = 24$.

Answer is C

9. If 99 pages each had a 2-digit page number (as, for example, p.10 and p.45), then the printer would print 99×2, or 198 digits. However, the first 9 pages (pp. 1-9) have only 1-digit page numbers, so in 99 pages, the printer would print $198 - 9$, or 189 digits. This means that there were 99 pages in the book.

Answer is B

10. You are given that the average of 3 numbers is 3. This means that their sum must be 9. That is,

$$\frac{x+y+6}{3} = 3,$$

$$\text{so } x + y + 6 = 9.$$

This means that $x + y = 3$,

$$\text{so } \frac{x+y}{2} = \frac{3}{2}.$$

Answer is C

11. You are given that the areas of the two regions are equal. It may help to let K stand for this number. You are therefore to compare

$$\frac{K}{h_1} \text{ with } \frac{K}{h_2}.$$

You do not know whether $h_1 = h_2$, $h_1 > h_2$, or $h_1 < h_2$. Therefore, $\frac{K}{h_1}$ may be equal to, less than, or greater than, $\frac{K}{h_2}$.

For example (trying some numbers and letting the areas be 24 in each case):

$$\frac{24}{4} = \frac{24}{4}, \text{ but } \frac{24}{6} < \frac{24}{4} \text{ and } \frac{24}{3} > \frac{24}{8}.$$
$$(h_1 = h_2) \qquad (h_1 > h_2) \qquad (h_1 < h_2)$$

Answer is D

12. You can think of

$$\frac{3 \cdot 3 \cdot 3}{6 \cdot 6 \cdot 6} \text{ as } \frac{3}{6} \cdot \frac{3}{6} \cdot \frac{3}{6}$$
$$= \frac{1}{2} \cdot \frac{1}{2} \cdot \frac{1}{2}$$
$$= \left(\frac{1}{2}\right)^3$$

Answer is C

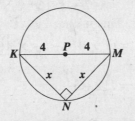

13. The area of a circular region is computed by the formula $A = \pi r^2$, where r is the length of the radius. In this case, since the area is given as 16π, r^2 must equal 16, and $r = 4$. Because KMN is a triangle, $x + x$, or $2x$, must be greater than the length of KM. That is, $2x > 8$, and $x > 4$. (Actually, by the Pythagorean Theorem, $x^2 + x^2 = 8^2$, which means that $2x^2 = 64$, or $x^2 = 32$. Since $x^2 = 32$, x must be between 5 and 6.)

Answer is A

14. You are given that m, p, and x are positive integers, which means they belong to the set $\{1, 2, 3, 4, \ldots\}$. You are also given that $mp = x$ and asked to compare the values of m and x. If you try some numbers, you can see that if $p = 1$, then $m = x$, but if $p > 1$, then $m < x$:

$$5(1) = 5$$
$$\text{but} \quad 5(2) = 10$$
$$5(3) = 15$$
$$5(4) = 20$$
$$\text{and so forth.}$$

Therefore, m may be equal to, or it may be less than, x.

Answer is D

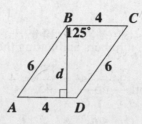

15. The area of the region enclosed by a parallelogram is computed by multiplying the lengths of the base and height. You are given that $\angle ABC$ measures $125°$, so $ABCD$ is not a rectangle, and its height, as shown, is less than 6. Therefore, the area is less than 4×6.

Answer is B

16. 72 seconds represents 7 ten-second intervals plus $\frac{1}{5}$ of such an interval.

Therefore, the person who takes 16 steps in 10 seconds will take $7\frac{1}{5} \times 16$ steps in 72 seconds.

$$7\frac{1}{5} \times 16$$

$$= (7 \times 16) + (\frac{1}{5} \times 16)$$

$$= 112 + 3\frac{1}{5}.$$

Since $\frac{1}{5}$ of a step is not a complete step, the answer is 115.

Answer is E

You can also solve this problem by setting up a proportion as follows, comparing steps to time:

$$\frac{16}{10} = \frac{x}{72}.$$

Therefore, $10x = (16)(72)$

or $10x = 1,152$

and $x = 115.2$.

Answer is E

17. The sum of the measures of the angles of a triangle is 180°. In the figure, therefore, $x + y + z = 180$, so
$$\frac{x + y + z}{45} = \frac{180}{45} = 4.$$

Answer is C

18. $52.68 \times \frac{1}{100}$ is the same as

$52.68 \div 100$, or 0.5268.

Answer is B

19. You are given the value of $b - c$ and $a + c$. If you note that
$(b - c) + (a + c) = b + a = a + b,$
this value must be
$(3) + (32) = 35.$

Answer is B

20. The dimensions of the floor are given in feet and the cost of carpeting in square yards. A way to compute the area of the floor in square yards is as follows:

$$\frac{18}{3} \times \frac{10}{3} = \frac{180}{9} = 20.$$

Therefore, the cost of the carpeting is $20x$.

Answer is A

Questions 21-25

These questions are based on two graphs, and it is a good idea to scan both of these before attempting the questions. The left-hand graph shows the number of students enrolled in the fall at College *R* for the five years, 1976-1980. The right-hand graph shows the allocation (in dollars) of contributions during the five academic years, 1976-1981.

21. This question asks about the number of students, and can be read directly from the graph. The total number of students who enrolled in the fall of 1979 was 700.

    Answer is E

22. This question asks about the percent increase in enrollment, and cannot be read directly from the graph.

    In the fall of 1979, 200 part-time students enrolled; in the fall of 1980, 350 part-time students enrolled. This was an increase of 150 over the 1979 enrollment.

    Since a percent is needed, it can be calculated as

$$\frac{150}{200} = \frac{75}{100}, \text{ which is } 75\%.$$

    Answer is D

23. This question asks about the increase in the number of full-time students from 1976 to 1977.

    In the fall of 1976, 300 full-time students enrolled (400 – 100); in the fall of 1977, there were also 300 full-time students (450 – 150).

    Therefore, there was no increase.

    Answer is A

24. This question refers to the allocation of contributions, so the right-hand graph is the source of information.

    If 12% of the amount of contributions was allocated to heating costs, then 88% was not. The amount of contributions for the 1978-1979 school year was about $233,000, and 88% of $233,000 is slightly more than $205,000.

    Answer is D

25. This question also refers to contributions, but asks for the total amount. You can read off the amount for each year and then add, but there is a somewhat easier way to determine the total. Notice that for the year 1979-1980, the contributions amounted to approximately $300,000. Looking at the year 1978-1979 and the year 1980-81, the contributions for those two years would total $700,000. That is, the contributions for 1978-79 are

$200,000 + $($\frac{1}{3}$) ($100,000), while the contributions for 1980-81 are

$400,000 + $($\frac{2}{3}$) ($100,000). Together, these total

$600,000 + $100,000 or $700,000. The sum for the three years is therefore about $300,000 + $700,000.

Answer is B

26. To simplify $\frac{x(x^2)^3}{x^2}$, it can be helpful to think of the expression as written this way:

$$\frac{x(x^2)(x^2)(x^2)}{x^2}$$

Since both numerator and denominator can be divided by x^2, the expression can also be written as $x(x^2)(x^2)$, or x^5.

Answer is D

27. One-third of seven is $\frac{7}{3}$, and the question asks how many thirds of 7 are in 7. As an equation, this is

$$7 = N \cdot \frac{7}{3}.$$

Clearly, $N = 3$.

Answer is C

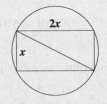

28. You are to find the circumference of the circle, which is equal to the diameter times π. Therefore, you need to determine the length of the diameter, which is not given in the problem. You are, however, given a rectangle inscribed in the circle. Since each angle of a rectangle is a right angle, $\angle KLM$ is inscribed in a semicircle. Therefore, a diagonal of the rectangle must be a diameter of the circle.

The diagonal of the inscribed rectangle is also the hypotenuse of one of the right triangles such as KLM. The legs of KLM have lengths x and $2x$ so if their lengths are known, the length of the diagonal KM can be calculated. The area of rectangular region $KLMN$ is given as 32, so $(x)(2x) = 2x^2 = 32$, or $x^2 = 16$, which means that $x = 4$ and $2x = 8$. By the Pythagorean Theorem,

$$(KM)^2 = (LM)^2 + (KL)^2$$
$$= 4^2 + 8^2 = 16 + 64 = 80.$$

Therefore, $KM = \sqrt{80} = \sqrt{16 \cdot 5} = 4\sqrt{5}$, and this is the diameter of the circle.

The circumference of the circle is therefore $(4\sqrt{5})(\pi)$, or $4\pi\sqrt{5}$.

Answer is B

29. The reciprocal of a nonzero number N is that number which, when multiplied by N, gives 1. For example, the reciprocal of 4 is $\frac{1}{4}$ and the reciprocal of $\frac{1}{4}$ is 4.

The given number is

$$x - \frac{1}{y} = \frac{xy}{y} - \frac{1}{y} = \frac{xy-1}{y}.$$

The number that multipled by $\frac{xy-1}{y}$ gives 1 is $\frac{y}{xy-1}$.

Answer is E

30. You need to determine whether each of the sentences I, II, and III is true or false.

n is a multiple of 5, so it must end in a 5 or a 0. n is also a multiple of 9. Some multiples of both 5 and 9 are 90, 180, 270, and so forth. Since all of these are even, I is false.

The same examples show that n may be greater than 45, so II is false.

III is true since in order that n be a multiple of both 5 and 9, there must be an integer w such that

$$n = 5 \times 9 \times w = 5 \times (3 \times 3) \times w$$
$$= (5 \times 3) \times (3 \times w)$$
$$= 15 \times (3 \times w).$$

Answer is A

SECTION 3

1. The sentence describes a chain of occurrences. The first missing word suggests what happened to mass literacy during the industrial revolution. The words "in turn, the new expansion of literacy" are a strong clue for the first missing word. The second missing word suggests what happened to popular literature as a result of the expansion of literacy and the advent of cheaper printing.

   (A) is not the answer. "Building" is an unlikely term to describe an expansion of literacy. It is also unlikely that cheaper printing would increase "mistrust" of popular literature. In addition, one would not be likely to nurture "mistrust."

   (B) is not the answer. The new expansion of mass literacy could be a "reappearance," but there is nothing in the sentence to suggest this. It is unlikely that mass literacy nurtured the "display" of popular literature; in fact, a "display" is not something that can be nurtured.

   (C) is not the answer. Mass literacy is not something that can be received, so "receipt" cannot be the first missing word. Printing does not directly affect the "source" of popular literature.

   (D) is not the answer. Mass literacy is not something that is ordinarily thought of as being selected, so "selection" cannot be the first missing word.

   (E) is the answer. The "emergence" of mass literacy corresponds to the "new expansion of literacy." It is reasonable to assume that increased literacy and cheaper printing are likely to have contributed to the "rise" of popular literature.

2. The first missing word describes how ancient tools were preserved. The phrase "enough have survived" indicates that not all survived, and the word "Although" indicates that the tools were preserved in a way that would not lead you to expect enough to survive. The second missing word describes a progress through prehistory. The word "but" suggests that the word that fills the second blank must contrast with the idea of occasional interruption.

   (A) is not the answer. In this context, "partially" must describe the incomplete preservation of particular tools, rather than of a number of tools, as "enough have survived" suggests. "Noticeable" does not present a direct contrast with "interrupted."

   (B) is not the answer. Superficial preservation would not permit tools to survive. There is no information in the sentence to suggest that a progress through prehistory is "necessary."

   (C) is not the answer. The ancient tools could have been "unwittingly" (inadvertently) preserved, but "documented" does not contrast with "occasionally interrupted."

(D) is the answer. It is logical to say that enough tools have survived in spite of their being "rarely" preserved. A "continual" progress contrasts with one that is occasionally interrupted.

(E) is not the answer. "Needlessly" suggests that there was no good reason to preserve the tools, but "enough have survived" suggests that their preservation was important. Since "needlessly" is not in keeping with the sense of the rest of the sentence, it cannot be the missing word. "Incessant" suggests that the progress through prehistory never ceased.

3. The missing word describes how land grades (levels off gradually and smoothly) into ice. It explains why you can walk off the coast without realizing that you have done so.

(A) is not the answer. The fact that land grades "permanently" into ice does not explain why you cannot detect the grading.

(B) is the answer. "Imperceptibly" means undetectably. The fact that you cannot detect the grading explains why you can walk off the coast without realizing it.

(C) is not the answer. It is likely that grading that occurs "irregularly" is detectable. In any case, it is unlikely that irregularity alone could explain your inability to detect grading.

(D) is not the answer. "Precariously" suggests abrupt change leading to danger, so it is likely that grading described as precarious is detectable.

(E) is not the answer. A slight grade might be undetectable, but in this question another answer choice indicates even more clearly why you can walk off the coast without realizing it.

4. The sentence contrasts the infant's reactions, part of a normal developmental process, with future unhappiness and anxiety. The missing word describes signs of adolescent anxiety as they relate to the infant.

(A) is the answer. "Prophetic" signs, like harbingers, foretell future occurrences. For the infant, adolescent anxiety is a future occurrence.

(B) is not the answer. "Normal" signs of adolescent anxiety cannot occur in an infant.

(C) is not the answer. Signs of adolescent anxiety could be "monotonous," but these signs could not occur as such in an infant.

(D) is not the answer. An infant's reactions are unlikely to be mistaken for signs of adolescent anxiety, as "virtual" suggests.

(E) is not the answer. "Typical" signs of adolescent anxiety are unlikely to occur in an infant.

5. The missing word describes an investigation that contrasts with a "search in a definite direction."

(A) is not the answer. "Timely" does not contrast with the idea of definite direction.

(B) is the answer. An "unguided" investigation contrasts with a search in a definite direction.

(C) is not the answer. A "consistent" investigation does not contrast with a search in a definite direction.

(D) is not the answer. An "uncomplicated" investigation does not contrast with a search in a definite direction.

(E) is not the answer. A "subjective" investigation does not contrast with a search in a definite direction.

6. The first missing word describes a gesture of comradeship of a kind that would neutralize the resentment of Winkelmann's peers. The second missing word explains Winkelmann's relationship with the high and mighty.

(A) is not the answer. A "quixotic" gesture is idealistic or romantic. There is no reason to suppose that such a gesture would neutralize resentment, or that Winkelmann indulged in "intrigue with" the high and mighty.

(B) is not the answer. It is unlikely that an "enigmatic" gesture, one that is puzzling or obscure, would neutralize resentment.

(C) is the answer. A "propitiatory" gesture is one intended to divert anger. Winkelmann's "involvement with" the high and mighty is indicated by the fact that he cultivated those in power.

(D) is not the answer. A "salutary" gesture, one that has a beneficial effect, could have helped Winkelmann. However, there is no indication that Winkelmann engaged in "questioning of" the high and mighty.

(E) is not the answer. An "unfeigned" gesture might have helped Winkelmann, but there is no information in the sentence to suggest that unfeignedness was a needed characteristic of the gesture. In addition, the sentence provides no suggestion that Winkelmann felt "sympathy for" those he cultivated.

7. The first missing word describes a society that worships efficiency. The second missing word describes the kinds of decisions that such a society requires, and contrasts with the words "sensitive" and "idealistic" that characterize a person trying with difficulty to make such decisions.

(A) is not the answer. A "bureaucratic" society might worship efficiency. However, "edifying" cannot be the second missing word because, if the decisions required were truly "edifying," a sensitive and idealistic person would not find them so difficult to make.

(B) is the answer. A "pragmatic" society is one that is more concerned with practical matters than with idealism. Such a society might well require "hardheaded" decisions rather than the idealistic ones preferred by a sensitive and idealistic person.

(C) is not the answer. A "rational" society might worship efficiency, but a sensitive and idealistic person would not have difficulty making decisions that are "well-intentioned."

(D) is not the answer. Worship of efficiency is not implicit in the definition of a "competitive" society. There is no way of knowing whether a sensitive and idealistic person would have difficulty making "evenhanded" decisions.

(E) is not the answer. A "modern" society might or might not worship efficiency, and there is no reason to suppose that such a society would require "dysfunctional" decisions.

8. A "tablecloth" is used to cover a "table," either to decorate it or to protect it. A rationale for this analogy could be "The purpose of X (a tablecloth) is to cover Y (a table)."

(A) is not the answer. A "tent" may cover "ground," but this is not a tent's purpose.

(B) is not the answer. A "shirt" may cover a "hanger," but this is not the shirt's purpose.

(C) is not the answer. A "sill" is part of a "window"; a window's purpose is not to cover a "sill."

(D) is the answer. A "sheet" is used to cover a "mattress."

(E) is not the answer. Clouds may cover portions of the Earth, but it is not the purpose of a "cloud" to cover "earth."

9. A "painter" often paints on "canvas." A rationale for this analogy could be "X is a material commonly used in the work of person Y."

(A) is not the answer. A "shoe" may be made of "leather," but a "shoe" is not a person, and cannot use "leather."

(B) is not the answer. A "brush" and a "palette" are commonly used at the same time, but a "palette" is not a person, and cannot use a "brush."

(C) is not the answer. A "chisel" may be used by a person working on "wood," but "wood" is not a person, and cannot use a "chisel."

(D) is the answer. "Marble" is a material commonly used by a "sculptor." As a "painter" uses "canvas" in creating a work of art, so a "sculptor" uses "marble."

(E) is not the answer. A "carpenter" uses a "hammer," but the "hammer" is not a material that the carpenter uses in his or her work.

10. A "mansion" is a large and usually expensive "residence." A rationale for this analogy could be "X is a large, expensive member of class Y."

(A) is the answer. A "limousine" is a special kind of "automobile," specifically, a large and expensive one.

(B) is not the answer. A "chandelier" is a larger and usually more expensive source of light than a "candle," but "candle" is not a class to which "chandelier" belongs.

(C) is not the answer. A "tuxedo" is often associated with wealth, and it may be a part of a "wardrobe," but it is not a kind of "wardrobe."

(D) is not the answer. A "diamond" is a more valuable kind of stone than a "rhinestone," but it is not a kind of "rhinestone."

(E) is not the answer. A "yacht" may be kept in a "harbor," but it is not a kind of "harbor."

11. A "door" is a barrier that can be used to close off (access to) a "room." A rationale for this analogy could be "X is a barrier that can be used to close off (prevent entry into) Y."

(A) is not the answer. A "rudder" and an "anchor" are both parts of a ship, but a "rudder" does not close off an "anchor."

(B) is not the answer. "Boat" and "ship" are names for vessels that are similar in some ways, but a "boat" does not close off a "ship."

(C) is not the answer. A "patio" does not close off a "terrace."

(D) is the answer. A "hatch" is a barrier that is used to close off a "hold" (a place where cargo is kept).

(E) is not the answer. A "basement" and an "attic" are both parts of a house, but a "basement" does not close off an "attic."

12. "Choreography" (the art of composing dances) provides a structure that determines what will happen during a "dance." A rationale for this analogy could be "X provides the organizing structure for creation Y."

(A) is not the answer. A "sermon" may be part of a "ceremony," but a "ceremony" does not usually provide structure for the "sermon."

(B) is not the answer. An "agenda" is a plan of things to be discussed or done. It provides an appropriate structure for a meeting, but not for an "advertisement."

(C) is not the answer. "Poetry" may be recited, but it does not provide structure for a "recitation."

(D) is not the answer. "Instrumentation" provides structure for music rather than for a "conductor."

(E) is the answer. The "plot" provides structure for a "story," a creative endeavor.

13. To "evaporate" means to change or be changed into a "vapor." A rationale for this analogy could be "To X means to change into Y."

(A) is the answer. To "petrify" means to turn into "stone."

(B) is not the answer. To "centrifuge" means to subject to the action of centrifugal force, a process that may sometimes separate out a "liquid." But to "centrifuge" something does not necessarily mean to change it into a "liquid."

(C) is not the answer. One meaning of "saturate" is to add "fluid" to something until it cannot hold more, but to "saturate" does not mean to turn into a "fluid."

(D) is not the answer. "Acid" can "corrode," but to "corrode" does not mean to turn into "acid."

(E) is not the answer. To "incinerate" means to consume by "fire," rather than to turn into "fire."

14. To "assuage" means to lessen the intensity of, or to relieve, something like pain or "sorrow." A rationale for this analogy could be "To X means to lessen the intensity of an emotion such as Y."

(A) is not the answer. To "retaliate" means to get back at or to get revenge. Retaliation is a result of "antipathy," rather than a lessening of its intensity.

(B) is the answer. To "dampen" can mean to diminish the intensity of an emotion such as "ardor."

(C) is not the answer. To "entrust" to someone is to depend on his or her "reliability" rather than to lessen it.

(D) is not the answer. In some circumstances, one might "counsel" in order to lessen "reluctance," but lessening the intensity of an emotion is not part of the definition of counseling.

(E) is not the answer. To "withhold" does not necessarily imply a lessening of intensity.

15. One way to make something "insensible" is to "numb" it. You can tell that "numb" is used as a verb, not as an adjective, because "reflect" in choice (A) is used only as a verb, not as an adjective. A rationale for this analogy could be "To X something means to render it Y."

(A) is not the answer. Something "luminous" may be reflected, but to "reflect" does not mean to make it "luminous."

(B) is the answer. To "burnish" means to polish something so that it is shiny, or "lustrous."

(C) is not the answer. One may "heckle" in a "raucous" way, but to "heckle" someone does not mean to make him or her "raucous."

(D) is not the answer. One may wish to "repulse" the "odious," or undesirable, but to "repulse" does not mean to render "odious."

(E) is not the answer. To "braid" means to put things together, but to "braid" something does not necessarily mean to make it "sinuous" (winding or complicated).

16. An "audacious" person acts boldly and fearlessly, that is, without "trepidation" (nervousness or fear). A rationale for this analogy could be "A person properly described as X is not characterized by Y."

(A) is not the answer. A "refractory" (stubborn) person is by definition characterized by "intransigence" (stubbornness).

(B) is the answer. "Laconic" means not characterized by "volubility" (talkativeness).

(C) is not the answer. One who is "sordid" (grasping, dirty, or generally awful) is not necessarily lacking in "aspiration"; to aspire does not necessarily imply reaching toward worthy or acceptable goals.

(D) is not the answer. Neither cursoriness nor "accumulation" is a word used to characterize people; to be "cursory" (to treat something superficially) does not mean to lack "accumulation."

(E) is not the answer. To be "derisive" (contemptuous or ridiculing) does not necessarily indicate a lack of "subordination." "Subordination" is not a personal quality like "trepidation."

17. This question asks you to identify the most appropriate title for the passage. You should consider the passage as a self-contained unit, not as part of a larger work.

(A) is not the answer. The passage is concerned not with influences on Woolf's work, but with its content and her approach to it.

(B) is not the answer. The passage is not about Woolf as a critic of the novel, but as a novelist.

(C) is not the answer. Though much of Woolf's work is, according to the passage, concerned with criticism of society, specific trends in contemporary reform movements are not mentioned in the passage.

(D) is not the answer. There is no discussion in the passage of any use of allegory in Woolf's work.

(E) is the answer. The topic of the passage is Woolf's novels, and the author emphasizes that the novels contain observations concerning "how individuals are shaped (or deformed) by their social environments" (lines 16-17).

18. The literary critics discussed in the first paragraph ignored Woolf's intention to criticize society and saw her as a "poetic" novelist unconcerned with the real world. This question asks you to identify the tone of the remarks made by the author of the passage concerning this assessment of Woolf's work.

(A) is the answer. The author's characterization of the critics' assessment as "cavalier" (line 13) can be described as "disparaging."

(B) is not the answer. There is no indication in the passage that the author is expressing an incongruity between actual and expected results or events, as "ironic" suggests.

(C) is not the answer. The author's attitude toward the critics is not "facetious." Rather, he takes the criticisms seriously, explaining why they cannot be correct.

(D) is not the answer. The author is "skeptical" of the critics' assessment, but that he is not "resigned" is shown in the pains he takes to prove that the claims are incorrect.

(E) is not the answer. The author is "disappointed" in the critics' assessment to the extent that he does not agree with it; but there is no indication that he expected better of them, nor does he expect them to change their assessment, as "hopeful" suggests.

19. The author discusses Woolf's literary models, emphasizing Chaucer, in the last paragraph. The reason why Woolf chose Chaucer as her model is not directly stated in the passage but must be inferred from the information there.

(A) is not the answer. The passage states that Chaucer understood his society, but there is no indication that he was the first to focus on society as a whole.

(B) is not the answer. Though Woolf criticized D. H. Lawrence's methods, there is no indication in the passage that she thought that Lawrence did not sincerely wish to change society.

(C) is not the answer. Though the last paragraph states that Chaucer was concerned with understanding his society, there is no information in the passage about his questioning of mores.

(D) is the answer. Line 49 indicates that Woolf's work as a moralist is subtle and done "by indirection." Woolf's statement that readers absorb morality at every pore despite the fact that no laws were changed because of Chaucer indicates that she believed Chaucer's influence to be subtle. Therefore, it is likely that it was Chaucer's subtle effectiveness that led Woolf to choose him as a model.

(E) is not the answer. There is no discussion in the passage of Woolf's beliefs concerning the acceptability of her own novels.

20. In lines 20-22, the author states that Woolf's novels presented social settings realistically. This question asks why Woolf did so.

(A) is not the answer. There is no indication in the passage either that critics considered the novel to be the most realistic genre or that Woolf believed that they thought so.

(B) is the answer. In lines 15-20, Woolf's interest in the effect of social environment on the individual is described. The juxtaposition of these lines with the statement in lines 20-22 strongly suggests that Woolf realistically described social settings because she was interested in their effect on character.

(C) is not the answer. Though it is conceivable that attention to detail could help Woolf advance her arguments, there is no information in the passage that suggests this.

(D) is not the answer. The passage indicates that Woolf's realistic rendering of society resulted from her interest in it, and not from a desire to prove that such a rendering was not a hindrance.

(E) is not the answer. The passage indicates that Woolf's realistic rendering of society resulted from her interest in it, and not from a desire to avoid criticism.

21. This question refers you to lines 43-44 of the passage so that you can evaluate the context in which the author uses the word "contemplative." You are to choose the definition of "contemplative" that is closest in meaning to the use of the word in that context.

(A) is not the answer. Since Woolf satirized society, it can be concluded that she did not find the structure of its mores to be rational.

(B) is not the answer. Though Woolf described rather than directly criticized society, the author's characterization of her as a satirist indicates that her work reflected emotional commitment.

(C) is the answer. Lines 41-44 suggest that a contemplative art is expressed indirectly, rather than by "aggressive assertion." Lines 44-48 point out that Woolf, as a contemplative novelist, encourages readers to make their own judgments.

(D) is not the answer. The author indicates that Woolf wished to criticize society rather than to focus on individual consciousness. However, the word "contemplative" in the context of lines 41-44 describes how she presented her criticism. (D) describes the objects of criticism rather than a method of criticism.

(E) is not the answer. The author indicates that Woolf believed the artist's view of the world to be an honest one. However, the passage does not imply that Woolf did not judge society in moral terms.

22. This question asks you to identify an element that the author thinks is important in the satirist's art. The colon in line 52 indicates that the information in lines 48-52 describing Woolf's work leads to the statement, "hers is the satirist's art." This statement indicates that conclusions about Woolf's work as a satirist can lead you to conclusions about the art of satirists in general.

(A) is not the answer. Though the author suggests that a satirist "works by indirection," there is no indication that "lofty disdain" underlies this method.

(B) is not the answer. The author discusses Woolf's interest in the influence of society on the individual, but there is no suggestion in the passage that Woolf as a satirist thought the individual helpless.

(C) is not the answer. The fact that Woolf was herself a "visionary" (line 12) suggests that she did not indulge in "cynical disbelief" concerning the influence of visionaries.

(D) is not the answer. There is no indication in the passage that satirists believe that a work of art must be ambiguous in order to be accurate.

(E) is the answer. Lines 48-52 describe Woolf's satirical art as providing the materials for judgments about mores in an indirect, subtle, and non-assertive way, that is, in a nonpolemical way.

23. This question asks you to determine which of the questions given can be answered using the information in the passage. To make this determination, you must first attempt to answer each question using only the information presented by the author.

(A) is not the answer. The author mentions Chekhov and Chaucer in the last paragraph as acute social observers who were models for Woolf. There is no mention of critics' treatment of their social criticism.

(B) is the answer. The answer to the question is "No." In lines 10-12, the author characterizes Woolf as realistic and satirical as well as introspective and visionary.

(C) is not the answer. Though the author characterizes Woolf as a social critic, he does not mention specific causes in which she is interested.

(D) is not the answer. The author mentions that Woolf criticized Lawrence's tendency to "preach," but there is no discussion of Lawrence's concern with realistic settings for his novels.

(E) is not the answer. Lines 15-20 suggest that Woolf believed social environment to be a force in shaping people's lives, but there is no comparison of her belief about the effect of this force with her belief about the effect of the force of history on people's lives.

24. This question asks you to determine the primary purpose of the passage. In order to do this, you must take into account all of the information in the passage.

(A) is not the answer. The author does not criticize scientists because they believe that the reaction may be a feasible energy source.

(B) is not the answer. The author states that miscalculation of the amount of lithium available is a problem, but he does not say who has miscalculated.

(C) is not the answer. The author does defend the continued short-term use of fossil fuels, but he mentions fossil fuels as one of several possible sources of energy.

(D) is the answer. The author mentions several reasons why nuclear fusion should not be accepted as a major source of energy at this time and recommends continued critical evaluation of its potential.

(E) is not the answer. The author does correct the misconception that nuclear fusion power is not radioactive, but to do so is not his primary purpose.

25. This question asks you to use the specific statements made in the passage to determine what the author believes about public awareness of nuclear fusion power.

(A) is not the answer. There is no information in the passage to indicate that the public has been misinformed deliberately, though several instances of misinformation are mentioned.

(B) is not the answer. No mention is made in the passage of the advantages of nuclear fusion as compared with those of nuclear fission.

(C) is the answer. The author specifically mentions two misconceptions about nuclear fusion that he believes are generally held, indicating that he believes that people's knowledge of the scientific facts is incomplete.

(D) is not the answer. The public's interest in increasing its awareness is not discussed.

(E) is not the answer. The author indicates, on the contrary, that the public is not aware of some of the limitations of nuclear fusion power.

26. This question asks you to determine which of the questions given can be answered using the information in the passage. To make this determination, you must first attempt to answer each question using only the information presented by the author.

(A) is the answer. The answer to the question posed in (A) is "the sea." The passage states that it is commonly believed that there is an enormous quantity of deuterium in the sea; the author does not deny this.

(B) is not the answer. The author states that radiation is produced by the deuterium-tritium reaction, but no amount is mentioned.

(C) is not the answer. The author mentions that scientists are studying the reaction with zeal, but no reason for their zeal is given.

(D) is not the answer. The author does not provide a rationale for the use of lithium to produce tritium.

(E) is not the answer. The author mentions that the deuterium-tritium reaction produces alpha particles and neutrons, but he does not explain why these are produced by the reaction.

27. The author mentions nuclear scientists only once, near the beginning of the passage. This question asks you to determine what the passage most directly suggests about them.

(A) is not the answer. It is probably true that scientists do not know all the facts, but the question asks what is suggested in the passage. Though the passage suggests that the public does not know all the facts, there is no information about how much scientists know.

(B) is not the answer. The author attributes zeal to nuclear scientists, but not particular misconceptions or errors. Thus, he does not associate misconceptions or errors with their zeal.

(C) is not the answer. The author does not say that the amount of lithium has been overestimated. He discusses only evaluations of the amount of deuterium available.

(D) is the answer. The author's statement that scientists are studying the deuterium-tritium reaction with "zeal" suggests that he believes that they are not dispassionate.

(E) is not the answer. The author cautions that scientists should continue to study nuclear fusion, but he does not single out the lithium-to-tritium reaction as one needing further study.

28. To "persevere" means to continue in an enterprise in spite of opposition or other difficulties.

(A) is not the answer. To "put into" could mean to invest, as energy, or, more generally, to insert.

(B) is not the answer. To "send out" means to emit.

(C) is not the answer. To "take away" means to subtract, to relieve someone of something, or to remove.

(D) is the answer. To "give up" can mean to cease to try to accomplish something.

(E) is not the answer. To "bring forward" can mean to move up or to carry over. It does not suggest a lack of perseverance.

29. Something that is "waterproof" cannot be penetrated by water.

(A) is not the answer. Something "soggy" has already been penetrated by a liquid. Something "soggy" is not "waterproof," but "soggy" implies more than being penetrable by water. It means having already absorbed a great deal of liquid.

(B) is not the answer. "Natural" does not indicate either resistance to water or lack of resistance.

(C) is not the answer. It is likely that an "unglazed" substance such as pottery is less "waterproof" than the same substance covered with a glaze. However, "unglazed" does not by definition mean lacking resistance to water.

(D) is not the answer. "Viscous" means gluey; it refers to the consistency of a material rather than to its resistance to water.

(E) is the answer. "Permeable" means capable of being penetrated, by water or other liquids.

30. To "amalgamate" means to mix together or unite.

(A) is the answer. To "separate" means to disunite.

(B) is not the answer. To "fixate" means to gaze steadily at something.

(C) is not the answer. To "terminate" means to put an end to or to come to an end. It does not necessarily imply dissolution.

(D) is not the answer. To "calibrate" means to adjust, as the markings on an instrument.

(E) is not the answer. To "correlate" means to show a relationship to something else.

31. In some contexts, "pungency" is a quality that is directly perceived. It implies sharpness, a stinging quality, and frequently applies to smells or tastes.

(A) is not the answer. Something that is the opposite of pungent might cause "boredom," but "boredom" is a feeling rather than a quality.

(B) is not the answer. "Redundancy" refers to that which is extra, unnecessary, or repetitive.

(C) is not the answer. "Pungency" is a quality that might provoke a response, but "unresponsiveness" is a characteristic of the perceiver, not of the thing perceived.

(D) is the answer. "Blandness" means lacking flavor, not irritating, stimulating, sharp, or stinging. It is frequently used to describe tastes.

(E) is not the answer. "Insignificance" is a quality, but it does not necessarily imply a lack of sharpness. It is not a common quality of tastes or smells.

32. "Anarchy" means absence of order.

(A) is not the answer. A lack of "courtesy" might well accompany a state of "anarchy," but this lack is not implied in the definition of "anarchy."

(B) is not the answer. "Hope" is an emotion, and not a state. It may or may not accompany "anarchy," but it is not the opposite of "anarchy."

(C) is the answer. "Order" is the opposite of a lack of order.

(D) is not the answer. "Neutrality," like "anarchy," can be a political state, but it does not necessarily imply orderliness.

(E) is not the answer. "Importance" is a quality that does not directly or necessarily have to do with order or the lack of it.

33. An "incursion" is an intrusion into another's territory. It suggests aggression, and is often used in a military context.

(A) is not the answer. To make an "incursion" does not necessarily inspire respect in those whose territory is invaded, so a "loss of respect" is not the opposite of "incursion."

(B) is not the answer. It is likely that "incursion" is preceded by a certain amount of resolve, but a "lack of resolve" is not the opposite of an intrusion.

(C) is not the answer. "Reparation" (repaying wartime damages, or making amends) may be required as a result of an "incursion," but repayment is not the opposite of an intrusion.

(D) is not the answer. A "relapse" is a return to a previous, undesirable state. It is not the opposite of an intrusion.

(E) is the answer. "Retreat" is often used in a military context to describe an end to formal aggression, a backing off from a former position. Though "retreat" is more general than "incursion" in that it does not necessarily refer to a position in another's territory, it is still the option most nearly opposite to "incursion."

34. To "abrogate" means to do away with, usually in a legal context, as when something official is done away with or when something is done away with by law.

(A) is the answer. To "uphold" means to support something. In a legal context, it is likely to mean to keep something (like a rule or law) in existence rather than to do away with it.

(B) is not the answer. In a legal context, to "defer" is most likely to mean to put off, or to delay.

(C) is not the answer. To "discuss secretly" is not necessarily to keep something in existence.

(D) is not the answer. To "admit willingly" does not necessarily mean to keep something in existence.

(E) is not the answer. To "read thoroughly" does not mean to keep something in existence.

35. "Hapless" means unlucky or unable to achieve success because of bad luck.

(A) is not the answer. "Excited" means stimulated, or showing strong feeling.

(B) is not the answer. One might feel "elated" if one were not "hapless," but elation is an emotional state rather than the state that causes emotion.

(C) is the answer. One who is "fortunate" is lucky.

(D) is not the answer. To be "completely self-reliant" means to be able to depend entirely on one's own abilities, and does not imply luck or lack of it.

(E) is not the answer. If one is "assured of success," one is not "hapless." However, luck or the lack of it is not a necessary element in the idea of being guaranteed success.

36. To "aver" means to state that something is certainly true, or to prove something positively to be true.

(A) is not the answer. To "collect" means to gather, and could refer to evidence in support of a position, but it does not refer to a statement or to proof.

(B) is not the answer. To "augment" means to make greater.

(C) is not the answer. To "placate" means to soothe. The ability of a statement to placate is not necessarily related to the certainty or truth of its content.

(D) is the answer. To "deny" is to state that something is false.

(E) is not the answer. To "encourage" is to inspire or to help along. Encouragement is not concerned with truth or the lack of it.

37. "Sedulous" means applying oneself faithfully to a task. It suggests continuing effort and attention to what is to be done.

(A) is not the answer. "Presumptuous" means showing arrogance by overstepping one's authority. Presumptuousness does not necessarily have to do with performance of a task.

(B) is not the answer. "Ponderous" means being hard to manage because of great weight or size. It does not suggest a lack of attention or application.

(C) is not the answer. "Treacherous" means likely to betray. It does not describe an approach to a task.

(D) is the answer. "Careless" can mean failing to apply due attention to performance of a task.

(E) is not the answer. Work might be made "useless" if effort and attention were not applied to it, but "useless" does not describe the worker's approach to the work.

38. "Insularity" means the state of being isolated or confined to a limited area. It often applies to nations or to peoples.

(A) is not the answer. "Overzealousness" is excessive concern over an issue. It might result from isolation or the lack of it, but it does not imply a lack of isolation.

(B) is the answer. "Cosmopolitanism" implies worldwide scope.

(C) is not the answer. "Insularity" might make a nation susceptible, but "susceptibility" means inability to resist some outside influence, and does not have to do directly with isolation.

(D) is not the answer. It is unlikely that an insular people would be characterized by "willing hospitality," but "willing hospitality" is not implied in the idea of a lack of isolation.

(E) is not the answer. "Insularity" might result from a lack of "knowledgeable consideration," but "knowledgeable consideration" is not itself a state like "insularity."

SECTION 4

1. Since $n + 3 = 8$, n must be 5.
   Since $k + n = k + 5 = 13$, k must be 8.

   Answer is A

2. Betty spent $102 on her bicycle ($75 + $27). Therefore, in selling the bicycle for $120, she got $18 in excess of what she spent.

   Answer is B

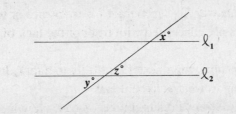

3. In the figure, $y = z$ because they are measures of a pair of vertical angles. Also, since $\ell_1 \parallel \ell_2$, $z = x$ because they are measures of a pair of corresponding angles. Therefore, $y = x$.

   Answer is C

4. $-2(-3)(-4) < 0$. You can determine this by calculating the product or by realizing that the product of an odd number of negative factors must be negative. On the other hand, $0(4)(8) = 0$ since the product of 0 and any number is 0.

   Answer is B

5. The value of $11 + x$ depends on the value of x. If $x \geq 0$, then $11 + x \geq 11$, but if $x < 0$, then $11 + x < 11$. For example,

   if $x = 0$, then $11 + x = 11$;
   if $x = -1$, then $11 + x = 10$;
   and if $x = -2$, then $11 + x = 9$.

   Therefore, $11 + x$ may be greater than, equal to, or less than 10.

   Answer is D

6. $\dfrac{1}{2} + \dfrac{3}{5} > 1$. You can determine this by computation or by noting that $\dfrac{3}{5}$ is

greater than $\dfrac{1}{2}$, so that

$$\frac{1}{2} + \frac{3}{5} > \frac{1}{2} + \frac{1}{2} = 1.$$

On the other hand,

$$\frac{1+3}{2+5} = \frac{4}{7} < 1.$$

Answer is A

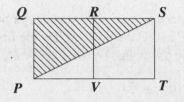

7. In the figure, the two squares have a common side, RV, so that $PQST$ is a 12 by 6 rectangle. Its area is therefore 72. You are asked to compare the area of region PQS with 36. Since diagonal PS splits region $PQST$ in half, the area of region PQS is $\dfrac{1}{2}$ of 72, or 36.

Answer is C

8. It is given that R, S, and T are consecutive **odd** integers, with $R < S < T$. This means that S is 2 more than R, and T is 2 more than S. (Examples of consecutive odd integers are 1, 3, and 5; and 19, 21, and 23.) You can use this to rewrite each of the expressions to be compared as follows:

$R + S + 1 = R + (R + 2) + 1 = \mathbf{2R + 3}$
$S + T - 1 = (R + 2) + (R + 4) - 1 = \mathbf{2R + 5}$

Since $5 > 3$, then $2R + 5 > 2R + 3$. You might also notice that both expressions to be compared contain S: $S + (R + 1)$ and $S + (T - 1)$.

Therefore, the real difference in the two expressions depends on the difference in value of $R + 1$ and $T - 1$. Since T is 4 more than R, $T - 1 > R + 1$.

Answer is B

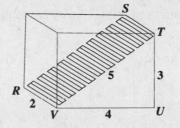

9. You need to determine the area of the shaded rectangular region. It is given that *VR* = 2, but the length of *VT* is not given. However, *UV* = 4 and *TU* = 3, and *VTU* is a right triangle, so by the Pythagorean theorem, *VT* = 5. Thus, the area of *RVTS* (the shaded region) is 5 × 2, or 10, which is greater than 9.

Answer is A

10. It is given that $x^2y > 0$ and $xy^2 < 0$, so neither *x* nor *y* can be 0. If neither *x* nor *y* is 0, then both x^2 and y^2 are positive. By the first equation ($x^2y > 0$), *y* must also be positive; by the second equation ($xy^2 < 0$), *x* must be negative. That is, $x < 0 < y$.

Answer is B

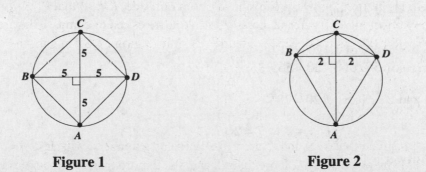

Figure 1   **Figure 2**

11. You are given no information about the location of points *A, B, C,* and *D* except that they are on a circle of diameter 10. In Figure 1 above, if *AC* and *BD* are perpendicular diameters, then:

$$\text{Area } \triangle ABC = \text{Area } \triangle ADC = \frac{10 \cdot 5}{2} = 25,$$

so the area of *ABCD* is 2 × 25 = 50.

181

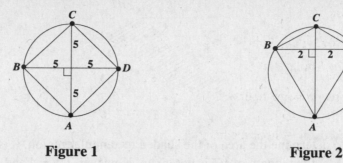

Figure 1   **Figure 2**

On the other hand, in Figure 2, although the bases of *ABC* and *ADC* are still 10, the altitude of each could be 2. In this case,

Area △ *ABC* = Area △ *ADC* = (10·2)/2 = 10, so the area of *ABCD* is 2 × 10 = 20. These examples show that the area of *ABCD* may be greater or less than 40.

Answer is D

12. If you made an error in computation, you might think of the problem this way, noting that

5 is $\frac{1}{2}$ of 10, and $2\frac{1}{2}$ is $\frac{1}{2}$ of 5:

$$10\% \text{ of } 1,120 = 112,$$
$$\text{so } 5\% \text{ of } 1,120 = 56,$$

and $2\frac{1}{2}\%$ of 1,120 = 28

$$= 4 \times 7 = 2^2 \cdot 7.$$

Answer is C

13. The number of records pressed by machine *R* in 3 hours is 6*x* — that is, (3 ÷ 0.5) times *x*. The number of records pressed by machine *S* in 4 hours is $\left(5\frac{1}{3}\right)x$ — that is, (4 ÷ 0.75) times *x*.

Answer is A

Alternate solution:

Machine R: x records in $\frac{1}{2}$ hour means

$2x$ records in 1 hour and

$3 \cdot 2x$ or $6x$ records in 3 hours.

Machine S: x records in $\frac{3}{4}$ hour means

$\frac{4}{3}x$ records in 1 hour and $4 \cdot \frac{4}{3}x$, or

$\left(5\frac{1}{3}\right)x$, records in 4 hours.

And $6x > \left(5\frac{1}{3}\right)x$.

Answer is A

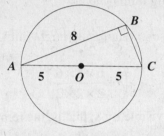

14. In the figure, since O is the center of the circle, AO and OC are radii, and
$AO = OC = 5$. Triangle ABC is a right triangle in which diameter AC
is the hypotenuse of the triangle. So by the Pythagorean theorem,
$BC^2 = 10^2 - 8^2 = 100 - 64 = 36$. Thus $BC = 6$, so the perimeter is
$6 + 8 + 10 = 24$.

Answer is C

15. If the three negative integers happen to be -1, -2, and -3, then
$$(-1)(-2)(-3) = (-1) + (-2) + (-3)$$
$$= -6;$$
that is, the product is equal to the sum. However, if the integers are -2, -3,
and -4, then

$$(-2)(-3)(-4) < (-2) + (-3) + (-4) \text{ because } -24 < -9.$$

In this case, the product is less than the sum. These examples show that the
relative values of the sum and product can vary according to the numbers
chosen.

Answer is D

16. $\sqrt{(42-6)(25+11)} =$

$\sqrt{(36)(36)} =$

$\sqrt{36} \times \sqrt{36} = 6 \times 6 = 36$

Answer is C

17. Since there are two brands of socks with different prices, the greatest number of pairs of socks that could be purchased for a given amount of money would be the cheaper brand — brand *X*. Since these are $2 per pair, at most 12 pairs could be bought for $25 if, as stated in the problem, there is no sales tax. Note that the customer could also buy 11 pairs at $2 each and 1 pair at $3 to use the entire $25, but this would still be 12 pairs of socks.

Answer is D

18. You can solve this problem by calculation, but you might notice that $8 = 2^3$, so if you think of writing it this way,

$$\frac{6^3}{8} = \frac{6^3}{2^3} = \left(\frac{6}{2}\right)^3$$

$$\left(\text{or } \frac{6 \times 6 \times 6}{2 \times 2 \times 2}\right)$$

you can see that 6^3 is divisible by 8; that is, the remainder is 0.

Answer is E

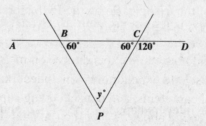

19. You are given that $x = 120$, so the measure of $\angle PCB$ must be 60°. You are also given that $BP = CP$, so $\angle PBC$ has the same measure as $\angle PCB$. Since the sum of the measures of the angles of $\triangle BPC$ is 180°, *y* must also be 60.

Answer is B

20.
Since $z = 2y$ and $y = 3x$, then
$z = 2(3x) = 6x$. Thus,
$x + y + z = x + (3x) + (6x)$
$= (1 + 3 + 6)x = 10x.$

Answer is A

Questions 21-25 refer to a graph and a chart. Since there are 5 questions based on these sources, it is wise to scan both of them first to get an overview. In this case, the graph shows the percent of annual income spent on six categories of some food and nonfood items. The chart, on the other hand, shows the percent of expenditures for food and household items spent on six subcategories of these item.

21. This question asks about percent of annual income, so the necessary information is given in the graph. "Food at Home" is indicated by the unshaded portion of each of the bars, and the lowest percent (shortest portion) was spent by professionals and managers.

Answer is B

22. This question asks about expenditures, so all the needed information is given in the chart. For professionals and managers, an average of 29% of weekly expenditures ($38.77) was for food away home. To estimate this amount, you could think of this as a bit less than 30% of $39. Since 30% of $39 is $11.70, the best of the answer choices given is $11.

Answer is C

23. This question also asks about expenditures; this time about expenditures for fruits and vegetables. This category is included with others (cereals, and bakery and dairy products), so it is not possible to estimate the percent spent only on fruits and vegetables.

Answer is E

24. For this question, you must use both the chart (meats, poultry, and seafood) and the graph (annual income). According to the chart, retirees spend about 23% of food and household expenditures on meats, poultry, and seafood. However, "household expenditures" includes food at home, food away from home, personal care items, and housekeeping supplies. According to the graph, retirees spend about 29% of their annual income on these four categories (about 23% for food and 6% for the other two categories). Therefore, they spend about 23% of 29% for meats, poultry, and seafood. $.23 \times .29 = .0667$, which is approximately 7%.

Answer is A

Alternate solution: According to the graph, retirees spent about 19.5% of their annual income on Food at Home. According to the table, they spent 23% of the 66% of their average weekly Food at Home budget on meats, poultry, and seafood. Therefore, they spent about $\frac{23}{66}$ (19.5), or $\frac{1}{3}$ (19.5) of their annual income, on these foods. Since $\frac{1}{3}$ (19.5) = 6.5, and (19.5) > $\frac{1}{3}$ (19.5), this is about 7%.

Answer is A

25. You are to determine which of three given statements can be inferred from the data. Statement I cannot properly be inferred since the graph shows percents of annual incomes. (Although the bar for retirees is tallest, this does not mean that their actual income was greater: rather, it means that they spend a greater percent of their annual incomes on these categories than the other occupations listed.) Statement II cannot be inferred either — although each group spends about the same percent of their income on housekeeping supplies, the expenditures differed. For example, 7% of $35.88 is less than 7% of $38.77. Thus, III is the only possible correct inference. This can be verified by actual calculation (23% of $35.44 is greater than any of the other combinations).

Answer is C

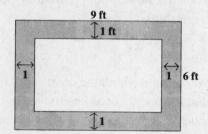

26. The rug is 9 feet by 6 feet. The border is 1 foot wide. This means that the portion of the rug that excludes the border is 7 feet by 4 feet. Its area is therefore 7 × 4.

Answer is A

27.
$$\frac{d-3n}{7n-d} = 1 \text{ means that}$$
$$d-3n = 7n-d.$$
$$d-3n = 7n-d$$
$$\text{means that } d = 10n-d$$
$$\text{or } 2d = 10n$$
$$\text{or } d = 5n.$$

Answer is D

28. There are 80 positive whole numbers that are less than 81. They include the squares of only the whole numbers 1 through 8 ($81 = 9^2$, and we're concerned with numbers less than 81). That is, there are 8 positive whole numbers less than 81 that are squares of whole numbers, and $80 - 8 = 72$ that are NOT squares of whole numbers.

Answer is D

29. If $2 - 5x \leq \dfrac{6x - 5}{-3}$, you should notice that $(-3)(2 - 5x) \geq 6x - 5$ because multipying an inequality by a negative number reverses the direction of the inequality.

Therefore, $-6 + 15x \geq 6x - 5$,

$$\text{or} \qquad 15x \geq 6x + 1$$
$$\text{or} \qquad 9x \geq 1.$$

That is, $\qquad x \geq \dfrac{1}{9}$.

Answer is C

30. The area of a circular region is usually given as $A = \pi r^2$, where r is the length of the radius.
Since

$$r = \frac{d}{2},$$

the formula, in terms of d,

is $A = \pi \left(\dfrac{d}{2}\right)^2 = \pi \dfrac{d^2}{4} = \dfrac{\pi d^2}{4}.$

Answer is E

NOTE: To ensure prompt processing of test results, it is important that you fill in the blanks exactly as directed.

GENERAL TEST

A. Print and sign your full name in this box:

PRINT: _____

            (LAST)   (FIRST)   (MIDDLE)

SIGN: _____

Copy this code in box 6 on your answer sheet. Then fill in the corresponding ovals exactly as shown.

6. TITLE CODE

Copy the Test Name and Form Code in box 7 on your answer sheet.

TEST NAME _General_

FORM CODE _GR86-2_

GRADUATE RECORD EXAMINATIONS GENERAL TEST

B. You will have 3 hours and 30 minutes in which to work on this test, which consists of seven sections. During the time allowed for one section, you may work only on that section. The time allowed for each section is 30 minutes.

Each of your scores will be determined by the number of questions for which you select the best answer from the choices given. Questions for which you mark no answer or more than one answer are not counted in scoring. Nothing is subtracted from a score if you answer a question incorrectly. Therefore, to maximize your scores it is better for you to guess at an answer than not to respond at all.

You are advised to work as rapidly as you can without losing accuracy. Do not spend too much time on questions that are too difficult for you. Go on to the other questions and come back to the difficult ones later.

There are several different types of questions; you will find special directions for each type in the test itself. Be sure you understand the directions before attempting to answer any questions.

YOU MUST INDICATE ALL YOUR ANSWERS ON THE SEPARATE ANSWER SHEET. No credit will be given for anything written in this examination book, but you may write in the book as much as you wish to work out your answers. After you have decided on your response to a question, fill in the corresponding oval on the answer sheet. BE SURE THAT EACH MARK IS DARK AND COMPLETELY FILLS THE OVAL. Mark only one answer to each question. No credit will be given for multiple answers. Erase all stray marks. If you change an answer, be sure that all previous marks are erased completely. Incomplete erasures may be read as intended answers. Do not be concerned if your answer sheet provides spaces for more answers than there are questions in each section.

Example:

What city is the capital of France?

(A) Rome
(B) Paris
(C) London
(D) Cairo
(E) Oslo

Sample Answer

BEST ANSWER
PROPERLY MARKED

IMPROPER MARKS

Some or all of the passages for this test have been adapted from published material to provide the examinee with significant problems for analysis and evaluation. To make the passages suitable for testing purposes, the style, content, or point of view of the original may have been altered in some cases. The ideas contained in the passages do not necessarily represent the opinions of the Graduate Record Examinations Board or Educational Testing Service.

DO NOT OPEN YOUR TEST BOOK UNTIL YOU ARE TOLD TO DO SO.

GENERAL TEST GR86-2 ONLY

Answer Key and Percentages* of Examinees Answering Each Question Correctly

VERBAL ABILITY						QUANTITATIVE ABILITY					
Section 1			Section 3			Section 2			Section 4		
Number	Answer	P+	Number	Answer	P+	Number	Answer	P+	Number	Answer	P+
1	C	87	1	E	88	1	A	87	1	A	91
2	E	86	2	D	80	2	A	87	2	B	94
3	A	66	3	B	79	3	D	82	3	C	93
4	E	61	4	A	69	4	B	83	4	B	87
5	B	52	5	B	69	5	B	84	5	D	86
6	D	44	6	C	51	6	C	82	6	A	85
7	D	18	7	B	41	7	A	72	7	C	75
8	B	91	8	D	94	8	C	74	8	B	70
9	E	76	9	D	87	9	B	59	9	A	77
10	D	50	10	A	81	10	C	44	10	B	51
11	C	51	11	D	70	11	D	59	11	D	53
12	A	38	12	E	59	12	C	64	12	C	59
13	E	41	13	A	42	13	A	47	13	A	61
14	C	38	14	B	37	14	D	42	14	C	55
15	A	27	15	B	22	15	B	27	15	D	41
16	C	14	16	B	30	16	F	89	16	C	87
17	B	83	17	E	66	17	C	84	17	D	81
18	C	79	18	A	50	18	B	87	18	E	86
19	A	54	19	D	54	19	B	79	19	B	86
20	D	55	20	B	71	20	A	42	20	A	71
21	E	78	21	C	40	21	E	93	21	B	85
22	C	60	22	E	38	22	D	62	22	C	56
23	A	75	23	B	42	23	A	60	23	E	59
24	E	52	24	D	70	24	D	58	24	A	21
25	D	76	25	C	84	25	B	46	25	C	26
26	E	29	26	A	51	26	D	50	26	A	62
27	E	60	27	D	19	27	C	40	27	D	45
28	E	86	28	D	86	28	B	39	28	D	32
29	A	78	29	E	84	29	E	33	29	C	32
30	B	81	30	A	80	30	A	27	30	E	34
31	C	77	31	D	71						
32	D	66	32	C	67						
33	C	51	33	E	44						
34	B	55	34	A	39						
35	A	42	35	C	38						
36	D	34	36	D	29						
37	C	26	37	D	28						
38	A	24	38	B	20						

*Estimated P+ for the group of examinees who took the GRE General Test in a recent three-year period.

SCORE CONVERSIONS FOR GRE GENERAL TEST, GR86-2

Raw Score	Scaled Score Verbal	Scaled Score Quantitative	Raw Score	Scaled Score Verbal	Scaled Score Quantitative
74-76	800		35	400	500
73	790		34	390	480
72	780		33	380	470
71	770		32	370	460
			31	360	440
70	750				
69	740		30	360	430
68	730		29	350	420
67	720		28	340	400
66	700		27	330	390
			26	320	380
65	690				
64	680		25	310	370
63	670		24	300	350
62	660		23	290	340
61	650		22	280	330
			21	280	310
60	640	800			
59	620	800	20	270	300
58	610	790	19	260	290
57	600	780	18	250	280
56	590	770	17	240	260
			16	230	250
55	580	750			
54	570	740	15	220	240
53	560	730	14	210	220
52	550	710	13	200	210
51	540	700	12	200	200
			11	200	200
50	530	690			
49	520	680	10	200	200
48	510	660	9	200	200
47	500	650	0-8	200	200
46	490	640			
45	480	620			
44	470	610			
43	460	600			
42	450	590			
41	450	570			
40	440	560			
39	430	550			
38	420	530			
37	410	520			
36	400	510			

THE GRADUATE RECORD EXAMINATIONS®

General Test

Do not break the seal
until you are told to do so.

The contents of this test are confidential.
Disclosure or reproduction of any portion
of it is prohibited.

THIS TEST BOOK MUST NOT BE TAKEN FROM THE ROOM.

NO TEST MATERIAL ON THIS PAGE

SECTION 1

Time—30 minutes

38 Questions

Directions: Each sentence below has one or two blanks, each blank indicating that something has been omitted. Beneath the sentence are five lettered words or sets of words. Choose the word or set of words for each blank that best fits the meaning of the sentence as a whole.

1. Agronomists are increasingly worried about "desertification," the phenomenon that is turning many of the world's ------- fields and pastures into ------- wastelands, unable to support the people living on them.

   (A) fertile. .barren
   (B) productive. .blooming
   (C) arid. .thriving
   (D) poorest. .marginal
   (E) largest. .saturated

2. Old beliefs die hard: even when jobs became -------, the long-standing fear that unemployment could return at a moment's notice -------.

   (A) vacant. .perished
   (B) easier. .changed
   (C) plentiful. .persisted
   (D) protected. .subsided
   (E) available. .receded

3. Intellectual ------- and flight from boredom have caused him to rush pell-mell into situations that less ------- spirits might hesitate to approach.

   (A) restlessness. .adventurous
   (B) agitation. .passive
   (C) resilience. .quiescent
   (D) tranquillity. .versatile
   (E) curiosity. .lethargic

4. Science advances in ------- spiral in that each new conceptual scheme ------- the phenomena explained by its predecessors and adds to those explanations.

   (A) a discontinuous . . . decries
   (B) a repetitive. .vitiates
   (C) a widening. .embraces
   (D) an anomalous. .captures
   (E) an explosive. .questions

5. Politeness is not a ------- attribute of human behavior, but rather a central virtue, one whose very existence is increasingly being ------- by the faddish requirement to "speak one's mind."

   (A) superficial. .threatened
   (B) pervasive. .undercut
   (C) worthless. .forestalled
   (D) precious. .repudiated
   (E) trivial. .affected

6. The painting was larger than it appeared to be, for, hanging in a darkened recess of the chapel, it was ------- by the perspective.

   (A) improved
   (B) aggrandized
   (C) embellished
   (D) jeopardized
   (E) diminished

7. Because folk art is neither completely rejected nor accepted as an art form by art historians, their final evaluations of it necessarily remain -------.

   (A) arbitrary
   (B) estimable
   (C) orthodox
   (D) unspoken
   (E) equivocal

GO ON TO THE NEXT PAGE.

Directions: In each of the following questions, a related pair of words or phrases is followed by five lettered pairs of words or phrases. Select the lettered pair that best expresses a relationship similar to that expressed in the original pair.

*8. REFEREE : FIELD :: (A) scientist : results
(B) mediator : deadlock   (C) gladiator : contest
(D) teacher : classroom   (E) judge : courtroom

9. BLUSH : EMBARRASSMENT ::
(A) scream : anger   (B) smile : pleasure
(C) laugh : outrage   (D) love : sentimentality
(E) whine : indecision

10. TANGO : DANCE ::
(A) arabesque : theme
(B) tonality : instrumentation
(C) rhyme : pattern
(D) stanza : line
(E) elegy : poem

11. CELL : MEMBRANE ::
(A) door : jamb
(B) yard : sidewalk
(C) seed : hull
(D) head : halo
(E) mountain : clouds

12. HYMN : PRAISE :: (A) waltz : joy
(B) liturgy : rite   (C) lullaby : child
(D) dirge : grief   (E) prayer : congregation

13. EMOLLIENT : SOOTHE ::
(A) dynamo : generate
(B) elevation : level
(C) precipitation : fall
(D) hurricane : track
(E) negative : expose

14. IMPLACABLE : COMPROMISE ::
(A) perfidious : conspire
(B) irascible : avenge
(C) honest : swindle
(D) amenable : deceive
(E) hasty : prevail

15. MISANTHROPE : PEOPLE ::
(A) patriot : country
(B) reactionary : government
(C) curmudgeon : children
(D) xenophobe : strangers
(E) miscreant : dogma

16. MILK : EXTRACT :: (A) squander : enjoy
(B) exploit : utilize   (C) research : investigate
(D) hire : manage   (E) wheedle : flatter

GO ON TO THE NEXT PAGE.

Directions: Each passage in this group is followed by questions based on its content. After reading a passage, choose the best answer to each question. Answer all questions following a passage on the basis of what is stated or implied in that passage.

Many critics of Emily Brontë's novel *Wuthering Heights* see its second part as a counterpoint that comments on, if it does not reverse, the first part,
Line where a "romantic" reading receives more confirmation.
(5) Seeing the two parts as a whole is encouraged by the novel's sophisticated structure, revealed in its complex use of narrators and time shifts. Granted that the presence of these elements need not argue an authorial awareness of novelistic construction comparable to that
(10) of Henry James, their presence does encourage attempts to unify the novel's heterogeneous parts. However, any interpretation that seeks to unify all of the novel's diverse elements is bound to be somewhat unconvincing. This is not because such an interpretation necessarily
(15) stiffens into a thesis (although rigidity in any interpretation of this or of any novel is always a danger), but because *Wuthering Heights* has recalcitrant elements of undeniable power that, ultimately, resist inclusion in an all-encompassing interpretation. In this respect, *Wuthering Heights* shares a feature of *Hamlet*.

17. According to the passage, which of the following is a true statement about the first and second parts of *Wuthering Heights*?

(A) The second part has received more attention from critics.
(B) The second part has little relation to the first part.
(C) The second part annuls the force of the first part.
(D) The second part provides less substantiation for a "romantic" reading.
(E) The second part is better because it is more realistic.

18. Which of the following inferences about Henry James's awareness of novelistic construction is best supported by the passage?

(A) James, more than any other novelist, was aware of the difficulties of novelistic construction.
(B) James was very aware of the details of novelistic construction.
(C) James's awareness of novelistic construction derived from his reading of Brontë.
(D) James's awareness of novelistic construction has led most commentators to see unity in his individual novels.
(E) James's awareness of novelistic construction precluded him from violating the unity of his novels.

19. The author of the passage would be most likely to agree that an interpretation of a novel should

(A) not try to unite heterogeneous elements in the novel
(B) not be inflexible in its treatment of the elements in the novel
(C) not argue that the complex use of narrators or of time shifts indicates a sophisticated structure
(D) concentrate on those recalcitrant elements of the novel that are outside the novel's main structure
(E) primarily consider those elements of novelistic construction of which the author of the novel was aware

20. The author of the passage suggests which of the following about *Hamlet*?

I. *Hamlet* has usually attracted critical interpretations that tend to stiffen into theses.
II. *Hamlet* has elements that are not amenable to an all-encompassing critical interpretation.
III. *Hamlet* is less open to an all-encompassing critical interpretation than is *Wuthering Heights*.
IV. *Hamlet* has not received a critical interpretation that has been widely accepted by readers.

(A) I only
(B) II only
(C) I and IV only
(D) III and IV only
(E) I, II, and III only

GO ON TO THE NEXT PAGE.

195

The determination of the sources of copper ore used in the manufacture of copper and bronze artifacts of Bronze Age civilizations would add greatly to our knowledge of cultural contacts and trade in that era.

Line
(5) Researchers have analyzed artifacts and ores for their concentrations of elements, but for a variety of reasons, these studies have generally failed to provide evidence of the sources of the copper used in the objects. Elemental composition can vary within the same copper-ore lode,

(10) usually because of varying admixtures of other elements, especially iron, lead, zinc, and arsenic. And high concentrations of cobalt or zinc, noticed in some artifacts, appear in a variety of copper-ore sources. Moreover, the processing of ores introduced poorly controlled

(15) changes in the concentrations of minor and trace elements in the resulting metal. Some elements evaporate during smelting and roasting; different temperatures and processes produce different degrees of loss. Finally, flux, which is sometimes added during smelting to

(20) remove waste material from the ore, could add quantities of elements to the final product.

An elemental property that is unchanged through these chemical processes is the isotopic composition of each metallic element in the ore. Isotopic composition,

(25) the percentages of the different isotopes of an element in a given sample of the element, is therefore particularly suitable as an indicator of the sources of the ore. Of course, for this purpose it is necessary to find an element whose isotopic composition is more or less constant

(30) throughout a given ore body, but varies from one copper ore body to another or, at least, from one geographic region to another.

The ideal choice, when isotopic composition is used to investigate the source of copper ore, would seem to

(35) be copper itself. It has been shown that small but measurable variations occur naturally in the isotopic composition of copper. However, the variations are large enough only in rare ores; between samples of the common ore minerals of copper, isotopic variations

(40) greater than the measurement error have not been found. An alternative choice is lead, which occurs in most copper and bronze artifacts of the Bronze Age in amounts consistent with the lead being derived from the copper ores and possibly from the fluxes. The

(45) isotopic composition of lead often varies from one source of common copper ore to another, with variations exceeding the measurement error; and preliminary studies indicate virtually uniform isotopic composition of the lead from a single copper-ore source. While

(50) some of the lead found in an artifact may have been introduced from flux or when other metals were added to the copper ore, lead so added in Bronze Age processing would usually have the same isotopic composition as the lead in the copper ore. Lead isotope studies

(55) may thus prove useful for interpreting the archaeological record of the Bronze Age.

21. The primary purpose of the passage is to

(A) discuss the techniques of analyzing lead isotope composition
(B) propose a way to determine the origin of the copper in certain artifacts
(C) resolve a dispute concerning the analysis of copper ore
(D) describe the deficiencies of a currently used method of chemical analysis of certain metals
(E) offer an interpretation of the archaeological record of the Bronze Age

22. The author first mentions the addition of flux during smelting (lines 18-21) in order to

(A) give a reason for the failure of elemental composition studies to determine ore sources
(B) illustrate differences between various Bronze Age civilizations
(C) show the need for using high smelting temperatures
(D) illustrate the uniformity of lead isotope composition
(E) explain the success of copper isotope composition analysis

23. The author suggests which of the following about a Bronze Age artifact containing high concentrations of cobalt or zinc?

(A) It could not be reliably tested for its elemental composition.
(B) It could not be reliably tested for its copper isotope composition.
(C) It could not be reliably tested for its lead isotope composition.
(D) It could have been manufactured from ore from any one of a variety of sources.
(E) It could have been produced by the addition of other metals during the processing of the copper ore.

GO ON TO THE NEXT PAGE.

24. According to the passage, possible sources of the lead found in a copper or bronze artifact include which of the following?

    I. The copper ore used to manufacture the artifact
    II. Flux added during processing of the copper ore
    III. Other metal added during processing of the copper ore

(A) I only
(B) II only
(C) III only
(D) II and III only
(E) I, II, and III

25. The author rejects copper as the "ideal choice" mentioned in line 33 because

(A) the concentration of copper in Bronze Age artifacts varies
(B) elements other than copper may be introduced during smelting
(C) the isotopic composition of copper changes during smelting
(D) among common copper ores, differences in copper isotope composition are too small
(E) within a single source of copper ore, copper isotope composition can vary substantially

26. The author makes which of the following statements about lead isotope composition?

(A) It often varies from one copper-ore source to another.
(B) It sometimes varies over short distances in a single copper-ore source.
(C) It can vary during the testing of artifacts, producing a measurement error.
(D) It frequently changes during smelting and roasting.
(E) It may change when artifacts are buried for thousands of years.

27. It can be inferred from the passage that the use of flux in processing copper ore can alter the lead isotope composition of the resulting metal EXCEPT when

(A) there is a smaller concentration of lead in the flux than in the copper ore
(B) the concentration of lead in the flux is equivalent to that of the lead in the ore
(C) some of the lead in the flux evaporates during processing
(D) any lead in the flux has the same isotopic composition as the lead in the ore
(E) other metals are added during processing

GO ON TO THE NEXT PAGE.

Each question below consists of a word printed in capital letters, followed by five lettered words or phrases. Choose the lettered word or phrase that is most nearly <u>opposite</u> in meaning to the word in capital letters.

Since some of the questions require you to distinguish fine shades of meaning, be sure to consider all the choices before deciding which one is best.

28. MUTTER: (A) please oneself
(B) resolve conflict   (C) speak distinctly
(D) digress randomly   (E) omit willingly

29. TRANSPARENT: (A) indelicate   (B) neutral
(C) opaque   (D) somber   (E) tangible

30. ENSEMBLE: (A) complement   (B) cacophony
(C) coordination   (D) preface   (E) solo

31. RETAIN: (A) allocate   (B) distract
(C) relegate   (D) discard   (E) misplace

32. RADIATE: (A) approach   (B) cool
(C) absorb   (D) tarnish   (E) vibrate

33. EPICURE:
(A) a person ignorant about art
(B) a person dedicated to a cause
(C) a person motivated by greed
(D) a person indifferent to food
(E) a person insensitive to emotions

34. PREVARICATION: (A) tact   (B) consistency
(C) veracity   (D) silence   (E) proof

*35. AMORTIZE:
(A) loosen
(B) denounce
(C) suddenly increase one's indebtedness
(D) wisely cause to flourish
(E) grudgingly make provision for

36. EMACIATION: (A) invigoration
(B) glorification   (C) amelioration
(D) inundation   (E) magnification

37. UNALLOYED: (A) destabilized
(B) unregulated   (C) assimilated
(D) adulterated   (E) condensed

38. MINATORY: (A) reassuring   (B) genuine
(C) creative   (D) obvious   (E) awkward

STOP

IF YOU FINISH BEFORE TIME IS CALLED, YOU MAY CHECK YOUR WORK ON THIS SECTION ONLY.
DO NOT TURN TO ANY OTHER SECTION IN THE TEST.

SECTION 2

Time—30 minutes

30 Questions

Numbers: All numbers used are real numbers.

Figures: Position of points, angles, regions, etc. can be assumed to be in the order shown; and angle measures can be assumed to be positive.

Lines shown as straight can be assumed to be straight.

Figures can be assumed to lie in a plane unless otherwise indicated.

Figures that accompany questions are intended to provide information useful in answering the questions. However, unless a note states that a figure is drawn to scale, you should solve these problems NOT by estimating sizes by sight or by measurement, but by using your knowledge of mathematics (see Example 2 below).

Directions: Each of the Questions 1-15 consists of two quantities, one in Column A and one in Column B. You are to compare the two quantities and choose

A if the quantity in Column A is greater;
B if the quantity in Column B is greater;
C if the two quantities are equal;
D if the relationship cannot be determined from the information given.

Note: Since there are only four choices, NEVER MARK (E).

Common Information: In a question, information concerning one or both of the quantities to be compared is centered above the two columns. A symbol that appears in both columns represents the same thing in Column A as it does in Column B.

	Column A	Column B	Sample Answers
Example 1:	2×6	$2 + 6$	● Ⓑ Ⓒ Ⓓ Ⓔ

Examples 2-4 refer to $\triangle PQR$.

	Column A	Column B	Sample Answers
Example 2:	PN	NQ	Ⓐ Ⓑ Ⓒ ● Ⓔ

(since equal measures cannot be assumed, even though PN and NQ appear equal)

	Column A	Column B	Sample Answers
Example 3:	x	y	Ⓐ ● Ⓒ Ⓓ Ⓔ

(since N is between P and Q)

	Column A	Column B	Sample Answers
Example 4:	$w + z$	180	Ⓐ Ⓑ ● Ⓓ Ⓔ

(since PQ is a straight line)

GO ON TO THE NEXT PAGE.

A if the quantity in Column A is greater;
B if the quantity in Column B is greater;
C if the two quantities are equal;
D if the relationship cannot be determined from the information given.

	Column A	Column B

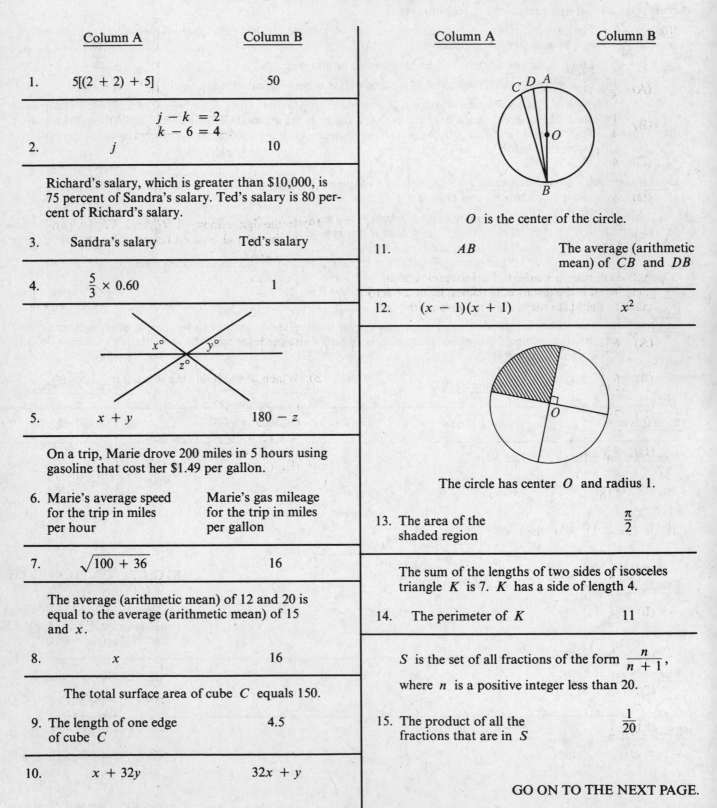

1. $5[(2 + 2) + 5]$ — 50

$$j - k = 2$$
$$k - 6 = 4$$

2. j — 10

Richard's salary, which is greater than $10,000, is 75 percent of Sandra's salary. Ted's salary is 80 percent of Richard's salary.

3. Sandra's salary — Ted's salary

4. $\frac{5}{3} \times 0.60$ — 1

5. $x + y$ — $180 - z$

On a trip, Marie drove 200 miles in 5 hours using gasoline that cost her $1.49 per gallon.

6. Marie's average speed for the trip in miles per hour — Marie's gas mileage for the trip in miles per gallon

7. $\sqrt{100 + 36}$ — 16

The average (arithmetic mean) of 12 and 20 is equal to the average (arithmetic mean) of 15 and x.

8. x — 16

The total surface area of cube C equals 150.

9. The length of one edge of cube C — 4.5

10. $x + 32y$ — $32x + y$

	Column A	Column B

O is the center of the circle.

11. AB — The average (arithmetic mean) of CB and DB

12. $(x - 1)(x + 1)$ — x^2

The circle has center O and radius 1.

13. The area of the shaded region — $\frac{\pi}{2}$

The sum of the lengths of two sides of isosceles triangle K is 7. K has a side of length 4.

14. The perimeter of K — 11

S is the set of all fractions of the form $\frac{n}{n + 1}$, where n is a positive integer less than 20.

15. The product of all the fractions that are in S — $\frac{1}{20}$

GO ON TO THE NEXT PAGE.

200

16. $\dfrac{5}{\frac{5}{4}} =$

   (A) $\dfrac{1}{5}$

   (B) $\dfrac{1}{4}$

   (C) 4

   (D) 5

   (E) $\dfrac{25}{4}$

17. A 12-inch ruler is marked off in sixteenths of an inch. What is the distance, in inches, from the zero mark to the 111th mark after the zero mark?

   (A) $6\dfrac{1}{4}$

   (B) $6\dfrac{15}{16}$

   (C) $7\dfrac{3}{4}$

   (D) $9\dfrac{1}{4}$

   (E) $11\dfrac{1}{16}$

18. If $(2x - 1)^2 = 0$, then $x =$

   (A) $-\dfrac{1}{4}$

   (B) $-\dfrac{1}{2}$

   (C) 0

   (D) $\dfrac{1}{2}$

   (E) $\dfrac{1}{4}$

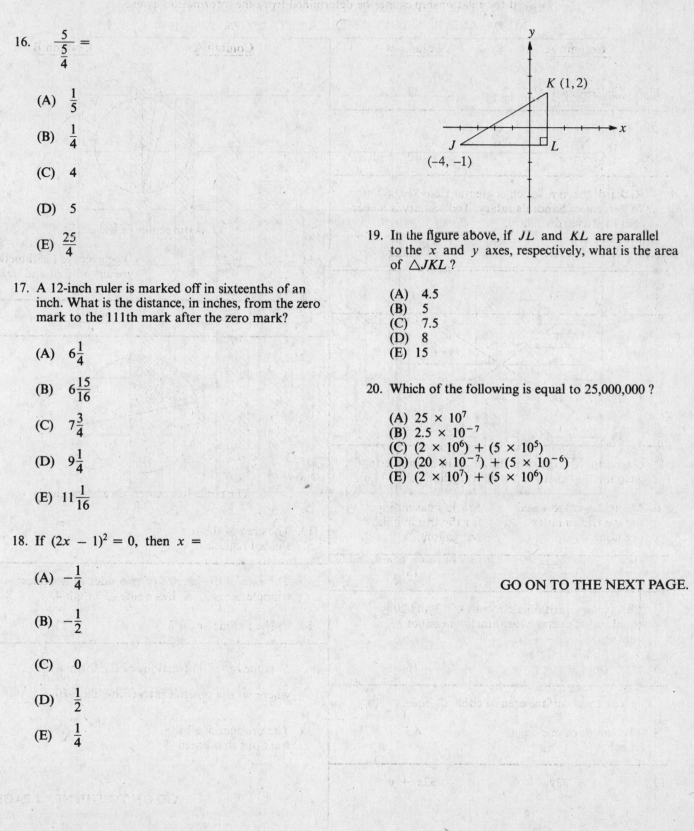

19. In the figure above, if JL and KL are parallel to the x and y axes, respectively, what is the area of $\triangle JKL$?

   (A) 4.5
   (B) 5
   (C) 7.5
   (D) 8
   (E) 15

20. Which of the following is equal to 25,000,000 ?

   (A) 25×10^7
   (B) 2.5×10^{-7}
   (C) $(2 \times 10^6) + (5 \times 10^5)$
   (D) $(20 \times 10^{-7}) + (5 \times 10^{-6})$
   (E) $(2 \times 10^7) + (5 \times 10^6)$

GO ON TO THE NEXT PAGE.

Questions 21-25 refer to the following graph. In these questions, all references to *charges* should be interpreted as the *average annual charges* shown on the graph.

AVERAGE ANNUAL TOTAL CHARGES* FOR UNDERGRADUATE TUITION,
ROOM, AND BOARD AT AMERICAN COLLEGES, 1974 - 1984

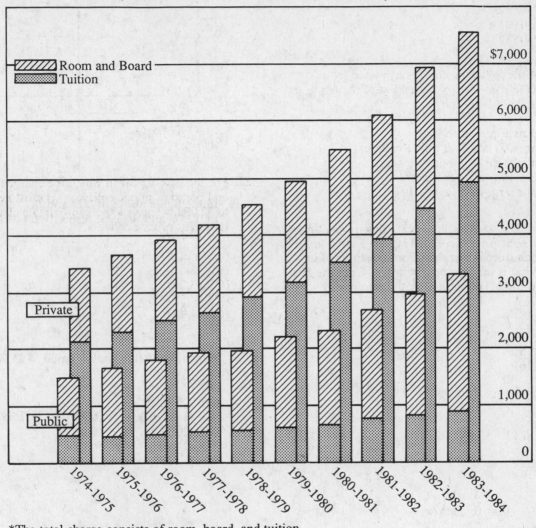

*The total charge consists of room, board, and tuition.

Note: Drawn to scale.

GO ON TO THE NEXT PAGE.

21. In which school year shown was the total charge for undergraduate tuition, room, and board at public colleges most nearly equal to $3,000 ?

    (A) 1983-1984
    (B) 1982-1983
    (C) 1981-1982
    (D) 1980-1981
    (E) 1979-1980

22. Which of the following charges increased by less than $1,000 from the first to the last of the ten years represented on the graph?

    (A) Tuition at public colleges
    (B) Room and board at public colleges
    (C) Total charge at public colleges
    (D) Tuition at private colleges
    (E) Total charge at private colleges

23. For how many of the school years shown was the total charge at private colleges at least $3,000 more than the total charge at public colleges?

    (A) Two
    (B) Three
    (C) Four
    (D) Five
    (E) Six

24. In the 1978-1979 school year, the ratio of the total charge at private colleges to the total charge at public colleges was closest to

    (A) $\frac{5}{3}$

    (B) $\frac{9}{5}$

    (C) $\frac{2}{1}$

    (D) $\frac{9}{4}$

    (E) $\frac{3}{1}$

25. For the school year in which the charge for room and board at public colleges was most nearly equal to $2,000, what was the approximate charge for tuition at private colleges?

    (A) $750
    (B) $3,500
    (C) $3,900
    (D) $4,500
    (E) $4,900

GO ON TO THE NEXT PAGE.

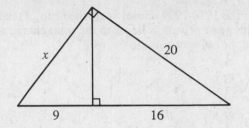

26. What is the value of x in the figure above?

(A) 12
(B) 12.5
(C) 15
(D) $9\sqrt{3}$
(E) 18

27. The number 10^{30} is divisible by all of the following EXCEPT

(A) 250
(B) 125
(C) 32
(D) 16
(E) 6

28. If $3x + 1$ represents an odd integer, which of the following represents the next larger odd integer?

(A) $3(x + 1)$
(B) $3(x + 2)$
(C) $3(x + 3)$
(D) $3x + 2$
(E) $3(x + 2) + 1$

29. In the sequence of numbers $x_1, x_2, x_3, x_4, x_5,$ each number after the first is twice the preceding number. If $x_5 - x_1$ is 20, what is the value of x_1?

(A) $\frac{4}{3}$

(B) $\frac{5}{4}$

(C) 2

(D) $\frac{5}{2}$

(E) 4

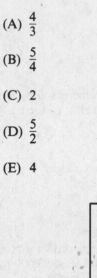

30. The rectangular garden represented in the figure above, with dimensions x feet by y feet, is surrounded by a walkway 2 feet wide. Which of the following represents the area of the walkway, in square feet?

(A) $2x + 2y + 4$
(B) $2x + 2y + 16$
(C) $4x + 4y + 8$
(D) $4x + 4y + 16$
(E) $4x + 4y + 32$

STOP

IF YOU FINISH BEFORE TIME IS CALLED, YOU MAY CHECK YOUR WORK ON THIS SECTION ONLY.
DO NOT TURN TO ANY OTHER SECTION IN THE TEST.

Section 3 starts on page 206.

SECTION 3

Time—30 minutes

30 Questions

Numbers: All numbers used are real numbers.

Figures: Position of points, angles, regions, etc. can be assumed to be in the order shown; and angle measures can be assumed to be positive.

Lines shown as straight can be assumed to be straight.

Figures can be assumed to lie in a plane unless otherwise indicated.

Figures that accompany questions are intended to provide information useful in answering the questions. However, unless a note states that a figure is drawn to scale, you should solve these problems NOT by estimating sizes by sight or by measurement, but by using your knowledge of mathematics (see Example 2 below).

Directions: Each of the <u>Questions 1-15</u> consists of two quantities, one in Column A and one in Column B. You are to compare the two quantities and choose

     A if the quantity in Column A is greater;
     B if the quantity in Column B is greater;
     C if the two quantities are equal;
     D if the relationship cannot be determined from the information given.

Note: Since there are only four choices, **NEVER MARK (E).**

Common Information: In a question, information concerning one or both of the quantities to be compared is centered above the two columns. A symbol that appears in both columns represents the same thing in Column A as it does in Column B.

	Column A	Column B	Sample Answers
Example 1:	2×6	$2 + 6$	● Ⓑ Ⓒ Ⓓ Ⓔ

Examples 2-4 refer to △ PQR.

	Column A	Column B	Sample Answers
Example 2:	PN	NQ	Ⓐ Ⓑ Ⓒ ● Ⓔ

(since equal measures cannot be assumed, even though PN and NQ appear equal)

	Column A	Column B	Sample Answers
Example 3:	x	y	Ⓐ ● Ⓒ Ⓓ Ⓔ

(since N is between P and Q)

	Column A	Column B	Sample Answers
Example 4:	$w + z$	180	Ⓐ Ⓑ ● Ⓓ Ⓔ

(since PQ is a straight line)

GO ON TO THE NEXT PAGE.

A if the quantity in Column A is greater;
B if the quantity in Column B is greater;
C if the two quantities are equal;
D if the relationship cannot be determined from the information given.

Column A	Column B

Each •——• represents a connection and
each • represents a joint.

1. The total number of   The total number of
   joints   connections

$$y = \frac{3x}{4}, \ x = \frac{2z}{3}, \ \text{and} \ z = 20.$$

2. y 11

3. The length of minor   The length of minor
   arc WX of the circle   arc YZ of the circle

4. 0.203×10^2 2.03×10

5.   40 percent of $250   80 percent of $125

Column A	Column B

$$x \neq 0$$

6. $3x^2$ $(3x)^2$

7. The greatest prime   The greatest prime
   factor of 15   factor of 14

8. The total savings on $1.80
   20 gallons of gasoline
   purchased for $1.169
   per gallon instead of
   $1.259 per gallon.

Three ships, X, Y, and Z, are near the equator.
X is 8 miles due west of Z, and Y is 7 miles due
north of Z.

9. The distance between   9 miles
   X and Y

10. AB BC

A retail business has determined that its net
income, in terms of x, the number of items
sold, is given by the expression $x^2 + x - 380$.

11. The number of items   10
    that must be sold for
    the net income to be
    zero

GO ON TO THE NEXT PAGE.

207

A if the quantity in Column A is greater;
B if the quantity in Column B is greater;
C if the two quantities are equal;
D if the relationship cannot be determined from the information given.

	Column A	Column B		Column A	Column B

Rectangular region R has area 30.

12. The perimeter of R — 25

$$x^2 = 16$$
$$y^3 = 64$$

14. x — y

$x < 90$

13. y — 70

15. $\dfrac{2^{30} - 2^{29}}{2}$ — 2^{28}

GO ON TO THE NEXT PAGE.

Directions: Each of the Questions 16-30 has five answer choices. For each of these questions, select the best of the answer choices given.

16. A certain post office imposes a service charge of $0.75 per order on any money order in the amount of $25.00 or less, and $1.00 per order on any money order in an amount from $25.01 through $700.00. If Dan purchases 3 money orders in the amounts of $18.25, $25.00, and $127.50, what is the total service charge for his money orders?

(A) $1.75
(B) $2.25
(C) $2.50
(D) $2.75
(E) $3.00

17. If $\frac{1}{4}(1 - x) = \frac{1}{16}$, then $x =$

(A) $\frac{15}{64}$

(B) $\frac{1}{4}$

(C) $\frac{3}{4}$

(D) $\frac{15}{16}$

(E) 4

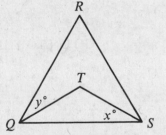

Note: Figure not drawn to scale.

18. In the figure above, QRS is an equilateral triangle and QTS is an isosceles triangle. If $x = 47$, what is the value of y?

(A) 13
(B) 23
(C) 30
(D) 47
(E) 53

19. $\frac{m + n}{4 + 5} =$

(A) $\frac{m + n}{4} + \frac{m + n}{5}$

(B) $\frac{m + n}{9} + \frac{m + n}{9}$

(C) $\frac{m}{5} + \frac{n}{4}$

(D) $\frac{m}{4} + \frac{n}{5}$

(E) $\frac{m}{9} + \frac{n}{9}$

20. What is the circumference of a circle with radius 8 ?

(A) $\frac{8}{\pi}$

(B) $\frac{16}{\pi}$

(C) 8π

(D) 16π

(E) 64π

GO ON TO THE NEXT PAGE.

Questions 21-25 refer to the following graph.

FOREIGN TRADE OF COUNTRY *X*, 1964-1980
(in United States dollars)

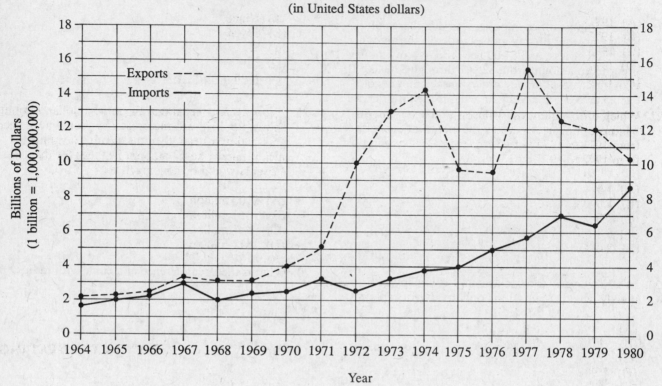

Note: Drawn to scale.

GO ON TO THE NEXT PAGE.

21. For which year shown on the graph did exports exceed the previous year's exports by the greatest dollar amount?

   (A) 1972
   (B) 1973
   (C) 1975
   (D) 1977
   (E) 1980

22. Which of the following is closest to the amount, in billions of dollars, by which the increase in exports from 1971 to 1972 exceeds the increase in exports from 1972 to 1973 ?

   (A) 1.9
   (B) 3.9
   (C) 5.0
   (D) 6.1
   (E) 8.0

23. In 1974 the dollar value of imports was approximately what percent of the dollar value of exports?

   (A)   4%
   (B) 17%
   (C) 27%
   (D) 79%
   (E) 367%

24. For how many years shown on the graph did exports exceed imports by more than 5 billion dollars?

   (A) Nine
   (B) Seven
   (C) Six
   (D) Five
   (E) Four

25. If it were discovered that the import dollar amount shown for 1978 was incorrect and should have been $5.3 billion instead, then the average (arithmetic mean) import dollar amount per year for the 17 years would be how much less?

   (A) $100 million
   (B) $53 million
   (C) $47 million
   (D) $17 million
   (E) $7 million

GO ON TO THE NEXT PAGE.

26. On the number line, 1.4 is halfway between which of the following pairs of numbers?

(A) −1.4 and 2.4
(B) −1 and 2
(C) −0.3 and 3.1
(D) 0.15 and 1.55
(E) 0.4 and 1

27. If a and b are both positive even integers, which of the following must be even?

I. a^b

II. $(a + 1)^b$

III. $a^{(b + 1)}$

(A) I only
(B) II only
(C) I and II only
(D) I and III only
(E) I, II, and III

28. If t tablets cost c cents, then at this rate how many cents will 5 tablets cost?

(A) $5ct$

(B) $\dfrac{5c}{t}$

(C) $\dfrac{c}{5t}$

(D) $\dfrac{5t}{c}$

(E) $\dfrac{t}{5c}$

29. If a rectangular block that is 4 inches by 4 inches by 10 inches is placed inside a right circular cylinder of radius 3 inches and height 10 inches, the volume of the unoccupied portion of the cylinder is how many cubic inches?

(A) $6\pi − 16$
(B) $9\pi − 16$
(C) $160 − 30\pi$
(D) $60\pi − 160$
(E) $90\pi − 160$

$$x − y + z = 0$$
$$2x + y + 3z = 0$$

30. In the system of equations above, if $z \neq 0$, then the ratio of x to z is

(A) $-\dfrac{2}{1}$

(B) $-\dfrac{4}{3}$

(C) $-\dfrac{1}{2}$

(D) $\dfrac{3}{4}$

(E) $\dfrac{4}{3}$

STOP

IF YOU FINISH BEFORE TIME IS CALLED, YOU MAY CHECK YOUR WORK ON THIS SECTION ONLY.
DO NOT TURN TO ANY OTHER SECTION IN THE TEST.

Section 4 starts on page 215.

NO TEST MATERIAL ON THIS PAGE

SECTION 4

Time—30 minutes

38 Questions

Directions: Each sentence below has one or two blanks, each blank indicating that something has been omitted. Beneath the sentence are five lettered words or sets of words. Choose the word or set of words for each blank that best fits the meaning of the sentence as a whole.

1. Because it is ------- to ------- all the business costs related to employee discontent, an accurate estimate of the magnitude of these costs is not easily calculated.

    (A) difficult. .measure
    (B) impossible. .justify
    (C) improper. .overlook
    (D) useless. .discover
    (E) necessary. .pinpoint

2. Consider the universal cannibalism of the sea, all of whose creatures ------- one another.

    (A) hide from
    (B) ferret out
    (C) prey on
    (D) glide among
    (E) compete against

3. How could words, confined as they individually are to certain ------- meanings specified in a dictionary, eventually come, when combined in groups, to create obscurity and actually to prevent thought from being -------?

    (A) indefinite. .articulated
    (B) conventional. .conceivable
    (C) unlikely. .classified
    (D) archaic. .expressed
    (E) precise. .communicable

4. Even though they tended to be ------- strangers, fifteenth-century Europeans did not automatically associate ------- and danger.

    (A) trusting of. .diversity
    (B) haughty with. .nonconformity
    (C) interested in. .enmity
    (D) antagonistic to. .rudeness
    (E) hostile to. .foreignness

5. The modern age is a permissive one in which things can be said explicitly, but the old tradition of ------- dies hard.

    (A) garrulousness
    (B) exaggeration
    (C) excoriation
    (D) bombast
    (E) euphemism

6. Although many findings of the Soviet and United States probes of Venus were complementary, the two sets of atmospheric results clearly could not be ------- without a major change of data or -------.

    (A) obtained. .experimentation
    (B) completed. .position
    (C) matched. .implementation
    (D) reconciled. .interpretation
    (E) produced. .falsification

7. While it is assumed that the mechanization of work has a ------- effect on the lives of workers, there is evidence available to suggest that, on the contrary, mechanization has served to ------- some of the traditional roles of women.

    (A) salutary. .improve
    (B) dramatic. .undermine
    (C) benign. .revise
    (D) debilitating. .weaken
    (E) revolutionary. .reinforce

GO ON TO THE NEXT PAGE.

Directions: In each of the following questions, a related pair of words or phrases is followed by five lettered pairs of words or phrases. Select the lettered pair that best expresses a relationship similar to that expressed in the original pair.

8. PILOT : SHIP :: (A) surveyor : landscape
(B) conductor : orchestra   (C) guard : stockade
   (D) actor : scene   (E) philosopher : inspiration

9. TOPSOIL : ERODE :: (A) leather : tan
(B) veneer : varnish   (C) roast : baste
   (D) grain : mash   (E) paint : peel

10. SCREEN : MOVIE :: (A) shelf : book
(B) frame : portrait   (C) shadow : object
   (D) stage : play   (E) score : performance

11. VOLCANO : LAVA ::
(A) geyser : water
(B) fault : tremor
(C) glacier : fissure
(D) avalanche : snow
(E) cavern : limestone

12. COGENT : CONVINCE ::
(A) irrational : disturb
(B) repugnant : repel
(C) dangerous : avoid
(D) eloquent : refine
(E) generous : appreciate

13. CHARY : CAUTION ::
(A) circumspect : recklessness
(B) imperturbable : composure
(C) meticulous : resourcefulness
(D) exigent : stability
(E) fortuitous : pluck

14. USURY : INTEREST ::
(A) fraud : property
(B) gouging : price
(C) monopoly : production
(D) foreclosure : mortgage
(E) embezzlement : savings

15. EPITHET : DISPARAGE ::
(A) abbreviation : proliferate
(B) hieroglyphic : mythologize
(C) diminutive : respect
(D) code : simplify
(E) alias : mislead

16. OFFENSE : PECCADILLO ::
(A) envy : resentment
(B) quarrel : tiff
(C) affinity : wish
(D) depression : regret
(E) homesickness : nostalgia

GO ON TO THE NEXT PAGE.

Directions: Each passage in this group is followed by questions based on its content. After reading a passage, choose the best answer to each question. Answer all questions following a passage on the basis of what is stated or implied in that passage.

Since the Hawaiian Islands have never been connected to other land masses, the great variety of plants in Hawaii must be a result of the long-distance dispersal
Line of seeds, a process that requires both a method of trans-
(5) port and an equivalence between the ecology of the source area and that of the recipient area.

There is some dispute about the method of transport involved. Some biologists argue that ocean and air currents are responsible for the transport of plant seeds
(10) to Hawaii. Yet the results of flotation experiments and the low temperatures of air currents cast doubt on these hypotheses. More probable is bird transport, either externally, by accidental attachment of the seeds to feathers, or internally, by the swallowing of fruit and
(15) subsequent excretion of the seeds. While it is likely that fewer varieties of plant seeds have reached Hawaii externally than internally, more varieties are known to be adapted to external than to internal transport.

17. The author of the passage is primarily concerned with

(A) discussing different approaches biologists have taken to testing theories about the distribution of plants in Hawaii
(B) discussing different theories about the transport of plant seeds to Hawaii
(C) discussing the extent to which air currents are responsible for the dispersal of plant seeds to Hawaii
(D) resolving a dispute about the adaptability of plant seeds to bird transport
(E) resolving a dispute about the ability of birds to carry plant seeds long distances

18. The author mentions the results of flotation experiments on plant seeds (lines 10-12) most probably in order to

(A) support the claim that the distribution of plants in Hawaii is the result of the long-distance dispersal of seeds
(B) lend credibility to the thesis that air currents provide a method of transport for plant seeds to Hawaii
(C) suggest that the long-distance dispersal of seeds is a process that requires long periods of time
(D) challenge the claim that ocean currents are responsible for the transport of plant seeds to Hawaii
(E) refute the claim that Hawaiian flora evolved independently from flora in other parts of the world

19. It can be inferred from information in the passage that the existence in alpine regions of Hawaii of a plant species that also grows in the southwestern United States would justify which of the following conclusions?

(A) The ecology of the southwestern United States is similar in important respects to the ecology of alpine regions of Hawaii.
(B) There are ocean currents that flow from the southwestern United States to Hawaii.
(C) The plant species discovered in Hawaii must have traveled from the southwestern United States only very recently.
(D) The plant species discovered in Hawaii reached there by attaching to the feathers of birds migrating from the southwestern United States.
(E) The plant species discovered in Hawaii is especially well adapted to transport over long distances.

20. The passage supplies information for answering which of the following questions?

(A) Why does successful long-distance dispersal of plant seeds require an equivalence between the ecology of the source area and that of the recipient area?
(B) Why are more varieties of plant seeds adapted to external rather than to internal bird transport?
(C) What varieties of plant seeds are birds that fly long distances most likely to swallow?
(D) What is a reason for accepting the long-distance dispersal of plant seeds as an explanation for the origin of Hawaiian flora?
(E) What evidence do biologists cite to argue that ocean and air currents are responsible for the transport of plant seeds to Hawaii?

GO ON TO THE NEXT PAGE.

A long-held view of the history of the English colonies that became the United States has been that England's policy toward these colonies before 1763 was dictated by commercial interests and that a change to a
(5) more imperial policy, dominated by expansionist militarist objectives, generated the tensions that ultimately led to the American Revolution. In a recent study, Stephen Saunders Webb has presented a formidable challenge to this view. According to Webb, England
(10) already had a military imperial policy for more than a century before the American Revolution. He sees Charles II, the English monarch between 1660 and 1685, as the proper successor of the Tudor monarchs of the sixteenth century and of Oliver Cromwell, all of
(15) whom were bent on extending centralized executive power over England's possessions through the use of what Webb calls "garrison government." Garrison government allowed the colonists a legislative assembly, but real authority, in Webb's view, belonged to the
(20) colonial governor, who was appointed by the king and supported by the "garrison," that is, by the local contingent of English troops under the colonial governor's command.

   According to Webb, the purpose of garrison govern-
(25) ment was to provide military support for a royal policy designed to limit the power of the upper classes in the American colonies. Webb argues that the colonial legislative assemblies represented the interests not of the common people but of the colonial upper classes, a
(30) coalition of merchants and nobility who favored self-rule and sought to elevate legislative authority at the expense of the executive. It was, according to Webb, the colonial governors who favored the small farmer, opposed the plantation system, and tried through taxation to break
(35) up large holdings of land. Backed by the military presence of the garrison, these governors tried to prevent the gentry and merchants, allied in the colonial assemblies, from transforming colonial America into a capitalistic oligarchy.

(40)   Webb's study illuminates the political alignments that existed in the colonies in the century prior to the American Revolution, but his view of the crown's use of the military as an instrument of colonial policy is not entirely convincing. England during the seventeenth
(45) century was not noted for its military achievements. Cromwell did mount England's most ambitious overseas military expedition in more than a century, but it proved to be an utter failure. Under Charles II, the English army was too small to be a major instrument
(50) of government. Not until the war with France in 1697 did William III persuade Parliament to create a professional standing army, and Parliament's price for doing so was to keep the army under tight legislative control. While it may be true that the crown attempted to curtail
(55) the power of the colonial upper classes, it is hard to imagine how the English army during the seventeenth century could have provided significant military support for such a policy.

21. The passage can best be described as a

   (A) survey of the inadequacies of a conventional viewpoint
   (B) reconciliation of opposing points of view
   (C) summary and evaluation of a recent study
   (D) defense of a new thesis from anticipated objections
   (E) review of the subtle distinctions between apparently similar views

22. The passage suggests that the view referred to in lines 1-7 argued that

   (A) the colonial governors were sympathetic to the demands of the common people
   (B) Charles II was a pivotal figure in the shift of English monarchs toward a more imperial policy in their governorship of the American colonies
   (C) the American Revolution was generated largely out of a conflict between the colonial upper classes and an alliance of merchants and small farmers
   (D) the military did not play a major role as an instrument of colonial policy until 1763
   (E) the colonial legislative assemblies in the colonies had little influence over the colonial governors

23. It can be inferred from the passage that Webb would be most likely to agree with which of the following statements regarding garrison government?

   (A) Garrison government gave legislative assemblies in the colonies relatively little authority, compared to the authority that it gave the colonial governors.
   (B) Garrison government proved relatively ineffective until it was used by Charles II to curb the power of colonial legislatures.
   (C) Garrison government became a less viable colonial policy as the English Parliament began to exert tighter legislative control over the English military.
   (D) Oliver Cromwell was the first English ruler to make use of garrison government on a large scale.
   (E) The creation of a professional standing army in England in 1697 actually weakened garrison government by diverting troops from the garrisons stationed in the American colonies.

GO ON TO THE NEXT PAGE.

24. According to the passage, Webb views Charles II as the "proper successor" (line 13) of the Tudor monarchs and Cromwell because Charles II

(A) used colonial tax revenues to fund overseas military expeditions
(B) used the military to extend executive power over the English colonies
(C) wished to transform the American colonies into capitalistic oligarchies
(D) resisted the English Parliament's efforts to exert control over the military
(E) allowed the American colonists to use legislative assemblies as a forum for resolving grievances against the crown

25. Which of the following, if true, would most seriously weaken the author's assertion in lines 54-58 ?

(A) Because they were poorly administered, Cromwell's overseas military expeditions were doomed to failure.
(B) Because it relied primarily on the symbolic presence of the military, garrison government could be effectively administered with a relatively small number of troops.
(C) Until early in the seventeenth century, no professional standing army in Europe had performed effectively in overseas military expeditions.
(D) Many of the colonial governors appointed by the crown were also commissioned army officers.
(E) Many of the English troops stationed in the American colonies were veterans of other overseas military expeditions.

26. According to Webb's view of colonial history, which of the following was (were) true of the merchants and nobility mentioned in line 30 ?

I. They were opposed to policies formulated by Charles II that would have transformed the colonies into capitalistic oligarchies.
II. They were opposed to attempts by the English crown to limit the power of the legislative assemblies.
III. They were united with small farmers in their opposition to the stationing of English troops in the colonies.

(A) I only
(B) II only
(C) I and II only
(D) II and III only
(E) I, II, and III

27. The author suggests that if William III had wanted to make use of the standing army mentioned in line 52 to administer garrison government in the American colonies, he would have had to

(A) make peace with France
(B) abolish the colonial legislative assemblies
(C) seek approval from the English Parliament
(D) appoint colonial governors who were more sympathetic to royal policy
(E) raise additional revenues by increasing taxation of large landholdings in the colonies

GO ON TO THE NEXT PAGE.

Each question below consists of a word printed in capital letters, followed by five lettered words or phrases. Choose the lettered word or phrase that is most nearly <u>opposite</u> in meaning to the word in capital letters.

Since some of the questions require you to distinguish fine shades of meaning, be sure to consider all the choices before deciding which one is best.

28. FLUCTUATE: (A) work for   (B) flow over
   (C) follow from   (D) remain steady
   (E) cling together

29. PRECARIOUS: (A) safe   (B) covert
   (C) rescued   (D) revived   (E) pledged

30. FUMBLE: (A) organize neatly   (B) say clearly
   (C) prepare carefully   (D) handle adroitly
   (E) replace immediately

31. AUTHENTIC: (A) ordinary   (B) criminal
   (C) unattractive   (D) inexpensive   (E) bogus

32. COWER: (A) swiftly disappear
   (B) brazenly confront   (C) assuage
   (D) coast   (E) invert

33. PRISTINE: (A) ruthless   (B) seductive
   (C) coarse   (D) commonplace
   (E) contaminated

34. LAMBASTE: (A) permit   (B) prefer
   (C) extol   (D) smooth completely
   (E) support openly

35. VISCID: (A) bent   (B) prone   (C) cool
   (D) slick   (E) slight

36. TURPITUDE: (A) saintly behavior
   (B) clever conversation   (C) lively imagination
   (D) agitation   (E) lucidity

37. PHILISTINE: (A) perfectionist   (B) aesthete
   (C) iconoclast   (D) critic   (E) cynic

38. ODIUM: (A) ease   (B) fragrance
   (C) resignation   (D) eccentricity
   (E) infatuation

STOP

**IF YOU FINISH BEFORE TIME IS CALLED, YOU MAY CHECK YOUR WORK ON THIS SECTION ONLY.
DO NOT TURN TO ANY OTHER SECTION IN THE TEST.**

GENERAL TEST

A. Print and sign your full name in this box:

PRINT: _____

(LAST)   (FIRST)   (MIDDLE)

SIGN: _____

6. TITLE CODE

Copy this code in box 6 on your answer sheet. Then fill in the corresponding ovals exactly as shown.

Copy the Test Name and Form Code in box 7 on your answer sheet.

TEST NAME _General_

FORM CODE _GR90-16_

GRADUATE RECORD EXAMINATIONS GENERAL TEST

B. You will have 3 hours and 30 minutes in which to work on this test, which consists of seven sections. During the time allowed for one section, you may work only on that section. The time allowed for each section is 30 minutes.

Each of your scores will be determined by the number of questions for which you select the best answer from the choices given. Questions for which you mark no answer or more than one answer are not counted in scoring. Nothing is subtracted from a score if you answer a question incorrectly. Therefore, to maximize your scores it is better for you to guess at an answer than not to respond at all.

You are advised to work as rapidly as you can without losing accuracy. Do not spend too much time on questions that are too difficult for you. Go on to the other questions and come back to the difficult ones later.

There are several different types of questions; you will find special directions for each type in the test itself. Be sure you understand the directions before attempting to answer any questions.

YOU MUST INDICATE ALL YOUR ANSWERS ON THE SEPARATE ANSWER SHEET. No credit will be given for anything written in this examination book, but you may write in the book as much as you wish to work out your answers. After you have decided on your response to a question, fill in the corresponding oval on the answer sheet. BE SURE THAT EACH MARK IS DARK AND COMPLETELY FILLS THE OVAL. Mark only one answer to each question. No credit will be given for multiple answers. Erase all stray marks. If you change an answer, be sure that all previous marks are erased completely. Incomplete erasures may be read as intended answers. Do not be concerned if your answer sheet provides spaces for more answers than there are questions in each section.

Example:

What city is the capital of France?

(A) Rome
(B) Paris
(C) London
(D) Cairo
(E) Oslo

Sample Answer

BEST ANSWER PROPERLY MARKED

IMPROPER MARKS

Some or all of the passages for this test have been adapted from published material to provide the examinee with significant problems for analysis and evaluation. To make the passages suitable for testing purposes, the style, content, or point of view of the original may have been altered in some cases. The ideas contained in the passages do not necessarily represent the opinions of the Graduate Record Examinations Board or Educational Testing Service.

DO NOT OPEN YOUR TEST BOOK UNTIL YOU ARE TOLD TO DO SO.

FOR GENERAL TEST, FORM GR90-16 ONLY
Answer Key and Percentages* of Examinees Answering Each Question Correctly

VERBAL ABILITY						QUANTITATIVE ABILITY					
Section 1			Section 4			Section 2			Section 3		
Number	Answer	P+	Number	Answer	P+	Number	Answer	P+	Number	Answer	P+
1	A	94	1	A	90	1	B	95	1	A	93
2	C	91	2	C	94	2	A	83	2	B	84
3	A	77	3	E	69	3	A	81	3	C	84
4	C	66	4	E	71	4	C	70	4	C	81
5	A	61	5	E	51	5	C	78	5	C	82
6	E	53	6	D	58	6	D	77	6	B	83
7	E	27	7	E	36	7	B	74	7	B	76
8	E	82	8	B	86	8	A	71	8	C	74
9	B	83	9	E	91	9	A	72	9	A	76
10	E	65	10	D	80	10	D	83	10	D	64
11	C	81	11	A	79	11	A	74	11	A	75
12	D	53	12	B	42	12	B	72	12	D	49
13	A	47	13	B	37	13	B	62	13	B	66
14	C	45	14	B	30	14	D	24	14	D	19
15	D	33	15	E	27	15	C	19	15	C	20
16	B	28	16	B	45	16	C	84	16	C	93
17	D	49	17	B	86	17	B	80	17	C	78
18	B	47	18	D	82	18	D	72	18	A	66
19	B	37	19	A	47	19	C	71	19	E	68
20	B	68	20	D	61	20	E	63	20	D	64
21	B	60	21	C	58	21	B	91	21	D	89
22	A	72	22	D	37	22	A	89	22	A	81
23	D	37	23	A	68	23	C	74	23	C	71
24	E	58	24	B	69	24	D	61	24	B	76
25	D	46	25	B	49	25	C	43	25	A	36
26	A	61	26	B	40	26	C	60	26	C	60
27	D	39	27	C	55	27	E	52	27	D	50
28	C	93	28	D	94	28	A	55	28	B	45
29	C	81	29	A	78	29	A	44	29	E	41
30	E	79	30	D	80	30	D	36	30	B	41
31	D	80	31	E	81						
32	C	79	32	B	84						
33	D	33	33	E	44						
34	C	31	34	C	36						
35	C	34	35	D	37						
36	A	22	36	A	38						
37	D	29	37	B	30						
38	A	17	38	E	22						

*Estimated P+ for the group of examinees who took the GRE General Test in a recent three-year period.

SCORE CONVERSIONS FOR GRE GENERAL TEST, GR90-16

Raw Score	Scaled Score Verbal	Scaled Score Quantitative	Raw Score	Scaled Score Verbal	Scaled Score Quantitative
73-76	800		39	430	540
72	780		38	420	530
71	770		37	410	520
70	750		36	400	500
			35	390	490
69	740		34	380	480
68	730		33	370	470
67	720		32	360	460
66	710		31	360	450
65	700		30	350	440
64	690				
63	670		29	340	430
62	660		28	340	420
61	650		27	330	400
60	640	800	26	310	390
			25	300	380
59	630	800	24	290	370
58	620	800	23	280	360
57	610	780	22	270	350
56	600	760	21	270	340
55	590	740	20	260	330
54	580	730			
53	570	710	19	250	320
52	560	700	18	240	310
51	550	680	17	230	290
50	540	670	16	200	280
			15	200	270
49	530	660	14	200	250
48	520	640	13	200	240
47	510	630	12	200	220
46	490	620	11	200	210
45	480	610			
44	470	590	10	200	200
43	460	580	9	200	200
42	450	570	8	200	200
41	450	560	0-7	200	200
40	440	550			

NO TEST MATERIAL ON THIS PAGE

THE GRADUATE RECORD
EXAMINATIONS®

GRE®

ETS®

General Test

Do not break the seal
until you are told to do so.

The contents of this test are confidential.
Disclosure or reproduction of any portion
of it is prohibited.

THIS TEST BOOK MUST NOT BE TAKEN FROM THE ROOM.

SECTION 1

Time—30 minutes

30 Questions

Numbers: All numbers used are real numbers.

Figures: Position of points, angles, regions, etc. can be assumed to be in the order shown; and angle measures can be assumed to be positive.

Lines shown as straight can be assumed to be straight.

Figures can be assumed to lie in a plane unless otherwise indicated.

Figures that accompany questions are intended to provide information useful in answering the questions. However, unless a note states that a figure is drawn to scale, you should solve these problems NOT by estimating sizes by sight or by measurement, but by using your knowledge of mathematics (see Example 2 below).

Directions: Each of the Questions 1-15 consists of two quantities, one in Column A and one in Column B. You are to compare the two quantities and choose

A if the quantity in Column A is greater;
B if the quantity in Column B is greater;
C if the two quantities are equal;
D if the relationship cannot be determined from the information given.

Note: Since there are only four choices, NEVER MARK (E).

Common
Information: In a question, information concerning one or both of the quantities to be compared is centered above the two columns. A symbol that appears in both columns represents the same thing in Column A as it does in Column B.

	Column A	Column B	Sample Answers
Example 1:	2×6	$2 + 6$	● Ⓑ Ⓒ Ⓓ Ⓔ

Examples 2-4 refer to $\triangle PQR$.

Example 2:	PN	NQ	Ⓐ Ⓑ Ⓒ ● Ⓔ

(since equal measures cannot be assumed, even though PN and NQ appear equal)

Example 3:	x	y	Ⓐ ● Ⓒ Ⓓ Ⓔ

(since N is between P and Q)

Example 4:	$w + z$	180	Ⓐ Ⓑ ● Ⓓ Ⓔ

(since PQ is a straight line)

GO ON TO THE NEXT PAGE.

A if the quantity in Column A is greater;
B if the quantity in Column B is greater;
C if the two quantities are equal;
D if the relationship cannot be determined from the information given.

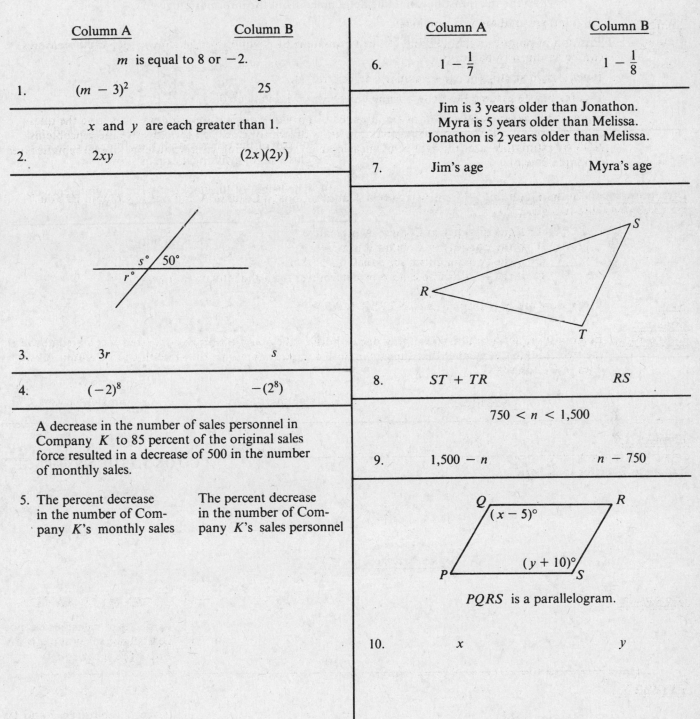

Column A   Column B

m is equal to 8 or -2.

1. $(m - 3)^2$ 25

x and y are each greater than 1.

2. $2xy$ $(2x)(2y)$

3. $3r$ s

4. $(-2)^8$ $-(2^8)$

A decrease in the number of sales personnel in Company K to 85 percent of the original sales force resulted in a decrease of 500 in the number of monthly sales.

5. The percent decrease   The percent decrease
    in the number of Com-   in the number of Com-
    pany K's monthly sales   pany K's sales personnel

Column A   Column B

6. $1 - \dfrac{1}{7}$ $1 - \dfrac{1}{8}$

Jim is 3 years older than Jonathon.
Myra is 5 years older than Melissa.
Jonathon is 2 years older than Melissa.

7.   Jim's age   Myra's age

8. $ST + TR$ RS

$750 < n < 1,500$

9. $1,500 - n$ $n - 750$

$PQRS$ is a parallelogram.

10. x y

GO ON TO THE NEXT PAGE.

227

A   if the quantity in Column A is greater;
B   if the quantity in Column B is greater;
C   if the two quantities are equal;
D   if the relationship cannot be determined from the information given.

Column A	Column B

$$\frac{x + 2y + z}{2} = y$$

11. x $-z$

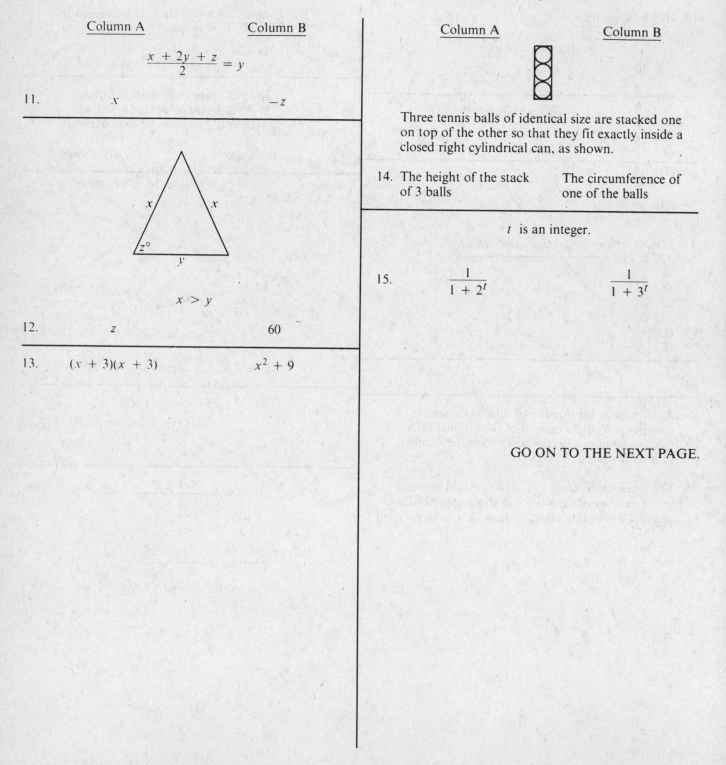

$$x > y$$

12. z 60

13. $(x + 3)(x + 3)$ $x^2 + 9$

Column A	Column B

Three tennis balls of identical size are stacked one on top of the other so that they fit exactly inside a closed right cylindrical can, as shown.

14.	The height of the stack of 3 balls	The circumference of one of the balls

t is an integer.

15. $\dfrac{1}{1 + 2^t}$ $\dfrac{1}{1 + 3^t}$

GO ON TO THE NEXT PAGE.

Directions: Each of the Questions 16-30 has five answer choices. For each of these questions, select the best of the answer choices given.

16. If $\frac{1}{6}n = \frac{1}{5}$, then $n =$

(A) $\frac{1}{30}$

(B) $\frac{5}{6}$

(C) $\frac{6}{5}$

(D) 6

(E) 30

17. If membership in the Elks Club increases from 120 to 150, what is the percent increase?

(A) 15%
(B) 25%
(C) 30%
(D) 40%
(E) 80%

18. The value of $\left(1 - \frac{5}{7}\right)\left(1 + \frac{3}{4}\right)$ is

(A) $\frac{1}{28}$

(B) $\frac{3}{14}$

(C) $\frac{9}{28}$

(D) $\frac{13}{28}$

(E) $\frac{1}{2}$

19. If the circumference of a circle is less than 10π, which of the following could be the area of the circle?

(A) 20π
(B) 25π
(C) 36π
(D) 81π
(E) 100π

20. If a, b, and c are consecutive positive integers and $a < b < c$, which of the following must be an odd integer?

(A) abc

(B) $a + b + c$

(C) $a + bc$

(D) $a(b + c)$

(E) $(a + b)(b + c)$

GO ON TO THE NEXT PAGE.

229

Questions 21-25 refer to the following graphs.

PHYSICIANS CLASSIFIED BY CATEGORY IN 1977

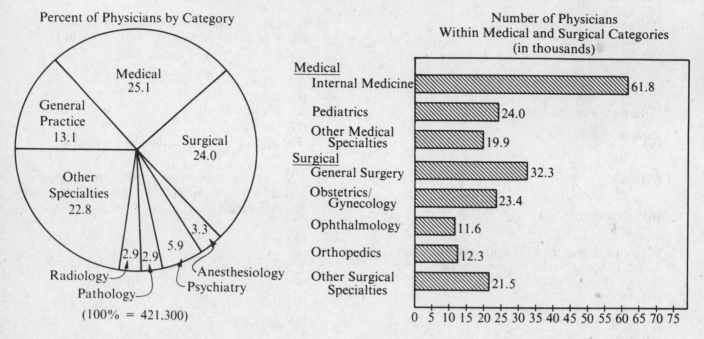

Percent of Physicians by Category

(100% = 421.300)

Number of Physicians
Within Medical and Surgical Categories
(in thousands)

21. Approximately what was the ratio of physicians in the surgical category to physicians in pathology?

    (A) 10 to 1
    (B) 8 to 1
    (C) 7 to 1
    (D) 5 to 6
    (E) 4 to 5

22. Approximately how many more physicians were in psychiatry than in radiology?

    (A) 3,000
    (B) 6,300
    (C) 12,600
    (D) 24,800
    (E) 37,000

23. Approximately how many of the physicians in the medical category were not in pediatrics?

    (A) 61,800
    (B) 76,000
    (C) 81,700
    (D) 92,600
    (E) 101,100

24. If there was a total of 334,000 physicians in 1970, what was the approximate percent increase in the number of physicians from 1970 to 1977 ?

    (A) 10%
    (B) 12%
    (C) 16%
    (D) 20%
    (E) 26%

25. In 1977, if twice as many anesthesiologists as orthopedists were sued for malpractice and 10 percent of the orthopedists were sued, approximately what percent of the anesthesiologists were sued?

    (A) 5%
    (B) 9%
    (C) 18%
    (D) 22%
    (E) 25%

GO ON TO THE NEXT PAGE.

26. If x can have only the values -3, 0, and 2, and y can have only the values -4, 2, and 3, what is the greatest possible value for $2x + y^2$?

(A) 13
(B) 15
(C) 16
(D) 20
(E) 22

27. If B is the midpoint of line segment AD and C is the midpoint of line segment BD, what is the value of $\frac{AB}{AC}$?

(A) $\frac{3}{4}$

(B) $\frac{2}{3}$

(C) $\frac{1}{2}$

(D) $\frac{1}{3}$

(E) $\frac{1}{4}$

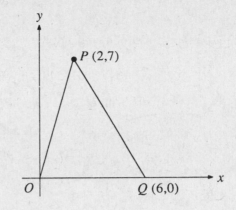

28. The area of $\triangle OPQ$ in the figure above is

(A) 6
(B) 12
(C) 14
(D) 21
(E) 42

29. What is the greatest positive integer n such that 2^n is a factor of 12^{10}?

(A) 10
(B) 12
(C) 16
(D) 20
(E) 60

30. For each of n people, Margie bought a hamburger and a soda at a restaurant. For each of n people, Paul bought 3 hamburgers and a soda at the same restaurant. If Margie spent a total of $5.40 and Paul spent a total of $12.60, how much did Paul spend just for hamburgers? (Assume that all hamburgers cost the same and all sodas cost the same.)

(A) $10.80
(B) $9.60
(C) $7.20
(D) $3.60
(E) $2.40

STOP

IF YOU FINISH BEFORE TIME IS CALLED, YOU MAY CHECK YOUR WORK ON THIS SECTION ONLY.
DO NOT TURN TO ANY OTHER SECTION IN THE TEST.

231

NO TEST MATERIAL ON THIS PAGE

Directions: Each sentence below has one or two blanks, each blank indicating that something has been omitted. Beneath the sentence are five lettered words or sets of words. Choose the word or set of words for each blank that best fits the meaning of the sentence as a whole.

1. Although economists have traditionally considered the district to be solely an agricultural one, the ------- of the inhabitants' occupations makes such a classification obsolete.

   (A) productivity   (B) diversity   (C) predictability
   (D) profitability   (E) stability

2. The author of this book ------- overlooks or minimizes some of the problems and shortcomings in otherwise highly successful foreign industries in order to ------- the points on which they excel and on which we might try to emulate them.

   (A) accidentally. .exaggerate
   (B) purposely. .emphasize
   (C) occasionally. .counterbalance
   (D) intentionally. .confuse
   (E) cleverly. .compound

3. Crosby's colleagues have never learned, at least not in time to avoid embarrassing themselves, that her occasional ------- air of befuddlement ------- a display of her formidable intelligence.

   (A) genuine. .dominates   (B) alert. .contradicts
   (C) acute. .precludes   (D) bogus. .presages
   (E) painstaking. .succeeds

4. To ensure the development and exploitation of a new technology, there must be a constant ------- of several nevertheless distinct activities.

   (A) interplay   (B) implementation
   (C) comprehending   (D) improvement
   (E) exploration

5. Some customs travel well; often, however, behavior that is considered the epitome of ------- at home is perceived as impossibly rude or, at the least, harmlessly bizarre abroad.

   (A) novelty   (B) eccentricity   (C) urbanity
   (D) coarseness   (E) tolerance

6. The ------- of the early Greek philosophers' attempts to explain the operations of the cosmos led certain later thinkers to inquire into the ------- of human reason.

   (A) difficulty. .origin
   (B) meaning. .supremacy
   (C) complexity. .reality
   (D) equivocations. .subtlety
   (E) failures. .efficacy

7. Ever prey to vagrant impulses that impelled him to ------- his talents on a host of unworthy projects, his very -------- nonetheless enhanced his reputation, for the sheer energy of his extravagance dazzled observers.

   (A) undermine. .enthusiasm
   (B) isolate. .selectiveness
   (C) display. .affability
   (D) squander. .dissipation
   (E) implicate. .genius

GO ON TO THE NEXT PAGE.

Directions: In each of the following questions, a related pair of words or phrases is followed by five lettered pairs of words or phrases. Select the lettered pair that best expresses a relationship similar to that expressed in the original pair.

8. MULTIPLY : DIVIDE ::
   (A) enumerate : count
   (B) speak : communicate
   (C) enter : leave
   (D) drive : ride
   (E) compute : estimate

9. RECLUSE : WITHDRAWN ::
   (A) isolationist : unreserved
   (B) pacifist : aggressive
   (C) miser : liberal
   (D) bigot : biased
   (E) procrastinator : unmanageable

10. CURATOR : ART ::
    (A) functionary : administration
    (B) archivist : documents
    (C) referee : laws
    (D) physician : research
    (E) raconteur : stories

*11. ABACUS : CALCULATE ::
    (A) organ : worship
    (B) patent : invent
    (C) calipers : regulate
    (D) manuscript : edit
    (E) sextant : navigate

12. STRAY : GROUP ::
    (A) miscalculate : solution
    (B) improvise : suggestion
    (C) slur : pronunciation
    (D) delete : change
    (E) digress : subject

13. ESCAPE : CAPTURE ::
    (A) warn : danger
    (B) immerse : dampness
    (C) feint : thrust
    (D) dodge : blow
    (E) invest : bankruptcy

14. LEVEE : RIVER ::
    (A) seam : fabric
    (B) corona : sun
    (C) cordon : crowd
    (D) petal : flower
    (E) moat : castle

15. MERCURIAL : MOOD ::
    (A) energetic : delirium
    (B) jovial : conviviality
    (C) fickle : affection
    (D) martial : anarchy
    (E) paranoid : suspicion

16. ENUNCIATE : WORDS ::
    (A) limn : lines
    (B) parse : sentences
    (C) hear : sounds
    (D) run : steps
    (E) stint : savings

GO ON TO THE NEXT PAGE.

Directions: Each passage in this group is followed by questions based on its content. After reading a passage, choose the best answer to each question. Answer all questions following a passage on the basis of what is stated or implied in that passage.

A serious critic has to comprehend the particular content, unique structure, and special meaning of a work of art. And here she faces a dilemma. The critic
Line must recognize the artistic element of uniqueness that
(5) requires subjective reaction; yet she must not be unduly prejudiced by such reactions. Her likes and dislikes are less important than what the work itself communicates, and her preferences may blind her to certain qualities of the work and thereby prevent an adequate under-
(10) standing of it. Hence, it is necessary that a critic develop a sensibility informed by familiarity with the history of art and aesthetic theory. On the other hand, it is insuffi- cient to treat the artwork solely historically, in relation to a fixed set of ideas or values. The critic's knowledge
(15) and training are, rather, a preparation of the cognitive and emotional abilities needed for an adequate personal response to an artwork's own particular qualities.

17. According to the author, a serious art critic may avoid being prejudiced by her subjective reactions if she

(A) treats an artwork in relation to a fixed set of ideas and values
(B) brings to her observation a knowledge of art history and aesthetic theory
(C) allows more time for the observation of each artwork
(D) takes into account the preferences of other art critics
(E) limits herself to that art with which she has adequate familiarity

18. The author implies that it is insufficient to treat a work of art solely historically because

(A) doing so would lead the critic into a dilemma
(B) doing so can blind the critic to some of the artwork's unique qualities
(C) doing so can insulate the critic from personally held beliefs
(D) subjective reactions can produce a biased response
(E) critics are not sufficiently familiar with art history

19. The passage suggests that the author would be most likely to agree with which of the following statements?

(A) Art speaks to the passions as well as to the intellect.
(B) Most works of art express unconscious wishes or desires.
(C) The best art is accessible to the greatest number of people.
(D) The art produced in the last few decades is of inferior quality.
(E) The meaning of art is a function of the social conditions in which it was produced.

20. The author's argument is developed primarily by the use of

(A) an attack on sentimentality
(B) an example of successful art criticism
(C) a critique of artists' training
(D) a warning against extremes in art criticism
(E) an analogy between art criticism and art production

GO ON TO THE NEXT PAGE.

Viruses, infectious particles consisting of nucleic acid packaged in a protein coat (the capsid), are difficult to resist. Unable to reproduce outside a living cell, viruses reproduce only by subverting the genetic mechanisms of a host cell. In one kind of viral life cycle, the virus first binds to the cell's surface, then penetrates the cell and sheds its capsid. The exposed viral nucleic acid produces new viruses from the contents of the cell. Finally, the cell releases the viral progeny, and a new (10) cell cycle of infection begins. The human body responds to a viral infection by producing antibodies: complex, highly specific proteins that selectively bind to foreign molecules such as viruses. An antibody can either interfere with a virus' ability to bind to a cell, or can prevent (15) it from releasing its nucleic acid.

Unfortunately, the common cold, produced most often by rhinoviruses, is intractable to antiviral defense. Humans have difficulty resisting colds because rhinoviruses are so diverse, including at least 100 strains. (20) The strains differ most in the molecular structure of the proteins in their capsids. Since disease-fighting antibodies bind to the capsid, an antibody developed to protect against one rhinovirus strain is useless against other strains. Different antibodies must be produced for (25) each strain.

A defense against rhinoviruses might nonetheless succeed by exploiting hidden similarities among the rhinovirus strains. For example, most rhinovirus strains bind to the same kind of molecule (delta-receptors) on (30) a cell's surface when they attack human cells. Colonno, taking advantage of these common receptors, devised a strategy for blocking the attachment of rhinoviruses to their appropriate receptors. Rather than fruitlessly searching for an antibody that would bind to all rhi- (35) noviruses, Colonno realized that an antibody binding to the common receptors of a human cell would prevent rhinoviruses from initiating an infection. Because human cells normally do not develop antibodies to components of their own cells, Colonno injected human cells (40) into mice, which did produce an antibody to the common receptor. In isolated human cells, this antibody proved to be extraordinarily effective at thwarting the rhinovirus. Moreover, when the antibody was given to chimpanzees, it inhibited rhinoviral growth, and in (45) humans it lessened both the severity and duration of cold symptoms.

Another possible defense against rhinoviruses was proposed by Rossman, who described rhinoviruses' detailed molecular structure. Rossman showed (50) that protein sequences common to all rhinovirus strains lie at the base of a deep "canyon" scoring each face of the capsid. The narrow opening of this canyon possibly prevents the relatively large antibody molecules from binding to the common sequence, but smaller molecules (55) might reach it. Among these smaller, nonantibody molecules, some might bind to the common sequence, lock the nucleic acid in its coat, and thereby prevent the virus from reproducing.

21. The primary purpose of the passage is to

(A) discuss viral mechanisms and possible ways of circumventing certain kinds of those mechanisms
(B) challenge recent research on how rhinoviruses bind to receptors on the surfaces of cells
(C) suggest future research on rhinoviral growth in chimpanzees
(D) defend a controversial research program whose purpose is to discover the molecular structure of rhinovirus capsids
(E) evaluate a dispute between advocates of two theories about the rhinovirus life cycle

22. It can be inferred from the passage that the protein sequences of the capsid that vary most among strains of rhinovirus are those

(A) at the base of the "canyon"
(B) outside of the "canyon"
(C) responsible for producing nucleic acid
(D) responsible for preventing the formation of delta-receptors
(E) preventing the capsid from releasing its nucleic acid

23. It can be inferred from the passage that a cell lacking delta-receptors will be

(A) unable to prevent the rhinoviral nucleic acid from shedding its capsid
(B) defenseless against most strains of rhinovirus
(C) unable to release the viral progeny it develops after infection
(D) protected from new infections by antibodies to the rhinovirus
(E) resistant to infection by most strains of rhinovirus

24. Which of the following research strategies for developing a defense against the common cold would the author be likely to find most promising?

(A) Continuing to look for a general antirhinoviral antibody
(B) Searching for common cell-surface receptors in humans and mice
(C) Continuing to look for similarities among the various strains of rhinovirus
(D) Discovering how the human body produces antibodies in response to a rhinoviral infection
(E) Determining the detailed molecular structure of the nucleic acid of a rhinovirus

GO ON TO THE NEXT PAGE.

25. It can be inferred from the passage that the purpose of Colonno's experiments was to determine whether

(A) chimpanzees and humans can both be infected by rhinoviruses
(B) chimpanzees can produce antibodies to human cell-surface receptors
(C) a rhinovirus' nucleic acid might be locked in its protein coat
(D) binding antibodies to common receptors could produce a possible defense against rhinoviruses
(E) rhinoviruses are vulnerable to human antibodies

26. According to the passage, Rossman's research suggests that

(A) a defense against rhinoviruses might exploit structural similarities among the strains of rhinovirus
(B) human cells normally do not develop antibodies to components of their own cells
(C) the various strains of rhinovirus differ in their ability to bind to the surface of a host cell
(D) rhinovirus versatility can work to the benefit of researchers trying to find a useful antibody
(E) Colonno's research findings are probably invalid

27. According to the passage, in order for a given antibody to bind to a given rhinoviral capsid, which of the following must be true?

(A) The capsid must have a deep "canyon" on each of its faces.
(B) The antibody must be specific to the molecular structure of the particular capsid.
(C) The capsid must separate from its nucleic acid before binding to an antibody.
(D) The antibody must bind to a particular cell-surface receptor before it can bind to a rhinovirus.
(E) The antibody must first enter a cell containing the particular rhinovirus.

GO ON TO THE NEXT PAGE.

Each question below consists of a word printed in capital letters, followed by five lettered words or phrases. Choose the lettered word or phrase that is most nearly <u>opposite</u> in meaning to the word in capital letters.

Since some of the questions require you to distinguish fine shades of meaning, be sure to consider all the choices before deciding which one is best.

28. DOMINANT: (A) defective   (B) multiple
    (C) inferred   (D) shifting   (E) recessive

29. DISPUTE: (A) accept   (B) simplify
    (C) frustrate   (D) silence   (E) understand

30. PERJURY:
    (A) truthful deposition
    (B) vivid recollection
    (C) voluntary testimony
    (D) inadvertent disclosure
    (E) inexplicable fabrication

31. DORMANCY: (A) momentum   (B) hysteria
    (C) availability   (D) activity   (E) cultivation

32. PLETHORA: (A) deterioration
    (B) embellishment   (C) scarcity
    (D) vacillation   (E) affirmation

33. STOCK: (A) unique   (B) unfounded
    (C) desirable   (D) unhealthy   (E) trustworthy

34. BURGEON: (A) retreat   (B) evolve
    (C) wither   (D) sever   (E) minimize

35. OCCULT: (A) foresee   (B) bare   (C) assert
    (D) transform   (E) presume

36. NASCENT: (A) widely displaced
    (B) completely clear   (C) totally natural
    (D) strongly contrary   (E) fully established

37. AMPLIFY: (A) condemn   (B) disburse
    (C) decipher   (D) garble   (E) abridge

38. EXTENUATING: (A) opposing   (B) severe
    (C) intractable   (D) aggravating   (E) internal

STOP

IF YOU FINISH BEFORE TIME IS CALLED, YOU MAY CHECK YOUR WORK ON THIS SECTION ONLY. DO NOT TURN TO ANY OTHER SECTION IN THE TEST.

Section 3 starts on page 240.

SECTION 3

Time—30 minutes

30 Questions

Numbers: All numbers used are real numbers.

Figures: Position of points, angles, regions, etc. can be assumed to be in the order shown; and angle measures can be assumed to be positive.

Lines shown as straight can be assumed to be straight.

Figures can be assumed to lie in a plane unless otherwise indicated.

Figures that accompany questions are intended to provide information useful in answering the questions. However, unless a note states that a figure is drawn to scale, you should solve these problems NOT by estimating sizes by sight or by measurement, but by using your knowledge of mathematics (see Example 2 below).

Directions: Each of the Questions 1-15 consists of two quantities, one in Column A and one in Column B. You are to compare the two quantities and choose

   A   if the quantity in Column A is greater;
   B   if the quantity in Column B is greater;
   C   if the two quantities are equal;
   D   if the relationship cannot be determined from the information given.

Note: Since there are only four choices, NEVER MARK (E).

Common Information: In a question, information concerning one or both of the quantities to be compared is centered above the two columns. A symbol that appears in both columns represents the same thing in Column A as it does in Column B.

	Column A	Column B	Sample Answers
Example 1:	2×6	$2 + 6$	● Ⓑ Ⓒ Ⓓ Ⓔ

Examples 2-4 refer to $\triangle PQR$.

	Column A	Column B	Sample Answers
Example 2:	PN	NQ	Ⓐ Ⓑ Ⓒ ● Ⓔ

(since equal measures cannot be assumed, even though PN and NQ appear equal)

	Column A	Column B	Sample Answers
Example 3:	x	y	Ⓐ ● Ⓒ Ⓓ Ⓔ

(since N is between P and Q)

	Column A	Column B	Sample Answers
Example 4:	$w + z$	180	Ⓐ Ⓑ ● Ⓓ Ⓔ

(since PQ is a straight line)

240

GO ON TO THE NEXT PAGE.

A if the quantity in Column A is greater;
B if the quantity in Column B is greater;
C if the two quantities are equal;
D if the relationship cannot be determined from the information given.

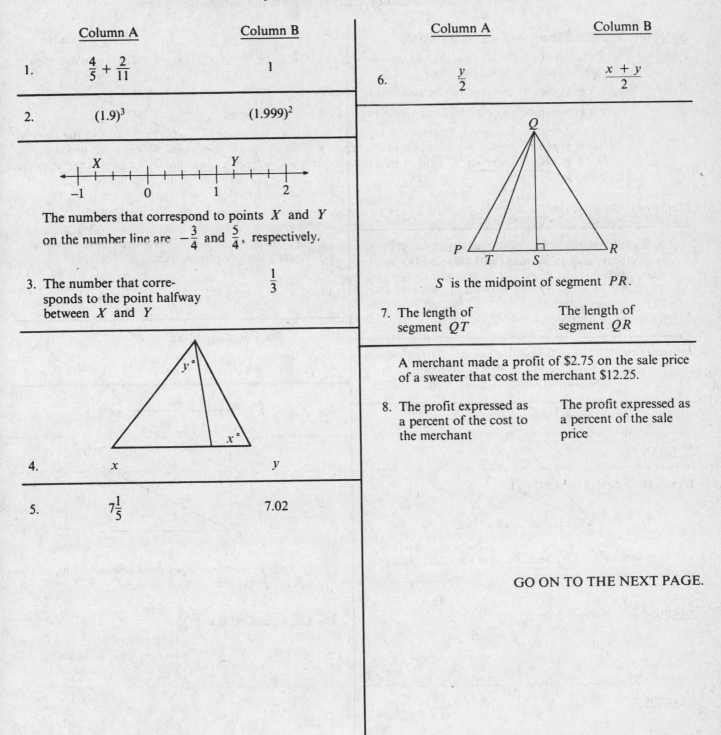

	Column A	Column B
1.	$\dfrac{4}{5} + \dfrac{2}{11}$	1
2.	$(1.9)^3$	$(1.999)^2$

The numbers that correspond to points X and Y on the number line are $-\dfrac{3}{4}$ and $\dfrac{5}{4}$, respectively.

3.	The number that corresponds to the point halfway between X and Y	$\dfrac{1}{3}$
4.	x	y
5.	$7\dfrac{1}{5}$	7.02

	Column A	Column B
6.	$\dfrac{y}{2}$	$\dfrac{x+y}{2}$

S is the midpoint of segment PR.

7.	The length of segment QT	The length of segment QR

A merchant made a profit of $2.75 on the sale price of a sweater that cost the merchant $12.25.

8.	The profit expressed as a percent of the cost to the merchant	The profit expressed as a percent of the sale price

GO ON TO THE NEXT PAGE.

241

A   if the quantity in Column A is greater;
B   if the quantity in Column B is greater;
C   if the two quantities are equal;
D   if the relationship cannot be determined from the information given.

Column A	Column B

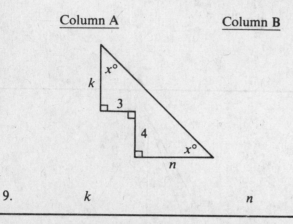

9. k n

A student has test scores of 85, x, and y, respectively, and an average (arithmetic mean) score of 95 on the three tests.

10. The average (arithmetic   100
    mean) of x and y

$$y^2 + 4y - 12 = 0$$

11. y^2 30

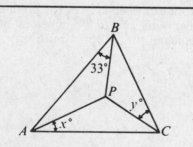

Segments PA, PB, and PC are the angle bisectors of $\triangle ABC$.

12. $x + y$ 57

Column A	Column B

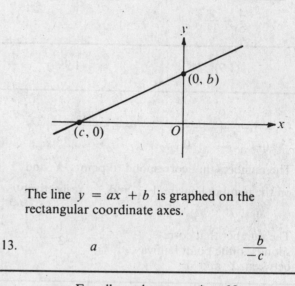

The line $y = ax + b$ is graphed on the rectangular coordinate axes.

13. a $\dfrac{b}{-c}$

For all numbers n, $n* = 32 - n$.

14. $(n*)*$ n

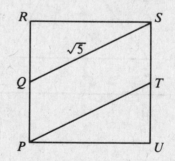

Q and T are the midpoints of opposite sides of square $PRSU$.

15. The area of region $PQST$ $\dfrac{3}{2}$

GO ON TO THE NEXT PAGE.

Directions: Each of the Questions 16-30 has five answer choices. For each of these questions, select the best of the answer choices given.

16. If a certain company purchased its computer terminals for a total of $540,400 and each of the terminals was purchased for $350, how many terminals did the company purchase?

    (A) 1,624
    (B) 1,544
    (C) 1,434
    (D) 1,384
    (E) 1,264

17. $\dfrac{\frac{2}{3} \times 9 \times \frac{2}{5} \times 15}{\frac{1}{3} \times 18 \times \frac{1}{5} \times 30} =$

    (A) 2

    (B) 1

    (C) $\frac{1}{2}$

    (D) $\frac{1}{3}$

    (E) $\frac{1}{4}$

18. If $2x = -10$, then $4x^2 - 6x - 5 =$

    (A) 65
    (B) 75
    (C) 125
    (D) 130
    (E) 135

19. If $3 < x < 8$ and $5 < y < 11$, which of the following represents all the possible values of xy?

    (A) $3 < xy < 11$
    (B) $8 < xy < 19$
    (C) $15 < xy < 88$
    (D) $24 < xy < 55$
    (E) $33 < xy < 40$

20. Chris gave Jane x cards. He gave Betty one card more than he gave Jane and he gave Paul two cards fewer than he gave Betty. In terms of x, how many cards did Chris give Betty, Jane, and Paul altogether?

    (A) $3x + 1$

    (B) $3x$

    (C) $3x - 1$

    (D) $x - 1$

    (E) $\frac{x}{3}$

GO ON TO THE NEXT PAGE.

Questions 21-25 refer to the following floor plan.

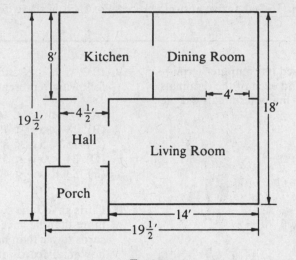

Front

Note: Figure drawn to scale.

The figure above shows the plan for the ground floor of a house. The thickness of the walls should be ignored in answering the questions. The dimensions are in feet, and each region is rectangular.

21. What is the area, in square feet, of the living room?

    (A) 161
    (B) 140
    (C) 133
    (D) 126
    (E) 115

22. If the ceilings and walls of the living room, dining room, kitchen, and hall are to be painted, how many square feet must be painted?

    (A) $231\frac{1}{4}$
    (B) 324
    (C) 333
    (D) $380\frac{1}{4}$
    (E) It cannot be determined from the information given.

23. If the hall is $6\frac{1}{2}$ feet long, what is the perimeter, in feet, of the porch area?

    (A) 18
    (B) 19
    (C) 20
    (D) 21
    (E) 22

24. How many more feet does the porch extend in front of the house than it does beyond the side of the house?

    (A) $\frac{1}{2}$
    (B) 1
    (C) $1\frac{1}{2}$
    (D) 2
    (E) It cannot be determined from the information given.

25. If the kitchen is square, what is the ratio of the area of the kitchen to the area of the dining room?

    (A) $\frac{16}{37}$
    (B) $\frac{3}{7}$
    (C) $\frac{4}{7}$
    (D) $\frac{8}{11}$
    (E) $\frac{16}{21}$

GO ON TO THE NEXT PAGE.

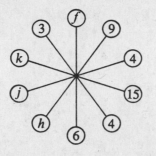

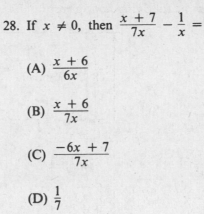

28. If $x \neq 0$, then $\dfrac{x + 7}{7x} - \dfrac{1}{x} =$

(A) $\dfrac{x + 6}{6x}$

(B) $\dfrac{x + 6}{7x}$

(C) $\dfrac{-6x + 7}{7x}$

(D) $\dfrac{1}{7}$

(E) $-\dfrac{1}{7}$

26. In the figure above, the product of any two numbers in adjacent circles is equal to the product of the two numbers that are opposite those circles. For example, $3 \cdot f = 4 \cdot 6$. What is the value of j?

(A) 3
(B) 4
(C) 6
(D) 12
(E) 20

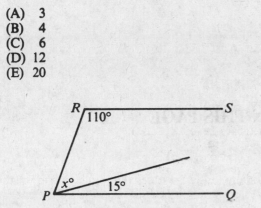

27. In the figure above, if $PQ \parallel RS$, then $x =$

(A) 95
(B) 85
(C) 75
(D) 65
(E) 55

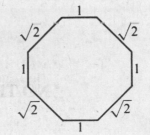

29. The figure above shows the lengths of the sides of an equiangular polygon. What is the area of the polygon?

(A) 7
(B) 8
(C) 9
(D) $14\sqrt{2}$
(E) It cannot be determined from the information given.

30. A certain recipe makes enough batter for exactly 8 circular pancakes that are each 10 inches in diameter. How many circular pancakes, each 5 inches in diameter and of the same thickness as the 10-inch pancakes, should the recipe make?

(A) 4
(B) 16
(C) 24
(D) 32
(E) 40

STOP

**IF YOU FINISH BEFORE TIME IS CALLED, YOU MAY CHECK YOUR WORK ON THIS SECTION ONLY.
DO NOT TURN TO ANY OTHER SECTION IN THE TEST.**

NO TEST MATERIAL ON THIS PAGE

SECTION 4

Time—30 minutes

38 Questions

Directions: Each sentence below has one or two blanks, each blank indicating that something has been omitted. Beneath the sentence are five lettered words or sets of words. Choose the word or set of words for each blank that best fits the meaning of the sentence as a whole.

1. Given the existence of so many factions in the field, it was unrealistic of Anna Freud to expect any ------- of opinion.

   (A) freedom   (B) reassessment   (C) uniformity
   (D) expression   (E) formation

2. Although specific concerns may determine the intent of a research project, its results are often -------.

   (A) unanticipated   (B) beneficial   (C) expensive
   (D) spectacular   (E) specialized

3. To list Reilly's achievements in a fragmentary way is -------, for it distracts our attention from the ------- themes of her work.

   (A) unproductive. .disparate
   (B) misleading. .integrating
   (C) pragmatic. .comprehensive
   (D) logical. .important
   (E) inevitable. .unsettling

4. People frequently denigrate books about recent catastrophes as morally ------- attempts to profit from misfortune, but in my view our desire for such books, together with the venerable tradition to which they belong, ------- them.

   (A) inopportune. .encourages
   (B) fortuitous. .fosters
   (C) treacherous. .safeguards
   (D) despicable. .legitimizes
   (E) corrupt. .generates

5. That many of the important laws of science were discovered during experiments designed to ------- other phenomena suggests that experimental results are the ------- of inevitable natural forces rather than of planning.

   (A) analyze. .foundations
   (B) disprove. .predecessors
   (C) alter. .adjuncts
   (D) illuminate. .consequence
   (E) verify. .essence

6. Although in eighteenth-century England an active cultural life accompanied the beginnings of middle-class consumerism, the ------- of literacy was ------- with the rise of such consumerism in the different areas of the country.

   (A) repudiation. .reconciled
   (B) renewal. .inconsistent
   (C) promotion. .combined
   (D) spread. .compatible
   (E) degree. .uncorrelated

7. The trainees were given copies of a finished manual to see whether they could themselves begin to ------- the inflexible, though tacit, rules for composing more of such instructional materials.

   (A) design   (B) revise   (C) disrupt
   (D) standardize   (E) derive

GO ON TO THE NEXT PAGE.

247

Directions: In each of the following questions, a related pair of words or phrases is followed by five lettered pairs of words or phrases. Select the lettered pair that best expresses a relationship similar to that expressed in the original pair.

8. BUTTER : MARGARINE ::
   (A) sugar : saccharin
   (B) porcelain : tile
   (C) photograph : painting
   (D) music : tape
   (E) signal : whistle

9. MUTED : COLOR ::
   (A) archaic : diction
   (B) pastoral : composition
   (C) muffled : sound
   (D) haunting : tune
   (E) unconcerned : interest

10. MUFFLER : NECK ::
    (A) sandal : foot
    (B) collar : blouse
    (C) earring : ear
    (D) mitten : hand
    (E) suspenders : trousers

11. PLANT : SOIL ::
    (A) germ : bacteria
    (B) organism : medium
    (C) sample : growth
    (D) nutrient : liquid
    (E) tree : root

12. POTTERY : SHARD ::
    (A) symphony : musician
    (B) bread : crumb
    (C) wall : brick
    (D) shoe : heel
    (E) building : architect

13. PURIFICATION : DROSS ::
    (A) distillation : vinegar
    (B) assay : gold
    (C) desalinization : salt
    (D) condensation : vapor
    (E) reaction : catalyst

14. DISGUISE : RECOGNITION ::
    (A) prevarication : statement
    (B) infidelity : marriage
    (C) camouflage : infiltration
    (D) espionage : diplomacy
    (E) padding : damage

15. GUST : WIND ::
    (A) rapids : river
    (B) blizzard : snowstorm
    (C) cloudburst : rainfall
    (D) mist : fog
    (E) surf : sea

16. DISABUSE : ERROR ::
    (A) rehabilitate : addiction
    (B) persevere : dereliction
    (C) belittle : imperfection
    (D) discredit : reputation
    (E) discern : discrimination

GO ON TO THE NEXT PAGE.

Directions: Each passage in this group is followed by questions based on its content. After reading a passage, choose the best answer to each question. Answer all questions following a passage on the basis of what is <u>stated</u> or <u>implied</u> in that passage.

Diamonds, an occasional component of rare igneous rocks called lamproites and kimberlites, have never been dated satisfactorily. However, some diamonds contain
Line
(5) minute inclusions of silicate minerals, commonly olivine, pyroxene, and garnet. These minerals can be dated by radioactive decay techniques because of the very small quantities of radioactive trace elements they, in turn, contain. Usually, it is possible to conclude that the inclusions are older than their diamond hosts, but with little
(10) indication of the time interval involved. Sometimes, however, the crystal form of the silicate inclusions is observed to resemble more closely the internal structure of diamond than that of other silicate minerals. It is not known how rare this resemblance is, or whether it is
(15) most often seen in inclusions of silicates such as garnet, whose crystallography is generally somewhat similar to that of diamond; but when present, the resemblance is regarded as compelling evidence that the diamonds and inclusions are truly cogenetic.

17. The author implies that silicate inclusions were most often formed

    (A) with small diamonds inside of them
    (B) with trace elements derived from their host minerals
    (C) by the radioactive decay of rare igneous rocks
    (D) at an earlier period than were their host minerals
    (E) from the crystallization of rare igneous material

18. According to the passage, the age of silicate minerals included in diamonds can be determined due to a feature of the

    (A) trace elements in the diamond hosts
    (B) trace elements in the rock surrounding the diamonds
    (C) trace elements in the silicate minerals
    (D) silicate minerals' crystal structure
    (E) host diamonds' crystal structure

19. The author states that which of the following generally has a crystal structure similar to that of diamond?

    (A) Lamproite   (B) Kimberlite   (C) Olivine
    (D) Pyroxene   (E) Garnet

20. The main purpose of the passage is to

    (A) explain why it has not been possible to determine the age of diamonds
    (B) explain how it might be possible to date some diamonds
    (C) compare two alternative approaches to determining the age of diamonds
    (D) compare a method of dating diamonds with a method used to date certain silicate minerals
    (E) compare the age of diamonds with that of certain silicate minerals contained within them

GO ON TO THE NEXT PAGE.

*Discussion of the assimilation of Puerto Ricans in the United States has focused on two factors: social standing and the loss of national culture. In general, excessive stress is placed on one factor or the other, depending on whether the commentator is North American or Puerto Rican. Many North American social scientists, such as Oscar Handlin, Joseph Fitzpatrick, and Oscar Lewis, consider Puerto Ricans as the most recent in a long line of ethnic entrants to occupy the lowest rung on the social ladder. Such a "sociodemographic" approach tends to regard assimilation as a benign process, taking for granted increased economic advantage and inevitable cultural integration, in a supposedly egalitarian context. However, this approach fails to take into account the colonial nature of the Puerto Rican case, with this group, unlike their European predecessors, coming from a nation politically subordinated to the United States. Even the "radical" critiques of this mainstream research model, such as the critique developed in *Divided Society*, attach the issue of ethnic assimilation too mechanically to factors of economic and social mobility and are thus unable to illuminate the cultural subordination of Puerto Ricans as a colonial minority.

In contrast, the "colonialist" approach of island-based writers such as Eduardo Seda-Bonilla, Manuel Maldonado-Denis, and Luis Nieves-Falcón tends to view assimilation as the forced loss of national culture in an unequal contest with imposed foreign values. There is, of course, a strong tradition of cultural accommodation among other Puerto Rican thinkers. The writings of Eugenio Fernández Méndez clearly exemplify this tradition, and many supporters of Puerto Rico's commonwealth status share the same universalizing orientation. But the Puerto Rican intellectuals who have written most about the assimilation process in the United States all advance cultural nationalist views, advocating the preservation of minority cultural distinctions and rejecting what they see as the subjugation of colonial nationalities.

This cultural and political emphasis is appropriate, but the colonialist thinkers misdirect it, overlooking the class relations at work in both Puerto Rican and North American history. They pose the clash of national cultures as an absolute polarity, with each culture understood as static and undifferentiated. Yet both the Puerto Rican and North American traditions have been subject to constant challenge from cultural forces within their own societies, forces that may move toward each other in ways that cannot be written off as mere "assimilation." Consider, for example, the indigenous and Afro-Caribbean traditions in Puerto Rican culture and how they influence and are influenced by other Caribbean cultures and Black cultures in the United States. The elements of coercion and inequality, so central to cultural contact according to the colonialist framework, play no role in this kind of convergence of racially and ethnically different elements of the same social class.

21. The author's main purpose is to

(A) criticize the emphasis on social standing in discussions of the assimilation of Puerto Ricans in the United States

(B) support the thesis that assimilation has not been a benign process for Puerto Ricans

(C) defend a view of the assimilation of Puerto Ricans that emphasizes the preservation of national culture

(D) indicate deficiencies in two schools of thought on the assimilation of Puerto Ricans in the United States

(E) reject the attempt to formulate a general framework for discussion of the assimilation of Puerto Ricans in the United States

22. According to the passage, cultural accommodation is promoted by

(A) Eduardo Seda-Bonilla
(B) Manuel Maldonado-Denis
(C) the author of *Divided Society*
(D) the majority of social scientists writing on immigration
(E) many supporters of Puerto Rico's commonwealth status

23. It can be inferred from the passage that a writer such as Eugenio Fernández Méndez would most likely agree with which of the following statements concerning members of minority ethnic groups?

(A) It is necessary for the members of such groups to adapt to the culture of the majority.

(B) The members of such groups generally encounter a culture that is static and undifferentiated.

(C) Social mobility is the most important feature of the experience of members of such groups.

(D) Social scientists should emphasize the cultural and political aspects of the experience of members of such groups.

(E) The assimilation of members of such groups requires the forced abandonment of their authentic national roots.

GO ON TO THE NEXT PAGE.

24. The author implies that the Puerto Rican writers who have written most about assimilation do NOT do which of the following?

    (A) Regard assimilation as benign.
    (B) Resist cultural integration.
    (C) Describe in detail the process of assimilation.
    (D) Take into account the colonial nature of the Puerto Rican case.
    (E) Criticize supporters of Puerto Rico's commonwealth status.

25. It can be inferred from the passage that the "colonialist" approach is so called because its practitioners

    (A) support Puerto Rico's commonwealth status
    (B) have a strong tradition of cultural accommodation
    (C) emphasize the class relations at work in both Puerto Rican and North American history
    (D) pose the clash of national cultures as an absolute polarity in which each culture is understood as static and undifferentiated
    (E) regard the political relation of Puerto Rico to the United States as a significant factor in the experience of Puerto Ricans

26. The author regards the emphasis by island-based writers on the cultural and political dimensions of assimilation as

    (A) ironic
    (B) dangerous
    (C) fitting but misdirected
    (D) illuminating but easily misunderstood
    (E) peculiar but benign

27. The example discussed in lines 51-54 is intended by the author to illustrate a

    (A) strength of the sociodemographic approach
    (B) strength of the "colonialist" approach
    (C) weakness of the sociodemographic approach
    (D) weakness of the "colonialist" approach
    (E) weakness of the cultural-accommodationist approach

GO ON TO THE NEXT PAGE.

Directions: Each question below consists of a word printed in capital letters, followed by five lettered words or phrases. Choose the lettered word or phrase that is most nearly <u>opposite</u> in meaning to the word in capital letters.

Since some of the questions require you to distinguish fine shades of meaning, be sure to consider all the choices before deciding which one is best.

28. OVERREACH:
    (A) disparage another's work
    (B) aim below one's potential
    (C) seek to buy at a lower price
    (D) say less than one intends
    (E) tend to overstate

29. BULGE: (A) depressed region   (B) tilted plane
    (C) steep slope   (D) rippled surface
    (E) short line

30. FACILITATE: (A) evict   (B) thwart
    (C) define   (D) make excuses for
    (E) call attention to

31. EULOGY: (A) defamation   (B) fluctuation
    (C) characterization   (D) hallucination
    (E) deprivation

32. FRACAS:
    (A) functional compromise
    (B) reasonable judgment
    (C) peaceable discussion
    (D) plausible exception
    (E) theoretical approach

33. HARROW: (A) assuage   (B) levy   (C) suffice
    (D) repel   (E) invert

34. BOOR: (A) forthright individual
    (B) brave fighter   (C) deceitful ally
    (D) civil person   (E) steadfast friend

35. HACKNEYED: (A) fresh   (B) illicit
    (C) careful   (D) unpopular   (E) dissenting

36. SODDEN: (A) barren   (B) desiccated
    (C) temperate   (D) expedient   (E) artificial

37. GAINSAY: (A) hesitate   (B) intercede
    (C) perceive   (D) concur   (E) praise

38. NICE: (A) indirect   (B) indecisive
    (C) imperceptible   (D) imprecise
    (E) imperturbable

STOP

**IF YOU FINISH BEFORE TIME IS CALLED, YOU MAY CHECK YOUR WORK ON THIS SECTION ONLY.
DO NOT TURN TO ANY OTHER SECTION IN THE TEST.**

NOTE: To ensure prompt processing of test results, it is important that you fill in the blanks exactly as directed.

GENERAL TEST

A. Print and sign your full name in this box:

PRINT: _____
          (LAST)   (FIRST)   (MIDDLE)

SIGN: _____

Copy this code in box 6 on your answer sheet. Then fill in the corresponding ovals exactly as shown.

6. TITLE CODE

Copy the Test Name and Form Code in box 7 on your answer sheet.

TEST NAME *General*

FORM CODE *GR 91-17*

GRADUATE RECORD EXAMINATIONS GENERAL TEST

You will have 3 hours and 30 minutes in which to work on this test, which consists of seven sections. During the time allowed for one section, you may work only on that section. The time allowed for each section is 30 minutes.

Each of your scores will be determined by the number of questions for which you select the best answer from the choices given. Questions for which you mark no answer or more than one answer are not counted in scoring. Nothing is subtracted from a score if you answer a question incorrectly. Therefore, to maximize your scores it is better for you to guess at an answer than not to respond at all.

You are advised to work as rapidly as you can without losing accuracy. Do not spend too much time on questions that are too difficult for you. Go on to the other questions and come back to the difficult ones later.

There are several different types of questions; you will find special directions for each type in the test itself. Be sure you understand the directions before attempting to answer any questions.

YOU MUST INDICATE ALL YOUR ANSWERS ON THE SEPARATE ANSWER SHEET. No credit will be given for anything written in this examination book, but you may write in the book as much as you wish to work out your answers. After you have decided on your response to a question, fill in the corresponding oval on the answer sheet. BE SURE THAT EACH MARK IS DARK AND COMPLETELY FILLS THE OVAL. Mark only one answer to each question. No credit will be given for multiple answers. Erase all stray marks. If you change an answer, be sure that all previous marks are erased completely. Incomplete erasures may be read as intended answers. Do not be concerned if your answer sheet provides spaces for more answers than there are questions in each section.

Example:

What city is the capital of France?

(A) Rome
(B) Paris
(C) London
(D) Cairo
(E) Oslo

Sample Answer

BEST ANSWER PROPERLY MARKED

IMPROPER MARKS

Some or all of the passages for this test have been adapted from published material to provide the examinee with significant problems for analysis and evaluation. To make the passages suitable for testing purposes, the style, content, or point of view of the original may have been altered in some cases. The ideas contained in the passages do not necessarily represent the opinions of the Graduate Record Examinations Board or Educational Testing Service.

DO NOT OPEN YOUR TEST BOOK UNTIL YOU ARE TOLD TO DO SO.

253

FOR GENERAL TEST, FORM GR91-17 ONLY
Answer Key and Percentages* of Examinees Answering Each Question Correctly

VERBAL ABILITY						QUANTITATIVE ABILITY					
Section 2			Section 4			Section 1			Section 3		
Number	Answer	P+	Number	Answer	P+	Number	Answer	P+	Number	Answer	P+
1	B	89	1	C	85	1	C	87	1	B	85
2	B	88	2	A	84	2	B	85	2	A	86
3	D	51	3	B	80	3	A	87	3	B	81
4	A	48	4	D	59	4	A	88	4	D	74
5	C	49	5	D	55	5	D	77	5	A	83
6	E	44	6	E	48	6	B	74	6	D	78
7	D	30	7	E	34	7	C	70	7	B	76
8	C	76	8	A	92	8	C	61	8	A	61
9	D	83	9	C	86	9	D	57	9	B	50
10	B	77	10	D	77	10	A	56	10	C	61
11	E	67	11	B	58	11	C	40	11	D	41
12	E	61	12	B	57	12	A	43	12	C	35
13	D	54	13	C	43	13	D	31	13	C	32
14	C	34	14	E	35	14	B	45	14	C	23
15	C	35	15	C	33	15	D	29	15	A	47
16	A	14	16	A	33	16	C	81	16	B	83
17	B	88	17	D	63	17	B	69	17	B	77
18	B	74	18	C	70	18	E	79	18	C	74
19	A	79	19	E	90	19	A	53	19	C	65
20	D	54	20	B	48	20	E	42	20	B	68
21	A	81	21	D	59	21	B	84	21	B	79
22	B	26	22	E	64	22	C	66	22	E	76
23	E	52	23	A	30	23	C	69	23	D	56
24	C	42	24	A	38	24	E	47	24	A	51
25	D	76	25	E	26	25	C	36	25	E	37
26	A	50	26	C	63	26	D	65	26	A	49
27	B	44	27	D	44	27	B	64	27	E	51
28	E	92	28	B	86	28	D	65	28	D	56
29	A	90	29	A	91	29	D	25	29	A	29
30	A	86	30	B	75	30	A	30	30	D	25
31	D	83	31	A	85						
32	C	75	32	C	74						
33	A	43	33	A	42						
34	C	39	34	D	45						
35	B	34	35	A	38						
36	E	29	36	B	30						
37	E	26	37	D	25						
38	D	7	38	D	20						

*Estimated P+ for the group of examinees who took the GRE General Test in a recent three-year period.

254

SCORE CONVERSIONS FOR GRE GENERAL TEST, GR91-17

Raw Score	Scaled Score Verbal	Scaled Score Quantitative	Raw Score	Scaled Score Verbal	Scaled Score Quantitative
73-76	800		39	440	590
72	790		38	430	580
71	780		37	420	570
70	760		36	410	560
			35	400	550
69	750		34	400	540
68	730		33	390	530
67	720		32	380	520
66	710		31	370	500
65	700		30	360	490
64	690				
63	680		29	350	480
62	670		28	350	470
61	660		27	340	460
60	650	800	26	330	450
			25	320	430
59	630	800	24	310	420
58	620	800	23	300	410
57	610	790	22	300	400
56	600	780	21	290	380
55	590	760	20	280	370
54	580	750			
53	570	740	19	270	350
52	560	730	18	260	340
51	550	730	17	250	330
50	540	720	16	240	310
			15	230	290
49	530	700	14	220	280
48	520	690	13	210	260
47	510	680	12	200	250
46	500	670	11	200	230
45	490	660	10	200	220
44	480	650			
43	470	640	9	200	200
42	460	620	8	200	200
41	450	610	7	200	200
40	450	600	0-6	200	200

NO TEST MATERIAL ON THIS PAGE

THE GRADUATE RECORD
EXAMINATIONS®

GRE®

(ETS)®

General Test

*Do not break the seal
until you are told to do so.*

*The contents of this test are confidential.
Disclosure or reproduction of any portion
of it is prohibited.*

THIS TEST BOOK MUST NOT BE TAKEN FROM THE ROOM.

SECTION 1

Time—30 minutes

38 Questions

Directions: Each sentence that follows has one or two blanks, each blank indicating that something has been omitted. Following the sentence are five lettered words or sets of words. Choose the word or set of words for each blank that best fits the meaning of the sentence as a whole.

1. The availability of oxygen is an essential ------- for animal life, while carbon dioxide is equally ------- for plant life.

   (A) choice. .optional
   (B) duplication. .selective
   (C) conversion. .exchangeable
   (D) condition. .necessary
   (E) luxury. .harmful

2. Prudery actually draws attention to the vice it is supposed to -------; the very act that forbids speech or prohibits sight ------- what is hidden.

   (A) condemn. .distorts
   (B) monitor. .signals
   (C) repress. .dramatizes
   (D) obviate. .fosters
   (E) divulge. .conceals

3. After thirty years of television, people have become "speed watchers"; consequently, if the camera lingers, the interest of the audience -------.

   (A) broadens   (B) begins   (C) varies
   (D) flags   (E) clears

4. Compared mathematically to smoking and driving, almost everything else seems relatively risk-free, ------- almost nothing seems worth regulating.

   (A) yet   (B) since   (C) so
   (D) even though   (E) as long as

5. Ironically, Carver's precision in sketching lives on the edge of despair ensures that his stories will sometimes be read too narrowly, much as Dickens' social-reformer role once caused his broader concerns to be -------.

   (A) ignored   (B) reinforced   (C) contradicted
   (D) diminished   (E) diversified

6. The demise of the rigorous academic curriculum in high school resulted, in part, from the progressive rhetoric that ------- the study of subjects previously thought ------- as part of school learning.

   (A) advocated. .necessary
   (B) enhanced. .indispensable
   (C) restricted. .impractical
   (D) undermined. .popular
   (E) sanctioned. .inappropriate

7. While some see in practical jokes a wish for mastery in miniature over a world that seems very -------, others believe that the jokes' purpose is to disrupt, by reducing all transactions to -------.

   (A) dubious. .confusion
   (B) disorderly. .symmetry
   (C) harmonious. .dissonance
   (D) unruly. .chaos
   (E) turbulent. .uniformity

GO ON TO THE NEXT PAGE.

258

Directions: In each of the following questions, a related pair of words or phrases is followed by five lettered pairs of words or phrases. Select the lettered pair that best expresses a relationship similar to that expressed in the original pair.

8. ATHLETE : TROPHY ::   (A) detective : badge
   (B) presenter : award   (C) soldier : medal
   (D) bettor : stake   (E) musician : instrument

9. ARTICULATE : UNCLEAR ::
   (A) assign : unencumbered
   (B) elaborate : sketchy
   (C) explain : lucid
   (D) grieve : somber
   (E) march : planned

10. INVENTORY : STOCK ::   (A) calculation : ledger
    (B) poll : balloting   (C) survey : territory
    (D) census : population   (E) petition : names

11. LOGIC : REASONING ::
    (A) sensitivity : morality
    (B) arrogance : leadership
    (C) ethics : behavior
    (D) creativity : enthusiasm
    (E) bravery : charisma

12. MIMICRY : CAMOUFLAGE ::
    (A) photosynthesis : pollination
    (B) territoriality : migration
    (C) hibernation : generation
    (D) mutation : variation
    (E) digestion : rumination

13. APPREHENSION : TERROR ::
    (A) interest : conspiracy
    (B) affection : adoration
    (C) indifference : animosity
    (D) reluctance : termination
    (E) anxiety : faith

14. LUMBER : GRACE ::   (A) dissemble : pretense
    (B) relent : energy   (C) castigate : justice
    (D) waver : resolution   (E) insinuate : subtlety

15. CAUSTIC : EAT AWAY ::
    (A) hormone : inhibit
    (B) reagent : bind
    (C) explosive : destroy
    (D) synthetic : substitute
    (E) desiccant : dry

16. MALINGERER : DUTY ::
    (A) scholar : pedantry   (B) recluse : humanity
    (C) rebel : responsibility   (D) miser : wealth
    (E) patron : criticism

GO ON TO THE NEXT PAGE.

Classical physics defines the vacuum as a state of absence: a vacuum is said to exist in a region of space if there is nothing in it. In the quantum field theories that describe the physics of elementary particles, the vacuum becomes somewhat more complicated. Even in empty space, particles can appear spontaneously as a result of fluctuations of the vacuum. For example, an electron and a positron, or antielectron, can be created out of the void. Particles created in this way have only a fleeting existence; they are annihilated almost as soon as they appear, and their presence can never be detected directly. They are called virtual particles in order to distinguish them from real particles, whose lifetimes are not constrained in the same way, and which can be detected. Thus it is still possible to define the vacuum as a space that has no real particles in it.

One might expect that the vacuum would always be the state of lowest possible energy for a given region of space. If an area is initially empty and a real particle is put into it, the total energy, it seems, should be raised by at least the energy equivalent of the mass of the added particle. A surprising result of some recent theoretical investigations is that this assumption is not invariably true. There are conditions under which the introduction of a real particle of finite mass into an empty region of space can reduce the total energy. If the reduction in energy is great enough, an electron and a positron will be spontaneously created. Under these conditions the electron and positron are not a result of vacuum fluctuations but are real particles, which exist indefinitely and can be detected. In other words, under these conditions the vacuum is an unstable state and can decay into a state of lower energy; i.e., one in which real particles are created.

The essential condition for the decay of the vacuum is the presence of an intense electric field. As a result of the decay of the vacuum, the space permeated by such a field can be said to acquire an electric charge, and it can be called a charged vacuum. The particles that materialize in the space make the charge manifest. An electric field of sufficient intensity to create a charged vacuum is likely to be found in only one place: in the immediate vicinity of a superheavy atomic nucleus, one with about twice as many protons as the heaviest natural nuclei known. A nucleus that large cannot be stable, but it might be possible to assemble one next to a vacuum for long enough to observe the decay of the vacuum. Experiments attempting to achieve this are now under way.

17. Which of the following titles best describes the passage as a whole?

(A) The Vacuum: Its Fluctuations and Decay
(B) The Vacuum: Its Creation and Instability
(C) The Vacuum: A State of Absence
(D) Particles That Materialize in the Vacuum
(E) Classical Physics and the Vacuum

18. According to the passage, the assumption that the introduction of a real particle into a vacuum raises the total energy of that region of space has been cast into doubt by which of the following?

(A) Findings from laboratory experiments
(B) Findings from observational field experiments
(C) Accidental observations made during other experiments
(D) Discovery of several erroneous propositions in accepted theories
(E) Predictions based on theoretical work

19. It can be inferred from the passage that scientists are currently making efforts to observe which of the following events?

(A) The decay of a vacuum in the presence of virtual particles
(B) The decay of a vacuum next to a superheavy atomic nucleus
(C) The creation of a superheavy atomic nucleus next to an intense electric field
(D) The creation of a virtual electron and a virtual positron as a result of fluctuations of a vacuum
(E) The creation of a charged vacuum in which only real electrons can be created in the vacuum's region of space

GO ON TO THE NEXT PAGE.

20. Physicists' recent investigations of the decay of the vacuum, as described in the passage, most closely resemble which of the following hypothetical events in other disciplines?

(A) On the basis of data gathered in a carefully controlled laboratory experiment, a chemist predicts and then demonstrates the physical properties of a newly synthesized polymer.

(B) On the basis of manipulations of macroeconomic theory, an economist predicts that, contrary to accepted economic theory, inflation and unemployment will both decline under conditions of rapid economic growth.

(C) On the basis of a rereading of the texts of Jane Austen's novels, a literary critic suggests that, contrary to accepted literary interpretations, Austen's plots were actually metaphors for political events in early nineteenth-century England.

(D) On the basis of data gathered in carefully planned observations of several species of birds, a biologist proposes a modification in the accepted theory of interspecies competition.

(E) On the basis of a study of observations incidentally recorded in ethnographers' descriptions of non-Western societies, an anthropologist proposes a new theory of kinship relations.

21. According to the passage, the author considers the reduction of energy in an empty region of space to which a real particle has been added to be

(A) a well-known process
(B) a frequent occurrence
(C) a fleeting aberration
(D) an unimportant event
(E) an unexpected outcome

22. According to the passage, virtual particles differ from real particles in which of the following ways?

   I. Virtual particles have extremely short lifetimes.
   II. Virtual particles are created in an intense electric field.
   III. Virtual particles cannot be detected directly.

(A) I only
(B) II only
(C) III only
(D) I and II only
(E) I and III only

23. The author's assertions concerning the conditions that lead to the decay of the vacuum would be most weakened if which of the following occurred?

(A) Scientists created an electric field next to a vacuum, but found that the electric field was not intense enough to create a charged vacuum.

(B) Scientists assembled a superheavy atomic nucleus next to a vacuum, but found that no virtual particles were created in the vacuum's region of space.

(C) Scientists assembled a superheavy atomic nucleus next to a vacuum, but found that they could not then detect any real particles in the vacuum's region of space.

(D) Scientists introduced a virtual electron and a virtual positron into a vacuum's region of space, but found that the vacuum did not then fluctuate.

(E) Scientists introduced a real electron and a real positron into a vacuum's region of space, but found that the total energy of the space increased by the energy equivalent of the mass of the particles.

GO ON TO THE NEXT PAGE.

Simone de Beauvoir's work greatly influenced Betty Friedan's—indeed, made it possible. Why, then, was it Friedan who became the prophet of women's emancipation in the United States? Political conditions, as well as a certain anti-intellectual bias, prepared Americans and the American media to better receive Friedan's deradicalized and highly pragmatic *The Feminine Mystique*, published in 1963, than Beauvoir's theoretical reading of women's situation in *The Second Sex*. In 1953 when *The Second Sex* first appeared in translation in the United States, the country had entered the silent, fearful fortress of the anticommunist McCarthy years (1950-1954), and Beauvoir was suspected of Marxist sympathies. Even *The Nation*, a generally liberal magazine, warned its readers against "certain political leanings" of the author. Open acknowledgement of the existence of women's oppression was too radical for the United States in the fifties, and Beauvoir's conclusion, that change in women's economic condition, though insufficient by itself, "remains the basic factor" in improving women's situation, was particularly unacceptable.

24. According to the passage, one difference between *The Feminine Mystique* and *The Second Sex* is that Friedan's book

    (A) rejects the idea that women are oppressed
    (B) provides a primarily theoretical analysis of women's lives
    (C) does not reflect the political beliefs of its author
    (D) suggests that women's economic condition has no impact on their status
    (E) concentrates on the practical aspects of the question of women's emancipation

25. The author quotes from *The Nation* most probably in order to

    (A) modify an earlier assertion
    (B) point out a possible exception to her argument
    (C) illustrate her central point
    (D) clarify the meaning of a term
    (E) cite an expert opinion

26. It can be inferred from the passage that which of the following is not a factor in the explanation of why *The Feminine Mystique* was received more positively in the United States than was *The Second Sex*?

    (A) By 1963 political conditions in the United States had changed.
    (B) Friedan's book was less intellectual and abstract than Beauvoir's.
    (C) Readers did not recognize the powerful influence of Beauvoir's book on Friedan's ideas.
    (D) Friedan's approach to the issue of women's emancipation was less radical than Beauvoir's.
    (E) American readers were more willing to consider the problem of the oppression of women in the sixties than they had been in the fifties.

27. According to the passage, Beauvoir's book asserted that the status of women

    (A) is the outcome of political oppression
    (B) is inherently tied to their economic condition
    (C) can be best improved under a communist government
    (D) is a theoretical, rather than a pragmatic, issue
    (E) is a critical area of discussion in Marxist economic theory

GO ON TO THE NEXT PAGE.

Each question below consists of a word printed in capital letters, followed by five lettered words or phrases. Choose the lettered word or phrase that is most nearly <u>opposite</u> in meaning to the word in capital letters.

Since some of the questions require you to distinguish fine shades of meaning, be sure to consider all the choices before deciding which one is best.

28. STERILIZE: (A) uncover (B) irritate
 (C) contaminate (D) operate (E) agitate

29. INADVERTENT: (A) well known
 (B) quite similar (C) fortunate
 (D) normal (E) intentional

30. SUBLIMINAL: (A) adroit (B) gentle
 (C) downcast (D) able to be manipulated
 (E) at a perceptible level

31. PLACATE: (A) avert (B) antagonize
 (C) procure (D) subside (E) revolt

32. INUNDATE: (A) drain (B) erupt (C) exit
 (D) decelerate (E) disturb

33. FLOURISH:
 (A) lack of consistency
 (B) lack of embellishment
 (C) lack of sense
 (D) lack of spontaneity
 (E) lack of substance

34. SUMMARILY:
 (A) after long deliberation
 (B) with benevolent intent
 (C) in general disagreement
 (D) under close scrutiny
 (E) from questionable premises

35. STOLID: (A) excitable (B) friendly
 (C) slender (D) brittle (E) weak

36. IDYLL:
 (A) negative appraisal
 (B) pedestrian argument
 (C) object created for a purpose
 (D) experience fraught with tension
 (E) action motivated by greed

37. ASPERITY:
 (A) failure of imagination
 (B) brevity of speech
 (C) sureness of judgment
 (D) mildness of temper
 (E) lack of beauty

38. DESULTORY:
 (A) highly inimical
 (B) cheerfully accepted
 (C) strongly highlighted
 (D) lightly considered
 (E) strictly methodical

STOP

**IF YOU FINISH BEFORE TIME IS CALLED, YOU MAY CHECK YOUR WORK ON THIS SECTION ONLY.
DO NOT TURN TO ANY OTHER SECTION IN THE TEST.**

SECTION 2
Time—30 minutes
30 Questions

Numbers: All numbers used are real numbers.

Figures: Position of points, angles, regions, etc. can be assumed to be in the order shown; and angle measures can be assumed to be positive.

Lines shown as straight can be assumed to be straight.

Figures can be assumed to lie in a plane unless otherwise indicated.

Figures that accompany questions are intended to provide information useful in answering the questions. However, unless a note states that a figure is drawn to scale, you should solve these problems NOT by estimating sizes by sight or by measurement, but by using your knowledge of mathematics (see Example 2 below).

Directions: Each of the Questions 1-15 consists of two quantities, one in Column A and one in Column B. You are to compare the two quantities and choose

    A if the quantity in Column A is greater;
    B if the quantity in Column B is greater;
    C if the two quantities are equal;
    D if the relationship cannot be determined from the information given.

Note: Since there are only four choices, NEVER MARK (E).

Common Information: In a question, information concerning one or both of the quantities to be compared is centered above the two columns. A symbol that appears in both columns represents the same thing in Column A as it does in Column B.

	Column A	Column B	Sample Answers
Example 1:	2×6	$2 + 6$	● Ⓑ Ⓒ Ⓓ Ⓔ

Examples 2-4 refer to $\triangle PQR$.

	Column A	Column B	Sample Answers
Example 2:	PN	NQ	Ⓐ Ⓑ Ⓒ ● Ⓔ

(since equal measures cannot be assumed, even though PN and NQ appear equal)

	Column A	Column B	Sample Answers
Example 3:	x	y	Ⓐ ● Ⓒ Ⓓ Ⓔ

(since N is between P and Q)

	Column A	Column B	Sample Answers
Example 4:	$w + z$	180	Ⓐ Ⓑ ● Ⓓ Ⓔ

(since PQ is a straight line)

GO ON TO THE NEXT PAGE.

A if the quantity in Column A is greater;
B if the quantity in Column B is greater;
C if the two quantities are equal;
D if the relationship cannot be determined from the information given.

Column A	Column B

1. $3,960 \div 65$ 60

Team X scored 10 points in the first half of a certain game. In the second half of the game, team Y scored 15 points more than team X.

2. The number of points scored by team X in the first half of the game   The number of points scored by team Y in the first half of the game

3. $\dfrac{5}{8}$ $\dfrac{7}{11}$

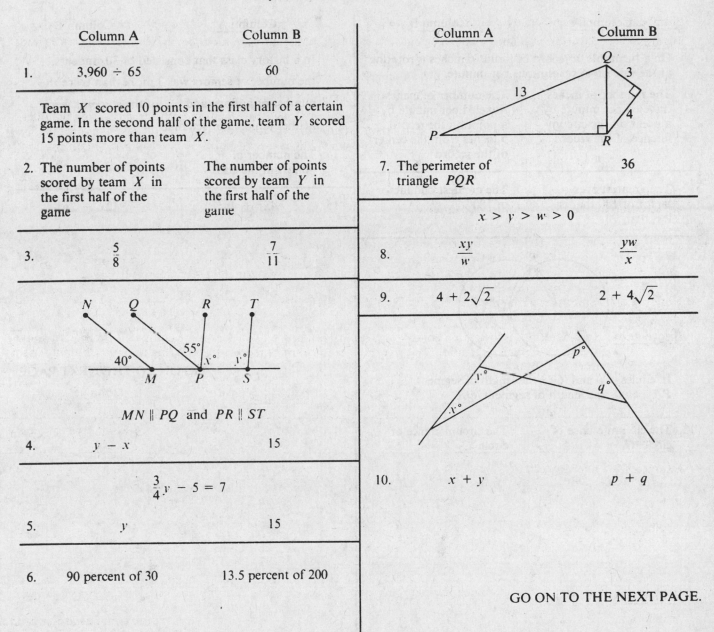

$MN \parallel PQ$ and $PR \parallel ST$

4. $y - x$ 15

$$\frac{3}{4}y - 5 = 7$$

5. y 15

6.   90 percent of 30   13.5 percent of 200

Column A	Column B

7. The perimeter of triangle PQR 36

$$x > y > w > 0$$

8. $\dfrac{xy}{w}$ $\dfrac{yw}{x}$

9. $4 + 2\sqrt{2}$ $2 + 4\sqrt{2}$

10. $x + y$ $p + q$

GO ON TO THE NEXT PAGE.

Column A	Column B

On a turntable, a record of radius 6 inches is rotating at the rate of 45 revolutions per minute.

11. The number of inches traveled per minute by a point on the circumference of the record | The number of inches traveled per minute by a point on the record 5 inches from the center of the record

12. The greatest even factor of 180 that is less than 90 | The greatest odd factor of 180

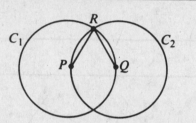

In circles C_1 and C_2, the length of segment PR equals the length of segment QR.

13. The circumference of circle C_1 | The circumference of circle C_2

Column A	Column B

In a history class that consisted of 30 students, the number of seniors was 3 more than twice the number of juniors, and $\frac{3}{10}$ of the students were neither juniors nor seniors.

14. The number of juniors in the class | 6

15. $4x^2 + 4y^2$ | $(2x + 2y)^2$

GO ON TO THE NEXT PAGE.

Directions: Each of the Questions 16-30 has five answer choices. For each of these questions, select the best of the answer choices given.

16. If 25 percent of a certain number is 1,600, what is 10 percent of the number?

   (A)   40
   (B)   400
   (C)   640
   (D) 1,440
   (E) 4,000

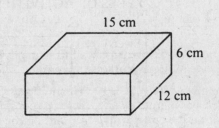

17. The ratio of 1.8 to 2 is equal to the ratio of

   (A) 9 to 1
   (B) 9 to 10
   (C) 9 to 20
   (D) 18 to 100
   (E) 18 to 200

20. What is the maximum number of cubes, each 3 centimeters on an edge, that can be packed into a rectangular box with inside dimensions as shown above?

   (A) 360   (B) 120   (C) 90   (D) 40   (E) 20

18. If $2x + 7 = 12$ then $4x - 7 =$

   (A) 2   (B) 2.5   (C) 3   (D) 10   (E) 13

GO ON TO THE NEXT PAGE.

19. If $x + y = n$, then $x^2 + 2xy + y^2 =$

   (A) $2n$

   (B) n^2

   (C) $n(x - y)$

   (D) $n^2 + 2y(n - y)$

   (E) $n^2 + xn - x^2$

Questions 21-25 refer to the following graphs.

AVERAGE NUMBER OF HOURS PER WEEK SPENT IN MAJOR TYPES OF ACTIVITIES BY EMPLOYED PERSONS

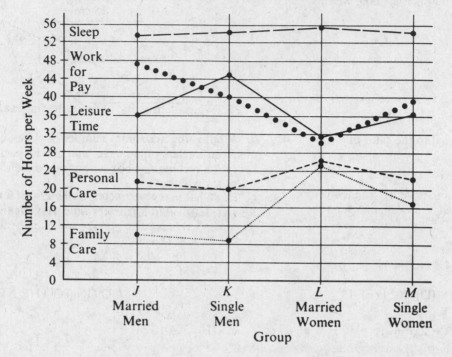

AVERAGE NUMBER OF HOURS PER WEEK SPENT IN LEISURE-TIME ACTIVITIES BY EMPLOYED PERSONS

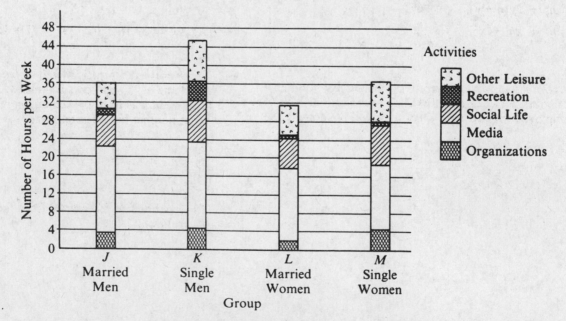

Note: Graphs drawn to scale.

GO ON TO THE NEXT PAGE.

268

21. In which major type of activity is the average number of hours spent per week most nearly the same for all four groups?

(A) Sleep
(B) Work for pay
(C) Leisure time
(D) Personal care
(E) Family care

22. Approximately what is the average number of hours per week that employed single women spend in leisure-time activities?

(A) 47   (B) 39   (C) 37   (D) 30   (E) 17

23. Approximately what is the average number of hours per week that employed married men spend on media activities?

(A) 12
(B) 16
(C) 19
(D) 22
(E) 25

24. Which of the following lists the four groups from least to greatest with respect to the average number of hours per week that each spends working for pay?

(A) J, K, M, L
(B) J, L, M, K
(C) L, J, M, K
(D) L, K, M, J
(E) L, M, K, J

25. Approximately what percent of the average number of hours per week spent in leisure-time activities by employed single men is spent on social-life activities?

(A) 5%   (B) 9%   (C) 15%
(D) 20%   (E) 27%

26. If x is an integer and $y = 9x + 13$, what is the greatest value of x for which y is less than 100 ?

(A) 12   (B) 11   (C) 10   (D) 9   (E) 8

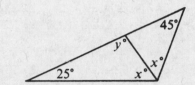

27. What is the value of y in the figure above?

(A) 70   (B) 80   (C) 90

(D) 100   (E) 110

28. What is the perimeter, in meters, of a rectangular playground 24 meters wide that has the same area as a rectangular playground 64 meters long and 48 meters wide?

(A) 112
(B) 152
(C) 224
(D) 256
(E) 304

29. Saplings are to be planted 30 feet apart along one side of a straight lane 455 feet long. If the first sapling is to be planted at one end of the lane, how many saplings are needed?

(A) 18   (B) 16   (C) $15\frac{1}{6}$ (D) 15   (E) 14

30. The average (arithmetic mean) of five numbers is 25. After one of the numbers is removed, the average (arithmetic mean) of the remaining numbers is 31. What number has been removed?

(A) 1
(B) 6
(C) 11
(D) 24
(E) It cannot be determined from the information given.

STOP

IF YOU FINISH BEFORE TIME IS CALLED, YOU MAY CHECK YOUR WORK ON THIS SECTION ONLY.
DO NOT TURN TO ANY OTHER SECTION IN THE TEST.

NO TEST MATERIAL ON THIS PAGE

Directions: Each sentence below has one or two blanks, each blank indicating that something has been omitted. Beneath the sentence are five lettered words or sets of words. Choose the word or set of words for each blank that best fits the meaning of the sentence as a whole.

1. Aspartame, a new artificial sugar substitute, is only ------- replacement for saccharin because, unlike saccharin, it breaks down and loses its sweetening characteristics at high temperatures, making it ------- for baking.

   (A) an interim. .ideal
   (B) an apparent. .excellent
   (C) a potential. .versatile
   (D) a significant. .problematic
   (E) a partial. .unsuitable

2. Trapped thousands of years ago in Antarctic ice, recently discovered air bubbles are ------- time capsules filled with information for scientists who chart the history of the atmosphere.

   (A) inconsequential   (B) broken   (C) veritable
   (D) resplendent   (E) impenetrable

3. In the days before the mass marketing of books, censorship was ------- source of -------, which helped the sale of the book and inspired Ralph Waldo Emerson to remark: "Every burned book enlightens the world."

   (A) a respected. .opinion
   (B) a constant. .guidance
   (C) a prime. .publicity
   (D) an unnoticed. .opposition
   (E) an unpromising. .criticism

4. It was not only the ------- of geologists that ------- earlier development of the revolutionary idea that the Earth's continents were moving plates; classical physicists, who could not then explain the mechanism, had declared continental movement impossible.

   (A) indecisiveness. .challenged
   (B) radicalism. .deterred
   (C) conservatism. .hindered
   (D) assumptions. .hastened
   (E) resistance. .mandated

5. Although often extremely critical of the medical profession as a whole, people are rarely willing to treat their personal doctors with equal -------.

   (A) impetuosity   (B) sarcasm   (C) mockery
   (D) contempt   (E) condescension

6. Aalto, like other modernists, believed that form follows function; consequently, his furniture designs asserted the ------- of human needs, and the furniture's form was ------- human use.

   (A) universality. .refined by
   (B) importance. .relegated to
   (C) rationale. .emphasized by
   (D) primacy. .determined by
   (E) variability. .reflected in

7. A ------- acceptance of contemporary forms of social behavior has misled a few into believing that values in conflict with the present age are for all practical purposes -------.

   (A) casual. .reliable
   (B) superficial. .trenchant
   (C) complacent. .superseded
   (D) cautious. .redemptive
   (E) plaintive. .redundant

GO ON TO THE NEXT PAGE.

Directions: In each of the following questions, a related pair of words or phrases is followed by five lettered pairs of words or phrases. Select the lettered pair that best expresses a relationship similar to that expressed in the original pair.

8. TEACHER : CERTIFICATION ::
    (A) driver : license   (B) officer : handcuffs
    (C) librarian : book   (D) mechanic : tool
    (E) architect : blueprint

9. FOOD : NOURISH ::   (A) organ : secrete
    (B) fluids : circulate   (C) cells : degenerate
    (D) antibodies : protect   (E) fats : saturate

10. HACK : CARVE ::   (A) grind : polish
    (B) snip : mince   (C) hew : fell
    (D) whet : blunt   (E) gouge : engrave

11. DETOXIFY : POISON ::   (A) determine : certainty
    (B) destabilize : deviance   (C) disguise : costume
    (D) dissolve : liquid   (E) dehydrate : water

12. SUPERIMPOSE : ABOVE ::
    (A) permeate : beside   (B) focus : around
    (C) insert : between   (D) splice : below
    (E) fuse : behind

13. TAMPER : ADJUST ::
    (A) misrepresent : communicate
    (B) warp : deform
    (C) confess : tell
    (D) mar : deface
    (E) undermine : stop

14. METAPHOR : LITERAL ::
    (A) biography : accurate
    (B) melody : spoken
    (C) poem : rhythmic
    (D) anthem : patriotic
    (E) ballet : intricate

15. COURAGE : RASHNESS ::
    (A) generosity : prodigality
    (B) temperance : modesty
    (C) mettle : spirit
    (D) honor : humility
    (E) compassion : contempt

16. PRESCIENCE : FUTURE ::
    (A) irrationality : sanity
    (B) predictability : past
    (C) irascibility : emotions
    (D) erudition : esoterica
    (E) talkativeness : loquacity

GO ON TO THE NEXT PAGE.

Directions: Each passage in this group is followed by questions based on its content. After reading a passage, choose the best answer to each question. Answer all questions following a passage on the basis of what is stated or implied in that passage.

One of the questions of interest in the study of the evolution of spiders is whether the weaving of orb webs evolved only once or several times. About half the 35,000 known kinds of spiders make webs; a third of the web weavers make orb webs. Since most orb weavers belong either to the Araneidae or the Uloboridae families, the origin of the orb web can be determined only by ascertaining whether the families are related.

Recent taxonomic analysis of individuals from both families indicates that the families evolved from different ancestors, thereby contradicting Wiehle's theory. This theory postulates that the families must be related, based on the assumption that complex behavior, such as web building, could evolve only once. According to Kullman, web structure is the only characteristic that suggests a relationship between families. The families differ in appearance, structure of body hair, and arrangement of eyes. Only Uloborids lack venom glands. Further identification and study of characteristic features will undoubtedly answer the question of the evolution of the orb web.

17. The primary purpose of the passage is to

(A) settle the question of whether orb webs evolved once or more than once
(B) describe scientific speculation concerning an issue related to the evolution of orb webs
(C) analyze the differences between the characteristic features of spiders in the Araneidae and Uloboridae families
(D) question the methods used by earlier investigators of the habits of spiders
(E) demonstrate that Araneidae spiders are not related to Uloboridae spiders

18. It can be inferred from the passage that all orb-weaving spiders belong to types of spiders that

(A) lack venom glands
(B) are included either in the Uloboridae or Araneidae families
(C) share few characteristic features with other spider types
(D) comprise less than a third of all known types of spiders
(E) are more recently evolved than other types of spiders

19. According to the passage, members of the Araneidae family can be distinguished from members of the Uloboridae family by all of the following EXCEPT

(A) the presence of venom glands
(B) the type of web they spin
(C) the structure of their body hair
(D) the arrangement of their eyes
(E) their appearance

20. Which of the following statements, if true, most weakens Wiehle's theory that complex behavior could evolve only once?

(A) Horses, introduced to the New World by the Spaniards, thrived under diverse climatic conditions.
(B) Plants of the Palmaceae family, descendants of a common ancestor, evolved unique seed forms even though the plants occupy similar habitats throughout the world.
(C) All mammals are descended from a small, rodentlike animal whose physical characteristics in some form are found in all its descendants.
(D) Plants in the Cactaceae and Euphorbiaceae families, although they often look alike and have developed similar mechanisms to meet the rigors of the desert, evolved independently.
(E) The Cuban anole, which was recently introduced in the Florida wilds, is quickly replacing the native Florida chameleon because the anole has no competitors.

GO ON TO THE NEXT PAGE.

273

"Popular art" has a number of meanings, impossible to define with any precision, which range from folklore to junk. The poles are clear enough, but the middle tends to blur. The Hollywood Western of the 1930's, for example, has elements of folklore, but is closer to junk than to high art or folk art. There can be great trash, just as there is bad high art. The musicals of George Gershwin are great popular art, never aspiring to high art. Schubert and Brahms, however, used elements of popular music—folk themes—in works clearly intended as high art. The case of Verdi is a different one: he took a popular genre—bourgeois melodrama set to music (an accurate definition of nineteenth-century opera)—and, without altering its fundamental nature, transmuted it into high art. This remains one of the greatest achievements in music, and one that cannot be fully appreciated without recognizing the essential trashiness of the genre.

As an example of such a transmutation, consider what Verdi made of the typical political elements of nineteenth-century opera. Generally in the plots of these operas, a hero or heroine—usually portrayed only as an individual, unfettered by class—is caught between the immoral corruption of the aristocracy and the doctrinaire rigidity or secret greed of the leaders of the proletariat. Verdi transforms this naïve and unlikely formulation with music of extraordinary energy and rhythmic vitality, music more subtle than it seems at first hearing. There are scenes and arias that still sound like calls to arms and were clearly understood as such when they were first performed. Such pieces lend an immediacy to the otherwise veiled political message of these operas and call up feelings beyond those of the opera itself.

Or consider Verdi's treatment of character. Before Verdi, there were rarely any characters at all in musical drama, only a series of situations which allowed the singers to express a series of emotional states. Any attempt to find coherent psychological portrayal in these operas is misplaced ingenuity. The only coherence was the singer's vocal technique: when the cast changed, new arias were almost always substituted, generally adapted from other operas. Verdi's characters, on the other hand, have genuine consistency and integrity, even if, in many cases, the consistency is that of pasteboard melodrama. The integrity of the character is achieved through the music: once he had become established, Verdi did not rewrite his music for different singers or countenance alterations or substitutions of somebody else's arias in one of his operas, as every eighteenth-century composer had done. When he revised an opera, it was only for dramatic economy and effectiveness.

21. The author refers to Schubert and Brahms in order to suggest

(A) that their achievements are no less substantial than those of Verdi
(B) that their works are examples of great trash
(C) the extent to which Schubert and Brahms influenced the later compositions of Verdi
(D) a contrast between the conventions of nineteenth-century opera and those of other musical forms
(E) that popular music could be employed in compositions intended as high art

22. According to the passage, the immediacy of the political message in Verdi's operas stems from the

(A) vitality and subtlety of the music
(B) audience's familiarity with earlier operas
(C) portrayal of heightened emotional states
(D) individual talents of the singers
(E) verisimilitude of the characters

23. According to the passage, all of the following characterize musical drama before Verdi EXCEPT

(A) arias tailored to a particular singer's ability
(B) adaptation of music from other operas
(C) psychological inconsistency in the portrayal of characters
(D) expression of emotional states in a series of dramatic situations
(E) music used for the purpose of defining a character

GO ON TO THE NEXT PAGE.

24. It can be inferred that the author regards Verdi's revisions to his operas with

(A) regret that the original music and texts were altered
(B) concern that many of the revisions altered the plots of the original work
(C) approval for the intentions that motivated the revisions
(D) puzzlement, since the revisions seem largely insignificant
(E) enthusiasm, since the revisions were aimed at reducing the conventionality of the operas' plots

25. According to the passage, one of Verdi's achievements within the framework of nineteenth-century opera and its conventions was to

(A) limit the extent to which singers influenced the musical composition and performance of his operas
(B) use his operas primarily as forums to protest both the moral corruption and dogmatic rigidity of the political leaders of his time
(C) portray psychologically complex characters shaped by the political environment surrounding them
(D) incorporate elements of folklore into both the music and plots of his operas
(E) introduce political elements into an art form that had traditionally avoided political content

26. Which of the following best describes the relationship of the first paragraph of the passage to the passage as a whole?

(A) It provides a group of specific examples from which generalizations are drawn later in the passage.
(B) It leads to an assertion that is supported by examples later in the passage.
(C) It defines terms and relationships that are challenged in an argument later in the passage.
(D) It briefly compares and contrasts several achievements that are examined in detail later in the passage.
(E) It explains a method of judging a work of art, a method that is used later in the passage.

27. It can be inferred that the author regards the independence from social class of the heroes and heroines of nineteenth-century opera as

(A) an idealized but fundamentally accurate portrayal of bourgeois life
(B) a plot convention with no real connection to political reality
(C) a plot refinement unique to Verdi
(D) a symbolic representation of the position of the bourgeoisie relative to the aristocracy and the proletariat
(E) a convention largely seen as irrelevant by audiences

GO ON TO THE NEXT PAGE.

Directions: Each question below consists of a word printed in capital letters, followed by five lettered words or phrases. Choose the lettered word or phrase that is most nearly <u>opposite</u> in meaning to the word in capital letters.

Since some of the questions require you to distinguish fine shades of meaning, be sure to consider all the choices before deciding which one is best.

28. PERISH: (A) move on   (B) survive
    (C) come after   (D) transgress   (E) strive

29. UNPREDICTABLE: (A) sensitive
    (B) compliant   (C) dependable   (D) mature
    (E) laudable

30. TRIBUTE: (A) denunciation   (B) torment
    (C) betrayal   (D) menace   (E) penalty

31. FINESSE: (A) indecision
    (B) heavy-handedness   (C) extroversion
    (D) extravagance   (E) competitiveness

32. SAP: (A) reinstate   (B) condone   (C) bolster
    (D) satiate   (E) facilitate

33. CONVOLUTED: (A) symmetrical
    (B) separate   (C) straightforward
    (D) completely flexible   (E) consistently calm

34. MITIGATE: (A) exacerbate   (B) preponderate
    (C) accelerate   (D) elevate   (E) extrapolate

35. TORPOR: (A) rigidity   (B) randomness
    (C) agility   (D) obscurity   (E) vigor

36. ZENITH: (A) decline   (B) anticlimax
    (C) foundation   (D) nadir   (E) abyss

37. VENAL: (A) pleasant   (B) clever
    (C) healthy   (D) unstinting   (E) incorruptible

38. PERIPATETIC: (A) stationary   (B) enclosed
    (C) discrete   (D) essential   (E) careful

STOP

**IF YOU FINISH BEFORE TIME IS CALLED, YOU MAY CHECK YOUR WORK ON THIS SECTION ONLY.
DO NOT TURN TO ANY OTHER SECTION IN THE TEST.**

Section 4 starts on page 278.

Time—30 minutes

30 Questions

Numbers: All numbers used are real numbers.

Figures: Position of points, angles, regions, etc. can be assumed to be in the order shown; and angle measures can be assumed to be positive.

Lines shown as straight can be assumed to be straight.

Figures can be assumed to lie in a plane unless otherwise indicated.

Figures that accompany questions are intended to provide information useful in answering the questions. However, unless a note states that a figure is drawn to scale, you should solve these problems NOT by estimating sizes by sight or by measurement, but by using your knowledge of mathematics (see Example 2 below).

Directions: Each of the <u>Questions 1-15</u> consists of two quantities, one in Column A and one in Column B. You are to compare the two quantities and choose

      A if the quantity in Column A is greater;
      B if the quantity in Column B is greater;
      C if the two quantities are equal;
      D if the relationship cannot be determined from the information given.

Note: Since there are only four choices, **NEVER MARK (E).**

Common Information: In a question, information concerning one or both of the quantities to be compared is centered above the two columns. A symbol that appears in both columns represents the same thing in Column A as it does in Column B.

Column A	Column B	Sample Answers

Example 1: 2×6 $2 + 6$ ● Ⓑ Ⓒ Ⓓ Ⓔ

Examples 2-4 refer to $\triangle PQR$.

Example 2: PN NQ Ⓐ Ⓑ Ⓒ ● Ⓔ

(since equal measures cannot be assumed, even though PN and NQ appear equal)

Example 3: x y Ⓐ ● Ⓒ Ⓓ Ⓔ

(since N is between P and Q)

Example 4: $w + z$ 180 Ⓐ Ⓑ ● Ⓓ Ⓔ

(since PQ is a straight line)

GO ON TO THE NEXT PAGE.

A if the quantity in Column A is greater;
B if the quantity in Column B is greater;
C if the two quantities are equal;
D if the relationship cannot be determined from the information given.

	Column A	Column B
1.	$\frac{2}{3}\left(1-\frac{1}{3}\right)$	$\frac{2}{9}$

$$n = \frac{1}{2} + \frac{1}{4} + \frac{1}{8} + \frac{1}{16}$$

	Column A	Column B
2.	$1 - n$	$\frac{1}{16}$
3.	5^3	3^5

R and S are distinct points on a circle of radius 1.

	Column A	Column B
4.	The length of line segment RS	2

$x < 5$ and $y > 12$.

	Column A	Column B
5.	$y - x$	7

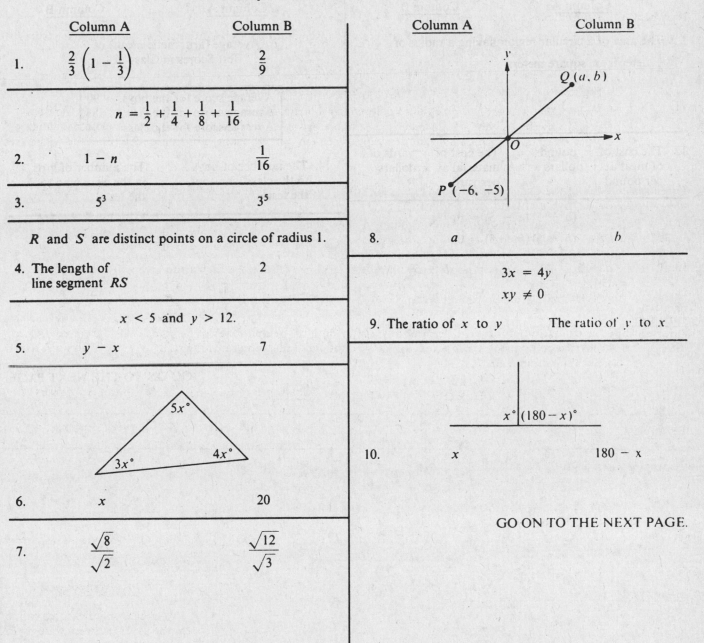

	Column A	Column B
6.	x	20
7.	$\dfrac{\sqrt{8}}{\sqrt{2}}$	$\dfrac{\sqrt{12}}{\sqrt{3}}$

	Column A	Column B
8.	a	b

$$3x = 4y$$
$$xy \neq 0$$

	Column A	Column B
9.	The ratio of x to y	The ratio of y to x
10.	x	$180 - x$

GO ON TO THE NEXT PAGE.

A if the quantity in Column A is greater;
B if the quantity in Column B is greater;
C if the two quantities are equal;
D if the relationship cannot be determined from the information given.

Column A	Column B

The area of a circular region having a radius of $\frac{1}{4}$ meter is x square meters.

11. x $\frac{1}{4}$

12. The cost of x pounds of meat at y dollars per pound   The cost of y yards of material at x dollars per yard

$$(a + 5)(a - 5) = 0$$
$$(b + 5)(b - 5) = 0$$

13. $a + 5$ $b + 5$

Column A	Column B

Average (arithmetic mean) of Test Scores in Class R

Average score for the boys	90
Average score for the girls	81
Average score for the class	84

14. The number of boys in the class who took the test   The number of girls in the class who took the test

$$x > 1$$
$$y > 1$$

15. $\dfrac{1}{\frac{1}{x} + \frac{1}{y}}$ $\dfrac{1}{x} + \dfrac{1}{y}$

GO ON TO THE NEXT PAGE.

16. If $\frac{1}{7}$ of a certain number is 4, then $\frac{1}{4}$ of the number is

    (A) $\frac{7}{16}$

    (B) 2

    (C) $\frac{16}{7}$

    (D) 7

    (E) 28

17. At College C there are from 2 to 4 introductory philosophy classes each semester, and each of these classes has from 20 to 30 students enrolled. If one semester 10 percent of the students enrolled in introductory philosophy failed, what is the greatest possible number who failed?

    (A) 12
    (B) 10
    (C) 8
    (D) 6
    (E) 3

18. The lengths of the sides of triangle T are $x + 1$, $2x$, and $3x$. The sum of the degree measures of the three interior angles of T is

    (A) $6x$
    (B) $60x$
    (C)   90
    (D)   180
    (E)   not determinable from the information given

19. Today is Jack's 12th birthday and his father's 40th birthday. How many years from today will Jack's father be twice as old as Jack is at that time?

    (A) 12
    (B) 14
    (C) 16
    (D) 18
    (E) 20

20. If $a + b = 10$, then $\left(a + \frac{b}{2}\right) + \left(b + \frac{a}{2}\right) =$

    (A) 5
    (B) 10
    (C) 15
    (D) 20
    (E) 25

GO ON TO THE NEXT PAGE.

Questions 21-25 refer to the following graphs.

PUBLIC AND PRIVATE SCHOOL EXPENDITURES
1965-1979
(in billions of dollars)
(1 billion = 1,000,000,000)

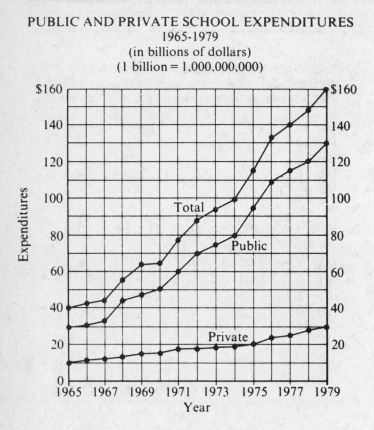

SCHOOL ENROLLMENT BY LEVEL OF INSTRUCTION
1965-1979
(in millions of students)

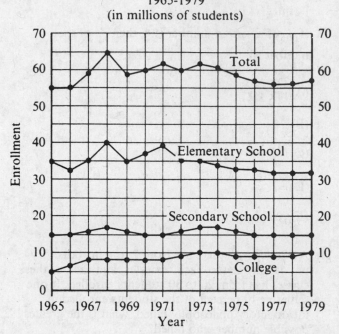

21. Of the following years, which showed the least difference between public school expenditures and private school expenditures?

(A) 1965
(B) 1970
(C) 1974
(D) 1978
(E) 1979

22. For each year from 1965 to 1979, the total enrollment in college, secondary school, and elementary school was in which of the following ranges?

(A) 50 to 60 million
(B) 55 to 60 million
(C) 55 to 65 million
(D) 60 to 65 million
(E) 60 to 70 million

23. In 1970, approximately how many billion dollars were spent on public elementary schools?

(A) 37
(B) 50
(C) 60
(D) 87
(E) It cannot be determined from the information given.

24. Which of the following periods showed a continual increase in the total school enrollment?

(A) 1967-1969
(B) 1969-1971
(C) 1971-1973
(D) 1973-1975
(E) 1975-1977

25. In 1972, public school expenditures were approximately what percent of the total school expenditures for that year?

(A) 20%
(B) 60%
(C) 70%
(D) 80%
(E) 90%

GO ON TO THE NEXT PAGE.

282

26. If the sum of the first n positive integers is equal to $\frac{n(n + 1)}{2}$, then the sum of the first 25 positive integers is

(A) 51
(B) 52
(C) 313
(D) 325
(E) 326

27. If $\frac{2x - 1}{3} = \frac{12}{9}$, then $x =$

(A) $\frac{3}{2}$

(B) $\frac{5}{2}$

(C) 4

(D) $\frac{13}{2}$

(E) 7

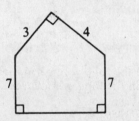

28. What is the perimeter of the pentagon above?

(A) 21
(B) 26
(C) 28
(D) 31
(E) 41

29. If x is positive and y is 1 less than the square of x, which of the following expresses x in terms of y?

(A) $x = y^2 - 1$
(B) $x = y^2 + 1$
(C) $x = \sqrt{y} + 1$
(D) $x = \sqrt{1 - y}$
(E) $x = \sqrt{y + 1}$

30. If the total surface area of a cube is 24, what is the volume of the cube?

(A) 8
(B) 24
(C) 64
(D) $48\sqrt{6}$
(E) 216

STOP

IF YOU FINISH BEFORE TIME IS CALLED, YOU MAY CHECK YOUR WORK ON THIS SECTION ONLY.
DO NOT TURN TO ANY OTHER SECTION IN THE TEST.

NO TEST MATERIAL ON THIS PAGE

NOTE: To ensure prompt processing of test results, it is important that you fill in the blanks exactly as directed.

GENERAL TEST

Copy this code in box 6 on your answer sheet. Then fill in the corresponding ovals exactly as shown.

6. TITLE CODE

Copy the Test Name and Form Code in box 7 on your answer sheet.

TEST NAME _General_

FORM CODE _GR91-18_

GRADUATE RECORD EXAMINATIONS GENERAL TEST

B. You will have 3 hours and 30 minutes in which to work on this test, which consists of seven sections. During the time allowed for one section, you may work only on that section. The time allowed for each section is 30 minutes.

Each of your scores will be determined by the number of questions for which you select the best answer from the choices given. Questions for which you mark no answer or more than one answer are not counted in scoring. Nothing is subtracted from a score if you answer a question incorrectly. Therefore, to maximize your scores it is better for you to guess at an answer than not to respond at all.

You are advised to work as rapidly as you can without losing accuracy. Do not spend too much time on questions that are too difficult for you. Go on to the other questions and come back to the difficult ones later.

There are several different types of questions; you will find special directions for each type in the test itself. Be sure you understand the directions before attempting to answer any questions.

YOU MUST INDICATE ALL YOUR ANSWERS ON THE SEPARATE ANSWER SHEET. No credit will be given for anything written in this examination book, but you may write in the book as much as you wish to work out your answers. After you have decided on your response to a question, fill in the corresponding oval on the answer sheet. BE SURE THAT EACH MARK IS DARK AND COMPLETELY FILLS THE OVAL. Mark only one answer to each question. No credit will be given for multiple answers. Erase all stray marks. If you change an answer, be sure that all previous marks are erased completely. Incomplete erasures may be read as intended answers. Do not be concerned if your answer sheet provides spaces for more answers than there are questions in each section.

Example:

What city is the capital of France?

(A) Rome
(B) Paris
(C) London
(D) Cairo
(E) Oslo

Sample Answer

BEST ANSWER PROPERLY MARKED

IMPROPER MARKS

Some or all of the passages for this test have been adapted from published material to provide the examinee with significant problems for analysis and evaluation. To make the passages suitable for testing purposes, the style, content, or point of view of the original may have been altered in some cases. The ideas contained in the passages do not necessarily represent the opinions of the Graduate Record Examinations Board or Educational Testing Service.

DO NOT OPEN YOUR TEST BOOK UNTIL YOU ARE TOLD TO DO SO.

285

FOR GENERAL TEST, FORM GR91-18 ONLY
Answer Key and Percentages* of Examinees Answering Each Question Correctly

VERBAL ABILITY						QUANTITATIVE ABILITY					
Section 1			Section 3			Section 2			Section 4		
Number	Answer	P+	Number	Answer	P+	Number	Answer	P+	Number	Answer	P+
1	D	97	1	E	91	1	A	82	1	A	87
2	C	62	2	C	74	2	D	82	2	C	80
3	D	63	3	C	80	3	B	80	3	B	90
4	C	60	4	C	61	4	B	76	4	D	78
5	A	47	5	D	55	5	A	74	5	A	77
6	E	47	6	D	50	6	C	72	6	B	76
7	D	45	7	C	41	7	B	76	7	C	74
8	C	95	8	A	98	8	A	74	8	A	44
9	B	85	9	D	92	9	B	60	9	A	56
10	D	76	10	E	84	10	C	48	10	D	48
11	C	71	11	E	79	11	A	63	11	B	45
12	D	58	12	C	73	12	A	70	12	C	37
13	B	65	13	A	37	13	D	39	13	D	33
14	D	48	14	B	47	14	C	43	14	B	38
15	E	34	15	A	36	15	D	28	15	D	21
16	B	18	16	D	29	16	C	86	16	D	90
17	A	53	17	B	67	17	B	79	17	A	87
18	E	73	18	D	29	18	C	85	18	D	76
19	B	59	19	B	79	19	B	66	19	C	81
20	B	51	20	D	65	20	D	63	20	C	65
21	E	63	21	E	76	21	A	89	21	A	97
22	E	62	22	A	59	22	C	88	22	C	85
23	C	37	23	E	55	23	C	70	23	E	57
24	E	50	24	C	64	24	E	61	24	B	80
25	C	63	25	A	23	25	D	49	25	D	63
26	C	35	26	B	40	26	D	71	26	D	69
27	B	69	27	B	29	27	D	48	27	B	73
28	C	95	28	B	91	28	E	38	28	B	63
29	E	84	29	C	88	29	B	33	29	E	54
30	E	86	30	A	83	30	A	29	30	A	47
31	B	68	31	B	80						
32	A	51	32	C	53						
33	B	46	33	C	63						
34	A	38	34	B	44						
35	A	36	35	E	34						
36	D	33	36	D	25						
37	D	24	37	E	28						
38	E	13	38	A	25						

*Estimated P+ for the group of examinees who took the GRE General Test in a recent three-year period.

SCORE CONVERSIONS FOR GRE GENERAL TEST, GR91-18

Raw Score	Scaled Score Verbal	Scaled Score Quantitative	Raw Score	Scaled Score Verbal	Scaled Score Quantitative
74-76	800		39	430	550
73	790		38	420	540
72	780		37	420	530
71	770		36	410	520
70	750		35	400	510
			34	390	500
69	740		33	380	480
68	730		32	370	470
67	720		31	370	460
66	710		30	360	450
65	690				
64	680		29	350	440
63	670		28	340	430
62	660		27	340	410
61	650		26	330	400
60	640	800	25	320	390
			24	310	380
59	630	790	23	300	370
58	620	780	22	290	360
57	610	760	21	280	340
56	590	750	20	270	330
55	580	740			
54	570	730	19	260	320
53	560	720	18	250	310
52	550	710	17	240	300
51	540	690	16	230	290
50	530	680	15	220	270
			14	210	260
49	520	670	13	200	250
48	520	660	12	200	240
47	510	650	11	200	230
46	500	640	10	200	220
45	490	620			
44	480	610	9	200	200
43	470	600	8	200	200
42	460	590	7	200	200
41	450	580	0-6	200	200
40	440	570			

NO TEST MATERIAL ON THIS PAGE

THE GRADUATE RECORD
EXAMINATIONS®

GRE®

(ETS)®

General Test

Do not break the seal
until you are told to do so.

The contents of this test are confidential.
Disclosure or reproduction of any portion
of it is prohibited.

THIS TEST BOOK MUST NOT BE TAKEN FROM THE ROOM.

SECTION 1

Time—30 minutes

30 Questions

Numbers: All numbers used are real numbers.

Figures: Position of points, angles, regions, etc. can be assumed to be in the order shown; and angle measures can be assumed to be positive.

Lines shown as straight can be assumed to be straight.

Figures can be assumed to lie in a plane unless otherwise indicated.

Figures that accompany questions are intended to provide information useful in answering the questions. However, unless a note states that a figure is drawn to scale, you should solve these problems NOT by estimating sizes by sight or by measurement, but by using your knowledge of mathematics (see Example 2 below).

Directions: Each of the Questions 1-15 consists of two quantities, one in Column A and one in Column B. You are to compare the two quantities and choose

A if the quantity in Column A is greater;
B if the quantity in Column B is greater;
C if the two quantities are equal;
D if the relationship cannot be determined from the information given.

Note: Since there are only four choices, **NEVER MARK (E)**.

Common
Information: In a question, information concerning one or both of the quantities to be compared is centered above the two columns. A symbol that appears in both columns represents the same thing in Column A as it does in Column B.

	Column A	Column B	Sample Answers
Example 1:	2×6	$2 + 6$	● Ⓑ Ⓒ Ⓓ Ⓔ

Examples 2-4 refer to $\triangle PQR$.

	Column A	Column B	Sample Answers
Example 2:	PN	NQ	Ⓐ Ⓑ Ⓒ ● Ⓔ

(since equal measures cannot be assumed, even though PN and NQ appear equal)

	Column A	Column B	Sample Answers
Example 3:	x	y	Ⓐ ● Ⓒ Ⓓ Ⓔ

(since N is between P and Q)

	Column A	Column B	Sample Answers
Example 4:	$w + z$	180	Ⓐ Ⓑ ● Ⓓ Ⓔ

(since PQ is a straight line)

290

GO ON TO THE NEXT PAGE.

A if the quantity in Column A is greater;
B if the quantity in Column B is greater;
C if the two quantities are equal;
D if the relationship cannot be determined from the information given.

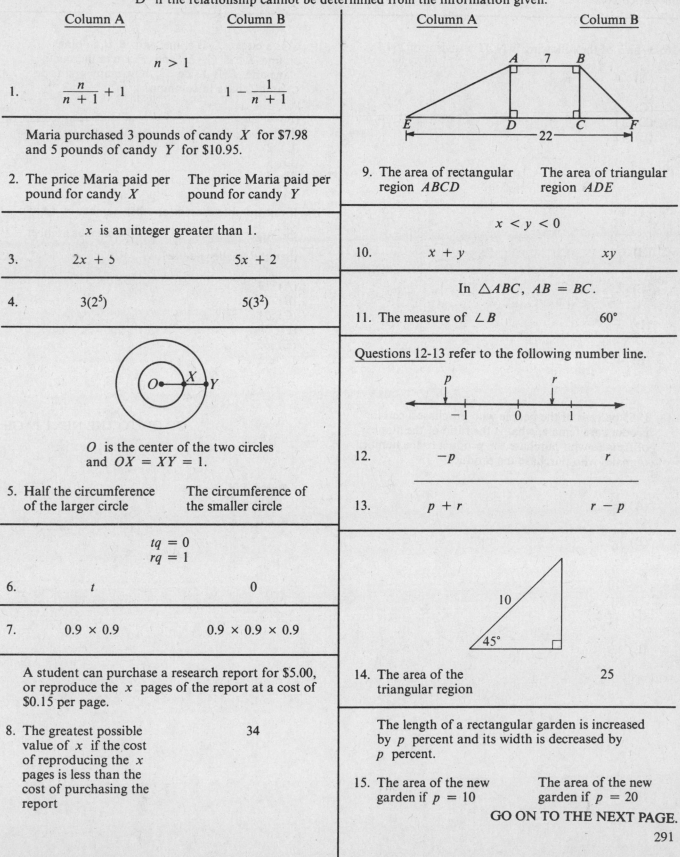

Column A	Column B

$n > 1$

1. $\dfrac{n}{n+1} + 1$ $1 - \dfrac{1}{n+1}$

Maria purchased 3 pounds of candy X for \$7.98 and 5 pounds of candy Y for \$10.95.

2. The price Maria paid per pound for candy X The price Maria paid per pound for candy Y

x is an integer greater than 1.

3. $2x + 5$ $5x + 2$

4. $3(2^5)$ $5(3^2)$

O is the center of the two circles and $OX = XY = 1$.

5. Half the circumference of the larger circle   The circumference of the smaller circle

$tq = 0$
$rq = 1$

6. t 0

7. 0.9×0.9 $0.9 \times 0.9 \times 0.9$

A student can purchase a research report for \$5.00, or reproduce the x pages of the report at a cost of \$0.15 per page.

8. The greatest possible value of x if the cost of reproducing the x pages is less than the cost of purchasing the report 34

9. The area of rectangular region $ABCD$ The area of triangular region ADE

$x < y < 0$

10. $x + y$ xy

In $\triangle ABC$, $AB = BC$.

11. The measure of $\angle B$ $60°$

Questions 12-13 refer to the following number line.

12. $-p$ r

13. $p + r$ $r - p$

14. The area of the triangular region 25

The length of a rectangular garden is increased by p percent and its width is decreased by p percent.

15. The area of the new garden if $p = 10$ The area of the new garden if $p = 20$

GO ON TO THE NEXT PAGE.

Directions: Each of the Questions 16-30 has five answer choices. For each of these questions, select the best of the answer choices given.

16. Which of the following is NOT a divisor of 264 ?

(A) 4
(B) 8
(C) 9
(D) 11
(E) 12

17. If $3(x + 1) = 4x - 1$, then $x =$

(A) $\frac{4}{7}$

(B) $\frac{3}{4}$

(C) 2

(D) 3

(E) 4

18. If 55 percent of the people who purchase a certain product are female, what is the ratio of the number of females who purchase the product to the number of males who purchase the product?

(A) $\frac{11}{9}$

(B) $\frac{10}{9}$

(C) $\frac{9}{10}$

(D) $\frac{9}{11}$

(E) $\frac{5}{9}$

19. C is a circle, L is a line, and P is a point on line L. If C, L, and P are in the same plane and P is inside C, how many points do C and L have in common?

(A) 0
(B) 1
(C) 2
(D) 3
(E) 4

20. If one number exceeds another number by 13 and the larger number is $\frac{3}{2}$ times the smaller number, then the smaller number is

(A) 13
(B) 26
(C) 31
(D) 39
(E) 65

GO ON TO THE NEXT PAGE.

Questions 21-25 refer to the following graph.

COUNTRY X'S TOTAL WHEAT IMPORTS
COMPARED TO ITS WHEAT IMPORTS
FROM THE UNITED STATES, 1973-1983

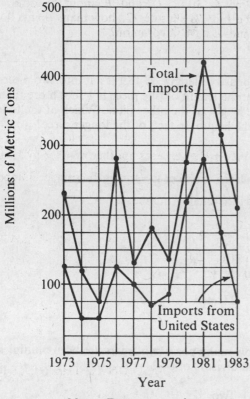

Note: Drawn to scale.

21. From 1973 to 1977, inclusive, how many million
metric tons of wheat did Country X import from
the United States?

(A) 450
(B) 400
(C) 350
(D) 320
(E) 250

22. For how many of the years shown did Country X
import more than 200 million metric tons of wheat?

(A) Two
(B) Five
(C) Six
(D) Seven
(E) Eight

23. The amount of wheat Country X imported from
countries other than the United States was greatest
in which of the following years?

(A) 1974
(B) 1976
(C) 1978
(D) 1981
(E) 1983

24. For the year in which total wheat imports and wheat
imports from the United States were most nearly
equal, how many million metric tons of wheat did
Country X import?

(A) 150
(B) 125
(C) 90
(D) 75
(E) 50

25. For the year in which the amount of Country X's
total wheat imports was greatest, approximately
what percent of that total was imported from the
United States?

(A) 35%
(B) 40%
(C) 50%
(D) 65%
(E) 75%

GO ON TO THE NEXT PAGE.

26. $\left(2 + \frac{3}{4}\right)^2 - \left(2 - \frac{1}{4}\right)^2 =$

(A) $\frac{37}{8}$

(B) $\frac{9}{2}$

(C) 3

(D) 1

(E) $\frac{1}{2}$

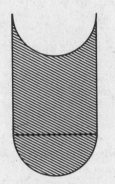

27. If each curved side in the figure above is a semicircle with radius 20, and the two parallel sides each have length 100, what is the area of the shaded region?

(A) 2,000
(B) 4,000
(C) $2,000 - 200\pi$
(D) $4,000 - 200\pi$
(E) $4,000 - 400\pi$

28. If the degree measures of the angles of a triangle are in the ratio $3 : 4 : 5$, what is the degree measure of the smallest angle?

(A) 15°
(B) 30°
(C) 45°
(D) 60°
(E) 75°

29. A board of length L feet is cut into two pieces such that the length of one piece is 1 foot more than twice the length of the other piece. Which of the following is the length, in feet, of the longer piece?

(A) $\frac{L + 2}{2}$

(B) $\frac{2L + 1}{2}$

(C) $\frac{L - 1}{3}$

(D) $\frac{2L + 3}{3}$

(E) $\frac{2L + 1}{3}$

30. How many positive integers are both multiples of 4 and divisors of 64 ?

(A) Two
(B) Three
(C) Four
(D) Five
(E) Six

STOP

IF YOU FINISH BEFORE TIME IS CALLED, YOU MAY CHECK YOUR WORK ON THIS SECTION ONLY.
DO NOT TURN TO ANY OTHER SECTION IN THE TEST.

Directions: Each sentence below has one or two blanks, each blank indicating that something has been omitted. Beneath the sentence are five lettered words or sets of words. Choose the word or set of words for each blank that best fits the meaning of the sentence as a whole.

1. With its maverick approach to the subject, Shere Hite's book has been more widely debated than most; the media throughout the country have brought the author's ------- opinions to the public's attention.

   (A) controversial
   (B) authoritative
   (C) popular
   (D) conclusive
   (E) articulate

2. Though many medieval women possessed devotional books that had belonged to their mothers, formal written evidence of women bequeathing books to their daughters is scarce, which suggests that such bequests were ------- and required no -------.

   (A) unselfish. .rationalization
   (B) tangential. .approval
   (C) customary. .documentation
   (D) covert. .discretion
   (E) spurious. .record

3. Although their initial anger had ------- somewhat, they continued to ------- the careless worker who had broken the machine.

   (A) blazed. .assail
   (B) diminished. .appease
   (C) abated. .berate
   (D) subsided. .condone
   (E) intensified. .torment

4. Borrowing a copyrighted book from a library amounts to a form of theft ------- by entrenched custom: the copyright owner's property, the book, is used repeatedly without ------- for such use.

   (A) engendered. .application
   (B) anticipated. .acknowledgment
   (C) sanctioned. .compensation
   (D) provoked. .adjustment
   (E) perpetrated. .permission

5. The notion that a parasite can alter the behavior of a host organism is not mere fiction; indeed, the phenomenon is not even -------.

   (A) observable   (B) real   (C) comprehended
    (D) rare   (E) imaginable

6. Although Shakespeare received little formal education, scholarship has in recent years ------- the view that he was ------- the work of classical authors.

   (A) substantiated. .unimpressed by
   (B) eroded. .obsessed by
   (C) supported. .oblivious to
   (D) questioned. .influenced by
   (E) undermined. .unfamiliar with

7. Darwin's method did not really ------- the idea of race as an important conceptual category; even the much more central idea of species was little more than a theoretical -------.

   (A) require. .convenience
   (B) apply. .measurement
   (C) exclude. .practice
   (D) subsume. .validation
   (E) reject. .fact

GO ON TO THE NEXT PAGE.

Directions: In each of the following questions, a related pair of words or phrases is followed by five lettered pairs of words or phrases. Select the lettered pair that best expresses a relationship similar to that expressed in the original pair.

8. DENTURE : TEETH :: (A) scarf : head
(B) toupee : hair   (C) fingernail : hand
(D) eyebrow : eye   (E) bandage : wound

9. PROFESSIONAL : ROOKIE :: (A) player : fan
(B) ranger : cowhand   (C) prisoner : thief
(D) soldier : recruit   (E) conductor : musician

10. SCRIPT : PLAY :: (A) refrain : song
(B) assignment : course   (C) score : symphony
(D) collection : story   (E) debate : candidate

11. BUOYANT : SINK :: (A) frozen : melt
(B) liquid : evaporate   (C) brittle : cleave
(D) insoluble : dissolve   (E) gaseous : expand

12. CRAWL : PROCEED :: (A) plummet : descend
(B) nurture : grow   (C) inundate : flood
(D) rampage : destroy   (E) dwindle : decrease

13. ELEGY : SORROW ::
(A) paean : distress
(B) encomium : criticism
(C) requiem : euphoria
(D) tirade : joy
(E) eulogy : admiration

14. FRIEZE : ORNAMENT :: (A) arch : divide
(B) relief : form   (C) arabesque : accentuate
(D) nave : border   (E) pillar : support

15. DECELERATE : SPEED ::
(A) desiccate : dryness
(B) extinguish : oxygen
(C) interpolate : interval
(D) decontaminate : sterility
(E) enervate : vitality

16. DESPOTIC : TYRANNY ::
(A) authoritarian : superiority
(B) skillful : celebrity
(C) generous : liberality
(D) suspect : illegality
(E) peaceful : benevolence

GO ON TO THE NEXT PAGE.

(The article from which the passage was taken appeared in 1982.)

Theorists are divided concerning the origin of the Moon. Some hypothesize that the Moon was formed in the same way as were the planets in the inner solar system (Mercury, Venus, Mars, and Earth)—from
(5) planet-forming materials in the presolar nebula. But, unlike the cores of the inner planets, the Moon's core contains little or no iron, while the typical planet-forming materials were quite rich in iron. Other theorists propose that the Moon was ripped out of the Earth's rocky mantle by the Earth's collison with another large
(10) celestial body after much of the Earth's iron fell to its core. One problem with the collision hypothesis is the question of how a satellite formed in this way could have settled into the nearly circular orbit that the Moon has
(15) today. Fortunately, the collision hypothesis is testable. If it is true, the mantlerocks of the Moon and the Earth should be the same geochemically.

17. The primary purpose of the passage is to

    (A) present two hypotheses concerning the origin of the Moon

    (B) discuss the strengths and weaknesses of the collision hypothesis concerning the origin of the Moon

    (C) propose that hypotheses concerning the Moon's origin be tested

    (D) argue that the Moon could not have been formed out of the typical planet-forming materials of the presolar nebula

    (E) describe one reason why the Moon's geochemical makeup should resemble that of the Earth

18. According to the passage, Mars and the Earth are similar in which of the following ways?

    I. Their satellites were formed by collisions with other celestial bodies.
    II. Their cores contain iron.
    III. They were formed from the presolar nebula.

    (A) III only
    (B) I and II only
    (C) I and III only
    (D) II and III only
    (E) I, II, and III

19. The author implies that a nearly circular orbit is unlikely for a satellite that

    (A) circles one of the inner planets
    (B) is deficient in iron
    (C) is different from its planet geochemically
    (D) was formed by a collision between two celestial bodies
    (E) was formed out of the planet-forming materials in the presolar nebula

20. Which of the following, if true, would be most likely to make it difficult to verify the collision hypothesis in the manner suggested by the author?

    (A) The Moon's core and mantlerock are almost inactive geologically.

    (B) The mantlerock of the Earth has changed in composition since the formation of the Moon, while the mantlerock of the Moon has remained chemically inert.

    (C) Much of the Earth's iron fell to the Earth's core long before the formation of the Moon, after which the Earth's mantlerock remained unchanged.

    (D) Certain of the Earth's elements, such as platinum, gold, and iridium, followed iron to the Earth's core.

    (E) The mantlerock of the Moon contains elements such as platinum, gold, and iridium.

GO ON TO THE NEXT PAGE.

Surprisingly enough, modern historians have rarely interested themselves in the history of the American South in the period before the South began to become self-consciously and distinctively "Southern"—the
(5) decades after 1815. Consequently, the cultural history of Britain's North American empire in the seventeenth and eighteenth centuries has been written almost as if the Southern colonies had never existed. The American culture that emerged during the Colonial and Revolu-
(10) tionary eras has been depicted as having been simply an extension of New England Puritan culture. However, Professor Davis has recently argued that the South stood apart from the rest of American society during this early period, following its own unique pattern of cultural
(15) development. The case for Southern distinctiveness rests upon two related premises: first, that the cultural similarities among the five Southern colonies were far more impressive than the differences, and second, that what made those colonies alike also made them different from
(20) the other colonies. The first, for which Davis offers an enormous amount of evidence, can be accepted without major reservations; the second is far more problematic.

What makes the second premise problematic is the use of the Puritan colonies as a basis for comparison.
(25) Quite properly, Davis decries the excessive influence ascribed by historians to the Puritans in the formation of American culture. Yet Davis inadvertently adds weight to such ascriptions by using the Puritans as the standard against which to assess the achievements and
(30) contributions of Southern colonials. Throughout, Davis focuses on the important, and undeniable, differences between the Southern and Puritan colonies in motives for and patterns of early settlement, in attitudes toward nature and Native Americans, and in the degree of
(35) receptivity to metropolitan cultural influences.

However, recent scholarship has strongly suggested that those aspects of early New England culture that seem to have been most distinctly Puritan, such as the strong religious orientation and the communal impulse,
(40) were not even typical of New England as a whole, but were largely confined to the two colonies of Massachusetts and Connecticut. Thus, what in contrast to the Puritan colonies appears to Davis to be peculiarly Southern—acquisitiveness, a strong interest in politics
(45) and the law, and a tendency to cultivate metropolitan cultural models—was not only more typically English than the cultural patterns exhibited by Puritan Massachusetts and Connecticut, but also almost certainly characteristic of most other early modern British colonies
(50) from Barbados north to Rhode Island and New Hampshire. Within the larger framework of American colonial life, then, not the Southern but the Puritan colonies appear to have been distinctive, and even they seem to have been rapidly assimilating to the dominant cultural patterns by the late Colonial period.

21. The author is primarily concerned with

   (A) refuting a claim about the influence of Puritan culture on the early American South
   (B) refuting a thesis about the distinctiveness of the culture of the early American South
   (C) refuting the two premises that underlie Davis' discussion of the culture of the American South in the period before 1815
   (D) challenging the hypothesis that early American culture was homogeneous in nature
   (E) challenging the contention that the American South made greater contributions to early American culture than Puritan New England did

22. The passage implies that the attitudes toward Native Americans that prevailed in the Southern colonies

   (A) were in conflict with the cosmopolitan outlook of the South
   (B) derived from Southerners' strong interest in the law
   (C) were modeled after those that prevailed in the North
   (D) differed from those that prevailed in the Puritan colonies
   (E) developed as a response to attitudes that prevailed in Massachusetts and Connecticut

23. According to the author, the depiction of American culture during the Colonial and Revolutionary eras as an extension of New England Puritan culture reflects the

   (A) fact that historians have overestimated the importance of the Puritans in the development of American culture
   (B) fact that early American culture was deeply influenced by the strong religious orientation of the colonists
   (C) failure to recognize important and undeniable cultural differences between New Hampshire and Rhode Island on the one hand and the Southern colonies on the other
   (D) extent to which Massachusetts and Connecticut served as cultural models for the other American colonies
   (E) extent to which colonial America resisted assimilating cultural patterns that were typically English

GO ON TO THE NEXT PAGE

24. The author of the passage is in agreement with which of the following elements of Davis' book?

    I. Davis' claim that acquisitiveness was a characteristic unique to the South during the Colonial period

   II. Davis' argument that there were significant differences between Puritan and Southern culture during the Colonial period

  III. Davis' thesis that the Southern colonies shared a common culture

    (A) I only
    (B) II only
    (C) III only
    (D) I and II only
    (E) II and III only

25. It can be inferred from the passage that the author would find Davis' second premise (lines 18-20) more plausible if it were true that

    (A) Puritan culture had displayed the tendency characteristic of the South to cultivate metropolitan cultural models
    (B) Puritan culture had been dominant in all the non-Southern colonies during the seventeenth and eighteenth centuries
    (C) the communal impulse and a strong religious orientation had been more prevalent in the South
    (D) the various cultural patterns of the Southern colonies had more closely resembled each other
    (E) the cultural patterns characteristic of most early modern British colonies had also been characteristic of the Puritan colonies

26. The passage suggests that by the late Colonial period the tendency to cultivate metropolitan cultural models was a cultural pattern that was

    (A) dying out as Puritan influence began to grow
    (B) self-consciously and distinctively Southern
    (C) spreading to Massachusetts and Connecticut
    (D) more characteristic of the Southern colonies than of England
    (E) beginning to spread to Rhode Island and New Hampshire

27. Which of the following statements could most logically follow the last sentence of the passage?

    (A) Thus, had more attention been paid to the evidence, Davis would not have been tempted to argue that the culture of the South diverged greatly from Puritan culture in the seventeenth century.
    (B) Thus, convergence, not divergence, seems to have characterized the cultural development of the American colonies in the eighteenth century.
    (C) Thus, without the cultural diversity represented by the American South, the culture of colonial America would certainly have been homogeneous in nature.
    (D) Thus, the contribution of Southern colonials to American culture was certainly overshadowed by that of the Puritans.
    (E) Thus, the culture of America during the Colonial period was far more sensitive to outside influences than historians are accustomed to acknowledge.

GO ON TO THE NEXT PAGE.

Directions: Each question below consists of a word printed in capital letters, followed by five lettered words or phrases. Choose the lettered word or phrase that is most nearly opposite in meaning to the word in capital letters.

Since some of the questions require you to distinguish fine shades of meaning, be sure to consider all the choices before deciding which one is best.

28. HARMONY: (A) dishonesty   (B) indignity
    (C) insecurity   (D) discord   (E) irritation

29. SLACK: (A) twisted   (B) taut
    (C) compact   (D) durable   (E) shattered

30. JOCULAR: (A) active   (B) serious
    (C) unknown   (D) equable   (E) destructive

31. IMPEDE: (A) assist   (B) entreat
    (C) dislodge   (D) ascribe   (E) avow

32. SAP: (A) fortify   (B) alleviate
    (C) lend credence   (D) hold fast
    (E) draw out

33. CONTROL:
    (A) minor variable
    (B) weak assumption
    (C) improper simulation
    (D) group experimented on
    (E) expression substituted for

34. RECONDITE: (A) intended   (B) defeated
    (C) widely understood   (D) freely dispensed
    (E) recently discovered

35. INIMITABLE: (A) inclined to disagree
    (B) unwilling to compete   (C) eager to advise
    (D) intelligible   (E) ordinary

36. DISINTER: (A) restrain   (B) confiscate
    (C) resist   (D) bury   (E) fund

37. DIATRIBE:
    (A) laudatory piece of writing
    (B) formal speech by one person
    (C) written agreement
    (D) farewell address
    (E) witty poem

38. HOODWINK: (A) explain   (B) shock
    (C) lead   (D) disregard   (E) disabuse

STOP

IF YOU FINISH BEFORE TIME IS CALLED, YOU MAY CHECK YOUR WORK ON THIS SECTION ONLY. DO NOT TURN TO ANY OTHER SECTION IN THE TEST.

Numbers: All numbers used are real numbers.

Figures: Position of points, angles, regions, etc. can be assumed to be in the order shown; and angle measures can be assumed to be positive.

Lines shown as straight can be assumed to be straight.

Figures can be assumed to lie in a plane unless otherwise indicated.

Figures that accompany questions are intended to provide information useful in answering the questions. However, unless a note states that a figure is drawn to scale, you should solve these problems NOT by estimating sizes by sight or by measurement, but by using your knowledge of mathematics (see Example 2 below).

Directions: Each of the Questions 1-15 consists of two quantities, one in Column A and one in Column B. You are to compare the two quantities and choose

  A if the quantity in Column A is greater;
  B if the quantity in Column B is greater;
  C if the two quantities are equal;
  D if the relationship cannot be determined from the information given.

Note: Since there are only four choices, NEVER MARK (E).

Common
Information: In a question, information concerning one or both of the quantities to be compared is centered above the two columns. A symbol that appears in both columns represents the same thing in Column A as it does in Column B.

	Column A	Column B	Sample Answers
Example 1:	2×6	$2 + 6$	● Ⓑ Ⓒ Ⓓ Ⓔ

Examples 2-4 refer to $\triangle PQR$.

	Column A	Column B	Sample Answers
Example 2:	PN	NQ	Ⓐ Ⓑ Ⓒ ● Ⓔ

(since equal measures cannot be assumed, even though PN and NQ appear equal)

Example 3:	x	y	Ⓐ ● Ⓒ Ⓓ Ⓔ

(since N is between P and Q)

Example 4:	$w + z$	180	Ⓐ Ⓑ ● Ⓓ Ⓔ

(since PQ is a straight line)

GO ON TO THE NEXT PAGE.

A if the quantity in Column A is greater;
B if the quantity in Column B is greater;
C if the two quantities are equal;
D if the relationship cannot be determined from the information given.

Column A	Column B

1. The number of seconds in an hour | The number of days in 10 years

2. The average (arithmetic mean) of 13, 31, and 81 | The average (arithmetic mean) of 13, 30, and 81

$x = 4$

3. $3x^2$ | 144

4. x | 88

5. $(598.95)^2$ | 360,000

6. $3.4(5.5)$ | $3(5.5) + 0.4(5.5)$

7. The cost of x apples at a cost of $y + 2$ cents apiece | The cost of y oranges at a cost of $x + 2$ cents apiece

8. $\sqrt{5^2}$ | $5\sqrt{5}$

Column A	Column B

A rectangular box is 2 feet wide and 3 feet long and has a volume of 15 cubic feet.

9. The height of the box | 3 feet

10. 24 percent of 75 | 75 percent of 24

The height of right circular cylinder C is 3 times the diameter of its base.

11. The circumference of the base of C | The height of C

12. The area of a square region with perimeter 24 | The area of a rectangular region with perimeter 28

$$2x + 3y = 10$$
$$x + 2y = 8$$

13. $x + y$ | 2

In the rectangular coordinate plane, points P, Q, and R have coordinates (2, 3), (5, 6), and (5, 3), respectively.

14. PQ | QR

x is an integer greater than 1.

15. 3^{x+1} | 4^x

GO ON TO THE NEXT PAGE.

302

Directions: Each of the Questions 16-30 has five answer choices. For each of these questions, select the best of the answer choices given.

16. If $n + n = k + k + k$ and $n + k = 5$, then $n =$

 (A) 2
 (B) 3
 (C) 5
 (D) 6
 (E) 9

17. What is the length of a rectangle that has width 10 and perimeter 60 ?

 (A) 15
 (B) 20
 (C) 25
 (D) 30
 (E) 40

18. A watch gains 7 minutes and 6 seconds every 6 days. If the rate of gain is constant, how much does the watch gain in one day?

 (A) 1 min 1 sec
 (B) 1 min 6 sec
 (C) 1 min 11 sec
 (D) 1 min 16 sec
 (E) 1 min 21 sec

19. If $2x = 7$ and $3y = 2$, then $9xy =$

 (A) 14
 (B) 18
 (C) 21
 (D) 28
 (E) 63

20. If $\sqrt{x} = 16$, then $x =$

 (A) 4
 (B) 8
 (C) 16
 (D) 32
 (E) 256

GO ON TO THE NEXT PAGE.

Questions 21-25 refer to the following graph.

PERCENT OF TOTAL MALE FACULTY AND PERCENT OF TOTAL
FEMALE FACULTY AT UNIVERSITY X BY FIELD

Males   (Total male faculty is 250.)
Females (Total female faculty is 200.)

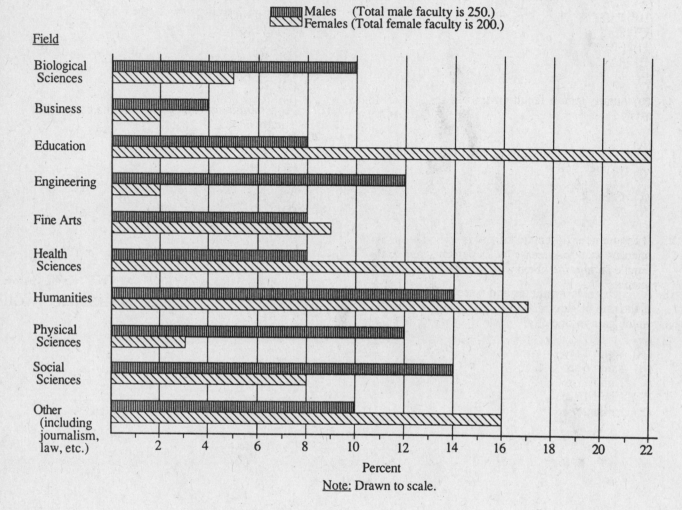

Note: Drawn to scale.

GO ON TO THE NEXT PAGE.

21. For how many of the fields is the percent of total male faculty at University X greater than 11 percent?

   (A) Two
   (B) Three
   (C) Four
   (D) Five
   (E) Six

22. How many female faculty members are there in fine arts?

   (A) 14
   (B) 16
   (C) 17
   (D) 18
   (E) 20

23. If the number of female faculty members in social sciences were to increase by 75 percent, how many female faculty members would there be in social sciences?

   (A) 12
   (B) 14
   (C) 21
   (D) 28
   (E) 30

24. If there are 275 students in engineering at University X, what is the approximate ratio of the number of engineering students to the number of engineering faculty?

   (A) 8 to 1
   (B) 12 to 1
   (C) 14 to 1
   (D) 18 to 1
   (E) 20 to 1

25. Approximately what percent of the humanities faculty is male?

   (A) 35%
   (B) 38%
   (C) 41%
   (D) 45%
   (E) 51%

GO ON TO THE NEXT PAGE.

26. If $2r - s = 3s - 2r$, what is s in terms of r?

(A) $\dfrac{r}{3}$

(B) $\dfrac{r}{2}$

(C) r

(D) $2r$

(E) $3r$

27. If $n \neq 0$, which of the following must be greater than n?

   I. $2n$
   II. n^3
   III. $4 - n$

(A) None
(B) I only
(C) II only
(D) I and II
(E) I and III

28. The distance from point X to point Y is 20 miles, and the distance from point X to point Z is 12 miles. If d is the distance, in miles, between points Y and Z, then the range of possible values for d is indicated by

(A) $8 \leqq d \leqq 20$
(B) $8 \leqq d \leqq 32$
(C) $12 \leqq d \leqq 20$
(D) $12 \leqq d \leqq 32$
(E) $20 \leqq d \leqq 32$

29. What is the least integer value of n such that $\dfrac{1}{2^n} < 0.01$?

(A) 7
(B) 11
(C) 50
(D) 51
(E) There is no such least value.

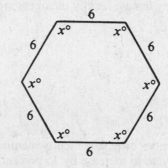

30. What is the area of the hexagonal region shown in the figure above?

(A) $54\sqrt{3}$

(B) 108

(C) $108\sqrt{3}$

(D) 216

(E) It cannot be determined from the information given.

STOP

IF YOU FINISH BEFORE TIME IS CALLED, YOU MAY CHECK YOUR WORK ON THIS SECTION ONLY.
DO NOT TURN TO ANY OTHER SECTION IN THE TEST.

306

NO TEST MATERIAL ON THIS PAGE

Time—30 minutes

38 Questions

Directions: Each sentence below has one or two blanks, each blank indicating that something has been omitted. Beneath the sentence are five lettered words or sets of words. Choose the word or set of words for each blank that best fits the meaning of the sentence as a whole.

1. The functions of the hands, eyes, and brain are so ------- that using the hands during early childhood helps to promote the child's entire ------- development.

    (A) intertwined. .perceptual
    (B) unalterable. .intellectual
    (C) enigmatic. .psychological
    (D) regulated. .adolescent
    (E) individualized. .social

2. Before 1500 North America was inhabited by more than 300 cultural groups, each with different customs, social structures, world views, and languages; such diversity -------- the existence of a single Native American culture.

    (A) complements   (B) implies   (C) reiterates
    (D) argues against   (E) explains away

3. That dealers ------- enough to nurture a young modern painter's career rather than plunder it exist is not impossible, but the public's ------- appetite for modern art makes such dealers less and less likely.

    (A) chivalrous. .discriminating
    (B) magnanimous. .quirky
    (C) patient. .insatiable
    (D) cynical. .finicky
    (E) reckless. .zealous

4. In the absence of any ------- caused by danger, hardship, or even cultural difference, most utopian communities deteriorate into ------- but enervating backwaters.

    (A) turmoil. .frantic
    (B) mistrust. .naïve
    (C) amelioration. .ignorant
    (D) decimation. .intrusive
    (E) stimulation. .placid

5. As Juanita argued, this new code of conduct is laughable; its principles are either -------, offering no wisdom but the obvious, or are so devoid of specific advice as to make almost any action -------.

    (A) irresolute. .unlikely
    (B) corroborative. .redundant
    (C) platitudinous. .justifiable
    (D) homogeneous. .impartial
    (E) labyrinthine. .unacceptable

6. Histocompatibility antigens that attack foreign tissue in the body cannot have been ------- through evolution expressly to ------- organ transplantation; on the contrary, they have been found to facilitate many essential biological functions.

    (A) designed. .retain
    (B) produced. .aid
    (C) developed. .enhance
    (D) selected. .promote
    (E) conserved. .foil

7. Their air of cheerful self-sacrifice and endless complaisance won them undeserved praise, for their seeming gallantry was wholly motivated by a ------- wish to avoid conflict of any sort.

    (A) poignant
    (B) sincere
    (C) plaintive
    (D) laudable
    (E) craven

GO ON TO THE NEXT PAGE.

Directions: In each of the following questions, a related pair of words or phrases is followed by five lettered pairs of words or phrases. Select the lettered pair that best expresses a relationship similar to that expressed in the original pair.

8. RUST : CORROSION ::
   (A) vapor : flammability
   (B) dew : condensation
   (C) crystal : purification
   (D) solution : precipitation
   (E) mold : disinfection

9. CLAIM : LEGITIMATED ::
   (A) hypothesis : confirmed
   (B) verdict : appealed
   (C) counterargument : doubted
   (D) proposition : repeated
   (E) speculation : disbelieved

10. ENCLOSE : PARENTHESES ::
    (A) abbreviate : brackets
    (B) emphasize : hyphen
    (C) separate : comma
    (D) join : period
    (E) omit : colon

11. ANTENNA : SIGNAL .. (A) bread : grain
    (B) story : reporter   (C) stem : flower
    (D) net : fish   (E) telegram : sender

12. WAG : HUMOROUS ::
    (A) ruffian : frightened
    (B) spendthrift : inattentive
    (C) dolt : stupid
    (D) pirate : merciless
    (E) sinner : repentant

13. FIRM : IRONCLAD :: (A) bruised : broken
    (B) polished : shining   (C) smart : brilliant
    (D) hard : stiff   (E) jovial : merry

14. FOIL : METAL :: (A) pebble : concrete
    (B) suede : leather   (C) glaze : pottery
    (D) veneer : wood   (E) paper : cardboard

15. LEAVE : ABSCOND :: (A) take : steal
    (B) evacuate : flee   (C) interest : astound
    (D) build : renovate   (E) evaluate : downgrade

16. QUAFF : SIP :: (A) bolt : run   (B) punch : hit
    (C) gnaw : nibble   (D) trudge : plod
    (E) stride : mince

GO ON TO THE NEXT PAGE.

309

For some time scientists have believed that cholesterol plays a major role in heart disease because people
with familial hypercholesterolemia, a genetic defect, have
Line six to eight times the normal level of cholesterol in their
(5) blood and they invariably develop heart disease. These
people lack cell-surface receptors for low-density lipo-
proteins (LDL's), which are the fundamental carriers
of blood cholesterol to the body cells that use cholesterol. Without an adequate number of cell-surface recep-
(10) tors to remove LDL's from the blood, the cholesterol-
carrying LDL's remain in the blood, increasing blood
cholesterol levels. Scientists also noticed that people
with familial hypercholesterolemia appear to produce
more LDL's than normal individuals. How, scientists
(15) wondered, could a genetic mutation that causes a slow-
down in the removal of LDL's from the blood also
result in an increase in the synthesis of this cholesterol-
carrying protein?

Since scientists could not experiment on human body
(20) tissue, their knowledge of familial hypercholesterolemia
was severely limited. However, a breakthrough came in
the laboratories of Yoshio Watanabe of Kobe University
in Japan in 1980. Watanabe noticed that a male rabbit
in his colony had ten times the normal concentration
(25) of cholesterol in its blood. By appropriate breeding,
Watanabe obtained a strain of rabbits that had very high
cholesterol levels. These rabbits spontaneously developed
heart disease. To his surprise, Watanabe further found
that the rabbits, like humans with familial hypercholes-
(30) terolemia, lacked LDL receptors. Thus, scientists could
study these Watanabe rabbits to gain a better understanding of familial hypercholesterolemia in humans.

Prior to the breakthrough at Kobe University, it
was known that LDL's are secreted from the liver in
(35) the form of a precursor, called very low-density lipo-
proteins (VLDL's), which carry triglycerides as well
as relatively small amounts of cholesterol. The triglycerides are removed from the VLDL's by fatty and other
tissues. What remains is a remnant particle that must
(40) be removed from the blood. What scientists learned by
studying the Watanabe rabbits is that the removal of
the VLDL remnant requires the LDL receptor. Normally, the majority of the VLDL remnants go to the
liver where they bind to LDL receptors and are de-
(45) graded. In the Watanabe rabbit, due to a lack of LDL
receptors on liver cells, the VLDL remnants remain in
the blood and are eventually converted to LDL's. The
LDL receptors thus have a dual effect in controlling
LDL levels. They are necessary to prevent oversynthesis
(50) of LDL's from VLDL remnants and they are necessary
for the normal removal of LDL's from the blood. With
this knowledge, scientists are now well on the way toward developing drugs that dramatically lower cholesterol levels in people afflicted with certain forms of
familial hypercholesterolemia.

17. In the passage, the author is primarily concerned
with

(A) presenting a hypothesis and describing
compelling evidence in support of it
(B) raising a question and describing an important
discovery that led to an answer
(C) showing that a certain genetically caused
disease can be treated effectively with drugs
(D) explaining what causes the genetic mutation
that leads to heart disease
(E) discussing the importance of research on
animals for the study of human disease

18. Which of the following drugs, if developed, would
most likely be an example of the kind of drug
mentioned in line 53 ?

(A) A drug that stimulates the production of VLDL
remnants
(B) A drug that stimulates the production of LDL
receptors on the liver
(C) A drug that stimulates the production of an
enzyme needed for cholesterol production
(D) A drug that suppresses the production of body
cells that use cholesterol
(E) A drug that prevents triglycerides from
attaching to VLDL's

19. The passage supplies information to answer which
of the following questions?

(A) Which body cells are the primary users of
cholesterol?
(B) How did scientists discover that LDL's are
secreted from the liver in the form of a
precursor?
(C) Where in the body are VLDL remnants
degraded?
(D) Which body tissues produce triglycerides?
(E) What techniques are used to determine the presence or absence of cell-surface receptors?

GO ON TO THE NEXT PAGE.

20. According to the passage, by studying the Watanabe rabbits scientists learned that

(A) VLDL remnants are removed from the blood by LDL receptors in the liver
(B) LDL's are secreted from the liver in the form of precursors called VLDL's
(C) VLDL remnant particles contain small amounts of cholesterol
(D) triglycerides are removed from VLDL's by fatty tissues
(E) LDL receptors remove LDL's from the blood

21. The development of drug treatments for some forms of familial hypercholesterolemia is regarded by the author as

(A) possible, but not very important
(B) interesting, but too costly to be practical
(C) promising, but many years off
(D) extremely unlikely
(E) highly probable

22. The passage implies that if the Watanabe rabbits had had as many LDL receptors on their livers as do normal rabbits, the Watanabe rabbits would have been

(A) less likely than normal rabbits to develop heart disease
(B) less likely than normal rabbits to develop high concentrations of cholesterol in their blood
(C) less useful than they actually were to scientists in the study of familial hypercholesterolemia in humans
(D) unable to secrete VLDL's from their livers
(E) immune to drugs that lower cholesterol levels in people with certain forms of familial hyper-cholesterolemia

23. The passage implies that Watanabe rabbits differ from normal rabbits in which of the following ways?

(A) Watanabe rabbits have more LDL receptors than do normal rabbits.
(B) The blood of Watanabe rabbits contains more VLDL remnants than does the blood of normal rabbits.
(C) Watanabe rabbits have fewer fatty tissues than do normal rabbits.
(D) Watanabe rabbits secrete lower levels of VLDL's than do normal rabbits.
(E) The blood of Watanabe rabbits contains fewer LDL's than does the blood of normal rabbits.

GO ON TO THE NEXT PAGE.

(The article from which this passage was taken appeared in 1981.)

When speaking of Romare Bearden, one is tempted to say, "A great Black American artist." The subject matter of Bearden's collages is certainly Black. Por-
Line
(5) trayals of the folk of Mecklenburg County, North Carolina, whom he remembers from early childhood, of the jazz musicians and tenement roofs of his Harlem days, of Pittsburgh steelworkers, and his reconstruction of classical Greek myths in the guise of the ancient Black kingdom of Benin, attest to this. In natural harmony
(10) with this choice of subject matter are the social sensibili-ties of the artist, who remains active today with the Cinque Gallery in Manhattan, which he helped found and which is devoted to showing the work of minority artists.
(15) Then why not call Bearden a Black American artist? Because ultimately this categorization is too narrow. "What stands up in the end is structure," Bearden says. "What I try to do is amplify. If I were just creating a picture of a farm woman from back home, it would have
(20) meaning to her and people there. But art amplifies itself to something universal."

24. According to the passage, all of the following are depicted in Bearden's collages EXCEPT

(A) workers in Pittsburgh's steel mills
(B) scenes set in the ancient kingdom of Benin
(C) people Bearden knew as a child
(D) traditional representations of the classical heroes of Greek mythology
(E) the jazz musicians of the Harlem Bearden used to know

25. The author suggests that Bearden should not be called a Black American artist because

(A) there are many collages by Bearden in which the subject matter is not Black
(B) Bearden's work reflects the Black American experience in a highly individual style
(C) through the structure of Bearden's art his Black subjects come to represent all of humankind
(D) Bearden's true significance lies not so much in his own work as in his efforts to help other minority artists
(E) much of Bearden's work uses the ancient Black kingdom of Benin for its setting

26. Bearden's social sensibilities and the subject matter of his collages are mentioned by the author in order to explain

(A) why one might be tempted to call Bearden a Black American artist
(B) why Bearden cannot be readily categorized
(C) why Bearden's appeal is thought by many to be ultimately universal
(D) how deeply an artist's artistic creations are influenced by the artist's social conscience
(E) what makes Bearden unique among contempo-rary Black American artists

27. The author of the passage is chiefly concerned with

(A) discussing Bearden's philosophy of art
(B) assessing the significance of the ethnic element in Bearden's work
(C) acknowledging Bearden's success in giving artistic expression to the Black American experience
(D) pointing out Bearden's helpfulness to other minority artists
(E) tracing Bearden's progress toward artistic matu-rity

GO ON TO THE NEXT PAGE.

Directions: Each question below consists of a word printed in capital letters, followed by five lettered words or phrases. Choose the lettered word or phrase that is most nearly opposite in meaning to the word in capital letters.

Since some of the questions require you to distinguish fine shades of meaning, be sure to consider all the choices before deciding which one is best.

28. INSERT: (A) remove (B) improve
    (C) revise (D) lessen (E) copy

29. BANKRUPTCY: (A) hypocrisy (B) solvency
    (C) advocacy (D) comparability (E) adversity

30. RELEVANT: (A) immaterial (B) random
    (C) hidden (D) false (E) inopportune

31. IMPLOSION:
    (A) high-frequency pitch
    (B) violent chemical reaction
    (C) rapid outward movement
    (D) complete change in composition
    (E) uncontrolled variation in temperature

32. SLAB: (A) nib (B) streak (C) husk
    (D) sliver (E) shield

33. RAREFY: (A) contract suddenly
    (B) converge slowly (C) blend thoroughly
    (D) make denser (E) cool quickly

34. IMPETUOUS: (A) appropriate (B) respectful
    (C) uninteresting (D) voracious (E) deliberate

35. VITUPERATIVE: (A) suggestive
    (B) complimentary (C) genuine
    (D) undirected (E) pessimistic

36. FOMENT: (A) squelch (B) sweeten
    (C) dilute (D) liberate (E) clear

37. INCHOATE: (A) explicit (B) dependable
    (C) pragmatic (D) therapeutic (E) enduring

38. TYRO: (A) underling (B) expert
    (C) eccentric (D) truthful person
    (E) beneficent ruler

STOP

IF YOU FINISH BEFORE TIME IS CALLED, YOU MAY CHECK YOUR WORK ON THIS SECTION ONLY.
DO NOT TURN TO ANY OTHER SECTION IN THE TEST.

I

GENERAL TEST

A. Print and sign your full name in this box:

PRINT: _____
               (LAST)   (FIRST)   (MIDDLE)

SIGN: _____

Copy this code in box 6 on your answer sheet. Then fill in the corresponding ovals exactly as shown.

6. TITLE CODE

Copy the Test Name and Form Code in box 7 on your answer sheet.

TEST NAME *General*

FORM CODE *GR91-19*

GRADUATE RECORD EXAMINATIONS GENERAL TEST

B. You will have 3 hours and 30 minutes in which to work on this test, which consists of seven sections. During the time allowed for one section, you may work <u>only</u> on that section. The time allowed for each section is 30 minutes.

Each of your scores will be determined by the number of questions for which you select the best answer from the choices given. Questions for which you mark no answer or more than one answer are not counted in scoring. Nothing is subtracted from a score if you answer a question incorrectly. Therefore, to maximize your scores it is better for you to guess at an answer than not to respond at all.

You are advised to work as rapidly as you can without losing accuracy. Do not spend too much time on questions that are too difficult for you. Go on to the other questions and come back to the difficult ones later.

There are several different types of questions; you will find special directions for each type in the test itself. <u>Be sure you understand the directions before attempting to answer any questions.</u>

YOU MUST INDICATE ALL YOUR ANSWERS ON THE SEPARATE ANSWER SHEET. No credit will be given for anything written in this examination book, but you may write in the book as much as you wish to work out your answers. After you have decided on your response to a question, fill in the corresponding oval on the answer sheet. BE SURE THAT EACH MARK IS DARK AND COMPLETELY FILLS THE OVAL. Mark <u>only one</u> answer to each question. No credit will be given for multiple answers. Erase all stray marks. If you change an answer, be sure that all previous marks are erased completely. Incomplete erasures may be read as intended answers. Do not be concerned if your answer sheet provides spaces for more answers than there are questions in each section.

Example:

What city is the capital of France?

(A) Rome
(B) Paris
(C) London
(D) Cairo
(E) Oslo

Sample Answer

Ⓐ ● Ⓒ Ⓓ Ⓔ   BEST ANSWER
                   PROPERLY MARKED

Ⓐ ⊠ Ⓒ Ⓓ Ⓔ
Ⓐ ⬮ Ⓒ Ⓓ Ⓔ   IMPROPER MARKS
Ⓐ ⬤ Ⓒ Ⓓ Ⓔ
Ⓐ Ⓕ Ⓒ Ⓓ Ⓔ

DO NOT OPEN YOUR TEST BOOK UNTIL YOU ARE TOLD TO DO SO.

FOR GENERAL TEST, FORM GR91-19 ONLY
Answer Key and Percentages* of Examinees Answering Each Question Correctly

VERBAL ABILITY						QUANTITATIVE ABILITY					
Section 2			Section 4			Section 1			Section 3		
Number	Answer	P+	Number	Answer	P+	Number	Answer	P+	Number	Answer	P+
1	A	96	1	A	89	1	A	90	1	B	88
2	C	74	2	D	75	2	A	83	2	A	85
3	C	71	3	C	59	3	B	88	3	B	85
4	C	55	4	E	50	4	A	83	4	A	81
5	D	59	5	C	57	5	C	84	5	B	80
6	E	43	6	E	39	6	C	68	6	C	77
7	A	28	7	E	24	7	A	83	7	D	77
8	B	94	8	B	81	8	B	71	8	B	77
9	D	83	9	A	86	9	D	70	9	B	67
10	C	75	10	C	84	10	B	76	10	C	64
11	D	63	11	D	57	11	D	52	11	A	48
12	E	49	12	C	51	12	A	64	12	D	41
13	E	39	13	C	43	13	B	74	13	C	46
14	E	37	14	D	30	14	C	33	14	A	60
15	E	32	15	A	32	15	A	32	15	D	20
16	C	27	16	E	14	16	C	86	16	B	77
17	A	75	17	B	54	17	E	76	17	B	84
18	D	71	18	B	74	18	A	78	18	C	72
19	D	80	19	C	52	19	C	63	19	C	74
20	B	68	20	A	57	20	B	62	20	E	80
21	B	42	21	E	83	21	A	76	21	C	90
22	D	69	22	C	53	22	C	68	22	D	83
23	A	47	23	B	54	23	B	59	23	D	65
24	E	38	24	D	65	24	D	64	24	A	68
25	B	41	25	C	83	25	D	64	25	E	44
26	C	31	26	A	45	26	B	53	26	C	64
27	B	41	27	B	33	27	B	45	27	A	54
28	D	89	28	A	98	28	C	37	28	B	47
29	B	82	29	B	81	29	E	20	29	A	37
30	B	72	30	A	83	30	D	19	30	A	21
31	A	74	31	C	76						
32	A	57	32	D	64						
33	D	42	33	D	39						
34	C	36	34	E	41						
35	E	31	35	B	31						
36	D	29	36	A	26						
37	A	29	37	A	28						
38	E	17	38	B	21						

*Estimated P+ for the group of examinees who took the GRE General Test in a recent three-year period.

315

SCORE CONVERSIONS FOR GRE GENERAL TEST, GR91-19

Raw Score	Scaled Score Verbal	Scaled Score Quantitative	Raw Score	Scaled Score Verbal	Scaled Score Quantitative
74-76	800		39	450	540
73	800		38	440	530
72	790		37	430	520
71	780		36	420	510
70	770		35	410	500
			34	400	490
69	750		33	390	470
68	740		32	390	460
67	730		31	380	450
66	720		30	370	440
65	710				
64	700		29	360	430
63	690		28	360	420
62	680		27	350	410
61	670		26	340	400
60	660	800	25	330	390
			24	320	370
59	650	800	23	310	360
58	640	800	22	300	350
57	630	800	21	290	340
56	620	780	20	280	330
55	610	760			
54	600	750	19	270	320
53	590	730	18	260	310
52	580	720	17	250	300
51	570	700	16	230	290
50	560	690	15	220	270
			14	200	250
49	550	670	13	200	240
48	540	660	12	200	230
47	520	640	11	200	210
46	510	630	10	200	200
45	500	610			
44	490	600	9	200	200
43	480	590	8	200	200
42	470	570	7	200	200
41	460	560	0-6	200	200
40	450	550			

THE GRADUATE RECORD EXAMINATIONS®

GRE®

ETS

General Test

*Do not break the seal
until you are told to do so.*

*The contents of this test are confidential.
Disclosure or reproduction of any portion
of it is prohibited.*

THIS TEST BOOK MUST NOT BE TAKEN FROM THE ROOM.

NO TEST MATERIAL ON THIS PAGE

SECTION 1

Time—30 minutes

38 Questions

Directions: Each sentence below has one or two blanks, each blank indicating that something has been omitted. Beneath the sentence are five lettered words or sets of words. Choose the word or set of words for each blank that best fits the meaning of the sentence as a whole.

1. Though some of the information the author reveals about Russian life might surprise Americans, her major themes are ------- enough.

   (A) familiar   (B) thorough   (C) vital
    (D) original   (E) interesting

2. In the early twentieth century, the discovery of radium ------- the popular imagination; not only was its discoverer, Marie Curie, idolized, but its market value ------- that of the rarest gemstone.

   (A) stormed. .sank to
   (B) horrified. .approached
   (C) taxed. .was equal to
   (D) enflamed. .exceeded
   (E) escaped. .was comparable to

3. The president's secretary and his chief aide adored him, and both wrote obsessively ------- personal memoirs about him; unfortunately, however, ------- does not make for true intimacy.

   (A) fatuous. .frankness
   (B) devoted. .idolatry
   (C) garrulous. .confidentiality
   (D) candid. .discretion
   (E) rancorous. .criticism

4. Despite claims that his philosophy can be traced to ------- source, the philosophy in fact draws liberally on several traditions and methodologies and so could justifiably be termed -------.

   (A) a particular. .consistent
   (B) a schematic. .multifaceted
   (C) a dominant. .cogent
   (D) an authoritative. .derivative
   (E) a single. .eclectic

5. Du Bois' foreign trips were the highlight, not the -------, of his travels; he was habitually on the go across and around the United States.

   (A) idiosyncrasy   (B) result   (C) precursor
    (D) culmination   (E) totality

6. Business forecasts usually prove reasonably accurate when the assumption that the future will be much like the past is -------; in times of major ------- in the business environment, however, forecasts can be dangerously wrong.

   (A) specified. .discontinuities
   (B) questioned. .surges
   (C) contradicted. .improvements
   (D) entertained. .risks
   (E) satisfied. .shifts

7. It is almost always desirable to increase the yield of a crop if ------- increases are not also necessary in energy, labor, and other inputs of crop production.

   (A) predetermined   (B) commensurate
    (C) compatible   (D) measured   (E) equivocal

GO ON TO THE NEXT PAGE.

Directions: In each of the following questions, a related pair of words or phrases is followed by five lettered pairs of words or phrases. Select the lettered pair that best expresses a relationship similar to that expressed in the original pair.

8. MISER : STINGY :: (A) porter : strong
(B) rebel : idle   (C) sage : docile
(D) friend : snide   (E) loner : solitary

9. AQUEDUCT : WATER :: (A) capillary : saliva
(B) artery : blood   (C) esophagus : breath
(D) corridor : aircraft   (E) tanker : fluids

10. ENZYME : CATALYST :: (A) vaccine : allergy
(B) bacterium : microbe   (C) gland : muscle
(D) vein : organ   (E) neuron : corpuscle

11. LIEN : CLAIM ::
(A) brief : investigation
(B) mortgage : interest
(C) foreclosure : pleading
(D) garnishment : presumption
(E) subpoena : command

12. VERBOSITY : WORDS ::
(A) harmoniousness : relationships
(B) floridness : embellishments
(C) interrogation : answers
(D) supposition : proposals
(E) condemnation : acts

13. QUIXOTIC : IDEALISTIC ::
(A) churlish : polite
(B) whimsical : steady
(C) disinterested : impartial
(D) touchy : sensitive
(E) central : random

14. PREEMPT : PRECEDENCE ::
(A) dissemble : diplomacy
(B) superintend : culpability
(C) preside : arbitration
(D) acquire : possession
(E) divest : implication

15. MALINGER : AIL :: (A) study : learn
(B) qualify : achieve   (C) sneer : respect
(D) flatter : appreciate   (E) clash : resolve

16. ARBOREAL : TREES :: (A) terrestrial : plains
(B) amphibious : rivers   (C) herbaceous : plants
(D) subterranean : caves   (E) sidereal : stars

GO ON TO THE NEXT PAGE.

Each passage in this group is followed by questions based on its content. After reading a passage, choose the best answer to each question. Answer all questions following a passage on the basis of what is <u>stated</u> or <u>implied</u> in that passage.

Zooplankton, tiny animals adapted to an existence in the ocean, have evolved clever mechanisms for obtaining their food, miniscule phytoplankton (plant plankton).
Line
(5) A very specialized feeding adaptation in zooplankton is that of the tadpolelike appendicularian who lives in a walnut-sized (or smaller) balloon of mucus equipped with filters that capture and concentrate phytoplankton. The balloon, a transparent structure that varies in design according to the type of appendicularian in-
(10) habiting it, also protects the animal and helps to keep it afloat. Water containing phytoplankton is pumped by the appendicularian's muscular tail into the balloon's incurrent filters, passes through the feeding filter where the appendicularian sucks the food into its mouth,
(15) and then goes through an exit passage. Found in all the oceans of the world, including the Arctic Ocean, appendicularians tend to remain near the water's surface where the density of phytoplankton is greatest.

17. It can be inferred from the passage that which of the following is true of appendicularians?

   (A) They are exclusively carnivorous.
   (B) They have more than one method of obtaining food.
   (C) They can tolerate frigid water.
   (D) They can disguise themselves by secreting mucus.
   (E) They are more sensitive to light than are other zooplankton.

18. The author is primarily concerned with

   (A) explaining how appendicularians obtain food
   (B) examining the flotation methods of appendicularians
   (C) mapping the distribution of appendicularians around the world
   (D) describing how appendicularians differ from other zooplankton
   (E) comparing the various types of balloons formed by appendicularians

19. According to the passage, all of the following are descriptive of appendicularians EXCEPT

   (A) tailed   (B) vegetarian   (C) small-sized
   (D) single-celled   (E) ocean-dwelling

20. The passage suggests that appendicularians tend to remain in surface waters because they

   (A) prefer the warmer water near the surface
   (B) are unable to secrete mucus at the lower levels of the ocean
   (C) use the contrast of light and shadow at the surface to hide from predators
   (D) live in balloons that cannot withstand the water pressure deeper in the ocean
   (E) eat food that grows more profusely near the surface

GO ON TO THE NEXT PAGE.

Students of United States history, seeking to identify the circumstances that encouraged the emergence of feminist movements, have thoroughly investigated the
Line
(5) mid-nineteenth-century American economic and social conditions that affected the status of women. These historians, however, have analyzed less fully the development of specifically feminist ideas and activities during the same period. Furthermore, the ideological origins of feminism in the United States have been obscured
(10) because, even when historians did take into account those feminist ideas and activities occurring within the United States, they failed to recognize that feminism was then a truly international movement actually centered in Europe. American feminist activists who have
(15) been described as "solitary" and "individual theorists" were in reality connected to a movement—utopian socialism—which was already popularizing feminist ideas in Europe during the two decades that culminated in the first women's rights conference held at Seneca
(20) Falls, New York, in 1848. Thus, a complete understanding of the origins and development of nineteenth-century feminism in the United States requires that the geographical focus be widened to include Europe and that the detailed study already made of social conditions
(25) be expanded to include the ideological development of feminism.

The earliest and most popular of the utopian socialists were the Saint-Simonians. The specifically feminist part of Saint-Simonianism has, however, been less studied
(30) ied than the group's contribution to early socialism. This is regrettable on two counts. By 1832 feminism was the central concern of Saint-Simonianism and entirely absorbed its adherents' energy; hence, by ignoring its feminism, European historians have misunder-
(35) stood Saint-Simonianism. Moreover, since many feminist ideas can be traced to Saint-Simonianism, European historians' appreciation of later feminism in France and the United States remained limited.

Saint-Simon's followers, many of whom were
(40) women, based their feminism on an interpretation of his project to reorganize the globe by replacing brute force with the rule of spiritual powers. The new world order would be ruled together by a male, to represent reflection, and a female, to represent sentiment. This
(45) complementarity reflects the fact that, while the Saint-Simonians did not reject the belief that there were innate differences between men and women, they nevertheless foresaw an equally important social and political role for both sexes in their utopia.
(50) Only a few Saint-Simonians opposed a definition of sexual equality based on gender distinction. This minority believed that individuals of both sexes were born similar in capacity and character, and they ascribed male-female differences to socialization and education.
(55) The envisioned result of both currents of thought, however, was that women would enter public life in the new age and that sexual equality would reward men as well as women with an improved way of life.

21. It can be inferred that the author considers those historians who describe early feminists in the United States as "solitary" to be

(A) insufficiently familiar with the international origins of nineteenth-century American feminist thought
(B) overly concerned with the regional diversity of feminist ideas in the period before 1848
(C) not focused narrowly enough in their geographical scope
(D) insufficiently aware of the ideological consequences of the Seneca Falls conference
(E) insufficiently concerned with the social conditions out of which feminism developed

22. According to the passage, which of the following is true of the Seneca Falls conference on women's rights?

(A) It was primarily a product of nineteenth-century Saint-Simonian feminist thought.
(B) It was the work of American activists who were independent of feminists abroad.
(C) It was the culminating achievement of the utopian socialist movement.
(D) It was a manifestation of an international movement for social change and feminism.
(E) It was the final manifestation of the women's rights movement in the United States in the nineteenth century.

23. The author's attitude toward most European historians who have studied the Saint-Simonians is primarily one of

(A) approval of the specific focus of their research
(B) disapproval of their lack of attention to the issue that absorbed most of the Saint-Simonians' energy after 1832
(C) approval of their general focus on social conditions
(D) disapproval of their lack of attention to links between the Saint-Simonians and their American counterparts
(E) disagreement with their interpretation of the Saint-Simonian belief in sexual equality

GO ON TO THE NEXT PAGE.

322

24. The author mentions all of the following as characteristic of the Saint-Simonians EXCEPT:

(A) The group included many women among its members.
(B) The group believed in a world that would be characterized by sexual equality.
(C) The group was among the earliest European socialist groups.
(D) Most members believed that women should enter public life.
(E) Most members believed that women and men were inherently similar in ability and character.

25. It can be inferred from the passage that the Saint-Simonians envisioned a utopian society having which of the following characteristics?

(A) It would be worldwide.
(B) It would emphasize dogmatic religious principles.
(C) It would most influence the United States.
(D) It would have armies composed of women rather than of men.
(E) It would continue to develop new feminist ideas.

26. It can be inferred from the passage that the author believes that study of Saint-Simonianism is necessary for historians of American feminism because such study

(A) would clarify the ideological origins of those feminist ideas that influenced American feminism
(B) would increase understanding of a movement that deeply influenced the utopian socialism of early American feminists
(C) would focus attention on the most important aspect of Saint-Simonian thought before 1832
(D) promises to offer insight into a movement that was a direct outgrowth of the Seneca Falls conference of 1848
(E) could increase understanding of those ideals that absorbed most of the energy of the earliest American feminists

27. According to the passage, which of the following would be the most accurate description of the society envisioned by most Saint-Simonians?

(A) A society in which women were highly regarded for their extensive education
(B) A society in which the two genders played complementary roles and had equal status
(C) A society in which women did not enter public life
(D) A social order in which a body of men and women would rule together on the basis of their spiritual power
(E) A social order in which distinctions between male and female would not exist and all would share equally in political power

GO ON TO THE NEXT PAGE.

323

Directions: Each question below consists of a word printed in capital letters, followed by five lettered words or phrases. Choose the lettered word or phrase that is most nearly <u>opposite</u> in meaning to the word in capital letters.

Since some of the questions require you to distinguish fine shades of meaning, be sure to consider all the choices before deciding which one is best.

28. TOY: (A) think over seriously
    (B) admire overtly   (C) use sporadically
    (D) praise unstintingly   (E) covet irrationally

29. QUACK: (A) hard worker   (B) true believer
    (C) honest practitioner   (D) careful employee
    (E) experienced planner

30. FRINGE: (A) center   (B) proximity
    (C) breadth   (D) outlet   (E) continuity

31. FALLACIOUS: (A) safe   (B) valid
    (C) energetic   (D) diverted   (E) persuasive

32. CRYPTIC: (A) resonant   (B) superficial
    (C) unobjectionable   (D) self-explanatory
    (E) other-directed

33. RENT: (A) in abeyance   (B) occupied
    (C) undeserved   (D) turned down
    (E) made whole

34. CONSIDER: (A) activate   (B) infer
    (C) table   (D) encourage   (E) deter

35. TENUOUS: (A) finite   (B) embedded
    (C) convinced   (D) substantial   (E) proximate

36. MERCURIAL: (A) earthy   (B) honest
    (C) thoughtful   (D) clumsy   (E) constant

37. OPPROBRIUM: (A) good repute
    (B) fair recompense   (C) fidelity
    (D) exposure   (E) patience

38. VENERATION: (A) derision   (B) blame
    (C) avoidance   (D) ostracism   (E) defiance

STOP

**IF YOU FINISH BEFORE TIME IS CALLED, YOU MAY CHECK YOUR WORK ON THIS SECTION ONLY.
DO NOT TURN TO ANY OTHER SECTION IN THE TEST.**

Section 2 starts on page 326.

Time—30 minutes

30 Questions

Numbers: All numbers used are real numbers.

Figures: Position of points, angles, regions, etc. can be assumed to be in the order shown; and angle measures can be assumed to be positive.

Lines shown as straight can be assumed to be straight.

Figures can be assumed to lie in a plane unless otherwise indicated.

Figures that accompany questions are intended to provide information useful in answering the questions. However, unless a note states that a figure is drawn to scale, you should solve these problems NOT by estimating sizes by sight or by measurement, but by using your knowledge of mathematics (see Example 2 below).

Directions: Each of the Questions 1-15 consists of two quantities, one in Column A and one in Column B. You are to compare the two quantities and choose

A if the quantity in Column A is greater;
B if the quantity in Column B is greater;
C if the two quantities are equal;
D if the relationship cannot be determined from the information given.

Note: Since there are only four choices, NEVER MARK (E).

Common Information: In a question, information concerning one or both of the quantities to be compared is centered above the two columns. A symbol that appears in both columns represents the same thing in Column A as it does in Column B.

	Column A	Column B	Sample Answers
Example 1:	2×6	$2 + 6$	● Ⓑ Ⓒ Ⓓ Ⓔ

Examples 2-4 refer to $\triangle PQR$.

	Column A	Column B	Sample Answers
Example 2:	PN	NQ	Ⓐ Ⓑ Ⓒ ● Ⓔ

(since equal measures cannot be assumed, even though PN and NQ appear equal)

	Column A	Column B	Sample Answers
Example 3:	x	y	Ⓐ ● Ⓒ Ⓓ Ⓔ

(since N is between P and Q)

	Column A	Column B	Sample Answers
Example 4:	$w + z$	180	Ⓐ Ⓑ ● Ⓓ Ⓔ

(since PQ is a straight line)

GO ON TO THE NEXT PAGE.

A if the quantity in Column A is greater;
B if the quantity in Column B is greater;
C if the two quantities are equal;
D if the relationship cannot be determined from the information given.

Column A	Column B

A hardware store purchased identical snow shovels at a cost of $9 apiece and sold each of them for 20 percent above cost.

1. The price at which the hardware store sold each shovel $10.80

$$n + \frac{2}{5} = 5 + \frac{7}{5}$$

2. n $6\frac{4}{5}$

$$x < 0$$

3. $x - 1$ $1 - x$

---

4. The total number of triangles shown above   6

---

5. 3^4 4^3

$$x + k = 8$$
$$x - k = 4$$

6. x k

Column A	Column B

Carol is c centimeters tall, and Diane is d centimeters <u>shorter</u> than Carol. ($d > 0$)

7. The sum of Carol's height and Diane's height $2c$ centimeters

---

8. $x + y + z$ 150

$$n = 105.873$$

9. $\dfrac{n \times 10^3}{10^5}$ 1

GO ON TO THE NEXT PAGE.

327

A if the quantity in Column A is greater;
B if the quantity in Column B is greater;
C if the two quantities are equal;
D if the relationship cannot be determined from the information given.

Column A	Column B	Column A	Column B

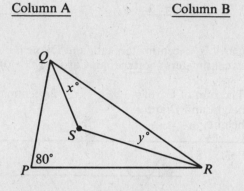

Segment QS bisects $\angle PQR$ and segment RS bisects $\angle PRQ$.

10.　　　　　x　　　　　　　　y

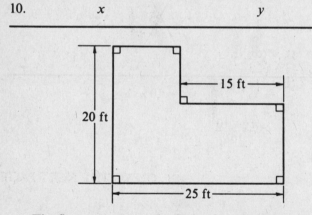

The figure represents the floor of a certain room.

11.　The area of the floor　　　350 square feet

$$x^2 - 3x + 2 = 0$$

12. Twice the sum of the　　　　　6
roots of the equation

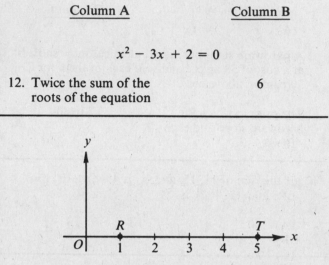

Point S (not shown) lies above the x-axis such that $\triangle RST$ has area equal to 6.

13. The x-coordinate of　　　The y-coordinate of
point S　　　　　　　point S

14.　　$\dfrac{10^5}{5^3}$　　　　　$2^5 \cdot 5^2$

$$rs \neq 0$$

15.　　$(r + s)^2$　　　　$r^2 + s^2$

GO ON TO THE NEXT PAGE.

16. If $9x - 3 = 15$, then $3x - 1 =$

(A) $\frac{5}{3}$

(B) 3

(C) 5

(D) 6

(E) 45

17. If the sum of 12, 15, and x is 45, then the product of 5 and $(x + 2)$ is

(A) 100
(B) 92
(C) 80
(D) 41
(E) 25

18. If the average (arithmetic mean) of two numbers is 20 and one of the numbers is x, what is the other number in terms of x?

(A) $40 - x$
(B) $40 - 2x$
(C) $20 + x$
(D) $20 - x$
(E) $20 - 2x$

19. $\dfrac{1}{\frac{1}{2}} + \dfrac{2}{\frac{2}{3}} + \dfrac{3}{\frac{3}{4}} =$

(A) $\frac{1}{9}$

(B) $\frac{13}{12}$

(C) $\frac{29}{12}$

(D) 8

(E) 9

20. What is the area of a circular region that has circumference 8π ?

(A) 4π
(B) 8π
(C) 16π
(D) 32π
(E) 64π

GO ON TO THE NEXT PAGE.

329

Questions 21-25 refer to the following graphs.

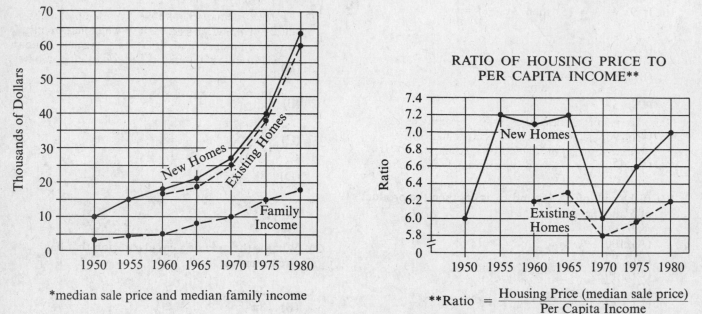

HOUSING PRICE AND FAMILY INCOME*

*median sale price and median family income

RATIO OF HOUSING PRICE TO PER CAPITA INCOME**

**Ratio = $\dfrac{\text{Housing Price (median sale price)}}{\text{Per Capita Income}}$

Note: Graphs drawn to scale.

21. Approximately what was the median sale price of an existing home in 1975 ?

(A) $15,000
(B) $35,000
(C) $36,000
(D) $38,000
(E) $40,000

22. In 1980, what was the approximate difference between the median sale price of an existing home and the median family income?

(A) $42,000
(B) $45,000
(C) $46,000
(D) $46,500
(E) $47,500

23. For which of the following years was the ratio of the median sale price of a new home minus the median sale price of an existing home to per capita income least?

(A) 1960
(B) 1965
(C) 1970
(D) 1975
(E) 1980

24. If in 1985 the per capita income was $7,200 and the ratio of the median sale price of an existing home to per capita income was the same as in 1980, what was the median sale price of an existing home in 1985 ?

(A) $50,040
(B) $44,640
(C) $11,600
(D) $5,040
(E) $1,160

25. By approximately what percent did the median sale price of a new home increase from 1955 to 1975 ?

(A) 26%

(B) $37\frac{1}{2}\%$

(C) $62\frac{1}{2}\%$

(D) 167%

(E) 267%

GO ON TO THE NEXT PAGE.

330

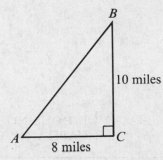

B

10 miles

A

8 miles

C

26. According to the figure above, traveling directly from point A to point B, rather than from point A to point C and then from point C to point B, would save approximately how many miles?

(A) 1
(B) 2
(C) 3
(D) 4
(E) 5

27.   0.50% =

(A) $\frac{1}{500}$

(B) $\frac{1}{200}$

(C) $\frac{1}{50}$

(D) $\frac{1}{20}$

(E) $\frac{1}{2}$

28. The rectangular solid above is made up of eight cubes of the same size, each of which has exactly one face painted blue. What is the greatest fraction of the total surface area of the solid that could be blue?

(A) $\frac{1}{6}$

(B) $\frac{3}{14}$

(C) $\frac{1}{4}$

(D) $\frac{2}{7}$

(E) $\frac{1}{3}$

29. If $a > 0$, $b > 0$, and $c > 0$, $a + \dfrac{1}{b + \frac{1}{c}} =$

(A) $\dfrac{a + b}{c}$

(B) $\dfrac{ac + bc + 1}{c}$

(C) $\dfrac{abc + b + c}{bc}$

(D) $\dfrac{a + b + c}{abc + 1}$

(E) $\dfrac{abc + a + c}{bc + 1}$

30. The buyer of a certain mechanical toy must choose 2 of 4 optional motions and 4 of 5 optional accessories. How many different combinations of motions and accessories are available to the buyer?

(A) 8
(B) 11
(C) 15
(D) 20
(E) 30

STOP

IF YOU FINISH BEFORE TIME IS CALLED, YOU MAY CHECK YOUR WORK ON THIS SECTION ONLY.
DO NOT TURN TO ANY OTHER SECTION IN THE TEST.

NO TEST MATERIAL ON THIS PAGE

SECTION 3

Time—30 minutes

38 Questions

Directions: Each sentence below has one or two blanks, each blank indicating that something has been omitted. Beneath the sentence are five lettered words or sets of words. Choose the word or set of words for each blank that best fits the meaning of the sentence as a whole.

1. Job failure means being fired from a job, being asked to resign, or leaving ------- to protect yourself because you had very strong evidence that one of the first two was ------- .

   (A) voluntarily. .impending
   (B) abruptly. .significant
   (C) knowingly. .operative
   (D) understandably. .pertinent
   (E) eventually. .intentional

2. The tone of Jane Carlyle's letter is guarded, and her feelings are always ------- by the wit and pride that made ------- plea for sympathy impossible for her.

   (A) masked. .a direct
   (B) bolstered. .a needless
   (C) controlled. .a circumspect
   (D) enhanced. .an intentional
   (E) colored. .an untimely

3. French folktales almost always take place within the basic ------- that correspond to the ------- setting of peasant life: on the one hand, the household and village and on the other, the open road.

   (A) contexts. .hierarchical
   (B) structures. .personal
   (C) frameworks. .dual
   (D) chronologies. .generic
   (E) narratives. .ambivalent

4. Nurturing the Royal Ballet's artistic growth while preserving its institutional stability has been difficult, because the claims of the latter seem inescapably to ------- development; apparently, attaining artistic success is simpler than ------- it.

   (A) ensure. .promoting
   (B) inhibit. .perpetuating
   (C) undermine. .resurrecting
   (D) modify. .appreciating
   (E) supplement. .confining

5. Inspired interim responses to hitherto unknown problems, New Deal economic stratagems became ------- as a result of bureaucratization, their flexibility and adaptibility destroyed by their transformation into rigid policies.

   (A) politicized
   (B) consolidated
   (C) ossified
   (D) ungovernable
   (E) streamlined

6. Biologists ------- isolated oceanic islands like the Galapagos, because, in such small, laboratory-like settings, the rich hurly-burly of continental plant and animal communities is reduced to a scientifically ------- complexity.

   (A) explore. .diverse
   (B) desert. .manageable
   (C) exploit. .intimidating
   (D) reject. .intricate
   (E) prize. .tractable

7. The startling finding that variations in the rate of the Earth's rotation depend to an ------- degree on the weather has necessitated a complete ------- of the world's time-keeping methods.

   (A) unexpected. .overhaul
   (B) anticipated. .recalibration
   (C) indeterminate. .rejection
   (D) unobservable. .review
   (E) estimated. .acceptance

GO ON TO THE NEXT PAGE.

Directions: In each of the following questions, a related pair of words or phrases is followed by five lettered pairs of words or phrases. Select the lettered pair that best expresses a relationship similar to that expressed in the original pair.

8. ORCHESTRA : INSTRUMENTAL ::
   (A) choir : vocal   (B) pianist : discordant
   (C) trio : harmonic   (D) singer : sacred
   (E) band : martial

9. TROPHY : CONTESTANT :: (A) baton : runner
   (B) pride : parent   (C) book : bibliography
   (D) loan : cashier   (E) honors : student

10. LISTENER : EAVESDROPPER ::
    (A) spectator : game   (B) viewer : gazer
    (C) observer : spy   (D) speaker : chatterbox
    (E) leader : demagogue

11. FIDGET : NERVOUSNESS :: (A) cringe : dread
    (B) stall : frustration   (C) regale : amusement
    (D) doubt : consternation   (E) nag : annoyance

12. DORMANT : INACTIVITY ::
    (A) stark : ornateness   (B) malleable : plasticity
    (C) prone : uprightness   (D) infuriating : tedium
    (E) slack : excess

13. WAFT : PLUMMET :: (A) skim : glide
    (B) dream : captivate   (C) toss : catch
    (D) flail : assault   (E) meander : dash

14. PRUDISH : PROPRIETY ::
    (A) fanatical : violence
    (B) authoritative : evidence
    (C) finicky : quality
    (D) obstinate : accuracy
    (E) fearful : comfort

15. POSEUR : SINCERITY :: (A) brat : insolence
    (B) flirt : decency   (C) grouch : patience
    (D) recluse : gregariousness   (E) rogue : empathy

16. MORALISTIC : PRINCIPLED ::
    (A) simplistic : unsophisticated
    (B) pedantic : learned
    (C) positivistic : empirical
    (D) dogmatic : prejudiced
    (E) fantastic : imaginative

GO ON TO THE NEXT PAGE.

Each passage in this group is followed by questions based on its content. After reading a passage, choose the best answer to each question. Answer all questions following a passage on the basis of what is <u>stated</u> or <u>implied</u> in that passage.

Historically, a cornerstone of classical empiricism has been the notion that every true generalization must be confirmable by specific observations. In classical em-
Line
(5) piricism, the truth of "All balls are red," for example, is assessed by inspecting balls; any observation of a *non*red ball refutes unequivocally the proposed generalization.

For W.V.O. Quine, however, this constitutes an overly "narrow" conception of empiricism. "All balls are red,"
he maintains, forms one strand within an entire web of
(10) statements (our knowledge); individual observations can be referred only to this web as a whole. As new observations are collected, he explains, they must be integrated into the web. Problems occur only if a contradiction develops between a new observation, say, "That ball
(15) is blue," and the preexisting statements. In that case, he argues, *any* statement or combination of statements (not merely the "offending" generalization, as in classical empiricism) can be altered to achieve the fundamental requirement, a system free of contradictions,
(20) even if, in some cases, the alteration consists of labeling the new observation a "hallucination."

17. The author of the passage is primarily concerned with presenting

    (A) criticisms of Quine's views on the proper conceptualization of empiricism
    (B) evidence to support Quine's claims about the problems inherent in classical empiricism
    (C) an account of Quine's counterproposal to one of the traditional assumptions of classical empiricism
    (D) an overview of classical empiricism and its contributions to Quine's alternate understanding of empiricism
    (E) a history of classical empiricism and Quine's reservations about it

18. According to Quine's conception of empiricism, if a new observation were to contradict some statement already within our system of knowledge, which of the following would be true?

    (A) The new observation would be rejected as untrue.
    (B) Both the observation and the statement in our system that it contradicted would be discarded.
    (C) New observations would be added to our web of statements in order to expand our system of knowledge.
    (D) The observation or some part of our web of statements would need to be adjusted to resolve the contradiction.
    (E) An entirely new field of knowledge would be created.

19. As described in the passage, Quine's specific argument against classical empiricism would be most strengthened if he did which of the following?

    (A) Provided evidence that many observations are actually hallucinations.
    (B) Explained why new observations often invalidate preexisting generalizations.
    (C) Challenged the mechanism by which specific generalizations are derived from collections of particular observations.
    (D) Mentioned other critics of classical empiricism and the substance of their approaches.
    (E) Gave an example of a specific generalization that has not been invalidated despite a contrary observation.

20. It can be inferred from the passage that Quine considers classical empircism to be "overly 'narrow'" (lines 7-8) for which of the following reasons?

    I. Classical empiricism requires that our system of generalizations be free of contradictions.
    II. Classical empiricism demands that in the case of a contradiction between an individual observation and a generalization, the generalization must be abandoned.
    III. Classical empiricism asserts that every observation will either confirm an existing generalization or initiate a new generalization.

    (A) II only
    (B) I and II only
    (C) I and III only
    (D) II and III only
    (E) I, II, and III

GO ON TO THE NEXT PAGE.

Until recently astronomers have been puzzled by the fate of red giant and supergiant stars. When the core of a giant star whose mass surpasses 1.4 times the present mass of our Sun ($M_\odot$) exhausts its nuclear fuel, it
(5) is unable to support its own weight and collapses into a tiny neutron star. The gravitational energy released during this implosion of the core blows off the remainder of the star in a gigantic explosion, or a supernova. Since around 50 percent of all stars are believed to
(10) begin their lives with masses greater than 1.4 $M_\odot$, we might expect that one out of every two stars would die as a supernova. But in fact, only one star in thirty dies such a violent death. The rest expire much more peacefully as planetary nebulas. Apparently most
(15) massive stars manage to lose sufficient material that their masses drop below the critical value of 1.4 $M_\odot$ before they exhaust their nuclear fuel.

Evidence supporting this view comes from observations of IRC + 10216, a pulsating giant star located
(20) 700 light-years away from Earth. A huge rate of mass loss (1 $M_\odot$ every 10,000 years) has been deduced from infrared observations of ammonia (NH_3) molecules located in the circumstellar cloud around IRC + 10216. Recent microwave observations of carbon monoxide
(25) (CO) molecules indicate a similar rate of mass loss and demonstrate that the escaping material extends outward from the star for a distance of at least one light-year. Because we know the size of the cloud around IRC + 10216 and can use our observations of either
(30) NH_3 or CO to measure the outflow velocity, we can calculate an age for the circumstellar cloud. IRC + 10216 has apparently expelled, in the form of molecules and dust grains, a mass equal to that of our entire Sun within the past ten thousand years. This
(35) implies that some stars can shed huge amounts of matter very quickly and thus may never expire as supernovas. Theoretical models as well as statistics on supernovas and planetary nebulas suggest that stars that begin their lives with masses around 6 $M_\odot$ shed sufficient
(40) material to drop below the critical value of 1.4 $M_\odot$. IRC + 10216, for example, should do this in a mere 50,000 years from its birth, only an instant in the life of a star.

But what place does IRC + 10216 have in stellar evo-
(45) lution? Astronomers suggest that stars like IRC + 10216 are actually "protoplanetary nebulas"—old giant stars whose dense cores have almost but not quite rid themselves of the fluffy envelopes of gas around them. Once the star has lost the entire envelope, its exposed core be-
(50) comes the central star of the planetary nebula and heats and ionizes the last vestiges of the envelope as it flows away into space. This configuration is a full-fledged planetary nebula, long familiar to optical astronomers.

21. The primary purpose of the passage is to

(A) offer a method of calculating the age of circum stellar clouds
(B) describe the conditions that result in a star's expiring as a supernova
(C) discuss new evidence concerning the composition of planetary nebulas
(D) explain why fewer stars than predicted expire a supernovas
(E) survey conflicting theories concerning the composition of circumstellar clouds

22. The passage implies that at the beginning of the life of IRC + 10216, its mass was approximately

(A) 7.0 $M_\odot$ (B) 6.0 $M_\odot$ (C) 5.0 $M_\odot$
(D) 1.4 $M_\odot$ (E) 1.0 $M_\odot$

23. The view to which line 18 refers serves to

(A) reconcile seemingly contradictory facts
(B) undermine a previously held theory
(C) take into account data previously held to be insignificant
(D) resolve a controversy
(E) question new methods of gathering data

24. It can be inferred from the passage that the author assumes which of the following in the discussion of the rate at which IRC + 10216 loses mass?

(A) The circumstellar cloud surrounding IRC + 10216 consists only of CO and NH_3 molecules.
(B) The circumstellar cloud surrounding IRC + 10216 consists of material expelled from that star.
(C) The age of a star is equal to that of its circum stellar cloud.
(D) The rate at which IRC + 10216 loses mass varies significantly from year to year.
(E) Stars with a mass greater than 6 $M_\odot$ lose mass at a rate faster than stars with a mass less than 6 $M_\odot$ do.

GO ON TO THE NEXT PAG

25. According to information provided by the passage, which of the following stars would astronomers most likely describe as a planetary nebula?

(A) A star that began its life with a mass of 5.5 $M_\odot$, has exhausted its nuclear fuel, and has a core that is visible to astronomers

(B) A star that began its life with a mass of 6 $M_\odot$, lost mass at a rate of 1 $M_\odot$ per 10,000 years, and exhausted its nuclear fuel in 40,000 years

(C) A star that has exhausted its nuclear fuel, has a mass of 1.2 $M_\odot$, and is surrounded by a circumstellar cloud that obscures its core from view

(D) A star that began its life with a mass greater than 6 $M_\odot$, has just recently exhausted its nuclear fuel, and is in the process of releasing massive amounts of gravitational energy

(E) A star that began its life with a mass of 5.5 $M_\odot$, has yet to exhaust its nuclear fuel, and exhibits a rate of mass loss similar to that of IRC + 10216

26. Which of the following statements would be most likely to follow the last sentence of the passage?

(A) Supernovas are not necessarily the most spectacular events that astronomers have occasion to observe.

(B) Apparently, stars that have a mass of greater than 6 $M_\odot$ are somewhat rare.

(C) Recent studies of CO and NH_3 in the circumstellar clouds of stars similar to IRC + 10216 have led astronomers to believe that the formation of planetary nebulas precedes the development of supernovas.

(D) It appears, then, that IRC + 10216 actually represents an intermediate step in the evolution of a giant star into a planetary nebula.

(E) Astronomers have yet to develop a consistently accurate method for measuring the rate at which a star exhausts its nuclear fuel.

27. Which of the following titles best summarizes the content of the passage?

(A) New Methods of Calculating the Age of Circumstellar Clouds
(B) New Evidence Concerning the Composition of Planetary Nebulas
(C) Protoplanetary Nebula: A Rarely Observed Phenomenon
(D) Planetary Nebulas: An Enigma to Astronomers
(E) The Diminution of a Star's Mass: A Crucial Factor in Stellar Evolution

GO ON TO THE NEXT PAGE.

28. SEND: (A) drop (B) lift (C) attempt
(D) receive (E) locate

29. INTERLOCKING: (A) independent
(B) internal (C) peripheral
(D) sequential (E) variable

30. REFLECT: (A) diffuse (B) polarize
(C) absorb (D) focus (E) propagate

31. LACKLUSTER: (A) necessary (B) descriptive
(C) radiant (D) organized (E) mature

32. ZENITH: (A) shortest line (B) furthest edge
(C) lowest point (D) roughest curve
(E) smallest surface

33. ENGENDER: (A) enumerate (B) emulate
(C) exculpate (D) eradicate (E) encapsulate

34. ANOMALOUS:
(A) veracious
(B) precise
(C) essential
(D) conforming to an established rule
(E) proceeding in a timely fashion

35. GRIEVOUS: (A) slight (B) stereotyped
(C) solicitous (D) sophisticated (E) sparkling

36. PRECIPITATE: (A) desperate (B) determined
(C) dissident (D) deliberate (E) divided

37. PROLIXITY: (A) intense devotion
(B) vehement protest (C) serious offense
(D) exact measurement (E) extreme brevity

38. DISABUSE: (A) afflict with pain
(B) lead into error (C) force into exile
(D) remove from grace (E) free from obligation

STOP

IF YOU FINISH BEFORE TIME IS CALLED, YOU MAY CHECK YOUR WORK ON THIS SECTION ONLY.
DO NOT TURN TO ANY OTHER SECTION IN THE TEST.

Section 4 starts on page 340.

SECTION 4

Time—30 minutes

30 Questions

Numbers: All numbers used are real numbers.

Figures: Position of points, angles, regions, etc. can be assumed to be in the order shown; and angle measures can be assumed to be positive.

Lines shown as straight can be assumed to be straight.

Figures can be assumed to lie in a plane unless otherwise indicated.

Figures that accompany questions are intended to provide information useful in answering the questions. However, unless a note states that a figure is drawn to scale, you should solve these problems NOT by estimating sizes by sight or by measurement, but by using your knowledge of mathematics (see Example 2 below).

Directions: Each of the <u>Questions 1-15</u> consists of two quantities, one in Column A and one in Column B. You are to compare the two quantities and choose

A if the quantity in Column A is greater;
B if the quantity in Column B is greater;
C if the two quantities are equal;
D if the relationship cannot be determined from the information given.

Note: Since there are only four choices, **NEVER MARK (E)**.

Common Information: In a question, information concerning one or both of the quantities to be compared is centered above the two columns. A symbol that appears in both columns represents the same thing in Column A as it does in Column B.

	Column A	Column B	Sample Answers
Example 1:	2×6	$2 + 6$	● Ⓑ Ⓒ Ⓓ Ⓔ

Examples 2-4 refer to $\triangle PQR$.

Example 2:	PN	NQ	Ⓐ Ⓑ Ⓒ ● Ⓔ

(since equal measures cannot be assumed, even though PN and NQ appear equal)

Example 3:	x	y	Ⓐ ● Ⓒ Ⓓ Ⓔ

(since N is between P and Q)

Example 4:	$w + z$	180	Ⓐ Ⓑ ● Ⓓ Ⓔ

(since PQ is a straight line)

GO ON TO THE NEXT PAGE.

A if the quantity in Column A is greater;
B if the quantity in Column B is greater;
C if the two quantities are equal;
D if the relationship cannot be determined from the information given.

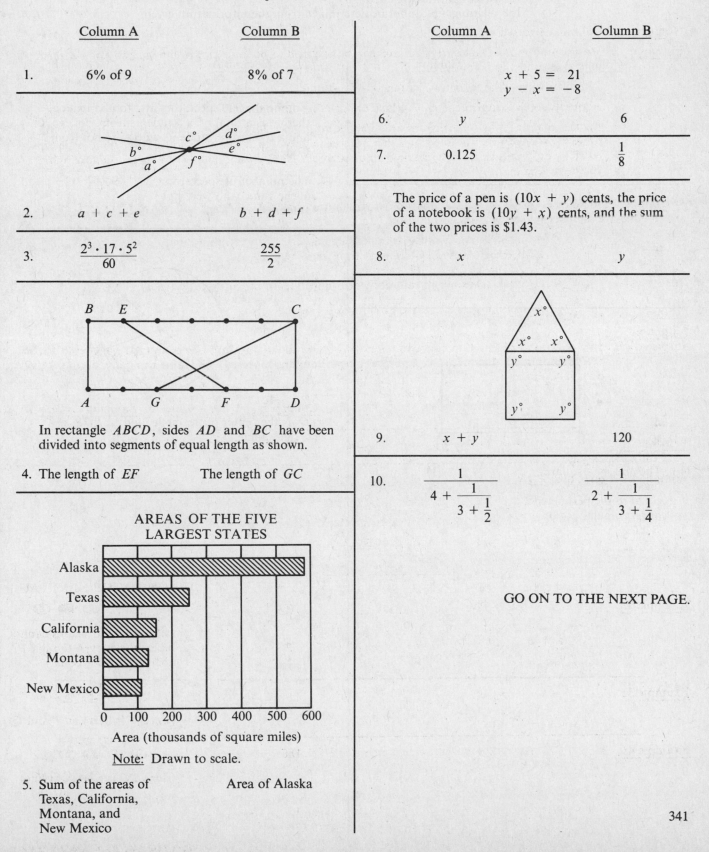

Column A	Column B

1. 6% of 9   8% of 7

2. $a + c + e$ $b + d + f$

3. $\dfrac{2^3 \cdot 17 \cdot 5^2}{60}$ $\dfrac{255}{2}$

In rectangle $ABCD$, sides AD and BC have been divided into segments of equal length as shown.

4. The length of EF The length of GC

AREAS OF THE FIVE
LARGEST STATES

Area (thousands of square miles)

Note: Drawn to scale.

5. Sum of the areas of Texas, California, Montana, and New Mexico   Area of Alaska

Column A	Column B

$x + 5 = 21$
$y - x = -8$

6. y 6

7. 0.125 $\dfrac{1}{8}$

The price of a pen is $(10x + y)$ cents, the price of a notebook is $(10y + x)$ cents, and the sum of the two prices is $1.43.

8. x y

9. $x + y$ 120

10. $\dfrac{1}{4 + \dfrac{1}{3 + \dfrac{1}{2}}}$ $\dfrac{1}{2 + \dfrac{1}{3 + \dfrac{1}{4}}}$

GO ON TO THE NEXT PAGE.

341

A   if the quantity in Column A is greater;
B   if the quantity in Column B is greater;
C   if the two quantities are equal;
D   if the relationship cannot be determined from the information given.

Column A	Column B

x and y are positive integers.
$$x > 1$$
$$y < 2$$

11. x $2y$

$$\frac{\dfrac{1}{r}}{\dfrac{1}{t}} = \frac{3}{5}$$

12. $\dfrac{r}{t}$ $\dfrac{t}{r}$

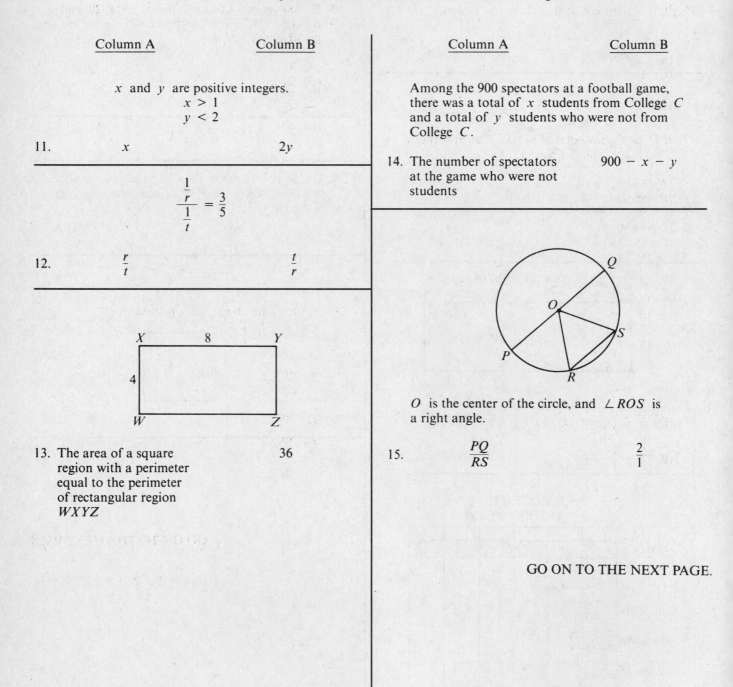

13. The area of a square   36
    region with a perimeter
    equal to the perimeter
    of rectangular region
    $WXYZ$

Column A	Column B

Among the 900 spectators at a football game, there was a total of x students from College C and a total of y students who were not from College C.

14. The number of spectators $900 - x - y$
    at the game who were not
    students

O is the center of the circle, and $\angle ROS$ is a right angle.

15. $\dfrac{PQ}{RS}$ $\dfrac{2}{1}$

GO ON TO THE NEXT PAGE.

Directions: Each of the Questions 16-30 has five answer choices. For each of these questions, select the best of the answer choices given.

16. If $\frac{x}{2} + 1 = 15$, then $x =$

    (A) 5
    (B) 7
    (C) 13
    (D) 28
    (E) 29

17. If 15 pies cost a total of $11.50, then at this rate, what is the cost of 9 pies?

    (A) $6.75
    (B) $6.90
    (C) $7.50
    (D) $8.50
    (E) $9.45

18. If $2(x + y) = 5$, then, in terms of x, $y =$

    (A) $\frac{5}{2} - x$

    (B) $\frac{5}{2} + x$

    (C) $5 - 2x$

    (D) $5 - \frac{x}{2}$

    (E) $\frac{5}{2} + \frac{x}{2}$

19. If the average (arithmetic mean) of 16, 20, and n is between 18 and 21, inclusive, what is the greatest possible value of n?

    (A) 18
    (B) 21
    (C) 27
    (D) 54
    (E) 63

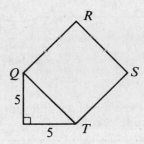

20. In the figure above, what is the area of square $QRST$?

    (A) 25
    (B) $20\sqrt{2}$
    (C) $25\sqrt{2}$
    (D) 50
    (E) $50\sqrt{2}$

GO ON TO THE NEXT PAGE.

343

Questions 21-25 refer to the following graphs.

DISTRIBUTION OF WORK FORCE BY OCCUPATIONAL CATEGORY FOR
COUNTRY X IN 1981 AND PROJECTED FOR 1995

Total Work Force: 150 Million   Total Work Force: 175 Million

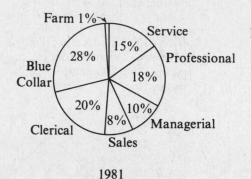
1981

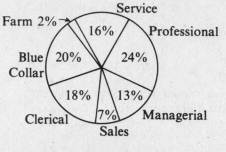
1995 (Projected)

21. In 1981, there were how many million Service
workers in the work force?

(A) 15.0
(B) 20.5
(C) 22.5
(D) 28.0
(E) 175.0

22. In 1981, how many categories each comprised more
than 25 million workers?

(A) One
(B) Two
(C) Three
(D) Four
(E) Five

23. What is the ratio of the number of workers in
the Professional category in 1981 to the projected
number of such workers in 1995 ?

(A) $\frac{4}{9}$

(B) $\frac{5}{14}$

(C) $\frac{9}{14}$

(D) $\frac{3}{4}$

(E) $\frac{14}{9}$

24. From 1981 to 1995, there is a projected increase in
the number of workers in which of the following
categories?

I. Sales
II. Service
III. Clerical

(A) None
(B) III only
(C) I and II only
(D) II and III only
(E) I, II, and III

25. Approximately what is the projected percent
decrease in the number of Blue-Collar workers
in the work force of Country X from 1981
to 1995 ?

(A) 42%
(B) 35%
(C) 20%
(D) 17%
(E) 7%

GO ON TO THE NEXT PAGE.

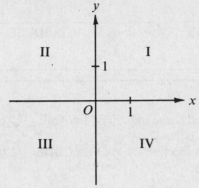

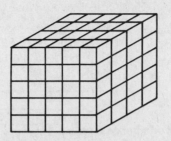

26. Points $(x, -3)$ and $(-2, y)$, not shown in the figure above, are in quadrants IV and II, respectively. If $xy \neq 0$, in which quadrant is point (x, y)?

(A) I
(B) II
(C) III
(D) IV
(E) It cannot be determined from the information given.

27. $(\sqrt{3} - \sqrt{2})^2 =$

(A) $1 - 2\sqrt{6}$
(B) $1 - \sqrt{6}$
(C) $5 - 2\sqrt{6}$
(D) $5 - 2\sqrt{3}$
(E) 1

28. If the figure above is a rectangular solid composed of cubes, each with edge of length 4 centimeters, what is the volume of the rectangular solid in cubic centimeters?

(A) 100
(B) 256
(C) 400
(D) 5,120
(E) 6,400

29. If $L = (a - b) - c$ and $R = a - (b - c)$, then $L - R =$

(A) $2b$
(B) $2c$
(C) 0
(D) $-2b$
(E) $-2c$

30. At the rate of 3,000 revolutions per minute, how many revolutions will a wheel make in k seconds?

(A) $3,000k$

(B) $50k$

(C) $\dfrac{50}{k}$

(D) $\dfrac{3,000}{k}$

(E) $\dfrac{180,000}{k}$

STOP

IF YOU FINISH BEFORE TIME IS CALLED, YOU MAY CHECK YOUR WORK ON THIS SECTION ONLY.
DO NOT TURN TO ANY OTHER SECTION IN THE TEST.

I

NOTE: To ensure prompt processing of test results, it is important that you fill in the blanks exactly as directed.

GENERAL TEST

A. Print and sign your full name in this box:

PRINT: _____
           (LAST)   (FIRST)   (MIDDLE)

SIGN: _____

Copy this code in box 6 on your answer sheet. Then fill in the corresponding ovals exactly as shown.

6. TITLE CODE

Copy the Test Name and Form Code in box 7 on your answer sheet.

TEST NAME _General_

FORM CODE _GR92-1_

GRADUATE RECORD EXAMINATIONS GENERAL TEST

B. You will have 3 hours and 30 minutes in which to work on this test, which consists of seven sections. During the time allowed for one section, you may work only on that section. The time allowed for each section is 30 minutes.

Each of your scores will be determined by the number of questions for which you select the best answer from the choices given. Questions for which you mark no answer or more than one answer are not counted in scoring. Nothing is subtracted from a score if you answer a question incorrectly. Therefore, to maximize your scores it is better for you to guess at an answer than not to respond at all.

You are advised to work as rapidly as you can without losing accuracy. Do not spend too much time on questions that are too difficult for you. Go on to the other questions and come back to the difficult ones later.

There are several different types of questions; you will find special directions for each type in the test itself. Be sure you understand the directions before attempting to answer any questions.

YOU MUST INDICATE ALL YOUR ANSWERS ON THE SEPARATE ANSWER SHEET. No credit will be given for anything written in this examination book, but you may write in the book as much as you wish to work out your answers. After you have decided on your response to a question, fill in the corresponding oval on the answer sheet. BE SURE THAT EACH MARK IS DARK AND COMPLETELY FILLS THE OVAL. Mark only one answer to each question. No credit will be given for multiple answers. Erase all stray marks. If you change an answer, be sure that all previous marks are erased completely. Incomplete erasures may be read as intended answers. Do not be concerned if your answer sheet provides spaces for more answers than there are questions in each section.

Example:

What city is the capital of France?

(A) Rome
(B) Paris
(C) London
(D) Cairo
(E) Oslo

Sample Answer

BEST ANSWER
PROPERLY MARKED

IMPROPER MARKS

Some or all of the passages for this test have been adapted from published material to provide the examinee with significant problems for analysis and evaluation. To make the passages suitable for testing purposes, the style, content, or point of view of the original may have been altered in some cases. The ideas contained in the passages do not necessarily represent the opinions of the Graduate Record Examinations Board or Educational Testing Service.

DO NOT OPEN YOUR TEST BOOK UNTIL YOU ARE TOLD TO DO SO.

FOR GENERAL TEST, FORM GR92-1 ONLY
Answer Key and Percentages* of Examinees Answering Each Question Correctly

VERBAL ABILITY						QUANTITATIVE ABILITY					
Section 1			Section 3			Section 2			Section 4		
Number	Answer	P+	Number	Answer	P+	Number	Answer	P+	Number	Answer	P+
1	A	85	1	A	95	1	C	88	1	B	81
2	D	71	2	A	79	2	B	83	2	C	85
3	B	74	3	C	79	3	B	81	3	B	81
4	E	59	4	B	64	4	A	84	4	B	81
5	E	51	5	C	45	5	A	87	5	A	89
6	E	40	6	E	58	6	A	71	6	A	87
7	B	37	7	A	50	7	B	74	7	C	87
8	E	83	8	A	90	8	A	76	8	D	68
9	B	87	9	E	88	9	A	77	9	A	72
10	B	54	10	C	83	10	D	59	10	B	65
11	E	58	11	A	59	11	D	52	11	D	67
12	B	42	12	B	54	12	C	44	12	A	63
13	D	35	13	E	57	13	D	50	13	C	50
14	D	44	14	C	48	14	C	33	14	C	49
15	D	28	15	D	36	15	D	29	15	B	30
16	E	11	16	B	31	16	C	88	16	D	85
17	C	64	17	C	63	17	A	78	17	B	77
18	A	84	18	D	61	18	A	64	18	A	74
19	D	79	19	E	45	19	E	64	19	C	71
20	E	90	20	A	14	20	C	64	20	D	57
21	A	74	21	D	61	21	D	87	21	C	79
22	D	38	22	B	65	22	A	83	22	C	75
23	B	53	23	A	40	23	C	63	23	C	40
24	E	47	24	B	49	24	B	59	24	E	42
25	A	57	25	A	22	25	D	38	25	D	35
26	A	49	26	D	61	26	E	52	26	A	53
27	B	67	27	E	47	27	B	48	27	C	39
28	A	77	28	D	94	28	D	43	28	E	52
29	C	78	29	A	88	29	E	33	29	E	32
30	A	79	30	C	76	30	E	28	30	B	49
31	B	73	31	C	79						
32	D	56	32	C	75						
33	E	38	33	D	51						
34	C	33	34	D	44						
35	D	35	35	A	32						
36	E	34	36	D	26						
37	A	22	37	E	33						
38	A	29	38	B	15						

*Estimated P+ for the group of examinees who took the GRE General Test in a recent three-year period.

347

SCORE CONVERSIONS FOR GRE GENERAL TEST, GR92-1

Raw Score	Scaled Score Verbal	Scaled Score Quantitative	Raw Score	Scaled Score Verbal	Scaled Score Quantitative
72-76	800		39	450	570
71	780		38	440	560
70	770		37	430	550
			36	420	540
69	750		35	410	530
68	740		34	400	520
67	730		33	400	510
66	720		32	390	500
65	710		31	380	490
64	690		30	370	470
63	680				
62	670		29	360	460
61	660		28	360	450
60	650	800	27	350	440
			26	340	430
59	640	800	25	340	410
58	630	800	24	330	400
57	620	790	23	320	390
56	610	780	22	310	380
55	600	770	21	300	370
54	590	750	20	290	360
53	580	740			
52	570	730	19	280	340
51	560	710	18	270	330
50	550	700	17	260	320
			16	250	310
49	540	690	15	250	290
48	530	680	14	240	280
47	520	660	13	230	260
46	510	650	12	220	250
45	500	640	11	210	230
44	490	630	10	200	210
43	480	620			
42	470	600	9	200	200
41	460	590	8	200	200
40	450	580	7	200	200
			0-6	200	200

THE GRADUATE RECORD
EXAMINATIONS®

GRE®

ⒺⓉⓈ®

General Test

*Do not break the seal
until you are told to do so.*

*The contents of this test are confidential.
Disclosure or reproduction of any portion
of it is prohibited.*

THIS TEST BOOK MUST NOT BE TAKEN FROM THE ROOM.

NO TEST MATERIAL ON THIS PAGE

Directions: Each sentence below has one or two blanks, each blank indicating that something has been omitted. Beneath the sentence are five lettered words or sets of words. Choose the word or set of words for each blank that best fits the meaning of the sentence as a whole.

1. In the British theater young people under thirty-five have not had much ------- getting recognition onstage, but offstage—in the ranks of playwrights, directors, designers, administrators—they have mostly been relegated to relative obscurity.

   (A) trouble   (B) satisfaction   (C) curiosity about
   (D) success at   (E) fear of

2. An institution concerned about its reputation is at the mercy of the actions of its members, because the misdeeds of individuals are often used to ------- the institutions of which they are a part.

   (A) reform   (B) coerce   (C) honor
   (D) discredit   (E) intimidate

3. Since many casual smokers develop lung cancer and many -------- smokers do not, scientists believe that individuals differ in their -------- the cancer-causing agents known to be present in cigarette smoke.

   (A) heavy. .susceptibility to
   (B) chronic. .concern about
   (C) habitual. .proximity to
   (D) devoted. .reliance upon
   (E) regular. .exposure to

4. We accepted the theory that as people become more independent of one another, they begin to feel so isolated and lonely that freedom becomes ------- condition that most will seek to -------.

   (A) a permanent. .postpone
   (B) a common. .enter
   (C) a negative. .escape
   (D) a political. .impose
   (E) an irreparable. .avoid

5. If animal parents were judged by human standards, the cuckoo would be one of nature's more ------- creatures, blithely laying its eggs in the nests of other birds, and leaving the incubating and nurturing to them.

   (A) mettlesome   (B) industrious   (C) domestic
   (D) lackluster   (E) feckless

6. The current penchant for ------- a product by denigrating a rival, named in the advertisement by brand name, seems somewhat -------:   suppose the consumer remembers only the rival's name?

   (A) criticizing. .inefficient
   (B) touting. .foolhardy
   (C) enhancing. .insipid
   (D) evaluating. .cumbersome
   (E) flaunting. .gullible

7. His imperturbability in the face of evidence indicating his deliberate fraud failed to reassure supporters of his essential ------- ; instead, it suggested a talent for ------- that they had never suspected.

   (A) culpability. .intrigue   (B) wisdom. .reproof
   (C) remorse. .loquacity   (D) probity. .guile
   (E) combativeness. .compromise

GO ON TO THE NEXT PAGE.

Directions: In each of the following questions, a related pair of words or phrases is followed by five lettered pairs of words or phrases. Select the lettered pair that best expresses a relationship similar to that expressed in the original pair.

8. JUDGE : GAVEL ::
   (A) detective : uniform
   (B) doctor : stethoscope
   (C) referee : whistle
   (D) soldier : insignia
   (E) lecturer : podium

9. ORGAN : KIDNEY ::
   (A) skeleton : kneecap
   (B) bone : rib
   (C) neuron : synapse
   (D) abdomen : stomach
   (E) blood : aorta

10. SOOT : COMBUSTION ::
    (A) lint : brushing
    (B) gravel : crushing
    (C) gristle : tenderizing
    (D) rubbish : housecleaning
    (E) sawdust : woodcutting

11. PURIFY : IMPERFECTION ::
    (A) align : adjustment
    (B) weary : boredom
    (C) disagree : controversy
    (D) verify : doubtfulness
    (E) hone : sharpness

12. CENTRIFUGE : SEPARATE ::
    (A) thermometer : calibrate
    (B) statue : chisel
    (C) floodgate : overflow
    (D) colander : drain
    (E) television : transmit

13. MOCK : IMITATE ::
    (A) satirize : charm
    (B) condense : summarize
    (C) placate : assuage
    (D) adapt : duplicate
    (E) taunt : challenge

14. MALADROIT : SKILL ::
    (A) intemperate : anger
    (B) unreasonable : intuition
    (C) sluggish : fatigue
    (D) glib : profundity
    (E) morose : depression

15. EQUIVOCATION : AMBIGUOUS ::
    (A) mitigation : severe
    (B) contradiction : peremptory
    (C) platitude : banal
    (D) precept : obedient
    (E) explanation : unintelligible

16. VOLATILE : TEMPER ::
    (A) prominent : notoriety
    (B) ready : wit
    (C) catastrophic : disaster
    (D) gentle : heart
    (E) expressive : song

GO ON TO THE NEXT PAGE.

Directions: Each passage in this group is followed by questions based on its content. After reading a passage, choose the best answer to each question. Answer all questions following a passage on the basis of what is <u>stated</u> or <u>implied</u> in that passage.

(This passage is from an article published in 1973)

The recent change to all-volunteer armed forces in the United States will eventually produce a gradual increase in the proportion of women in the armed forces and in the variety of women's assignments, but probably
Line
(5) not the dramatic gains for women that might have been expected. This is so even though the armed forces operate in an ethos of institutional change oriented toward occupational equality and under the federal sanction of equal pay for equal work. The difficulty is that women are
(10) unlikely to be trained for any direct combat operations. A significant portion of the larger society remains uncomfortable as yet with extending equality in this direction. Therefore, for women in the military, the search for equality will still be based on functional equivalence, not
(15) identity or even similarity of task. Opportunities seem certain to arise. The growing emphasis on deterrence is bound to offer increasing scope for women to become involved in novel types of noncombat military assignments.

17. The primary purpose of the passage is to

(A) present an overview of the different types of assignments available to women in the new United States all-volunteer armed forces
(B) present a reasoned prognosis of the status of women in the new United States all-volunteer armed forces
(C) present the new United States all-volunteer armed forces as a model case of equal employment policies in action
(D) analyze reforms in the new United States all-volunteer armed forces necessitated by the increasing number of women in the military
(E) analyze the use of functional equivalence as a substitute for occupational equality in the new United States all-volunteer armed forces

18. According to the passage, despite the United States armed forces' commitment to occupational equality for women in the military, certain other factors preclude women's

(A) receiving equal pay for equal work
(B) having access to positions of responsibility at most levels
(C) drawing assignments from a wider range of assignments than before
(D) benefiting from opportunities arising from new noncombat functions
(E) being assigned all of the military tasks that are assigned to men

19. The passage implies that which of the following is a factor conducive to a more equitable representation of women in the United States armed forces than has existed in the past?

(A) The all-volunteer character of the present armed forces
(B) The past service records of women who had assignments functionally equivalent to men's assignments
(C) The level of awareness on the part of the larger society of military issues
(D) A decline in the proportion of deterrence-oriented noncombat assignments
(E) Restrictive past policies governing the military assignments open to women

20. The "dramatic gains for women" (line 5) and the attitude, as described in lines 11-12, of a "significant portion of the larger society" are logically related to each other inasmuch as the author puts forward the latter as

(A) a public response to achievement of the former
(B) the major reason for absence of the former
(C) a precondition for any prospect of achieving the former
(D) a catalyst for a further extension of the former
(E) a reason for some of the former being lost again

GO ON TO THE NEXT PAGE.

Of the thousands of specimens of meteorites found on Earth and known to science, only about 100 are igneous; that is, they have undergone melting by volcanic action at some time since the planets were first
Line
(5) formed. These igneous meteorites are known as achondrites because they lack chondrules— small stony spherules found in the thousands of meteorites (called "chondrites") composed primarily of unaltered minerals that condensed from dust and gas at the origin of the
(10) solar system. Achondrites are the only known samples of volcanic rocks originating outside the Earth-Moon system. Most are thought to have been dislodged by interbody impact from asteroids, with diameters of from 10 to 500 kilometers, in solar orbit between Mars and
(15) Jupiter.

Shergottites, the name given to three anomalous achondrites so far discovered on Earth, present scientists with a genuine enigma. Shergottites crystallized from molten rock less than 1.1 billion years ago (some
(20) 3.5 billion years later than typical achondrites) and were presumably ejected into space when an object impacted on a body similar in chemical composition to Earth.

While most meteorites appear to derive from comparatively small bodies, shergottites exhibit properties that
(25) indicate that their source was a large planet, conceivably Mars. In order to account for such an unlikely source, some unusual factor must be invoked, because the impact needed to accelerate a fragment of rock to escape the gravitational field of a body even as small as the
(30) Moon is so great that no meteorites of lunar origin have been discovered.

While some scientists speculate that shergottites derive from Io (a volcanically active moon of Jupiter), recent measurements suggest that since Io's surface is
(35) rich in sulfur and sodium, the chemical composition of its volcanic products would probably be unlike that of the shergottites. Moreover, any fragments dislodged from Io by interbody impact would be unlikely to escape the gravitational pull of Jupiter.
(40) The only other logical source of shergottites is Mars. Space-probe photographs indicate the existence of giant volcanoes on the Martian surface. From the small number of impact craters that appear on Martian lava flows, one can estimate that the planet was volcanically
(45) active as recently as a half-billion years ago—and may be active today. The great objection to the Martian origin of shergottites is the absence of lunar meteorites on Earth. An impact capable of ejecting a fragment of the Martian surface into an Earth-intersecting orbit is
(50) even less probable than such an event on the Moon, in view of the Moon's smaller size and closer proximity to Earth. A recent study suggests, however, that permafrost ices below the surface of Mars may have altered the effects of impact on it. If the ices had been rapidly vapor-
(55) ized by an impacting object, the expanding gases might have helped the ejected fragments reach escape velocity. Finally, analyses performed by space probes show a remarkable chemical similarity between Martian soil and the shergottites.

21. The passage implies which of the following about shergottites?

   I. They are products of volcanic activity.
   II. They derive from a planet larger than Earth.
   III. They come from a planetary body with a chemical composition similar to that of Io.

(A) I only
(B) II only
(C) I and II only
(D) II and III only
(E) I, II, and III

22. According to the passage, a meteorite discovered on Earth is unlikely to have come from a large planet for which of the following reasons?

(A) There are fewer large planets in the solar system than there are asteroids.
(B) Most large planets have been volcanically inactive for more than a billion years.
(C) The gravitational pull of a large planet would probably prohibit fragments from escaping its orbit.
(D) There are no chondrites occurring naturally on Earth and probably none on other large planets.
(E) Interbody impact is much rarer on large than on small planets because of the density of the atmosphere on large planets.

23. The passage suggests that the age of shergottites is probably

(A) still entirely undetermined
(B) less than that of most other achondrites
(C) about 3.5 billion years
(D) the same as that of typical achondrites
(E) greater than that of the Earth

GO ON TO THE NEXT PAGE.

356

24. According to the passage, the presence of chondrules in a meteorite indicates that the meteorite

(A) has probably come from Mars
(B) is older than the solar system itself
(C) has not been melted since the solar system formed
(D) is certainly less than 4 billion years old
(E) is a small fragment of an asteroid

25. The passage provides information to answer which of the following questions?

(A) What is the precise age of the solar system?
(B) How did shergottites get their name?
(C) What are the chemical properties shared by shergottites and Martian soils?
(D) How volcanically active is the planet Jupiter?
(E) What is a major feature of the Martian surface?

26. It can be inferred from the passage that each of the following is a consideration in determining whether a particular planet is a possible source of shergottites that have been discovered on Earth EXCEPT the

(A) planet's size
(B) planet's distance from Earth
(C) strength of the planet's field of gravity
(D) proximity of the planet to its moons
(E) chemical composition of the planet's surface

27. It can be inferred from the passage that most meteorites found on Earth contain which of the following?

(A) Crystals   (B) Chondrules   (C) Metals
 (D) Sodium   (E) Sulfur

GO ON TO THE NEXT PAGE.

Each question below consists of a word printed in capital letters, followed by five lettered words or phrases. Choose the lettered word or phrase that is most nearly <u>opposite</u> in meaning to the word in capital letters.

Since some of the questions require you to distinguish fine shades of meaning, be sure to consider all the choices before deciding which one is best.

28. LIMP: (A) true   (B) firm   (C) clear
    (D) stark   (E) endless

29. GLOBAL: (A) local   (B) unusual
    (C) unpredictable   (D) hot-headed
    (E) single-minded

30. STABILITY: (A) disparity   (B) inconstancy
    (C) opposition   (D) carelessness   (E) weariness

31. DILATE: (A) narrow   (B) strengthen
    (C) bend   (D) push   (E) soften

32. CONSOLE: (A) pretend sympathy
    (B) reveal suffering   (C) aggravate grief
    (D) betray   (E) vilify

33. EXCULPATE: (A) attribute guilt
    (B) avoid responsibility   (C) establish facts
    (D) control hostilities   (E) show anxiety

34. ACCRETION:
    (A) ingestion of a nutrient
    (B) loss of the security on a loan
    (C) discernment of subtle differences
    (D) reduction in substance caused by erosion
    (E) sudden repulsion from an entity

35. CADGE: (A) conceal   (B) influence
    (C) reserve   (D) earn   (E) favor

36. ABJURE: (A) commingle   (B) arbitrate
    (C) espouse   (D) appease   (E) pardon

37. SPECIOUS: (A) unfeigned   (B) significant
    (C) valid   (D) agreeable   (E) restricted

38. QUOTIDIAN: (A) extraordinary   (B) certain
    (C) wishful   (D) secret   (E) premature

STOP

IF YOU FINISH BEFORE TIME IS CALLED, YOU MAY CHECK YOUR WORK ON THIS SECTION ONLY.
DO NOT TURN TO ANY OTHER SECTION IN THE TEST.

Section 2 starts on page 360

Time—30 minutes

30 Questions

Numbers: All numbers used are real numbers.

Figures: Position of points, angles, regions, etc. can be assumed to be in the order shown; and angle measures can be assumed to be positive.

Lines shown as straight can be assumed to be straight.

Figures can be assumed to lie in a plane unless otherwise indicated.

Figures that accompany questions are intended to provide information useful in answering the questions. However, unless a note states that a figure is drawn to scale, you should solve these problems NOT by estimating sizes by sight or by measurement, but by using your knowledge of mathematics (see Example 2 below).

Directions: Each of the Questions 1-15 consists of two quantities, one in Column A and one in Column B. You are to compare the two quantities and choose

A   if the quantity in Column A is greater;
B   if the quantity in Column B is greater;
C   if the two quantities are equal;
D   if the relationship cannot be determined from the information given.

Note: Since there are only four choices, NEVER MARK (E).

Common
Information: In a question, information concerning one or both of the quantities to be compared is centered above the two columns. A symbol that appears in both columns represents the same thing in Column A as it does in Column B.

	Column A	Column B	Sample Answers
Example 1:	2×6	$2 + 6$	● Ⓑ ⒸⒹⒺ

Examples 2-4 refer to $\triangle PQR$.

	Column A	Column B	Sample Answers
Example 2:	PN	NQ	ⒶⒷⒸ ● Ⓔ

(since equal measures cannot be assumed, even though PN and NQ appear equal)

Example 3:	x	y	Ⓐ ● ⒸⒹⒺ

(since N is between P and Q)

Example 4:	$w + z$	180	ⒶⒷ ● ⒹⒺ

(since PQ is a straight line)

GO ON TO THE NEXT PAGE.

A if the quantity in Column A is greater;
B if the quantity in Column B is greater;
C if the two quantities are equal;
D if the relationship cannot be determined from the information given.

	Column A	Column B
1.	0.8	$\frac{1}{2} + \frac{1}{3}$

Pat is older than Lee, and Lee is younger than Maria.

	Column A	Column B
2.	Maria's age	Pat's age

A farmer has two large plots of land that are equal in area. The first is divided into 16 parcels with n acres in each and the second is divided into 20 parcels with m acres in each.

	Column A	Column B
3.	n	m

$$x > 1$$

	Column A	Column B
4.	$x - 4$	-2

Rectangular region R has width 8 and perimeter 40.

	Column A	Column B
5.	The area of R	256
6.	$4n^2$	$(2n + 1)(2n - 1)$

a and b are both greater than 0 and less than 1.

	Column A	Column B
7.	$a^2 + b^2$	$a + b$

	Column A	Column B
8.	$x + y$	z
9.	3^x	4^x

$PQRS$ is a parallelogram.

	Column A	Column B
10.	x	y
11.	The sum of all the integers from 19 to 59, inclusive	The sum of all the integers from 22 to 60, inclusive

GO ON TO THE NEXT PAGE.

361

A if the quantity in Column A is greater;
B if the quantity in Column B is greater;
C if the two quantities are equal;
D if the relationship cannot be determined from the information given.

Column A	Column B	Column A	Column B

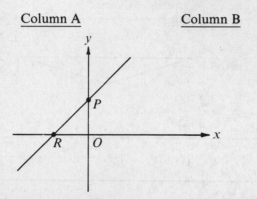

The equation of the line graphed on the rectangular coordinate system above is:

$$y = \frac{8x}{9} + 3$$

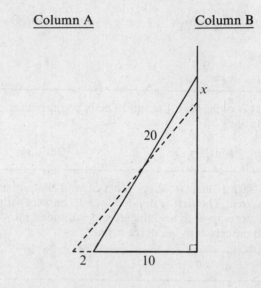

A 20-foot ladder leaning against a vertical wall with the base of the ladder 10 feet from the wall is pulled 2 feet farther out from the wall, causing the top of the ladder to drop x feet.

12. PO RO

14. x 2

$$0 > a > b$$

13. ab $(ab)^2$

15. $\dfrac{99^9}{9^{99}}$ $\dfrac{11^9}{9^{90}}$

GO ON TO THE NEXT PAGE.

362

16. If the sales tax on an appliance priced at $300 is between 5 percent and 8 percent, then the cost (price plus sales tax) of the appliance could be

(A) $310
(B) $312
(C) $314
(D) $318
(E) $325

17. $2[2x + (3x + 5x)] - (3x + 5x) =$

(A) $4x$
(B) $8x$
(C) $10x$
(D) $12x$
(E) $22x$

18. Which of the following is the product of two positive integers whose sum is 3 ?

(A) 0
(B) 1
(C) 2
(D) 3
(E) 4

19. If an integer y is subtracted from an integer x and the result is greater than x , then y must be

(A) equal to x
(B) less than 0
(C) less than x
(D) greater than 0
(E) greater than x

20. A circle with radius 2 is intersected by a line at points R and T . The maximum possible distance between R and T is

(A) 1
(B) 2
(C) π
(D) 4
(E) 4π

GO ON TO THE NEXT PAGE.

363

INCOME AND EXPENDITURES OF AN INTERNATIONAL SERVICE AGENCY—YEAR X

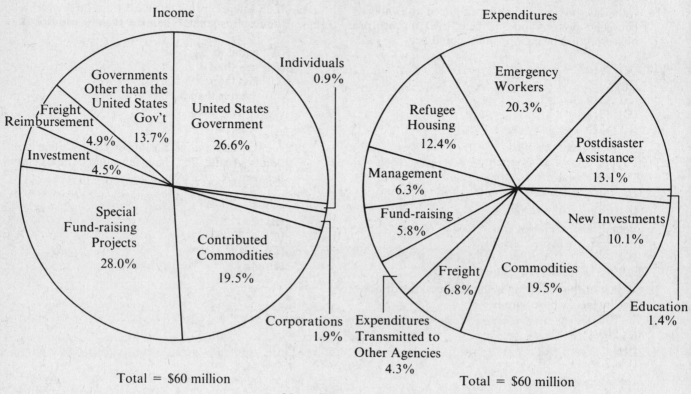

Income

Individuals
0.9%

Governments
Other than the
United States
Gov't
13.7%

United States
Government
26.6%

Freight
Reimbursement
4.9%

Investment
4.5%

Special
Fund-raising
Projects
28.0%

Contributed
Commodities
19.5%

Corporations
1.9%

Total = $60 million

Expenditures

Emergency
Workers
20.3%

Refugee
Housing
12.4%

Postdisaster
Assistance
13.1%

Management
6.3%

Fund-raising
5.8%

New Investments
10.1%

Freight
6.8%

Commodities
19.5%

Education
1.4%

Expenditures
Transmitted to
Other Agencies
4.3%

Total = $60 million

Note: Drawn to scale.

GO ON TO THE NEXT PAGE.

21. Approximately how much of the agency's income was provided by contributed commodities?

(A) $12 million
(B) $14 million
(C) $15 million
(D) $17 million
(E) $19 million

22. Of the following, the category that had expenditures most nearly equal to the average (arithmetic mean) expenditures per category was

(A) refugee housing
(B) emergency workers
(C) postdisaster assistance
(D) new investments
(E) commodities

23. Income from which of the following sources was most nearly equal to $2.9 million?

(A) United States government
(B) Freight reimbursement
(C) Investment
(D) Individuals
(E) Corporations

24. In year X, $\frac{1}{3}$ of the agency's refugee housing expenditures, $\frac{1}{5}$ of its emergency workers expenditures, $\frac{1}{4}$ of its commodities expenditures, and $\frac{2}{3}$ of its post-disaster assistance expenditures were directly related to one earthquake. The total of these expenditures was approximately how many millions of dollars?

(A) 5
(B) 7
(C) 9
(D) 11
(E) 13

25. Of the following, which is the closest appproximation to the percent of freight expenditures NOT covered by freight reimbursement income?

(A) 12%
(B) 28%
(C) 35%
(D) 39%
(E) 72%

GO ON TO THE NEXT PAGE.

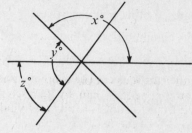

26. In the figure above, if $x = 110$ and $y = 120$, then $z =$

(A) 10
(B) 40
(C) 50
(D) 60
(E) 70

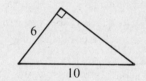

27. What is the area of the triangular region above?

(A) 24
(B) 30
(C) 40
(D) 48
(E) 60

28. A widow received $\frac{1}{3}$ of her husband's estate, and each of her three sons received $\frac{1}{3}$ of the balance. If the widow and one of her sons received a total of $60,000 from the estate, what was the amount of the estate?

(A) $90,000
(B) $96,000
(C) $108,000
(D) $135,000
(E) $180,000

29. If $\dfrac{x + 2}{y - 3} = 0$, which of the following must be true?

(A) $x = 2$ and $y = 3$
(B) $x = 2$ and $y \neq 3$
(C) $x = 0$ and $y = 0$
(D) $x = -2$ and $y = 3$
(E) $x = -2$ and $y \neq 3$

30. If $x = 0.888$, $y = \sqrt{0.888}$, and $z = (0.888)^2$, then which of the following is true?

(A) $x < y < z$
(B) $x < z < y$
(C) $y < x < z$
(D) $y < z < x$
(E) $z < x < y$

STOP

**IF YOU FINISH BEFORE TIME IS CALLED, YOU MAY CHECK YOUR WORK ON THIS SECTION ONLY.
DO NOT TURN TO ANY OTHER SECTION IN THE TEST.**

Time—30 minutes

38 Questions

Directions: Each sentence below has one or two blanks, each blank indicating that something has been omitted. Beneath the sentence are five lettered words or sets of words. Choose the word or set of words for each blank that best fits the meaning of the sentence as a whole.

1. Although providing wild chimpanzees with food makes them less ------- and easier to study, it is also known to ------- their normal social patterns.

   (A) interesting. .reinforce   (B) manageable. .upset
   (C) shy. .disrupt   (D) poised. .inhibit
   (E) accessible. .retard

2. There is something ------- about the way the building of monasteries proliferated in eighteenth-century Bavaria, while in the rest of the Western world religious ardor was ------- and church building was consequently declining.

   (A) enigmatic. .coalescing
   (B) destructive. .changing
   (C) immutable. .dissipating
   (D) incongruous. .diminishing
   (E) momentous. .diversifying

3. Because they had various meanings in nineteenth-century biological thought, "mechanism" and "vitalism" ought not to be considered ------- terms; thus, I find the recent insistence that the terms had single definitions to be entirely ------- .

   (A) univocal. .erroneous
   (B) problematic. .anachronistic
   (C) intractable. .obtuse
   (D) congruent. .suspect
   (E) multifaceted. .vapid

4. Many Americans believe that individual initiative epitomized the 1890's and see the entrepreneur as the ------- of that age.

   (A) caricature   (B) salvation   (C) throwback
   (D) aberration   (E) personification

5. Neither the ideas of philosophers nor the practices of ordinary people can, by themselves, ------- reality; what in fact changes reality and kindles revolution is the ------- of the two.

   (A) constitute. .divergence
   (B) affect. .aim
   (C) transform. .interplay
   (D) preserve. .conjunction
   (E) alter. .intervention

6. There has been a tendency among art historians not so much to revise as to eliminate the concept of the Renaissance—to ------- not only its uniqueness, but its very existence.

   (A) explain   (B) extol   (C) transmute
   (D) regret   (E) contest

7. Employees had become so inured to the caprices of top management's personnel policies that they greeted the announcement of a company-wide dress code with-------.

   (A) astonishment   (B) impassivity
   (C) resentment   (D) apprehension   (E) confusion

GO ON TO THE NEXT PAGE.

Directions: In each of the following questions, a related pair of words or phrases is followed by five lettered pairs of words or phrases. Select the lettered pair that best expresses a relationship similar to that expressed in the original pair.

8. SURGEON : DEXTERITY ::
   (A) engineer : clarity
   (B) sailor : navigation
   (C) magistrate : precedent
   (D) industrialist : capital
   (E) acrobat : agility

9. PRUNE : HEDGE ::
   (A) shuck : corn
   (B) trim : hair
   (C) cut : bouquet
   (D) reap : crop
   (E) shave : mustache

10. PHOTOGRAPH : LIGHT ::
   (A) script : scene
   (B) film : negative
   (C) recording : sound
   (D) rehearsal : practice
   (E) concert : song

11. ANTIBIOTIC : INFECTION ::
   (A) hormone : modification
   (B) enzyme : digestion
   (C) narcotic : dependency
   (D) coagulant : bleeding
   (E) stimulant : relaxation

12. EULOGY : PRAISE ::
   (A) comedy : laughter
   (B) epic : contempt
   (C) tirade : awe
   (D) elegy : lament
   (E) parody : respect

13. DAMP : VIBRATION ::
   (A) drench : moisture
   (B) concentrate : extraction
   (C) boil : liquid
   (D) seal : perforation
   (E) stanch : flow

14. ABRADED : FRICTION ::
   (A) refined : distillate
   (B) anodized : metal
   (C) diluted : gas
   (D) strengthened : pressure
   (E) vaporized : heat

15. QUARRY : STONE ::
   (A) fell : timber
   (B) dredge : canal
   (C) assay : gold
   (D) bale : hay
   (E) mold : clay

16. CREDULOUS : DUPE ::
   (A) wealthy : monarch
   (B) insensitive : boor
   (C) argumentative : lawyer
   (D) spontaneous : extrovert
   (E) extravagant : miser

GO ON TO THE NEXT PAGE.

The transplantation of organs from one individual to another normally involves two major problems: (1) organ rejection is likely unless the transplantation
Line antigens of both individuals are nearly identical, and
(5) (2) the introduction of any unmatched transplantation antigens induces the development by the recipient of donor-specific lymphocytes that will produce violent rejection of further transplantations from that donor. However, we have found that among many strains of
(10) rats these "normal" rules of transplantation are not obeyed by liver transplants. Not only are liver transplants never rejected, but they even induce a state of donor-specific unresponsiveness in which subsequent transplants of other organs, such as skin, from that
(15) donor are accepted permanently. Our hypothesis is that (1) many strains of rats simply cannot mount a sufficiently vigorous destructive immune-response (using lymphocytes) to outstrip the liver's relatively great capacity to protect itself from immune-response
(20) damage and that (2) the systemic unresponsiveness observed is due to concentration of the recipient's donor-specific lymphocytes at the site of the liver transplant.

17. The primary purpose of the passage is to treat the accepted generalizations about organ transplantation in which of the following ways?

   (A) Explicate their main features
   (B) Suggest an alternative to them
   (C) Examine their virtues and limitations
   (D) Criticize the major evidence used to support them
   (E) Present findings that qualify them

18. It can be inferred from the passage that the author believes that an important difference among strains of rats is the

   (A) size of their livers
   (B) constitution of their skin
   (C) strength of their immune-response reactions
   (D) sensitivity of their antigens
   (E) adaptability of their lymphocytes

19. According to the hypothesis of the author, after a successful liver transplant, the reason that rats do not reject further transplants of other organs from the same donor is that the

   (A) transplantation antigens of the donor and the recipient become matched
   (B) lymphocytes of the recipient are weakened by the activity of the transplanted liver
   (C) subsequently transplanted organ is able to repair the damage caused by the recipient's immune-response reaction
   (D) transplanted liver continues to be the primary locus for the recipient's immune-response reaction
   (E) recipient is unable to manufacture the lymphocytes necessary for the immune-response reaction

20. Which of the following new findings about strains of rats that do not normally reject liver transplants, if true, would support the authors' hypothesis?

   I. Stomach transplants are accepted by the recipients in all cases.
   II. Increasing the strength of the recipient's immune-response reaction can induce liver-transplant rejection.
   III. Organs from any other donor can be transplanted without rejection after liver transplantation.
   IV. Preventing lymphocytes from being concentrated at the liver transplant produces acceptance of skin transplants.

   (A) II only
   (B) I and III only
   (C) II and IV only
   (D) I, II, and III only
   (E) I, III, and IV only

GO ON TO THE NEXT PAGE.

Practically speaking, the artistic maturing of the cinema was the single-handed achievement of David W. Griffith (1875-1948). Before Griffith, photography *Line* in dramatic films consisted of little more than placing *(5)* the actors before a stationary camera and showing them in full length as they would have appeared on stage. From the beginning of his career as a director, however, Griffith, because of his love of Victorian painting, employed composition. He conceived of *(10)* the camera image as having a foreground and a rear ground, as well as the middle distance preferred by most directors. By 1910 he was using close-ups to reveal significant details of the scene or of the acting and extreme long shots to achieve a sense of spectacle *(15)* and distance. His appreciation of the camera's possibilities produced novel dramatic effects. By splitting an event into fragments and recording each from the most suitable camera position, he could significantly vary the emphasis from camera shot to camera shot.

(20) Griffith also achieved dramatic effects by means of creative editing. By juxtaposing images and varying the speed and rhythm of their presentation, he could control the dramatic intensity of the events as the story progressed. Despite the reluctance of his producers, who *(25)* feared that the public would not be able to follow a plot that was made up of such juxtaposed images, Griffith persisted, and experimented as well with other elements of cinematic syntax that have become standard ever since. These included the flashback, permitting broad *(30)* psychological and emotional exploration as well as narrative that was not chronological, and the crosscut between two parallel actions to heighten suspense and excitement. In thus exploiting fully the possibilities of editing, Griffith transposed devices of the Victorian *(35)* novel to film and gave film mastery of time as well as space.

Besides developing the cinema's language, Griffith immensely broadened its range and treatment of subjects. His early output was remarkably eclectic: it *(40)* included not only the standard comedies, melodramas, westerns, and thrillers, but also such novelties as adaptations from Browning and Tennyson, and treatments of social issues. As his successes mounted, his ambitions grew, and with them the whole of American cinema. *(45)* When he remade *Enoch Arden* in 1911, he insisted that a subject of such importance could not be treated in the then conventional length of one reel. Griffith's introduction of the American-made multireel picture began an immense revolution. Two years later, *Judith of Bethulia,* *(50)* an elaborate historicophilosophical spectacle, reached the unprecedented length of four reels, or one hour's running time. From our contemporary viewpoint, the pretensions of this film may seem a trifle ludicrous, but at the time it provoked endless debate and discussion and gave a new intellectual respectability to the cinema.

21. The primary purpose of the passage is to

    (A) discuss the importance of Griffith to the development of the cinema
    (B) describe the impact on cinema of the flashback and other editing innovations
    (C) deplore the state of American cinema before the advent of Griffith
    (D) analyze the changes in the cinema wrought by the introduction of the multireel film
    (E) document Griffith's impact on the choice of subject matter in American films

22. The author suggests that Griffith's film innovations had a direct effect on all of the following EXCEPT

    (A) film editing　　(B) camera work
    (C) scene composing　　(D) sound editing
    (E) directing

23. It can be inferred from the passage that before 1910 the normal running time of a film was

    (A) 15 minutes or less
    (B) between 15 and 30 minutes
    (C) between 30 and 45 minutes
    (D) between 45 minutes and 1 hour
    (E) 1 hour or more

24. The author asserts that Griffith introduced all of the following into American cinema EXCEPT

    (A) consideration of social issues
    (B) adaptations from Tennyson
    (C) the flashback and other editing techniques
    (D) photographic approaches inspired by Victorian painting
    (E) dramatic plots suggested by Victorian theater

GO ON TO THE NEXT PAGE.

25. The author suggests that Griffith's contributions to the cinema had which of the following results?

   I. Literary works, especially Victorian novels, became popular sources for film subjects.
   II. Audience appreciation of other film directors' experimentations with cinematic syntax was increased.
   III. Many of the artistic limitations thought to be inherent in filmmaking were shown to be really nonexistent.

   (A) II only
   (B) III only
   (C) I and II only
   (D) II and III only
   (E) I, II, and III

26. It can be inferred from the passage that Griffith would be most likely to agree with which of the following statements?

   (A) The good director will attempt to explore new ideas as quickly as possible.
   (B) The most important element contributing to a film's success is the ability of the actors.
   (C) The camera must be considered an integral and active element in the creation of a film.
   (D) The cinema should emphasize serious and sober examinations of fundamental human problems.
   (E) The proper composition of scenes in a film is more important than the details of their editing.

27. The author's attitude toward photography in the cinema before Griffith can best be described as

   (A) sympathetic (B) nostalgic (C) amused
   (D) condescending (E) hostile

GO ON TO THE NEXT PAGE.

Directions: Each question below consists of a word printed in capital letters, followed by five lettered words or phrases. Choose the lettered word or phrase that is most nearly <u>opposite</u> in meaning to the word in capital letters.

Since some of the questions require you to distinguish fine shades of meaning, be sure to consider all the choices before deciding which one is best.

28. ADHERE: (A) detach (B) cleanse (C) engulf (D) incise (E) contain

29. UNCONVENTIONALITY: (A) perceptibility (B) inscrutability (C) imperturbability (D) fidelity to custom (E) formality of discourse

30. PINCH: (A) important accomplishment (B) apt translation (C) abundant amount (D) opportune acquisition (E) unfamiliar period

31. OUTSET: (A) regression (B) series (C) exit (D) interruption (E) termination

32. RAREFY:
(A) make less humid
(B) make less opaque
(C) make more voluminous
(D) make more dense
(E) make more oily

33. EFFRONTERY: (A) charity (B) deference (C) simplicity (D) deceitfulness (E) stupidity

34. SCURVY: (A) completely centered (B) above reproach (C) imaginative (D) valiant (E) carefree

35. OBDURATE: (A) complaisant (B) similar (C) commensurate (D) uncommunicative (E) transitory

36. AVER:
(A) resign indignantly (B) condemn unjustly (C) refuse (D) deny (E) resent

37. PITH: (A) untimely action (B) insufficient attention (C) routine treatment (D) rigid formulation (E) superficial element

38. SUPINE: (A) vigilant (B) flustered (C) distorted (D) brittle (E) awkward

STOP

IF YOU FINISH BEFORE TIME IS CALLED, YOU MAY CHECK YOUR WORK ON THIS SECTION ONLY.
DO NOT TURN TO ANY OTHER SECTION IN THE TEST.

Section 4 starts on page 374

SECTION 4

Time—30 minutes

30 Questions

Numbers: All numbers used are real numbers.

Figures: Position of points, angles, regions, etc. can be assumed to be in the order shown; and angle measures can be assumed to be positive.

Lines shown as straight can be assumed to be straight.

Figures can be assumed to lie in a plane unless otherwise indicated.

Figures that accompany questions are intended to provide information useful in answering the questions. However, unless a note states that a figure is drawn to scale, you should solve these problems NOT by estimating sizes by sight or by measurement, but by using your knowledge of mathematics (see Example 2 below).

Directions: Each of the Questions 1-15 consists of two quantities, one in Column A and one in Column B. You are to compare the two quantities and choose

    A if the quantity in Column A is greater;
    B if the quantity in Column B is greater;
    C if the two quantities are equal;
    D if the relationship cannot be determined from the information given.

Note: Since there are only four choices, NEVER MARK (E).

Common Information: In a question, information concerning one or both of the quantities to be compared is centered above the two columns. A symbol that appears in both columns represents the same thing in Column A as it does in Column B.

	Column A	Column B	Sample Answers
Example 1:	2×6	$2 + 6$	● Ⓑ Ⓒ Ⓓ Ⓔ

Examples 2-4 refer to $\triangle PQR$.

Example 2:	PN	NQ	Ⓐ Ⓑ Ⓒ ● Ⓔ

(since equal measures cannot be assumed, even though PN and NQ appear equal)

Example 3:	x	y	Ⓐ ● Ⓒ Ⓓ Ⓔ

(since N is between P and Q)

Example 4:	$w + z$	180	Ⓐ Ⓑ ● Ⓓ Ⓔ

(since PQ is a straight line)

374

GO ON TO THE NEXT PAGE.

A if the quantity in Column A is greater;
B if the quantity in Column B is greater;
C if the two quantities are equal;
D if the relationship cannot be determined from the information given.

	Column A	Column B
1.	$\dfrac{4}{5} - \dfrac{4}{7}$	$\dfrac{4}{7} - \dfrac{2}{5}$
2.	The average (arithmetic mean) of 87, 95, and 130	The average (arithmetic mean) of 88, 95, and 129
3.	The time that it takes Jim to drive 300 miles at a speed of 52 miles per hour	The time that it takes Lila to drive 240 miles at a speed of 40 miles per hour
4.	$(-5)^6$	$(-6)^5$

Ms. Rogers bought an electric range on the installment plan. The cash price of the range was $400. The amount she paid was $120 down and 12 monthly payments of $28 each.

	Column A	Column B
5.	The amount she paid for the electric range in excess of the cash price	$56

Circle with center O

	Column A	Column B
6.	The length of chord PQ	The length of chord XY

$\dfrac{n}{x} = 428$ and $\dfrac{n}{y} = 107$.

$n > 0$

	Column A	Column B
7.	x	y

$\ell_1 \parallel \ell_2$

	Column A	Column B
8.	s	60

6 is x percent of 24.
y is 25 percent of 96.

	Column A	Column B
9.	x	y

$2x + y < 3$
$x > 2$

	Column A	Column B
10.	y	0

GO ON TO THE NEXT PAGE.

A if the quantity in Column A is greater;
B if the quantity in Column B is greater;
C if the two quantities are equal;
D if the relationship cannot be determined from the information given.

| Column A | Column B | | Column A | Column B |

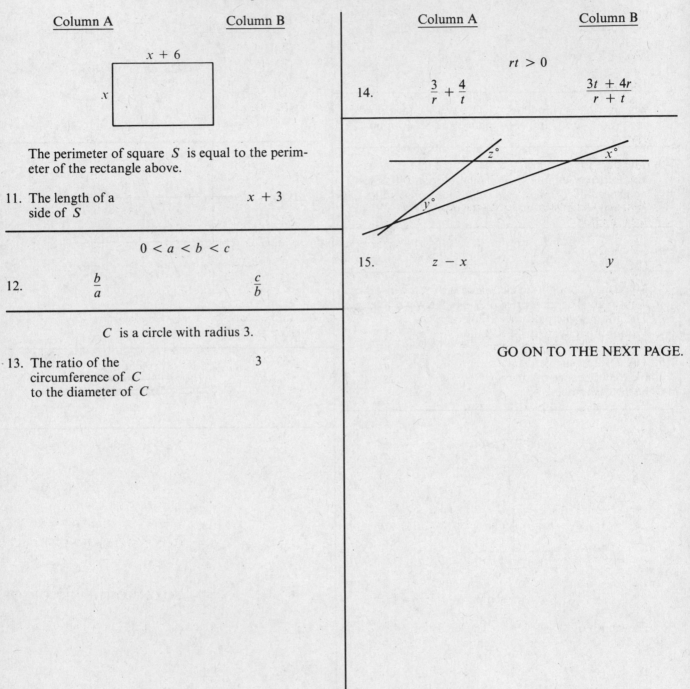

$x + 6$

x

The perimeter of square S is equal to the perimeter of the rectangle above.

11. The length of a $x + 3$
    side of S

$0 < a < b < c$

12. $\dfrac{b}{a}$ $\dfrac{c}{b}$

C is a circle with radius 3.

13. The ratio of the   3
    circumference of C
    to the diameter of C

$rt > 0$

14. $\dfrac{3}{r} + \dfrac{4}{t}$ $\dfrac{3t + 4r}{r + t}$

15. $z - x$ y

GO ON TO THE NEXT PAGE.

376

16. $\dfrac{9^2 - 6^2}{3} =$

   (A) 1

   (B) $\dfrac{15}{9}$

   (C) 5

   (D) 8

   (E) 15

17. What is 0.423658 rounded to the nearest thousandth?

   (A) 0.42
   (B) 0.423
   (C) 0.424
   (D) 0.4236
   (E) 0.4237

18. If $3(x + 2) = x - 4$, then $x =$

   (A) -5
   (B) -3
   (C)   1
   (D)   3
   (E)   5

19. If $x^2 + 2xy + y^2 = 9$, then $(x + y)^4 =$

   (A)   3
   (B) 18
   (C) 27
   (D) 36
   (E) 81

20. In the rectangular coordinate system above, if $x = 4.8$, then $y =$

   (A) 3.0
   (B) 3.2
   (C) 3.4
   (D) 3.6
   (E) 3.8

GO ON TO THE NEXT PAGE.

Questions 21-25 refer to the following graphs.

NATIONAL HEALTH EXPENDITURES FOR COUNTRY *X*, 1975-1986
(1 billion = 1,000,000,000)

Total National Health Expenditures
(in billions of dollars)

Private *vs.* Public National Health Expenditures
as a Percent of Total National Health Expenditures

Private

Public

National Health Expenditure Per Capita
(in dollars)

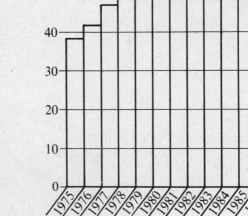

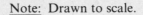

<u>Note:</u> Drawn to scale.

GO ON TO THE NEXT PAGE.

378

21. For how many of the years shown was the amount of private health expenditures at least double the amount of public health expenditures?

(A) None
(B) One
(C) Two
(D) Three
(E) Four

22. In which of the years from 1975 through 1986 was the national health expenditure per capita most nearly equal to half the per capita expenditure for 1984 ?

(A) 1975
(B) 1977
(C) 1979
(D) 1980
(E) 1982

23. Of the following, which is the best approximation of the percent increase in the national health expenditure per capita from 1981 to 1982 ?

(A) 35%
(B) 30%
(C) 20%
(D) 10%
(E) 5%

24. Of the following, which is closest to the amount of public national health expenditures, in billions of dollars, in 1980 ?

(A) 25
(B) 30
(C) 35
(D) 45
(E) 70

25. It can be inferred from the graphs that in 1977 the population of Country X, in millions, was closest to which of the following?

(A) 120
(B) 150
(C) 190
(D) 240
(E) 250

26. If x is the number on the number line between 5 and 15 that is twice as far from 5 as from 15, then x is

(A) $5\frac{2}{3}$

(B) 10

(C) $11\frac{2}{3}$

(D) $12\frac{1}{2}$

(E) $13\frac{1}{3}$

27. Jane has exactly 3 times as many Canadian as non-Canadian stamps in her collection. Which of the following CANNOT be the number of stamps in Jane's collection?

(A) 96
(B) 80
(C) 72
(D) 68
(E) 54

GO ON TO THE NEXT PAGE.

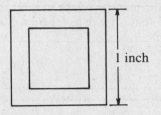

1 inch

28. In the figure above, if the area of the smaller square region is $\frac{1}{2}$ the area of the larger square region, then the diagonal of the larger square is how many inches longer than the diagonal of the smaller square?

(A) $\sqrt{2} - 1$

(B) $\frac{1}{2}$

(C) $\frac{\sqrt{2}}{2}$

(D) $\frac{\sqrt{2} + 1}{2}$

(E) $\sqrt{2}$

29. A distillate flows into an empty 64-gallon drum at spout A and out of the drum at spout B. If the rate of flow through A is 2 gallons per hour, how many gallons per hour must flow out at spout B so that the drum is full in exactly 96 hours?

(A) $\frac{3}{8}$

(B) $\frac{1}{2}$

(C) $\frac{2}{3}$

(D) $\frac{4}{3}$

(E) $\frac{8}{3}$

30. A farmer has two rectangular fields. The larger field has twice the length and 4 times the width of the smaller field. If the smaller field has area K, then the area of the larger field is greater than the area of the smaller field by what amount?

(A) $2K$
(B) $6K$
(C) $7K$
(D) $8K$
(E) $12K$

STOP

IF YOU FINISH BEFORE TIME IS CALLED, YOU MAY CHECK YOUR WORK ON THIS SECTION ONLY.
DO NOT TURN TO ANY OTHER SECTION IN THE TEST.

I

NOTE: To ensure prompt processing of test results, it is important that you fill in the blanks exactly as directed.

GENERAL TEST

A. Print and sign your full name in this box:

PRINT: _____
          (LAST)   (FIRST)   (MIDDLE)

SIGN: _____

Copy this code in box 6 on your answer sheet. Then fill in the corresponding ovals exactly as shown.

6. TITLE CODE

Copy the Test Name and Form Code in box 7 on your answer sheet.

TEST NAME _General_

FORM CODE _GR 92-2_

GRADUATE RECORD EXAMINATIONS GENERAL TEST

B. You will have 3 hours and 30 minutes in which to work on this test, which consists of seven sections. During the time allowed for one section, you may work only on that section. The time allowed for each section is 30 minutes.

Each of your scores will be determined by the number of questions for which you select the best answer from the choices given. Questions for which you mark no answer or more than one answer are not counted in scoring. Nothing is subtracted from a score if you answer a question incorrectly. Therefore, to maximize your scores it is better for you to guess at an answer than not to respond at all.

You are advised to work as rapidly as you can without losing accuracy. Do not spend too much time on questions that are too difficult for you. Go on to the other questions and come back to the difficult ones later.

There are several different types of questions; you will find special directions for each type in the test itself. Be sure you understand the directions before attempting to answer any questions.

YOU MUST INDICATE ALL YOUR ANSWERS ON THE SEPARATE ANSWER SHEET. No credit will be given for anything written in this examination book, but you may write in the book as much as you wish to work out your answers. After you have decided on your response to a question, fill in the corresponding oval on the answer sheet. BE SURE THAT EACH MARK IS DARK AND COMPLETELY FILLS THE OVAL. Mark only one answer to each question. No credit will be given for multiple answers. Erase all stray marks. If you change an answer, be sure that all previous marks are erased completely. Incomplete erasures may be read as intended answers. Do not be concerned if your answer sheet provides spaces for more answers than there are questions in each section.

Example:

What city is the capital of France?

(A) Rome
(B) Paris
(C) London
(D) Cairo
(E) Oslo

Sample Answer

BEST ANSWER
PROPERLY MARKED

IMPROPER MARKS

Some or all of the passages for this test have been adapted from published material to provide the examinee with significant problems for analysis and evaluation. To make the passages suitable for testing purposes, the style, content, or point of view of the original may have been altered in some cases. The ideas contained in the passages do not necessarily represent the opinions of the Graduate Record Examinations Board or Educational Testing Service.

381

DO NOT OPEN YOUR TEST BOOK UNTIL YOU ARE TOLD TO DO SO.

FOR GENERAL TEST, FORM GR92-2 ONLY
Answer Key and Percentages* of Examinees Answering Each Question Correctly

VERBAL ABILITY						QUANTITATIVE ABILITY					
Section 1			Section 3			Section 2			Section 4		
Number	Answer	P+	Number	Answer	P+	Number	Answer	P+	Number	Answer	P+
1	A	79	1	C	76	1	B	80	1	A	82
2	D	95	2	D	70	2	D	82	2	C	89
3	A	88	3	A	57	3	A	78	3	B	77
4	C	75	4	E	72	4	D	80	4	A	86
5	E	56	5	C	63	5	B	81	5	C	79
6	B	57	6	E	55	6	A	76	6	B	70
7	D	42	7	B	52	7	B	72	7	B	66
8	C	82	8	E	89	8	A	62	8	D	72
9	B	87	9	B	83	9	D	59	9	A	65
10	E	86	10	C	85	10	A	56	10	B	77
11	D	83	11	D	76	11	C	36	11	C	61
12	D	66	12	D	52	12	B	38	12	D	47
13	E	38	13	E	51	13	D	34	13	A	61
14	D	35	14	E	38	14	B	27	14	D	39
15	C	27	15	A	26	15	C	22	15	C	30
16	B	20	16	B	25	16	D	94	16	E	92
17	B	72	17	E	34	17	D	79	17	C	88
18	E	76	18	C	77	18	C	78	18	A	80
19	A	52	19	D	45	19	B	74	19	E	71
20	B	48	20	A	36	20	D	72	20	B	53
21	A	46	21	A	92	21	A	82	21	C	78
22	C	79	22	D	83	22	D	75	22	B	81
23	B	73	23	A	79	23	B	69	23	D	62
24	C	47	24	E	59	24	E	52	24	A	21
25	E	32	25	B	40	25	B	40	25	C	42
26	D	47	26	C	75	26	C	61	26	C	52
27	B	59	27	D	55	27	A	52	27	E	52
28	B	94	28	A	96	28	C	48	28	A	27
29	A	88	29	D	82	29	E	40	29	D	35
30	B	80	30	C	92	30	E	39	30	C	20
31	A	82	31	E	63						
32	C	76	32	D	34						
33	A	42	33	B	37						
34	D	36	34	B	38						
35	D	23	35	A	37						
36	C	26	36	D	31						
37	C	27	37	E	27						
38	A	20	38	A	26						

*Estimated P+ for the group of examinees who took the GRE General Test in a recent three-year period.

SCORE CONVERSIONS FOR GRE GENERAL TEST, GR92-2

Raw Score	Scaled Score Verbal	Scaled Score Quantitative	Raw Score	Scaled Score Verbal	Scaled Score Quantitative
72-76	800		39	430	590
71	790		38	420	580
70	780		37	410	570
			36	400	560
69	760		35	390	550
68	740		34	380	540
67	730		33	370	520
66	720		32	360	510
65	710		31	350	500
64	690		30	350	490
63	680				
62	670		29	340	480
61	660		28	330	470
60	650	800	27	320	460
			26	310	440
59	640	800	25	310	430
58	630	800	24	300	420
57	610	790	23	290	410
56	600	780	22	280	400
55	590	770	21	280	380
54	580	750	20	270	370
53	570	740			
52	560	730	19	260	360
51	550	720	18	250	340
50	540	710	17	250	330
			16	240	310
49	530	700	15	230	300
48	520	690	14	220	280
47	510	680	13	210	270
46	500	670	12	200	250
45	480	660	11	200	240
44	470	650	10	200	220
43	460	640			
42	450	630	9	200	210
41	440	620	8	200	200
40	430	620	7	200	200
			6	200	200
			0-5	200	200

General Test Interpretive Data[1]

Scaled Score	VERBAL % Below	QUANTITATIVE % Below	Scaled Score	VERBAL % Below	QUANTITATIVE % Below
800	90	95	500	57	26
790	99	93	490	55	24
780	99	91	480	51	22
770	99	88	470	48	20
760	99	86	460	45	19
750	99	84	450	41	17
740	99	82	440	38	15
730	99	80	430	35	14
720	98	78	420	32	12
710	98	75	410	28	11
700	97	73	400	25	10
690	96	71	390	22	8
680	96	69	380	19	7
670	95	67	370	17	6
660	94	65	360	14	5
650	93	62	350	12	4
640	91	60	340	10	4
630	90	57	330	8	3
620	88	55	320	6	3
610	87	52	310	4	2
600	85	50	300	3	2
590	83	47	290	2	1
580	81	45	280	1	1
570	78	43	270	1	1
560	75	40	260	1	1
550	72	38	250	1	1
540	69	35	240	1	1
530	66	33	230	1	1
520	64	31	220	1	1
510	61	29	210	1	1
			200	1	1

Verbal and Quantitative Mean Scores Classified by Broad Intended Graduate Major Field

(Based on the performance of seniors and nonenrolled college graduates[2] who tested between October 1, 1998, and September 30, 2001)

Broad Intended Graduate Major Field	Approximate Number of Examinees	Verbal Ability	Quantitative Ability
Life Sciences	107,600	464	568
Physical Sciences	45,700	491	694
Engineering	46,600	474	721
Social Sciences	79,500	484	548
Humanities and Arts	39,300	541	549
Education	36,200	450	521
Business	6,500	444	570

[1] Percent scoring below the scaled score is based on the performance of all examinees who took the General Test between October 1, 1998, and September 30, 2001. This percent below information is used for score reports during the 2002-03 testing year.

[2] Limited to those who earned their college degrees up to two years prior to the test date. Note that this table does not include summary information on the approximately 45,388 examinees whose response was invalid (misgrids, blanks, etc.) or the approximately 17,474 examinees whose response was "undecided." Most of the standard deviations of the score distribution represented by the means in this table are between 90 and 125.

GRADUATE RECORD EXAMINATIONS®

GRE®

ANALYTICAL WRITING SECTION

THE GRADUATE RECORD EXAMINATIONS®

Analytical Writing 1

PRESENT YOUR PERSPECTIVE ON AN ISSUE

45 minutes

You will have 45 minutes to plan and compose a response that presents your perspective on the topic you select. A response on any topic other than the one you select will receive a score of zero. You will have a choice between two Issue topics. Each topic will appear as a brief quotation that states or implies an issue of general interest. You are free to accept, reject, or qualify the claim made in the topic, as long as the ideas you present are clearly relevant to the topic you select. Support your views with reasons and examples drawn from such areas as your reading, experience, observations, or academic studies.

Before you make your choice, read each topic carefully. Then decide on which topic you could write a more effective and well-reasoned response. GRE readers who are college and university faculty will read your response and evaluate its overall quality, based on how well you

- consider the complexities and implications of the issue

- organize, develop, and express your ideas about the issue

- support your ideas with relevant reasons and examples

- control the elements of standard written English

You may want to take a few minutes to think about the issue you have chosen and to plan a response before you begin writing. Because the space for writing your response is limited, **use the next page to plan your response.** Be sure to develop your ideas fully and organize them coherently, but leave time to read what you have written and make any revisions that you think are necessary.

Present your perspective on <u>one</u> of the issues below, using relevant reasons and/or examples to support your views.

Topic
No:

P101.

> "Too much time, money, and energy are spent developing new and more elaborate technology. Society should instead focus on maximizing the use of existing technology for the immediate benefit of its citizens."

P102.

> "Most of the people we consider heroic today were, in fact, very ordinary people who happened to be in the right place at the right time."

Write the topic number of the issue you choose on the line at the top right corner of the answer booklet labeled "Analytical Writing 1: Issue."

Plan your response on this page. This page will not be scored. **WRITE YOUR RESPONSE IN THE ANSWER BOOKLET LABELED "Analytical Writing 1: Issue."**

STOP

IF YOU FINISH BEFORE TIME IS CALLED, YOU MAY CHECK YOUR WORK ON THIS SECTION ONLY.
DO NOT TURN TO ANY OTHER SECTION IN THE TEST.

THE GRADUATE RECORD EXAMINATIONS®

Analytical Writing 2

ANALYZE AN ARGUMENT

30 minutes

You will have 30 minutes to plan and write a critique of an argument presented in the form of a short passage. A critique of any other argument will receive a score of zero.

Analyze the line of reasoning in the argument. Be sure to consider what, if any, questionable assumptions underlie the thinking and, if evidence is cited, how well it supports the conclusion.

You can also discuss what sort of evidence would strengthen or refute the argument, what changes in the argument would make it more logically sound, and what additional information might help you better evaluate its conclusion. *Note that you are NOT being asked to present your views on the subject.*

GRE readers who are college and university faculty will read your critique and evaluate its overall quality, based on how well you

- identify and analyze important features of the argument

- organize, develop, and express your critique of the argument

- support your critique with relevant reasons and examples

- control the elements of standard written English

Before you begin writing, you may want to take a few minutes to evaluate the argument and to plan a response. Because the space for writing your response is limited, **use the next page to plan your response.** Be sure to develop your ideas fully and organize them coherently, but leave time to read what you have written and make any revisions that you think are necessary.

Discuss how well reasoned you find this argument.

Topic
No:

P103.

> The country Myria, which charges fees for the use of national parks, reports little evidence of environmental damage. This strongly suggests that for the country Illium, the best way to preserve public lands is to charge people more money when they are using national parks and wilderness areas for activities with heavy environmental impact. By collecting fees from those people who overuse public lands, Illium will help preserve those lands for present and future generations.

Write the topic number of the argument on the line at the top right corner of the answer booklet labeled "Analytical Writing 2: Argument."

Plan your response on this page. This page will not be scored. **WRITE YOUR RESPONSE IN THE ANSWER BOOKLET LABELED "Analytical Writing 2: Argument."**

STOP

IF YOU FINISH BEFORE TIME IS CALLED, YOU MAY CHECK YOUR WORK ON THIS SECTION ONLY.
DO NOT TURN TO ANY OTHER SECTION IN THE TEST.

NO TEST MATERIAL ON THIS PAGE

GRADUATE RECORD EXAMINATIONS®

ANALYTICAL WRITING SECTION

THE GRADUATE RECORD EXAMINATIONS®

Analytical Writing 1

PRESENT YOUR PERSPECTIVE ON AN ISSUE

45 minutes

You will have 45 minutes to plan and compose a response that presents your perspective on the topic you select. A response on any topic other than the one you select will receive a score of zero. You will have a choice between two Issue topics. Each topic will appear as a brief quotation that states or implies an issue of general interest. You are free to accept, reject, or qualify the claim made in the topic, as long as the ideas you present are clearly relevant to the topic you select. Support your views with reasons and examples drawn from such areas as your reading, experience, observations, or academic studies.

Before you make your choice, read each topic carefully. Then decide on which topic you could write a more effective and well-reasoned response. GRE readers who are college and university faculty will read your response and evaluate its overall quality, based on how well you

- consider the complexities and implications of the issue

- organize, develop, and express your ideas about the issue

- support your ideas with relevant reasons and examples

- control the elements of standard written English

You may want to take a few minutes to think about the issue you have chosen and to plan a response before you begin writing. Because the space for writing your response is limited, **use the next page to plan your response.** Be sure to develop your ideas fully and organize them coherently, but leave time to read what you have written and make any revisions that you think are necessary.

Present your perspective on <u>one</u> of the issues below, using relevant reasons and/or examples to support your views.

Topic
No:

P201. | "Great advances in knowledge necessarily involve the rejection of authority."

P202. | "What is called human nature is really a reflection of the human condition: if all people had a reasonable share of territory and resources, such products of 'human nature' as war and crime would become extremely rare."

Write the topic number of the issue you choose on the line at the top right corner of the answer booklet labeled "Analytical Writing 1: Issue."

Plan your response on this page. This page will not be scored. **WRITE YOUR RESPONSE IN THE ANSWER BOOKLET LABELED "Analytical Writing 1: Issue."**

STOP

IF YOU FINISH BEFORE TIME IS CALLED, YOU MAY CHECK YOUR WORK ON THIS SECTION ONLY.
DO NOT TURN TO ANY OTHER SECTION IN THE TEST.

Analytical Writing 2

ANALYZE AN ARGUMENT

30 minutes

You will have 30 minutes to plan and write a critique of an argument presented in the form of a short passage. A critique of any other argument will receive a score of zero.

Analyze the line of reasoning in the argument. Be sure to consider what, if any, questionable assumptions underlie the thinking and, if evidence is cited, how well it supports the conclusion.

You can also discuss what sort of evidence would strengthen or refute the argument, what changes in the argument would make it more logically sound, and what additional information might help you better evaluate its conclusion. *Note that you are NOT being asked to present your views on the subject.*

GRE readers who are college and university faculty will read your critique and evaluate its overall quality, based on how well you

- identify and analyze important features of the argument

- organize, develop, and express your critique of the argument

- support your critique with relevant reasons and examples

- control the elements of standard written English

Before you begin writing, you may want to take a few minutes to evaluate the argument and to plan a response. Because the space for writing your response is limited, **use the next page to plan your response.** Be sure to develop your ideas fully and organize them coherently, but leave time to read what you have written and make any revisions that you think are necessary.

Discuss how well reasoned you find this argument.

Topic
No:

P203.

Write the topic number of the argument on the line at the top right corner of the answer booklet labeled "Analytical Writing 2: Argument."

Plan your response on this page. This page will not be scored. **WRITE YOUR RESPONSE IN THE ANSWER BOOKLET LABELED "Analytical Writing 2: Argument."**

STOP

IF YOU FINISH BEFORE TIME IS CALLED, YOU MAY CHECK YOUR WORK ON THIS SECTION ONLY.
DO NOT TURN TO ANY OTHER SECTION IN THE TEST.

GRE Essay Scoring Guide: Present Your Perspective on an Issue

SCORE

6   A 6 paper presents a cogent, well-articulated analysis of the complexities of the issue and conveys meaning skillfully.

A typical paper in this category

– presents an insightful position on the issue
– develops the position with compelling reasons and/or persuasive examples
– sustains a well-focused, well-organized analysis, connecting ideas logically
– expresses ideas fluently and precisely, using effective vocabulary and sentence variety
– demonstrates facility with the conventions (i.e., grammar, usage, and mechanics) of standard written English but may have minor errors

---

5   A 5 paper presents a generally thoughtful, well-developed analysis of the complexities of the issue and conveys meaning clearly.

A typical paper in this category

– presents a well-considered position on the issue
– develops the position with logically sound reasons and/or well-chosen examples
– is focused and generally well organized, connecting ideas appropriately
– expresses ideas clearly and well, using appropriate vocabulary and sentence variety
– demonstrates facility with the conventions of standard written English but may have minor errors

---

4   A 4 paper presents a competent analysis of the issue and conveys meaning adequately.

A typical paper in this category

– presents a clear position on the issue
– develops the position on the issue with relevant reasons and/or examples
– is adequately focused and organized
– expresses ideas with reasonable clarity
– generally demonstrates control of the conventions of standard written English but may have some errors

GRE Scoring Guide: Issue (continued)

SCORE

3 A 3 paper demonstrates some competence in its analysis of the issue and in conveying meaning but is obviously flawed.

A typical paper in this category exhibits ONE OR MORE of the following characteristics:

- is vague or limited in presenting or developing a position on the issue
- is weak in the use of relevant reasons or examples
- is poorly focused and/or poorly organized
- has problems in language and sentence structure that result in a lack of clarity
- contains occasional major errors or frequent minor errors in grammar, usage, or mechanics that can interfere with meaning

---

2 A 2 paper demonstrates serious weaknesses in analytical writing.

A typical paper in this category exhibits ONE OR MORE of the following characteristics:

- is unclear or seriously limited in presenting or developing a position on the issue
- provides few, if any, relevant reasons or examples
- is unfocused and/or disorganized
- has serious problems in the use of language and sentence structure that frequently interfere with meaning
- contains serious errors in grammar, usage, or mechanics that frequently obscure meaning

---

1 A 1 paper demonstrates fundamental deficiencies in analytical writing.

A typical paper in this category exhibits ONE OR MORE of the following characteristics:

- provides little or no evidence of the ability to understand and analyze the issue
- provides little or no evidence of the ability to develop an organized response
- has severe problems in language and sentence structure that persistently interfere with meaning
- contains pervasive errors in grammar, usage, or mechanics that result in incoherence

---

0 Off topic, (i.e., provides no evidence of an attempt to respond to the assigned topic), in a foreign language, merely copies the topic, consists of only keystroke characters, or is illegible, or nonverbal

---

NS Blank

GRE Scoring Guide: Analyze an Argument

SCORE

6   A 6 paper presents a cogent, well-articulated critique of the argument and conveys meaning skillfully.

A typical paper in this category

- clearly identifies important features of the argument and analyzes them insightfully
- develops ideas cogently, organizes them logically, and connects them with clear transitions
- effectively supports the main points of the critique
- demonstrates control of language, including appropriate word choice and sentence variety
- demonstrates facility with the conventions (i.e., grammar, usage, and mechanics) of standard written English but may have minor errors

---

5   A 5 paper presents a generally thoughtful, well-developed critique of the argument and conveys meaning clearly.

A typical paper in this category

- clearly identifies important features of the argument and analyzes them in a generally perceptive way
- develops ideas clearly, organizes them logically, and connects them with appropriate transitions
- sensibly supports the main points of the critique
- demonstrates control of language, including appropriate word choice and sentence variety
- demonstrates facility with the conventions of standard written English but may have minor errors

---

4   A 4 paper presents a competent critique of the argument and conveys meaning adequately.

A typical paper in this category

- identifies and analyzes important features of the argument
- develops and organizes ideas satisfactorily but may not connect them with transitions
- supports the main points of the critique
- demonstrates sufficient control of language to express ideas with reasonable clarity
- generally demonstrates control of the conventions of standard written English but may have some errors

SCORE

3 A 3 paper demonstrates some competence in its critique of the argument and in conveying meaning but is obviously flawed.

A typical paper in this category exhibits ONE OR MORE of the following characteristics:

- does not identify or analyze most of the important features of the argument, although some analysis of the argument is present
- mainly analyzes tangential or irrelevant matters, or reasons poorly
- is limited in the logical development and organization of ideas
- offers support of little relevance and value for points of the critique
- lacks clarity in expressing ideas
- contains occasional major errors or frequent minor errors in grammar, usage, or mechanics that can interfere with meaning

---

2 A 2 paper demonstrates serious weaknesses in analytical writing.

A typical paper in this category exhibits ONE OR MORE of the following characteristics:

- does not present a critique based on logical analysis, but may instead present the writer's own views on the subject
- does not develop ideas, or is disorganized and illogical
- provides little, if any, relevant or reasonable support
- has serious problems in the use of language and in sentence structure that frequently interfere with meaning
- contains serious errors in grammar, usage, or mechanics that frequently obscure meaning

---

1 A 1 paper demonstrates fundamental deficiencies in analytical writing.

A typical paper in this category exhibits MORE THAN ONE of the following characteristics:

- provides little or no evidence of the ability to understand and analyze the argument
- provides little or no evidence of the ability to develop an organized response
- has severe problems in language and sentence structure that persistently interfere with meaning
- contains pervasive errors in grammar, usage, or mechanics that result in incoherence

---

0 Off topic, (i.e., provides no evidence of an attempt to respond to the assigned topic), in a foreign language, merely copies the topic, consists of only keystroke characters, or is illegible, or nonverbal

---

NS Blank

Analytical Writing Section Score Level Descriptions

Although the analytical writing section contains two discrete analytical writing tasks, a single combined score is reported because it is more reliable than is a score for either task alone. The reported score, the average of the scores for the two tasks, ranges from 0 to 6, in half-point increments.

The statements below describe, for each score level, the overall quality of analytical writing demonstrated across both the Issue and Argument tasks. Because the test assesses "analytical writing," critical thinking skills (the ability to reason, assemble evidence to develop a position, and communicate complex ideas) weigh more heavily than the writer's control of fine points of grammar or the mechanics of writing (e.g., spelling).

SCORES 6 and 5.5 – Sustains insightful, in-depth analysis of complex ideas; develops and supports main points with logically compelling reasons and/or highly persuasive examples; is well focused and well organized; skillfully uses sentence variety and precise vocabulary to convey meaning effectively; demonstrates superior facility with sentence structure and language usage but may have minor errors that do not interfere with meaning.

SCORES 5 and 4.5 – Provides generally thoughtful analysis of complex ideas; develops and supports main points with logically sound reasons and/or well-chosen examples; is generally focused and well organized; uses appropriate sentence variety and vocabulary to convey meaning clearly; demonstrates good control of sentence structure and language usage but may have minor errors that do not interfere with meaning.

SCORES 4 and 3.5 – Provides competent analysis of complex ideas; develops and supports main points with relevant reasons and/or examples; is adequately organized; conveys meaning with reasonable clarity; demonstrates satisfactory control of sentence structure and language usage but may have some errors that affect clarity.

SCORES 3 and 2.5 – Displays some competence in analytical writing, although the writing is flawed in at least one of the following ways: limited analysis or development; weak organization; weak control of sentence structure or language usage, with errors that often result in vagueness or lack of clarity.

SCORES 2 and 1.5 – Displays serious weaknesses in analytical writing. The writing is seriously flawed in at least one of the following ways: serious lack of analysis or development; lack of organization; serious and frequent problems in sentence structure or language usage, with errors that obscure meaning.

SCORES 1 and .5 – Displays fundamental deficiencies in analytical writing. The writing is fundamentally flawed in at least one of the following ways: content that is extremely confusing or mostly irrelevant to the assigned tasks; little or no development; severe and pervasive errors that result in incoherence.

SCORE 0 – The examinee's analytical writing performance cannot be evaluated because the responses do not address any part of the assigned tasks, are merely attempts to copy the assignments, are in a foreign language, or display only indecipherable text or no text whatsoever.

SCORE NS – The examinee produced no text whatsoever.

Analytical Writing Topics and Sample Scored Essay Responses* at Selected Score Points

Test 1: Issue Topic 1

"Too much time, money, and energy are spent developing new and more elaborate technology. Society should instead focus on maximizing the use of existing technology for the immediate benefit of its citizens."

Essay Response – Score 6

I must say that I reject this statement. While it is true that we need to support society as much as possible with current technology, that does not in any way mean that we should stop progressing simply because our current technology cannot handle all the problems we have brought to it. Does that mean that we should simply accept the status quo and make do? No, I don't think so. To do so would be tantamount to adopting a fatalistic approach; I think most people would reject that.

Technology has helped, and it has hurt. Without it, we would never have our standard of living, nor quality of nutrition, expectation of a long and productive life span, and the unshakable belief that our lives can be made even better. But it has also brought us universal pollution, weapons so powerful as to be capable of rendering us extinct, and the consequent fear for our survival as a species and as a planet. Technology is indeed a double-edged sword. And yet, I still have to argue in its favor, because without it, we have no hope.

Some might argue that we would be better off without technology. They might say that a return to a less technologically driven approach to life would have the benefits of reducing stress and allowing us to live simpler, happier lives, like those of our forebears. Such an idea is seductive, so much so that much of art and all of nostalgia are devoted to it. But upon closer inspection, one realizes that such a move would only return us to a life of different kinds of stress, one of false simplicity, one fraught with danger. It would be a life without antibiotics where a minor cut could prove deadly. It would be a life where childbirth is the main killer of women, and where an emergency is dealt with in terms of hours and days instead of minutes and hours; a life where there are no phones or cars or airplanes or central heating, no proven drug therapies to treat mental illness, no computers. Would this world really make people happy?

What we already have, we have. And since the only way to move is forward, instead of allowing ourselves to be paralyzed by fear and worry, we need to learn how to clean up the pollution we have caused, and how to deal with a world that feeds on weapons of mass destruction. Doing these things means having to move away from technology into a more difficult realm, that of diplomacy and compromise; to move from the bully stance of "I am bigger and better and I have more toys and so I win" to a place where everyone wins.

Technology is the thing that will allow people to do that. But, advanced as it is, it is still in its infancy. We have to allow it to grow up and mature in order to reap the real rewards that it can bring. And there are even greater rewards ahead of us than what the world has already experienced. When technology is pushed to the outer edge, that is where serendipitous discoveries can occur. This has been seen throughout technological advancement, but the easiest example is probably the space program which made us think, really hard, about how to do things in a different environment. It gave us telecommunications, new fabrics and international cooperation. Paramedical devices, so that people can be treated even as they are being transported to the hospital, are a direct development of that technology. None of this would have happened in the time frame that it did if we had not pushed for technological advancement. If we had decided to "focus on maximizing the use of existing technology" instead of foolishly reaching for the stars, we would not have made those discoveries which now are the bedrock of the 21st century.

It is the same with the technology which we have now. Yes, we could stop, and put all our effort into just trying to patch things with what we have. And it would probably make a lot of people foolishly happy. But in the long run, it would be the most expensive thing we've ever done because we would thereby forestall the discovery that cures cancer, or brings world peace, or cleans and restores the environment. And we would all suffer from that shortsightedness, for far too long.

Essay Response – Score 4

Over history, technology has moved society into a world of bigger, better, and amazing things. It is not a question of whether we are spending too much money in creating new technologies while not maximizing the potential of the technologies that exist; what it is the question is whether we are spending our money on new technologies and our time on older technologies wisely and in a beneficial manner.

The technologies that open the doors to find cures for diseases such as MS, cancer, and AIDS are prime examples of beneficial technologies which should continue to be researched. Spending vast amounts of time, money, and energy on technologies with the potential to cure millions of people of terminal diseases is by no means a waste. Perhaps there are some advances out there already which can be improved for a cheaper price, and that is fine. However, I do not believe it is safe to restrain technology from growing and perhaps prospering. If that is done, only negative things will remain.

When we start spending billions of dollars on research and technologies whose benefits do not outwiegh their consts, we start stepping on some shaky ground. Not only are we using hard earned money and valuable time on developing technologies of questionable auspiciousness, we are also draining our resources for the advancement of more plausible technologies of much needed monies and qualified personnel. Sure, it is nice to have a twenty-four speed super vacuum to get that tough stain out of the rug. But wouldn't it be nicer to use the minds of those design engineers to design a virtually perfect solar energy house that costs only $15 thousand? Wouldn't it serve more purpose to use those monies allocated to developing this 'super-vac' to developing a vaccine to cancer or an cure for diabetes?

So, technology is good, technology is bad. Technology is much needed in certain aspects, while in others the time and energies used truly are a waste. Instead of spending vast amounts of money in order to procure newer, better advancements, or trying to improve old technology, we should conduct research in order to determine what technologies are the most needed, and how can we develop those technologies most efficiently.

Essay Response – Score 2

So much time and money are spent on continuously developing technology that we forget to look and appreciate what we already have available and we somehow lose sight or refuse to see the impact of each newly-developed, more sophisticated technology is doing to our society and the world we live in. Too quickly do we throw things away without using them to advantage - always looking for something newer, something faster, something more exciting.

Technology is indeed an asset and and a major contributor to th world's comfort. The negative is it rushes us forward when we least expect it.

Test 1: Issue Topic 2

"Most of the people we consider heroic today were, in fact, very ordinary people who happened to be in the right place at the right time."

Essay Response – Score 6

This statement expresses, sadly, a basic lack of faith in the ineffable quality of human courage, and the transcendant desire - often buried deep within us - to give of ourselves to one another.

"Ordinary people who happen to be in the right place at the right time" - this is a fine description of those of us who happen across the right partner, the perfect job, the ideal house. That is called luck, not heroism.

I expect, to some extent, that this issue depends on how one defines heroism. Heroism - to me - qualifies as such when it exemplifies courage above and beyond ordinary bounds, and particularly when it entails sacrifice. Overcoming fear is one of the greatest challenges we as humans face, and the heroic are those who manage to overcome this obstacle. They rise above base human behavior and overcome their instinctive fear of death, poverty, imprisonment, alienation, and more.

When we think of heroes, whom do we most often cite? Mother Thesera, for one; a woman from a well-to-do background who sacrificed all to serve the greater good and bring redress to the lives of the hopelessly poor and marginalized. She renounced all that most of us hold dear - family, wealth, comfort - in the service of others, risking disease and death all the while. How many of us could follow her example? Can one honestly claim that she was simply in the right place at the right time? How many others were, and did nothing? How many of us sought out her place of work in Calcutta, to offer help?

Was the Arlington firefighter who plunged recently into a burning building merely in the right place at the right time, or did he summon superhuman resolve to place himself squarely in the face of danger and death? Was Audie Murphy, the most-decorated soldier of the Korean War, simply in the right place at the right time? Yes, he was there, in the right place, at the right time, but he could have shrunk back - instead, he risked death to save the lives of others. Many others were with him; why were they not equally recognized? Perhaps, because they did less. Was Vaclav Havel merely fortunate in time and circumstance when he led the Czech "Velvet Revolution" - a man who had already suffered long confinement in Communist prisons, and who knew he was risking?

I would argue that these people, whom indeed may have been perfectly ordinary, nonetheless went a step further and found within themselves reserves of enormous courage and commitment, which allowed them to triumph over instinct and rise to the level of heroism.

This statement above fails to take into account much of the enormous complexity of what it is that makes us human, and fails to consider that some people possess a highly developed moral instinct and are willing to commit themselves to the good of the many.

Any of us can be in the right place at the right time, yet most of us fail to step forward to do what is heroic. Those who exemplify heroism are those who take that frightening step. Being in the right place at the right time is not - cannot be - enough to constitute heroism.

Since before antiquity society has recognized this, and thus developed complex mechanisms to honor and reward heroic behavior: Medals of Honor and the Croix de Guerre; personal rewards such as promotions, power and money; and laudatory public events such as ticker-tape parades and eternal flames in Arlington Cemetery. These are but outward symbols of an inner reality: that heroism is something far greater and infinitely more transcendant than "being in the right place at the right time," and so ought to be, as it is, accorded dignity, reward, and respect.

Essay Response – Score 4

Heroes come in all shapes, colors, sizes and kinds. There are sports heroes, war heroes, personal heroes and everyday heroes. A hero is someone who is looked up to, someone who has exhibited principles or actions that go beyond the ordinary.

Naming a sports figure like Michael Jordan as a hero indicates that his physical abilities are so far ahead of his competitors that he stands apart from the rank and file of the sports world. He conducts himself in a manner that is dignified and wholesome. Children are encouraged to "be like Mike." As he proved by his questionable performance on the baseball field, his heroic abilities are largely restricted to a basketball court. Clearly, he happened to be in the right place at the right time, but there is little if anything ordinary about him in that environment.

War heroes are another issue altogether. They have occasionally been described as people who react instead of think. Having to save lives while under battlefield conditions would hardly be described as being in the right place. But fortunately for those around him or her, they are there at the right time. These heroes are, for the most part, ordinary people caught in extraordinary circumstances.

Asking children who their heroes are, one can expect a myriad of choices, from the fireman on the truck to an astronaut. For little children, Barney or Mr. Rogers may be the most important person in their lives besides their parents. A teenager may be more likely to select an athlete or musician. For children, heroes can be anyone or anything from "your neighbor" to a large Purple dinosaur, Dion Sanders to Snoop Doggy Dog.

Everyday heroes are exactly what they sound like. They are the John and Jane Doe's of the world who happen to come across a burning building and rush in to help rescue a child from an upper story. He or she might also be an ordinary person, minding his or her own business, when they stumble into a situation that lets them have a positive impact on the life of another. These are those very ordinary people who happened to be in the rightplace at the right time.

Realistically, to say that most people can fit into a tidy descriptor like the claim stated above is too confining to be true. Generalities about heroes are unfair to their actions, and unfair to those mere mortals who admire them. Each individual has the potential to be a hero. Whether he or she lives up to that potential is a matter of choice, in the case of physical prowess or talent, and circumstance, being in the right place at the right time.

Essay Response – Score 2

Today's world, through a broader perspective of understanding heroism, people whom are perceived to be heroic are average common people. The men and women who serve to increase the betterment of people health and lifestyle are heros. People who at an instint make the right decision of to save other in a dangerous situation. Common people whom report the location of criminals to American Most Wanted TV Show and the police, help protect future victims from being hurt. Everday doctors work extreme hours to save lives in the ER. Young boy scout helping senior citizen crossing the street or helping their parents around the house. The men and women who save lost cats are heros. These are some of million of issue that fix the criteria of commiting a heroic act.

In my field of work, when people who are in need and I help get through it and start a new life for themselves. I help them cope with the anger of facing life and try to show them that the world is not against them. It always works when I ask them to listen to music. The music help them relax, and give them the will to solve their problems on their own. I consider myself a hero, and I am sure there are many other like me in this world helping people everyday. The perspective I feel about this issue is clear; there are heros who take up their time to help other without reward happens everyday. Sometime, it is good to have good luck and little petience. To be in the right place and time to help others involvles a little luck.

Test 1: Argument Topic

The country Myria, which charges fees for the use of national parks, reports little evidence of environmental damage. This strongly suggests that for the country Illium, the best way to preserve public lands is to charge people more money when they are using national parks and wilderness areas for activities with heavy environmental impact. By collecting fees from those people who overuse public lands, Illium will help preserve those lands for present and future generations.

Essay Response – Score 6

This argument is not cogent because it assumes that the stated correlation implies causation, which is not necessarily the case. The argument asserts that because the country of Myria charges fees for the use of its national parks, there is little evidence of environmental damage. But there are several reasons why one cannot assume that the lack of evidence of environmental damage is a result of the fact that individuals are charged to use these parks.

First, just because there is a lack of evidence does not preclude the fact that environmental damage may in fact be occurring. The individuals who are testing the area for evidence of damage may not have the proper scientific instruments or educational training necessary to detect damage that may be present. In fact, certain kinds of environmental damage may not be detectable in the short term even using the most sophisticated scientific methods. Imbalance in ecosystems, for example, may only become apparent over a long period of time.

Second, even if we concede that there is in fact negligible amounts of environmental damage, this does not necessarily mean that by collecting money from individuals who are using the parks one can use these funds to maintain the land for future generations. An alternative explanation may be that because the country charges a fee to use the national parks, people are less inclined to use the parks. It then stands to reason that with fewer people in the parks, there will be less of a detrimental impact on the environment. In addition, even if people are willing to pay the fee, the funds collected may be insufficient to cover the costs of maintaining and preserving the parkland.

Finally, even if we accept that the situation in Myria is successful in that country, we cannot assume that this same scenario will work in Illium. There are a myriad of variables that can contribute to the success of this type of environmental maintenance and restoration program. Pre-exisiting and uncontrollable environmental conditions such as the rate of erosion and the overall climate may cause damage that cannot be rectified by monetary solutions. In addition, cultural norms regarding how one views his or her responsibility and role in terms of preserving the environment may influence the intensity of environmental damage that may be sustained.

Thus, although the strategy of charging citizens of Myria for the use of its parks in order to collect funds for any restoration that may be required may be successful in Myria, this reality alone does not conclusively suggest that such a strategy would be effective in Illium or any other country.

Essay Response – Score 4

This argument suggests that if people are required to pay fees to use their national parks that they will appreciate them and take better care of them. There is some validity to this argument in that if a payment is required, some consideration will be given as to why one is there and how one should behave while there. However, there will occasionally be people who vandalize the park and payment will not necessarily be a deterrent for that.

Additionally, this article assumes that people in the country of Myria are raised with the same value for parks as the people in Illium. The cultures of these two countries may be vastly different in respecting public lands.

Another factor in Myria besides the fees could be the existence of park rangers or some kind of patrolling system to monitor the use of the parks. These factors may be adequate to stop problems in parks in Myria but not in parks in Illium.

Economic conditions in these two countries also may be different. A greater percentage of people may be able to afford the park fees in Illium but in Myria the fees might have imposed severe limitation on the use of these lands.

Also the argument is assuming that no natural or man-made disasters will cause Illium's parks any harm.

The argument also assumes that those with money also have an appreciation for preserving public lands, that somehow having money causes one to take care of a place. This is not always the case.

In conclusion, charging fees for the use of national parks may have little if any effect on the presevation of these lands. Other factors: culture, economy, natural or man-made disasters, or monitoring devices or patrols may have greater impact on saving these lands for the future.

Essay Response – Score 2

The assumption made is that there is a lot of environmental damage in Illium. Therefore, more money should be charged to preserve the parks. However the argument states that there is little environmental damage in Myria. There certainly is a lack of evidence that there is a need to increase the fees in Illium. Perhaps a study could be completed on the extent of environmental damage and the cost to avoid the projected rate of damage. The income from the present fee system could be analyzed to determine if it is an adequate amount or if a higher price is in order.

The recommendation made about the best way to preserve the public lands in Illium is very weak. No other evidence is suggested at all to support the recommendation.

This argument is not effective or persuasive. It is not smoothly connected or written. It jumps from having a fee for use of the parks to having an increased fee for people who overuse the parks with no connecting data to support the leap.

The conclusion remains invalid because of the lack of supporting evidence from the beginning. A better conclusion might have been to discuss how the fees are presently being utilized to improve the environment. A better argument would be to discuss the exact nature of the environmental damage and the ways to stop people who are causing the damage in the parks.

Test 2: Issue Topic 1

"Great advances in knowledge necessarily involve the rejection of authority."

Essay Response – Score 6

The central tenant of history is change. History is the documentation of how things were, before new events and ideas emerged to revolutionize the status quo. As a species, we homo sapiens are equipped with faculties of intelligence and free will that allow us to develop an individual identity. As individuals, we establish an individual identity based on our interests, likes, dislikes, etc. As a species, we establish a collective identity that is the aggregate of all individual identities. What is the link between these two roles that we play, as individuals and as a collective member of society? It has to do with power, authority, and the subjugation of the individual will to what has been called "the general will."

In the 17th century, the emergence of social contract theory helped to explain (at least in a theoretical way) how individuals came to live under an authority such as the modern state. One of the most important of these social contract theorists, John Locke, took a cue from the earlier theorist Thomas Hobbes and postulated that there was an original condition, in which all humans once existed, called the "state of nature." In the state of nature, there was no collective power, but only scattered individuals, who had absolute freedom to do whatever they saw fit. The state of nature was to be governed by the "law of nature," ordained by a omnipotent creator, that individuals should not infringe upon the natural rights of others, specifically their life, liberty or property. However, there was no guarantee of this, for in the state of nature there is no controlling force of restraint, and the most powerful could easily exploit the weak. This led to the creation of a social contract, whereby a group of individuals banded together and agreed to give up some of their individual power in order to gain protection from their collectivity, the state, which would act as an executive, legislative and judicial authority to preserve justice and natural rights.

This social contract theory reflected an increase in knowledge - the increasingly humanistic philosophy that was overtaking Europe at the time advocated the eminence of the individual, and that no power, not even the sovereign state, should be able to infringe on the rights of the individual. Indeed, it was upon this very theory that Thomas Jefferson based his arguments against the tyrannies of King George in the Declaration of Independence, perhaps one of the greatest rejections of authority ever. By fighting the Revolutionary War, the 13 colonies demonstrated to the world that a people dedicated to the cause of justice could overthow tyranny - it was a revolutionary idea, that there should be government by, for and of the people, rather than by divine right.

The Americans were the obvious outlet for rebellion against European power. Many came here for religious freedom, to escape the forced recognition of a particular, state-sanctioned religion. Indeed, the whole concept of religion underwent a radical change in the 16th century, when a Catholic clergyman from what is now Germany went and nailed his arguments against the Catholic churches' selling of indulgences to the door of the church in Wurtenburg. Martin Luther was excommunicated from the church for his heresy, for his rejection of what he saw as the illegitimate exercise of authority by the Catholic church in Rome. Yet his act of defiance led to the creation of a huge branch of Christianity, Protestantism and all its variations. Upon this defection of some of its following, the Catholic church began the counterreformation, which was an attempt to get rid of the abuses of the Catholic church and restore it to its original sanctity. This represented change, brought on by the catalyst of dissent against the theretofore unchallenged dominance of the authority of the Catholic church.

Another groundbreaking advance in knowledge that has created a continuing struggle with the authority of religion occured late in the 19th century when Charles Darwin, aboard the H.M.S. Beagle, traveled to the Galapagos Islands of the coast of Ecuador to study the plant and animal life there. Shortly after, Darwin published his theory of evolution, stating that life was not created by an omnipotent god, but rather that all life evolved from the elements that were here on Earth after the Universe came into being. After about a century of continuing experiments that seem to conclusively prove the theory of evolution, there are still those in the religious sphere that reject the idea out of hand simply because the Book of Genesis (in the Bible, or Torah, Old Testament), says that God created life.

Essay Response – Score 4

When one thinks of the many advances in knowledge that have been made, it would seem that those who strove to reach beyond the simple reality of just what we deemed acceptable were also those who rejected the power of authority.

If we reflect back on some of the great minds in history such as, the Wright brothers, Albert Einstein, Christopher Columbus and Thomas Edison we see that each of them changed some part of the world in their own manner of greatness, but yet they never seemed to fit within the given realm of established authority. Their hunger for knowledge seemed to intimidate others to a point of ostricizing them from the mainline of society. Therefore making it seem as though they rebelled against authority.

Rejection of authority can be a very dangerous step toward the greater advancement of knowledge if it beganis to threaten our very existence. But we must always consider that without those who extend their minds beyond what is deemed acceptable, would we be where we are today? Would we have the advances in technology and medicine today if individuals had not gone against what others believed? Knowledge is never gained without chance.

With every great advance that has been taken conflict has existed. Such as today, cloning and stem cell research are two issues caught between the battle of morality and advancement for the greater good. So with change there will always be resistance and rejection. But to advance will always require those who will reach beyond the limiting powers of authority.

So is it really rejection of authority that is being displayed or is it fear and instability from those in authority that creates an illusion to discredit those who are reaching beyond today.

Essay Response – Score 2

To gain a perspective on a subject, or to learn something new, authority generally allow learners to have initial hints at the biginning of understanding and learning.

In the basic process of education or schooling, a right to authorize a class has been in teacher's hands, which at the same time means students are absolute to be obeyful them. These days, however, a class needs no longer teachers as their info icon. Instead, TV and PC can seem to give the knowledge-seekers all kinds of viewpoints. The digitalized almighty tools enable them to have their teachers, or authorities, in their own mind. Then, learners have to teach themselves through such informational devices like the Internet.

Does that mentioned above mean authority in earning the reasonable way of life has gone away? No. Whatever and whoever it should be, whether teachers or PC, we cannot come it through without examples, or histric and experienced views. After all, a dog in a cage could never go out unless his master orders him to. So - like the student need authority.

Test 2: Issue Topic 2

"What is called human nature is really a reflection of the human condition: if all people had a reasonable share of territory and resources, such products of 'human nature' as war and crime would become extremely rare."

Essay Response – Score 6

While it is true that human nature is a reflection of the human condition, it is not logical to assume that creating the illusion of an equitable set of circumstances for all humans would diminish things such as war and crime. Human nature is comprised of all the innate qualities that exist within human beings, including but not limited to the instinct of survival, the drive to be competitive, and the characteristic of envy.

Self-preservation is a fundamental quality that exists within all human beings. The desire to first and foremost protect oneself is an instinct that all people are born with. The act of surviving requires that human beings must, at times, conquer other people in order to promote their own self-interest. War, in its most basic, justified form is merely an act of survival. When humans feel threatened, the natural reaction is to lash out in self-defense. The threat need not be real; an imagined sense of insecurity can easily escalate into what is perceived as a dangerous situation. The build-up of nuclear weapons is an example of how insecurity can sow the seeds for military action. As one world power, the United States for example, accumulates weapons, other countries, such as the former Soviet Union, feel compelled to accumulate their weapons as well. To stand idly by while another group of humans is perceived as becoming more powerful is contrary to the instinct that drives human beings: to survive at any cost. Even if each country is equally well-armed, in possession of the same resources, the result is not peace and harmony. The result of these propensities is a war - not necessarily an arms war, but a war of the will.

The war of the will extends into even the most harmless aspects of life. The competitive drive is a part of the instict of survival that compels humans to reach beyond their present circumstances. This competitive spirit is a double-edged sword. The spirit of competition is what pushes individuals to succeed in every arena: sports, academics, medical advances, technological gains, etc. However, this competitive drive can also be fundamentally damaging and lead to violence as well. This innate spirit of competition is nurtured at an early age - even when humans are assumed to be on the same level. Parents push their children to succeed at every level - from pre-school to pee-wee soccer. Children learn from the example of their parents that competition is a desirable thing; or children learn that competing means winning at any cost. The recent outbreak of violence among parents at youth sporting events demonstrates that the spirit of competition can lead to dangerous confrontation, even murder.

Competition in and of itself is not a negative activity, but in human terms, everything is colored by those things which make up human nature. Human nature is also made up of vices; one of these vices is envy. It is fundamental to humans to look to others to assess the value of their particular standard of living. The idea of absolute equality is an illusion. Because of the human need to compete and survive, there will always be some that have more than others. It is not natural for humans to see others who they perceive to be similar to themselves possess more than they do and not react to it. The reaction comes in the form of seeking to gain at any cost, to "keep up with the Jones." Envy leads to a desire to dominate, to conquer, to cheat to get ahead, to steal to have more if one does not possess any other means.

If we lived in a Utopian society and all the world was an even playing field, that still could not conquer the problems inherent in the human condition. The human condition is exactly that: a condition. It is not something that individuals can escape from or remedy. Part of being human is acknowledging the problems that are inherent to being human. War and crime will always exist because they are the direct results of some of the most basic parts of human nature. The instinct of survival, the competitive drive, and envy will continue to cause humans - in any society - to stumble and fall.

Essay Response – Score 4

The statement that human nature is really a reflection of the human condition is not valid. If everyone was given a reasonable share of territory and resources, there would still be an abundance of war and crime because people are greedy. First of all, people would not be satisfied with what they were given but they will always want more. Secondly, people would still use war and crime to get more territoy and resources.

People would not be satisfied with what they were given because no matter how much anyone has, they always want more. However, this is not a bad thing, because this is what keeps people productive. People are always striving to do better at their jobs so that they can either keep their jobs or possibly get a promotion so that they can make more money. For example, someone in my math class at school already has a master's degree in teaching, but she is going back to get a science degree so that she will not lose her job and so that she can get a raise. Therefore, it is not a bad thing for people to want more than what they have, but nevertheless it can lead to crime and war.

People would still use war and crime to get more territory and resources even if everyone had a reasonable share. People are very greedy and will do horrible things to other people to get what they want. One example is that last semester at college, I left my wallet in the cafeteria for approximately one hour. When I remembered that I had left it there and went back to get it, I discovered that one hundred dollars had been stolen from my wallet. Therefore, some-one stole from me to help themselves. It did not matter whether I needed the money or not or whether it hurt someone else. People are greedy and will continue to be that way no matter what their situation is. Another example is that no matter how much any one country has, there will always be war because there will be a greedy leader who wants to own more land and wealth. No matter how many countries that Hitler took over, he still wanted more.

In conclusion, human nature is not a reflection of the human condtion. People just always want more than what they have, and some people go about getting more resources and territory in ways that they should not. There will always be war and crime, no matter if people were given reasonable share of territory and resources.

Essay Response – Score 2

I agee with the statement that "human nature": reflects the human condition. But it is difficult to say that even with equal resources like money and food and territory that war and crime would be rare or even nonexistant War and crime take place not just due to money and territory conflicts but because of other elements as well.

People with vast resources still commit crime, just look at the Enron scandal. War takes place not only over territory disputes but over other conflicts as well. So, it is hard to determine whether equal territory and resources would have any influence on indivdual acts. War and crime most definitely would decrease but, would it become rare is very hard to say. What makes people commit crime or encourage war is unknown. Many would probably argue that it takes a certain kind of person to do such things. What influences that person it is enviromental or genetic. This is uncertain. If a person exhibits a certain personality characteristic that propels him or her to commit a crime it would not make a difference whether he or she had ample resources. Basically, I believe there are many other influences that make up human nature.

Test 2: Argument Topic

The following appeared in a memo from the human resources department of Rifco Computer Company to the company president.

"In order to prevent conflicts in the workplace, Rifco Computer Company should require all its employees to attend workshops that teach the technique of "active listening," a technique in which people express feelings without assigning blame. This technique has clearly benefited Terland Publishing Company: five years ago, two hundred recently hired Terland employees volunteered to participate in a one-day active-listening workshop. Five years later, only five percent of these employees had filed formal complaints with the human resources department, whereas the company as a whole had a fifteen percent complaint rate during that period."

Essay Response – Score 6

The Rifco Company president should not require its employees to attend these workshops based solely upon the information she receives in this memo. In fact, she can draw very few conclusions regarding the efficacy of this workshop without requesting additional information from the human resource department at Terland Publishing Company.

Several variables have been left out of this report which, if included, would have made this claim more valid. For example, the company president needs to know what percentage of the employees who attended this workshop five years ago are still with the company at the present time. It is possible that this workshop had disastrous effects which resulted in 175 of the participants' quitting their jobs. Granted, this possibility may be unlikely, but it is certainly not impossible given the information provided by the memo. Similarly, the company president needs to know how many employees work at Terland Publishing Company overall. Even if all 200 employees who attended the seminar were still working there, the numbers mean little if there are only 220 employees in the company. If this were the case, and if one can assume that the 15% of the company as a whole excludes those who participated in the original workshop, than the 15% overall complaint rate would be explained by 3 disgruntled employees. If the 15% includes the employees who attended the workshop, the numbers are even less meaningful. This argument would be strengthened if it was discovered that the majority of employees who attended this workshop were still employed at Terland, and the overall employee population numbered in the thousands.

The argument appears to assume that the workshop attendees were representative of all of Terland employees. There is nothing in the argument to establish this representativeness, and the assumption seems suspect, since the attendees differed in an important respect from other Terland employees: they were newly hired. People tend to be especially cooperative when they are first hired for a job and this alone might explain their willingness to volunteer, unlike other employees.

Even if Terland's workshop participants could be shown to be representative of all Terland employees, there is no reason to assume that they would be representative of Rifco's employees. Before such an assumption could be warranted, comparisons would need to be made between Rifco and Terland in order to determine whether or not these results could be generalized. Are the companies (one is a computer company and the other is a publishing company) even similar enough to justify the assumption that the workshops would be equally successful with both groups of employees? Perhaps listening is a more important and valued skill in the publishing industry than it is in the computer industry. Perhaps Rifco's staff listens so actively that they succeed in avoiding conflicts the majority of the time--this memo does not even tell the reader whether conflicts are a problem in the Rifco workplace.

The company president should in fact become suspicious. Perhaps the author of this memo has just purchased a great deal of stock in the company which performs these workshops! The Rifco human resource department could, in fact, be correct in its argument that these workshops have benefitted Terland. This argument, however, is not well-supported by the paucity of details they have provided in this memo. Based upon the information here, the company president can certainly discount the claim that all employees should be required to attend this workshop. The only action that should be incited by this memo would be a deeper investigation of its claims.

Essay Response – Score 4

I believe the argument has some merit, however, there is some significant information that is omitted from in this argument.

First, there is no information provided about the two hundred employees who participated in the one-day workshop. There is no baseline to determine if these two hundred people had a tendencey to complain. It is quite possible they did not. They also were volunteers, which could mean these people were willing to learn and apply the active listening techniques. The age and sex of the participants is not available either. The group that went through the workshop may not be representative of the workplace as a whole.

Also, there is no information provided about the previous compliant rates for employees of the Terland Company as a whole. The fifteen percent complaint rate could be a decrease from previously higher complaint rates. Which could indicate that there are other factors playing a role in reducing the rate of complaints from employees, besides the participation in a active listening workshop.

To strengthen this argument, the human resources department should include information about Terland's workshop participants and about previous complaint rates at the company as a whole. If the workshop volunteers do not acurately reflect the complaining tendencies of the whole company, then their rate of complaints after the workshop does not reflect the way in which the employees of the company, as a whole, would have responded to the workshop. Also, if the rate of complaining for the whole company is down, then there might have been other factors at play.

Essay Response – Score 2

I thoroughly agree with the reasoning of this arguement! Usually, in the context of the work place, arguments do occur and these are generally the result of the lack of listening. I am a firm believer that the best way to learn is to listen. Sure, debate and discussion does promote a certain level of learning, but not to the same degree as listening. Furthermore, it is hard to understand another's viewpoint or logic if you are not listening. "Ears open, mouth closed" is a motto I personally live by. I can relate to the reasoning of the Rifco Computer Company in requiring employees to attend certain workshops that sharpen their listening skills, for this will prepare them for listening rather that arguing. If disagreements should exist, they should follow listening. Just imagine how much quieter the work place would be if the majority of people would listen instead of talking. There would be an increase in understanding, proper communication, and more than likely a decrease in stress levels for the employees. When it comes to listening and requring your employees who are in social positions to sharpen their listening skills, I can only that the plan will yield positive results.

TOPIC Number _____

Test Date _____

GRE® ANALYTICAL WRITING 1-ISSUE

LAST NAME (first four letters) ☐ ☐ ☐ ☐   FIRST INITIAL ☐   DATE OF BIRTH ☐ ☐   ☐ ☐
                                                                          M M   D D

REGISTRATION NUMBER ☐ ☐ ☐ ☐ ☐ ☐ ☐ ☐

BEGIN WRITING

_____

_____

_____

_____

_____

_____

_____

_____

_____

_____

_____

_____

_____

_____

_____

_____

_____

_____

_____

DO NOT WRITE BEYOND THIS BORDER (left margin)

DO NOT WRITE BEYOND THIS BORDER (right margin)

1 ☐ ☐ ☐ ☐ ☐ ☐   ☐   2 ☐ ☐ ☐ ☐ ☐ ☐   ☐   3 ☐ ☐ ☐ ☐ ☐ ☐   ☐

CONTINUE WRITING

CONTINUE WRITING

CONTINUE WRITING

DO NOT WRITE BEYOND THIS BORDER

DO NOT WRITE BEYOND THIS BORDER

TOPIC Number _____

Test Date _____

GRE® ANALYTICAL WRITING 2-ARGUMENT

LAST NAME (first four letters) ☐☐☐☐   FIRST INITIAL ☐   DATE OF BIRTH ☐☐ ☐☐
                                                                          M M   D D

REGISTRATION NUMBER ☐☐☐☐☐☐☐☐

BEGIN WRITING

1 ☐☐☐☐☐☐ ☐   2 ☐☐☐☐☐☐ ☐   3 ☐☐☐☐☐ ☐

CONTINUE WRITING

CONTINUE WRITING

CONTINUE WRITING

CONTINUE WRITING

STOP

☐ ☐ ☐ ☐ ☐ ☐ ☐ ☐ ☐ ☐ ☐ ☐ ☐ ☐ ☐ ☐ ☐ ☐

TOPIC Number _____

Test Date _____

GRE® ANALYTICAL WRITING 1-ISSUE

LAST NAME (first four letters) ☐☐☐☐   FIRST INITIAL ☐   DATE OF BIRTH ☐☐ ☐☐
                                                                        M M   D D

REGISTRATION NUMBER ☐☐☐☐☐☐☐☐

BEGIN WRITING

_____
_____
_____
_____
_____
_____
_____
_____
_____
_____
_____
_____
_____
_____
_____
_____
_____
_____
_____
_____

1 ☐☐☐☐☐ ☐   2 ☐☐☐☐☐ ☐   3 ☐☐☐☐☐ ☐

CONTINUE WRITING

CONTINUE WRITING

CONTINUE WRITING

TOPIC Number _____

Test Date _____

GRE® ANALYTICAL WRITING 2-ARGUMENT

LAST NAME (first four letters) ☐ ☐ ☐ ☐   FIRST INITIAL ☐   DATE OF BIRTH ☐ ☐ ☐ ☐
                                                                     M M   D D

REGISTRATION NUMBER ☐ ☐ ☐ ☐ ☐ ☐ ☐ ☐

BEGIN WRITING

_____
_____
_____
_____
_____
_____
_____
_____
_____
_____
_____
_____
_____
_____
_____
_____
_____
_____
_____
_____
_____

THE AREA BELOW IS FOR ETS USE ONLY. DO NOT WRITE IN THIS SPACE.

1 ☐ ☐ ☐ ☐ ☐ ☐ ☐   2 ☐ ☐ ☐ ☐ ☐ ☐ ☐   3 ☐ ☐ ☐ ☐ ☐ ☐ ☐

CONTINUE WRITING

DO NOT WRITE BEYOND THIS BORDER

DO NOT WRITE BEYOND THIS BORDER

CONTINUE WRITING

CONTINUE WRITING

DO NOT WRITE BEYOND THIS BORDER

DO NOT WRITE BEYOND THIS BORDER

STOP

DO NOT USE INK

Use only a pencil with soft black lead (No. 2 or HB) to complete this answer sheet.
Be sure to fill in completely the space that corresponds to your answer choice.
Completely erase any errors or stray marks.

1. NAME

Enter your last name, first name initial (given name), and middle initial if you have one.
Omit spaces, apostrophes, Jr., II., etc.

Last Name (Family Name or Surname) - First 15 Letters

First Name Initial

Middle Initial

BE SURE EACH MARK IS DARK AND COMPLETELY FILLS THE INTENDED SPACE AS ILLUSTRATED HERE:
YOU MAY FIND MORE RESPONSE SPACES THAN YOU NEED. IF SO, PLEASE LEAVE THEM BLANK.

SECTION 1 — items 1–38, choices (A) (B) (C) (D) (E)

SECTION 2 — items 1–38, choices (A) (B) (C) (D) (E)

SECTION 3 — items 1–38, choices (A) (B) (C) (D) (E)

2.

YOUR NAME:
(Print) Last Name (Family or Surname)   First Name (Given)   M.I.

MAILING ADDRESS:
(Print)   P.O. Box or Street Address

City   State or Province

Country   Zip or Postal Code

CENTER:
City   State or Province

Country   Center Number   Room Number

SIGNATURE:

3. DATE OF BIRTH

Month	Day	Year
Jan.		
Feb.		
Mar.		
April		
May		
June		
July		
Aug.		
Sept.		
Oct.		
Nov.		
Dec.		

4. SOCIAL SECURITY NUMBER
(U.S.A. only)

5. REGISTRATION NUMBER
(from your admission ticket)

6. TITLE CODE
(on back cover of your test book)

7. TEST NAME (on back cover of your test book)

FORM CODE (on back cover of your test book)

8. TEST BOOK SERIAL NUMBER
(red number in upper right corner of front cover of your test book)

SHADED AREA FOR ETS USE ONLY

DO NOT WRITE IN THIS AREA.

0

BE SURE EACH MARK IS DARK AND COMPLETELY FILLS THE INTENDED SPACE AS ILLUSTRATED HERE: ●

YOU MAY FIND MORE RESPONSE SPACES THAN YOU NEED. IF SO, PLEASE LEAVE THEM BLANK.

SECTION 4

1. (A) (B) (C) (D) (E)
2. (A) (B) (C) (D) (E)
3. (A) (B) (C) (D) (E)
4. (A) (B) (C) (D) (E)
5. (A) (B) (C) (D) (E)
6. (A) (B) (C) (D) (E)
7. (A) (B) (C) (D) (E)
8. (A) (B) (C) (D) (E)
9. (A) (B) (C) (D) (E)
10. (A) (B) (C) (D) (E)
11. (A) (B) (C) (D) (E)
12. (A) (B) (C) (D) (E)
13. (A) (B) (C) (D) (E)
14. (A) (B) (C) (D) (E)
15. (A) (B) (C) (D) (E)
16. (A) (B) (C) (D) (E)
17. (A) (B) (C) (D) (E)
18. (A) (B) (C) (D) (E)
19. (A) (B) (C) (D) (E)
20. (A) (B) (C) (D) (E)
21. (A) (B) (C) (D) (E)
22. (A) (B) (C) (D) (E)
23. (A) (B) (C) (D) (E)
24. (A) (B) (C) (D) (E)
25. (A) (B) (C) (D) (E)
26. (A) (B) (C) (D) (E)
27. (A) (B) (C) (D) (E)
28. (A) (B) (C) (D) (E)
29. (A) (B) (C) (D) (E)
30. (A) (B) (C) (D) (E)
31. (A) (B) (C) (D) (E)
32. (A) (B) (C) (D) (E)
33. (A) (B) (C) (D) (E)
34. (A) (B) (C) (D) (E)
35. (A) (B) (C) (D) (E)
36. (A) (B) (C) (D) (E)
37. (A) (B) (C) (D) (E)
38. (A) (B) (C) (D) (E)

SECTION 5

1. (A) (B) (C) (D) (E)
2. (A) (B) (C) (D) (E)
3. (A) (B) (C) (D) (E)
4. (A) (B) (C) (D) (E)
5. (A) (B) (C) (D) (E)
6. (A) (B) (C) (D) (E)
7. (A) (B) (C) (D) (E)
8. (A) (B) (C) (D) (E)
9. (A) (B) (C) (D) (E)
10. (A) (B) (C) (D) (E)
11. (A) (B) (C) (D) (E)
12. (A) (B) (C) (D) (E)
13. (A) (B) (C) (D) (E)
14. (A) (B) (C) (D) (E)
15. (A) (B) (C) (D) (E)
16. (A) (B) (C) (D) (E)
17. (A) (B) (C) (D) (E)
18. (A) (B) (C) (D) (E)
19. (A) (B) (C) (D) (E)
20. (A) (B) (C) (D) (E)
21. (A) (B) (C) (D) (E)
22. (A) (B) (C) (D) (E)
23. (A) (B) (C) (D) (E)
24. (A) (B) (C) (D) (E)
25. (A) (B) (C) (D) (E)
26. (A) (B) (C) (D) (E)
27. (A) (B) (C) (D) (E)
28. (A) (B) (C) (D) (E)
29. (A) (B) (C) (D) (E)
30. (A) (B) (C) (D) (E)
31. (A) (B) (C) (D) (E)
32. (A) (B) (C) (D) (E)
33. (A) (B) (C) (D) (E)
34. (A) (B) (C) (D) (E)
35. (A) (B) (C) (D) (E)
36. (A) (B) (C) (D) (E)
37. (A) (B) (C) (D) (E)
38. (A) (B) (C) (D) (E)

CERTIFICATION STATEMENT

Please write the following statement below, DO NOT PRINT.

"I certify that I am the person whose name appears on this answer sheet. I also agree not to disclose the contents of the test I am taking today to anyone."

Sign and date where indicated.

DATE: _____ / _____ / _____
                Month   Day   Year

SIGNATURE: _____

IF YOU DO NOT WANT THIS TEST TO BE SCORED

If you want to cancel your scores from this test administration, complete A and B below. You will not receive scores for this test; however, you will receive confirmation of this cancellation. No record of this test or the cancellation will be sent to the recipients you indicated, and there will be no scores for this test on your GRE file. Once a score is canceled, it cannot be reinstated.

To cancel your scores from this test administration, you must:

A. Fill in both ovals here   ○   B. Sign your full name here.

FOR ETS USE ONLY	V1R	V2R	VTR	VCS	Q1R	Q2R	QTR	QCS	A1R	A2R	ATR	ACS

GRADUATE RECORD EXAMINATIONS® - **GRE**® - GENERAL TEST

SIDE 1

Use only a pencil with soft, black lead (No. 2 or H-B) to complete this answer sheet.
Be sure to fill in completely the space that corresponds to your answer choice.
Completely erase any errors or stray marks.

1. NAME Enter your last name, first name initial (given name), and
middle initial if you have one.
Omit spaces, apostrophes, Jr., II., etc.

Last Name (Family Name or Surname) - First 15 Letters

| First Name Initial | Middle Initial |

BE SURE EACH MARK IS DARK AND COMPLETELY FILLS THE INTENDED SPACE AS ILLUSTRATED HERE: ●
YOU MAY FIND MORE RESPONSE SPACES THAN YOU NEED. IF SO, PLEASE LEAVE THEM BLANK.

SECTION 1

SECTION 2

SECTION 3

2.

YOUR NAME:
(Print)
Last Name (Family or Surname)   First Name (Given)   M.I.

MAILING ADDRESS:
(Print)
P.O. Box or Street Address

City   State or Province

Country   Zip or Postal Code

CENTER:
City   State or Province

Country   Center Number   Room Number

SIGNATURE:

3. DATE OF BIRTH

Month	Day	Year
Jan.		
Feb.		
Mar.		
April		
May		
June		
July		
Aug.		
Sept		
Oct.		
Nov.		
Dec.		

4. SOCIAL SECURITY NUMBER
(U.S.A. only)

5. REGISTRATION NUMBER
(from your admission ticket)

6. TITLE CODE
(on back cover of your test book)

7. TEST NAME (on back cover of your test book)

FORM CODE (on back cover of your test book)

8. TEST BOOK SERIAL NUMBER
(red number in upper right corner of front cover of your test book)

SHADED AREA FOR ETS USE ONLY

I.N. 994464

54074 • 011644 • CV82R200   MH/CHW02162   2986-06,07

ETS

SIDE 2

GENERAL TEST

BE SURE EACH MARK IS DARK AND COMPLETELY FILLS THE INTENDED SPACE AS ILLUSTRATED HERE: ● .

YOU MAY FIND MORE RESPONSE SPACES THAN YOU NEED. IF SO, PLEASE LEAVE THEM BLANK.

SECTION 4

1 (A) (B) (C) (D) (E)
2 (A) (B) (C) (D) (E)
3 (A) (B) (C) (D) (E)
4 (A) (B) (C) (D) (E)
5 (A) (B) (C) (D) (E)
6 (A) (B) (C) (D) (E)
7 (A) (B) (C) (D) (E)
8 (A) (B) (C) (D) (E)
9 (A) (B) (C) (D) (E)
10 (A) (B) (C) (D) (E)
11 (A) (B) (C) (D) (E)
12 (A) (B) (C) (D) (E)
13 (A) (B) (C) (D) (E)
14 (A) (B) (C) (D) (E)
15 (A) (B) (C) (D) (E)
16 (A) (B) (C) (D) (E)
17 (A) (B) (C) (D) (E)
18 (A) (B) (C) (D) (E)
19 (A) (B) (C) (D) (E)
20 (A) (B) (C) (D) (E)
21 (A) (B) (C) (D) (E)
22 (A) (B) (C) (D) (E)
23 (A) (B) (C) (D) (E)
24 (A) (B) (C) (D) (E)
25 (A) (B) (C) (D) (E)
26 (A) (B) (C) (D) (E)
27 (A) (B) (C) (D) (E)
28 (A) (B) (C) (D) (E)
29 (A) (B) (C) (D) (E)
30 (A) (B) (C) (D) (E)
31 (A) (B) (C) (D) (E)
32 (A) (B) (C) (D) (E)
33 (A) (B) (C) (D) (E)
34 (A) (B) (C) (D) (E)
35 (A) (B) (C) (D) (E)
36 (A) (B) (C) (D) (E)
37 (A) (B) (C) (D) (E)
38 (A) (B) (C) (D) (E)

SECTION 5

1 (A) (B) (C) (D) (E)
2 (A) (B) (C) (D) (E)
3 (A) (B) (C) (D) (E)
4 (A) (B) (C) (D) (E)
5 (A) (B) (C) (D) (E)
6 (A) (B) (C) (D) (E)
7 (A) (B) (C) (D) (E)
8 (A) (B) (C) (D) (E)
9 (A) (B) (C) (D) (E)
10 (A) (B) (C) (D) (E)
11 (A) (B) (C) (D) (E)
12 (A) (B) (C) (D) (E)
13 (A) (B) (C) (D) (E)
14 (A) (B) (C) (D) (E)
15 (A) (B) (C) (D) (E)
16 (A) (B) (C) (D) (E)
17 (A) (B) (C) (D) (E)
18 (A) (B) (C) (D) (E)
19 (A) (B) (C) (D) (E)
20 (A) (B) (C) (D) (E)
21 (A) (B) (C) (D) (E)
22 (A) (B) (C) (D) (E)
23 (A) (B) (C) (D) (E)
24 (A) (B) (C) (D) (E)
25 (A) (B) (C) (D) (E)
26 (A) (B) (C) (D) (E)
27 (A) (B) (C) (D) (E)
28 (A) (B) (C) (D) (E)
29 (A) (B) (C) (D) (E)
30 (A) (B) (C) (D) (E)
31 (A) (B) (C) (D) (E)
32 (A) (B) (C) (D) (E)
33 (A) (B) (C) (D) (E)
34 (A) (B) (C) (D) (E)
35 (A) (B) (C) (D) (E)
36 (A) (B) (C) (D) (E)
37 (A) (B) (C) (D) (E)
38 (A) (B) (C) (D) (E)

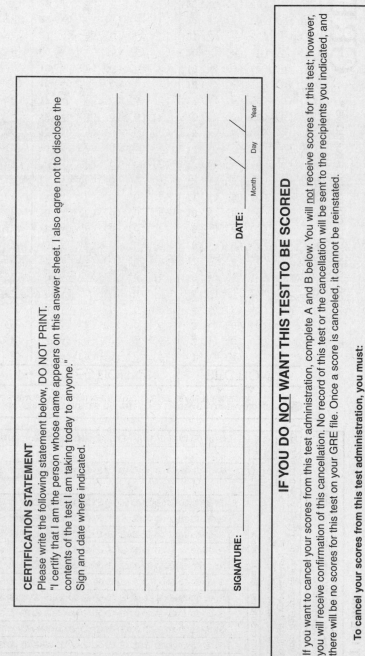

CERTIFICATION STATEMENT
Please write the following statement below, DO NOT PRINT. "I certify that I am the person whose name appears on this answer sheet. I also agree not to disclose the contents of the test I am taking today to anyone." Sign and date where indicated.

DATE: _____ Month / Day / Year

SIGNATURE: _____

IF YOU DO NOT WANT THIS TEST TO BE SCORED

If you want to cancel your scores from this test administration, complete A and B below. You will not receive scores for this test; however, you will receive confirmation of this cancellation. No record of this test or the cancellation will be sent to the recipients you indicated, and there will be no scores for this test on your GRE file. Once a score is canceled, it cannot be reinstated.

To cancel your scores from this test administration, you must:

A. Fill in both ovals here.   B. sign your full name here.

FOR ETS USE ONLY	V1R	V2R	VTR	VCS	Q1R	Q2R	QTR	QCS	A1R	A2R	ATR	ACS

Use only a pencil with soft, black lead (No. 2 or HB) to complete this answer sheet.
Be sure to fill in completely the space that corresponds to your answer choice.
Completely erase any errors or stray marks.

1. NAME Enter your last name, first name initial (given name), and middle initial if you have one.
Omit spaces, apostrophes, Jr., II., etc.

Last Name (Family Name or Surname) - First 15 Letters

First Name Initial | Middle Initial

2.

YOUR NAME:
(Print)

Last Name (Family or Surname)   First Name (Given)   M.I.

MAILING ADDRESS:
(Print)

P.O. Box or Street Address

City   State or Province

Country   Zip or Postal Code

CENTER:

City   State or Province

Country   Center Number   Room Number

SIGNATURE:

GRADUATE RECORD EXAMINATIONS® - **GRE**® - GENERAL TEST   SIDE 1

BE SURE EACH MARK IS DARK AND COMPLETELY FILLS THE INTENDED SPACE AS ILLUSTRATED HERE.
YOU MAY FIND MORE RESPONSE SPACES THAN YOU NEED. IF SO, PLEASE LEAVE THEM BLANK.

SECTION 1
SECTION 2
SECTION 3

(Answer bubbles numbered 1–38, choices A B C D E for each section)

3. DATE OF BIRTH

Month | Day | Year

Jan. Feb. Mar. April May June July Aug. Sept. Oct. Nov. Dec.

4. SOCIAL SECURITY NUMBER (U.S.A. only)

5. REGISTRATION NUMBER (from your admission ticket)

6. TITLE CODE (on back cover of your test book)

7. TEST NAME (on back cover of your test book)

FORM CODE (on back cover of your test book)

8. TEST BOOK SERIAL NUMBER (red number in upper right corner of front cover of your test book)

SHADED AREA FOR ETS USE ONLY

2986-06.07   54074 • 011644 • CV82R200 · MH/CHW02162   I.N. 9944464

1 2 3 4

SIDE 2

GENERAL TEST

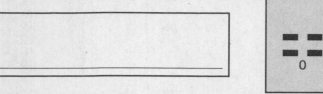

BE SURE EACH MARK IS DARK AND COMPLETELY FILLS THE INTENDED SPACE AS ILLUSTRATED HERE: ● .

YOU MAY FIND MORE RESPONSE SPACES THAN YOU NEED. IF SO, PLEASE LEAVE THEM BLANK.

SECTION 4	SECTION 5
1 (A) (B) (C) (D) (E)	1 (A) (B) (C) (D) (E)
2 (A) (B) (C) (D) (E)	2 (A) (B) (C) (D) (E)
3 (A) (B) (C) (D) (E)	3 (A) (B) (C) (D) (E)
4 (A) (B) (C) (D) (E)	4 (A) (B) (C) (D) (E)
5 (A) (B) (C) (D) (E)	5 (A) (B) (C) (D) (E)
6 (A) (B) (C) (D) (E)	6 (A) (B) (C) (D) (E)
7 (A) (B) (C) (D) (E)	7 (A) (B) (C) (D) (E)
8 (A) (B) (C) (D) (E)	8 (A) (B) (C) (D) (E)
9 (A) (B) (C) (D) (E)	9 (A) (B) (C) (D) (E)
10 (A) (B) (C) (D) (E)	10 (A) (B) (C) (D) (E)
11 (A) (B) (C) (D) (E)	11 (A) (B) (C) (D) (E)
12 (A) (B) (C) (D) (E)	12 (A) (B) (C) (D) (E)
13 (A) (B) (C) (D) (E)	13 (A) (B) (C) (D) (E)
14 (A) (B) (C) (D) (E)	14 (A) (B) (C) (D) (E)
15 (A) (B) (C) (D) (E)	15 (A) (B) (C) (D) (E)
16 (A) (B) (C) (D) (E)	16 (A) (B) (C) (D) (E)
17 (A) (B) (C) (D) (E)	17 (A) (B) (C) (D) (E)
18 (A) (B) (C) (D) (E)	18 (A) (B) (C) (D) (E)
19 (A) (B) (C) (D) (E)	19 (A) (B) (C) (D) (E)
20 (A) (B) (C) (D) (E)	20 (A) (B) (C) (D) (E)
21 (A) (B) (C) (D) (E)	21 (A) (B) (C) (D) (E)
22 (A) (B) (C) (D) (E)	22 (A) (B) (C) (D) (E)
23 (A) (B) (C) (D) (E)	23 (A) (B) (C) (D) (E)
24 (A) (B) (C) (D) (E)	24 (A) (B) (C) (D) (E)
25 (A) (B) (C) (D) (E)	25 (A) (B) (C) (D) (E)
26 (A) (B) (C) (D) (E)	26 (A) (B) (C) (D) (E)
27 (A) (B) (C) (D) (E)	27 (A) (B) (C) (D) (E)
28 (A) (B) (C) (D) (E)	28 (A) (B) (C) (D) (E)
29 (A) (B) (C) (D) (E)	29 (A) (B) (C) (D) (E)
30 (A) (B) (C) (D) (E)	30 (A) (B) (C) (D) (E)
31 (A) (B) (C) (D) (E)	31 (A) (B) (C) (D) (E)
32 (A) (B) (C) (D) (E)	32 (A) (B) (C) (D) (E)
33 (A) (B) (C) (D) (E)	33 (A) (B) (C) (D) (E)
34 (A) (B) (C) (D) (E)	34 (A) (B) (C) (D) (E)
35 (A) (B) (C) (D) (E)	35 (A) (B) (C) (D) (E)
36 (A) (B) (C) (D) (E)	36 (A) (B) (C) (D) (E)
37 (A) (B) (C) (D) (E)	37 (A) (B) (C) (D) (E)
38 (A) (B) (C) (D) (E)	38 (A) (B) (C) (D) (E)

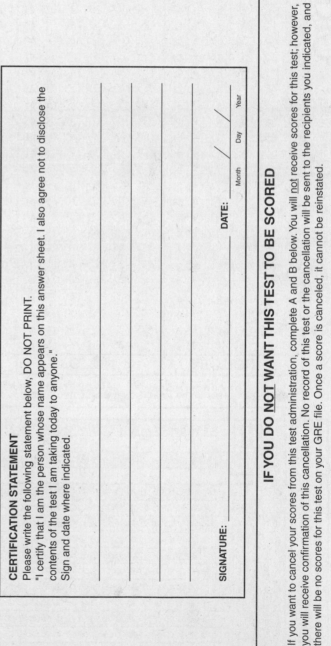

CERTIFICATION STATEMENT
Please write the following statement below, DO NOT PRINT.
"I certify that I am the person whose name appears on this answer sheet. I also agree not to disclose the contents of the test I am taking today to anyone."
Sign and date where indicated.

DATE: _____ / _____ / _____
Month   Day   Year

SIGNATURE: _____

IF YOU DO NOT WANT THIS TEST TO BE SCORED

If you want to cancel your scores from this test administration, complete A and B below. You will not receive scores for this test; however, you will receive confirmation of this cancellation. No record of this test or the cancellation will be sent to the recipients you indicated, and there will be no scores for this test on your GRE file. Once a score is canceled, it cannot be reinstated.

To cancel your scores from this test administration, you must:

A. Fill in both ovals here. ○   ○   B. Sign your full name here:

FOR ETS USE ONLY	V1R	V2R	VTR	VCS	Q1R	Q2R	QTR	QCS	A1R	A2R	ATR	ACS

SIDE 1

GRADUATE RECORD EXAMINATIONS® · **GRE**® – GENERAL TEST

BE SURE EACH MARK IS DARK AND COMPLETELY FILLS THE INTENDED SPACE AS ILLUSTRATED HERE:
YOU MAY FIND MORE RESPONSE SPACES THAN YOU NEED. IF SO, PLEASE LEAVE THEM BLANK.

SECTION 1 · SECTION 2 · SECTION 3
(items 1–38, answer bubbles A B C D E)

DO NOT USE INK

Use only a pencil with soft, black lead (No. 2 or HB) to complete this answer sheet.
Be sure to fill in completely the space that corresponds to your answer choice.
Completely erase any errors or stray marks.

1. NAME
Enter your last name, first name initial (given name), and middle initial if you have one.
Omit spaces, apostrophes, Jr., II, etc.
Last Name (Family Name or Surname) – First 15 Letters   First Name Initial   Middle Initial

2.
YOUR NAME:
(Print)   Last Name (Family or Surname)   First Name (Given)   M.I.

MAILING ADDRESS:
(Print)   P.O. Box or Street Address
City   State or Province
Country   Zip or Postal Code

CENTER:
City   State or Province
Country   Center Number   Room Number

SIGNATURE:

3. DATE OF BIRTH
Month   Day   Year
Jan. Feb. Mar. April May June July Aug. Sept. Oct. Nov. Dec.

4. SOCIAL SECURITY NUMBER (U.S.A. only)

5. REGISTRATION NUMBER (from your admission ticket)

6. TITLE CODE (on back cover of your test book)

7. TEST NAME (on back cover of your test book)
FORM CODE (on back cover of your test book)

8. TEST BOOK SERIAL NUMBER (red number in upper right corner of front cover of your test book)

SHADED AREA FOR ETS USE ONLY

I.N. 994464

MH/CHW02162

54074 · 011644 · CV82R200
1 2 3 4

2986-06,07

ETS Copyright © 2002 by Educational Testing Service, Princeton, NJ 08541
All rights reserved. Printed in U.S.A.

SIDE 2

GENERAL TEST

BE SURE EACH MARK IS DARK AND COMPLETELY FILLS THE INTENDED SPACE AS ILLUSTRATED HERE: ●.

YOU MAY FIND MORE RESPONSE SPACES THAN YOU NEED. IF SO, PLEASE LEAVE THEM BLANK.

SECTION 4 | SECTION 5

#	Section 4	#	Section 5
1	Ⓐ Ⓑ Ⓒ Ⓓ Ⓔ	1	Ⓐ Ⓑ Ⓒ Ⓓ Ⓔ
2	Ⓐ Ⓑ Ⓒ Ⓓ Ⓔ	2	Ⓐ Ⓑ Ⓒ Ⓓ Ⓔ
3	Ⓐ Ⓑ Ⓒ Ⓓ Ⓔ	3	Ⓐ Ⓑ Ⓒ Ⓓ Ⓔ
4	Ⓐ Ⓑ Ⓒ Ⓓ Ⓔ	4	Ⓐ Ⓑ Ⓒ Ⓓ Ⓔ
5	Ⓐ Ⓑ Ⓒ Ⓓ Ⓔ	5	Ⓐ Ⓑ Ⓒ Ⓓ Ⓔ
6	Ⓐ Ⓑ Ⓒ Ⓓ Ⓔ	6	Ⓐ Ⓑ Ⓒ Ⓓ Ⓔ
7	Ⓐ Ⓑ Ⓒ Ⓓ Ⓔ	7	Ⓐ Ⓑ Ⓒ Ⓓ Ⓔ
8	Ⓐ Ⓑ Ⓒ Ⓓ Ⓔ	8	Ⓐ Ⓑ Ⓒ Ⓓ Ⓔ
9	Ⓐ Ⓑ Ⓒ Ⓓ Ⓔ	9	Ⓐ Ⓑ Ⓒ Ⓓ Ⓔ
10	Ⓐ Ⓑ Ⓒ Ⓓ Ⓔ	10	Ⓐ Ⓑ Ⓒ Ⓓ Ⓔ
11	Ⓐ Ⓑ Ⓒ Ⓓ Ⓔ	11	Ⓐ Ⓑ Ⓒ Ⓓ Ⓔ
12	Ⓐ Ⓑ Ⓒ Ⓓ Ⓔ	12	Ⓐ Ⓑ Ⓒ Ⓓ Ⓔ
13	Ⓐ Ⓑ Ⓒ Ⓓ Ⓔ	13	Ⓐ Ⓑ Ⓒ Ⓓ Ⓔ
14	Ⓐ Ⓑ Ⓒ Ⓓ Ⓔ	14	Ⓐ Ⓑ Ⓒ Ⓓ Ⓔ
15	Ⓐ Ⓑ Ⓒ Ⓓ Ⓔ	15	Ⓐ Ⓑ Ⓒ Ⓓ Ⓔ
16	Ⓐ Ⓑ Ⓒ Ⓓ Ⓔ	16	Ⓐ Ⓑ Ⓒ Ⓓ Ⓔ
17	Ⓐ Ⓑ Ⓒ Ⓓ Ⓔ	17	Ⓐ Ⓑ Ⓒ Ⓓ Ⓔ
18	Ⓐ Ⓑ Ⓒ Ⓓ Ⓔ	18	Ⓐ Ⓑ Ⓒ Ⓓ Ⓔ
19	Ⓐ Ⓑ Ⓒ Ⓓ Ⓔ	19	Ⓐ Ⓑ Ⓒ Ⓓ Ⓔ
20	Ⓐ Ⓑ Ⓒ Ⓓ Ⓔ	20	Ⓐ Ⓑ Ⓒ Ⓓ Ⓔ
21	Ⓐ Ⓑ Ⓒ Ⓓ Ⓔ	21	Ⓐ Ⓑ Ⓒ Ⓓ Ⓔ
22	Ⓐ Ⓑ Ⓒ Ⓓ Ⓔ	22	Ⓐ Ⓑ Ⓒ Ⓓ Ⓔ
23	Ⓐ Ⓑ Ⓒ Ⓓ Ⓔ	23	Ⓐ Ⓑ Ⓒ Ⓓ Ⓔ
24	Ⓐ Ⓑ Ⓒ Ⓓ Ⓔ	24	Ⓐ Ⓑ Ⓒ Ⓓ Ⓔ
25	Ⓐ Ⓑ Ⓒ Ⓓ Ⓔ	25	Ⓐ Ⓑ Ⓒ Ⓓ Ⓔ
26	Ⓐ Ⓑ Ⓒ Ⓓ Ⓔ	26	Ⓐ Ⓑ Ⓒ Ⓓ Ⓔ
27	Ⓐ Ⓑ Ⓒ Ⓓ Ⓔ	27	Ⓐ Ⓑ Ⓒ Ⓓ Ⓔ
28	Ⓐ Ⓑ Ⓒ Ⓓ Ⓔ	28	Ⓐ Ⓑ Ⓒ Ⓓ Ⓔ
29	Ⓐ Ⓑ Ⓒ Ⓓ Ⓔ	29	Ⓐ Ⓑ Ⓒ Ⓓ Ⓔ
30	Ⓐ Ⓑ Ⓒ Ⓓ Ⓔ	30	Ⓐ Ⓑ Ⓒ Ⓓ Ⓔ
31	Ⓐ Ⓑ Ⓒ Ⓓ Ⓔ	31	Ⓐ Ⓑ Ⓒ Ⓓ Ⓔ
32	Ⓐ Ⓑ Ⓒ Ⓓ Ⓔ	32	Ⓐ Ⓑ Ⓒ Ⓓ Ⓔ
33	Ⓐ Ⓑ Ⓒ Ⓓ Ⓔ	33	Ⓐ Ⓑ Ⓒ Ⓓ Ⓔ
34	Ⓐ Ⓑ Ⓒ Ⓓ Ⓔ	34	Ⓐ Ⓑ Ⓒ Ⓓ Ⓔ
35	Ⓐ Ⓑ Ⓒ Ⓓ Ⓔ	35	Ⓐ Ⓑ Ⓒ Ⓓ Ⓔ
36	Ⓐ Ⓑ Ⓒ Ⓓ Ⓔ	36	Ⓐ Ⓑ Ⓒ Ⓓ Ⓔ
37	Ⓐ Ⓑ Ⓒ Ⓓ Ⓔ	37	Ⓐ Ⓑ Ⓒ Ⓓ Ⓔ
38	Ⓐ Ⓑ Ⓒ Ⓓ Ⓔ	38	Ⓐ Ⓑ Ⓒ Ⓓ Ⓔ

CERTIFICATION STATEMENT

Please write the following statement below, DO NOT PRINT.

"I certify that I am the person whose name appears on this answer sheet. I also agree not to disclose the contents of the test I am taking today to anyone."

Sign and date where indicated.

DATE: _____ Month / Day / Year

SIGNATURE: _____

IF YOU DO NOT WANT THIS TEST TO BE SCORED

If you want to cancel your scores from this test administration, complete A and B below. You will not receive scores for this test; however, you will receive confirmation of this cancellation. No record of this test or the cancellation will be sent to the recipients you indicated, and there will be no scores for this test on your GRE file. Once a score is canceled, it cannot be reinstated.

To cancel your scores from this test administration, you must:

A. Fill in both ovals here . . . ◯ ◯   B. Sign your full name here:

DO NOT USE INK

Use only a pencil with soft, black lead (No. 2 or HB) to complete this answer sheet.
Be sure to fill in completely the space that corresponds to your answer choice.
Completely erase any errors or stray marks.

GRADUATE RECORD EXAMINATIONS® - GRE® - GENERAL TEST

SIDE 1

1. NAME Enter your last name, first name initial (given name), and middle initial if you have one. Omit spaces, apostrophes, Jr., II., etc.

Last Name (Family Name or Surname) - First 15 Letters | First Name Initial | Middle Initial

BE SURE EACH MARK IS DARK AND COMPLETELY FILLS THE INTENDED SPACE AS ILLUSTRATED HERE:
YOU MAY FIND MORE RESPONSE SPACES THAN YOU NEED. IF SO, PLEASE LEAVE THEM BLANK.

SECTION 3 — 1–38 (A) (B) (C) (D) (E)

SECTION 2 — 1–38 (A) (B) (C) (D) (E)

SECTION 1 — 1–38 (A) (B) (C) (D) (E)

2.

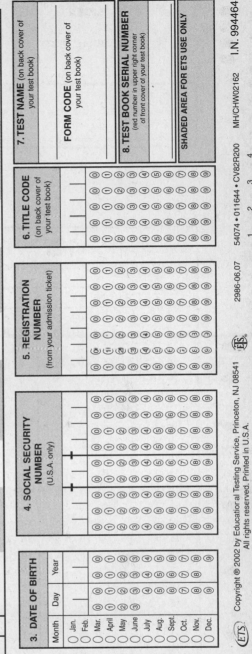

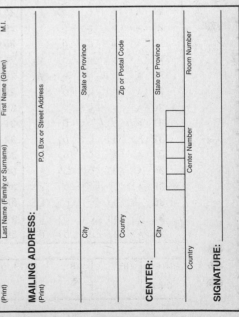

YOUR NAME: (Print) Last Name (Family or Surname) First Name (Given) M.I.

MAILING ADDRESS: (Print) P.O. Box or Street Address

City State or Province

Country Zip or Postal Code

CENTER: City State or Province

Country Center Number Room Number

SIGNATURE:

3. DATE OF BIRTH

Month: Jan. Feb. Mar. April May June July Aug. Sept. Oct. Nov. Dec. | Day | Year

4. SOCIAL SECURITY NUMBER (U.S.A. only)

5. REGISTRATION NUMBER (from your admission ticket)

6. TITLE CODE (on back cover of your test book)

7. TEST NAME (on back cover of your test book)

FORM CODE (on back cover of your test book)

8. TEST BOOK SERIAL NUMBER (red number in upper right corner of front cover of your test book)

SHADED AREA FOR ETS USE ONLY

2986-06,07 54074 • 011644 • CV82R200 MH/CHW02162 I.N. 994464

1 2 3 4

SIDE 2

GENERAL TEST

0

BE SURE EACH MARK IS DARK AND COMPLETELY FILLS THE INTENDED SPACE AS ILLUSTRATED HERE: ● .

YOU MAY FIND MORE RESPONSE SPACES THAN YOU NEED. IF SO, PLEASE LEAVE THEM BLANK.

SECTION 4	SECTION 5
1 Ⓐ Ⓑ Ⓒ Ⓓ Ⓔ	1 Ⓐ Ⓑ Ⓒ Ⓓ Ⓔ
2 Ⓐ Ⓑ Ⓒ Ⓓ Ⓔ	2 Ⓐ Ⓑ Ⓒ Ⓓ Ⓔ
3 Ⓐ Ⓑ Ⓒ Ⓓ Ⓔ	3 Ⓐ Ⓑ Ⓒ Ⓓ Ⓔ
4 Ⓐ Ⓑ Ⓒ Ⓓ Ⓔ	4 Ⓐ Ⓑ Ⓒ Ⓓ Ⓔ
5 Ⓐ Ⓑ Ⓒ Ⓓ Ⓔ	5 Ⓐ Ⓑ Ⓒ Ⓓ Ⓔ
6 Ⓐ Ⓑ Ⓒ Ⓓ Ⓔ	6 Ⓐ Ⓑ Ⓒ Ⓓ Ⓔ
7 Ⓐ Ⓑ Ⓒ Ⓓ Ⓔ	7 Ⓐ Ⓑ Ⓒ Ⓓ Ⓔ
8 Ⓐ Ⓑ Ⓒ Ⓓ Ⓔ	8 Ⓐ Ⓑ Ⓒ Ⓓ Ⓔ
9 Ⓐ Ⓑ Ⓒ Ⓓ Ⓔ	9 Ⓐ Ⓑ Ⓒ Ⓓ Ⓔ
10 Ⓐ Ⓑ Ⓒ Ⓓ Ⓔ	10 Ⓐ Ⓑ Ⓒ Ⓓ Ⓔ
11 Ⓐ Ⓑ Ⓒ Ⓓ Ⓔ	11 Ⓐ Ⓑ Ⓒ Ⓓ Ⓔ
12 Ⓐ Ⓑ Ⓒ Ⓓ Ⓔ	12 Ⓐ Ⓑ Ⓒ Ⓓ Ⓔ
13 Ⓐ Ⓑ Ⓒ Ⓓ Ⓔ	13 Ⓐ Ⓑ Ⓒ Ⓓ Ⓔ
14 Ⓐ Ⓑ Ⓒ Ⓓ Ⓔ	14 Ⓐ Ⓑ Ⓒ Ⓓ Ⓔ
15 Ⓐ Ⓑ Ⓒ Ⓓ Ⓔ	15 Ⓐ Ⓑ Ⓒ Ⓓ Ⓔ
16 Ⓐ Ⓑ Ⓒ Ⓓ Ⓔ	16 Ⓐ Ⓑ Ⓒ Ⓓ Ⓔ
17 Ⓐ Ⓑ Ⓒ Ⓓ Ⓔ	17 Ⓐ Ⓑ Ⓒ Ⓓ Ⓔ
18 Ⓐ Ⓑ Ⓒ Ⓓ Ⓔ	18 Ⓐ Ⓑ Ⓒ Ⓓ Ⓔ
19 Ⓐ Ⓑ Ⓒ Ⓓ Ⓔ	19 Ⓐ Ⓑ Ⓒ Ⓓ Ⓔ
20 Ⓐ Ⓑ Ⓒ Ⓓ Ⓔ	20 Ⓐ Ⓑ Ⓒ Ⓓ Ⓔ
21 Ⓐ Ⓑ Ⓒ Ⓓ Ⓔ	21 Ⓐ Ⓑ Ⓒ Ⓓ Ⓔ
22 Ⓐ Ⓑ Ⓒ Ⓓ Ⓔ	22 Ⓐ Ⓑ Ⓒ Ⓓ Ⓔ
23 Ⓐ Ⓑ Ⓒ Ⓓ Ⓔ	23 Ⓐ Ⓑ Ⓒ Ⓓ Ⓔ
24 Ⓐ Ⓑ Ⓒ Ⓓ Ⓔ	24 Ⓐ Ⓑ Ⓒ Ⓓ Ⓔ
25 Ⓐ Ⓑ Ⓒ Ⓓ Ⓔ	25 Ⓐ Ⓑ Ⓒ Ⓓ Ⓔ
26 Ⓐ Ⓑ Ⓒ Ⓓ Ⓔ	26 Ⓐ Ⓑ Ⓒ Ⓓ Ⓔ
27 Ⓐ Ⓑ Ⓒ Ⓓ Ⓔ	27 Ⓐ Ⓑ Ⓒ Ⓓ Ⓔ
28 Ⓐ Ⓑ Ⓒ Ⓓ Ⓔ	28 Ⓐ Ⓑ Ⓒ Ⓓ Ⓔ
29 Ⓐ Ⓑ Ⓒ Ⓓ Ⓔ	29 Ⓐ Ⓑ Ⓒ Ⓓ Ⓔ
30 Ⓐ Ⓑ Ⓒ Ⓓ Ⓔ	30 Ⓐ Ⓑ Ⓒ Ⓓ Ⓔ
31 Ⓐ Ⓑ Ⓒ Ⓓ Ⓔ	31 Ⓐ Ⓑ Ⓒ Ⓓ Ⓔ
32 Ⓐ Ⓑ Ⓒ Ⓓ Ⓔ	32 Ⓐ Ⓑ Ⓒ Ⓓ Ⓔ
33 Ⓐ Ⓑ Ⓒ Ⓓ Ⓔ	33 Ⓐ Ⓑ Ⓒ Ⓓ Ⓔ
34 Ⓐ Ⓑ Ⓒ Ⓓ Ⓔ	34 Ⓐ Ⓑ Ⓒ Ⓓ Ⓔ
35 Ⓐ Ⓑ Ⓒ Ⓓ Ⓔ	35 Ⓐ Ⓑ Ⓒ Ⓓ Ⓔ
36 Ⓐ Ⓑ Ⓒ Ⓓ Ⓔ	36 Ⓐ Ⓑ Ⓒ Ⓓ Ⓔ
37 Ⓐ Ⓑ Ⓒ Ⓓ Ⓔ	37 Ⓐ Ⓑ Ⓒ Ⓓ Ⓔ
38 Ⓐ Ⓑ Ⓒ Ⓓ Ⓔ	38 Ⓐ Ⓑ Ⓒ Ⓓ Ⓔ

CERTIFICATION STATEMENT

Please write the following statement below, DO NOT PRINT.

"I certify that I am the person whose name appears on this answer sheet. I also agree not to disclose the contents of the test I am taking today to anyone."
Sign and date where indicated.

DATE: _____ / _____ / _____
             Month   Day   Year

SIGNATURE: _____

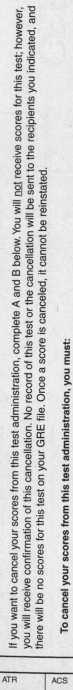

IF YOU DO NOT WANT THIS TEST TO BE SCORED

If you want to cancel your scores from this test administration, complete A and B below. You will not receive scores for this test; however, you will receive confirmation of this cancellation. No record of this test or the cancellation will be sent to the recipients you indicated, and there will be no scores for this test on your GRE file. Once a score is canceled, it cannot be reinstated.

To cancel your scores from this test administration, you must:

A. Fill in both ovals here ....   B. Sign your full name here:

FOR ETS USE ONLY	V1R	V2R	VTR	VCS	Q1R	Q2R	QTR	QCS	A1R	A2R	ATR	ACS

GRADUATE RECORD EXAMINATIONS® - GRE® - GENERAL TEST

SIDE 1

Use only a pencil with soft, black lead (No. 2 or HB) to complete this answer sheet.
Be sure to fill in completely the space that corresponds to your answer choice.
Completely erase any errors or stray marks.

1. NAME Enter your last name, first name initial (given name), and middle initial if you have one.
Omit spaces, apostrophes, Jr., II., etc.

First Name Initial
Middle Initial

Last Name (Family or Surname) - First 15 Letters

BE SURE EACH MARK IS DARK AND COMPLETELY FILLS THE INTENDED SPACE AS ILLUSTRATED HERE.
YOU MAY FIND MORE RESPONSE SPACES THAN YOU NEED. IF SO, PLEASE LEAVE THEM BLANK.

SECTION 1

SECTION 2

SECTION 3

3. DATE OF BIRTH
Month | Day | Year
Jan. Feb. Mar. April May June July Aug. Sept. Oct. Nov. Dec.

4. SOCIAL SECURITY NUMBER (U.S.A. only)

5. REGISTRATION NUMBER (from your admission ticket)

6. TITLE CODE (on back cover of your test book)

7. TEST NAME (on back cover of your test book)

FORM CODE (on back cover of your test book)

8. TEST BOOK SERIAL NUMBER (red number in upper right corner of front cover of your test book)

SHADED AREA FOR ETS USE ONLY

I.N. 994464

54074 • 011644 • CV82R200   MH/CHW02162

1   2   3   4

2986-06,07

2. YOUR NAME:
(Print) Last Name (Family or Surname)   First Name (Given)   M.I.

MAILING ADDRESS:
(Print) P.O. Box or Street Address
City   State or Province
Country   Zip or Postal Code

CENTER:
City   State or Province
Country   Center Number   Room Number

SIGNATURE:

a   b

c   d

DO NOT WRITE IN THIS AREA.

0

BE SURE EACH MARK IS DARK AND COMPLETELY FILLS THE INTENDED SPACE AS ILLUSTRATED HERE: ● .

YOU MAY FIND MORE RESPONSE SPACES THAN YOU NEED. IF SO, PLEASE LEAVE THEM BLANK.

SECTION 4

1 (A) (B) (C) (D) (E)
2 (A) (B) (C) (D) (E)
3 (A) (B) (C) (D) (E)
4 (A) (B) (C) (D) (E)
5 (A) (B) (C) (D) (E)
6 (A) (B) (C) (D) (E)
7 (A) (B) (C) (D) (E)
8 (A) (B) (C) (D) (E)
9 (A) (B) (C) (D) (E)
10 (A) (B) (C) (D) (E)
11 (A) (B) (C) (D) (E)
12 (A) (B) (C) (D) (E)
13 (A) (B) (C) (D) (E)
14 (A) (B) (C) (D) (E)
15 (A) (B) (C) (D) (E)
16 (A) (B) (C) (D) (E)
17 (A) (B) (C) (D) (E)
18 (A) (B) (C) (D) (E)
19 (A) (B) (C) (D) (E)
20 (A) (B) (C) (D) (E)
21 (A) (B) (C) (D) (E)
22 (A) (B) (C) (D) (E)
23 (A) (B) (C) (D) (E)
24 (A) (B) (C) (D) (E)
25 (A) (B) (C) (D) (E)
26 (A) (B) (C) (D) (E)
27 (A) (B) (C) (D) (E)
28 (A) (B) (C) (D) (E)
29 (A) (B) (C) (D) (E)
30 (A) (B) (C) (D) (E)
31 (A) (B) (C) (D) (E)
32 (A) (B) (C) (D) (E)
33 (A) (B) (C) (D) (E)
34 (A) (B) (C) (D) (E)
35 (A) (B) (C) (D) (E)
36 (A) (B) (C) (D) (E)
37 (A) (B) (C) (D) (E)
38 (A) (B) (C) (D) (E)

SECTION 5

1 (A) (B) (C) (D) (E)
2 (A) (B) (C) (D) (E)
3 (A) (B) (C) (D) (E)
4 (A) (B) (C) (D) (E)
5 (A) (B) (C) (D) (E)
6 (A) (B) (C) (D) (E)
7 (A) (B) (C) (D) (E)
8 (A) (B) (C) (D) (E)
9 (A) (B) (C) (D) (E)
10 (A) (B) (C) (D) (E)
11 (A) (B) (C) (D) (E)
12 (A) (B) (C) (D) (E)
13 (A) (B) (C) (D) (E)
14 (A) (B) (C) (D) (E)
15 (A) (B) (C) (D) (E)
16 (A) (B) (C) (D) (E)
17 (A) (B) (C) (D) (E)
18 (A) (B) (C) (D) (E)
19 (A) (B) (C) (D) (E)
20 (A) (B) (C) (D) (E)
21 (A) (B) (C) (D) (E)
22 (A) (B) (C) (D) (E)
23 (A) (B) (C) (D) (E)
24 (A) (B) (C) (D) (E)
25 (A) (B) (C) (D) (E)
26 (A) (B) (C) (D) (E)
27 (A) (B) (C) (D) (E)
28 (A) (B) (C) (D) (E)
29 (A) (B) (C) (D) (E)
30 (A) (B) (C) (D) (E)
31 (A) (B) (C) (D) (E)
32 (A) (B) (C) (D) (E)
33 (A) (B) (C) (D) (E)
34 (A) (B) (C) (D) (E)
35 (A) (B) (C) (D) (E)
36 (A) (B) (C) (D) (E)
37 (A) (B) (C) (D) (E)
38 (A) (B) (C) (D) (E)

CERTIFICATION STATEMENT

Please write the following statement below, DO NOT PRINT.
"I certify that I am the person whose name appears on this answer sheet. I also agree not to disclose the contents of the test I am taking today to anyone."
Sign and date where indicated.

DATE: _____ / _____ / _____
Month   Day   Year

SIGNATURE: _____

IF YOU DO NOT WANT THIS TEST TO BE SCORED

If you want to cancel your scores from this test administration, complete A and B below. You will not receive scores for this test; however, you will receive confirmation of this cancellation. No record of this test or the cancellation will be sent to the recipients you indicated, and there will be no scores for this test on your GRE file. Once a score is canceled, it cannot be reinstated.

To cancel your scores from this test administration, you must:

A. Fill in both ovals here   B. Sign your full name here

FOR ETS USE ONLY	V1R	V2R	VTR	VCS	Q1R	Q2R	QTR	QCS	A1R	A2R	ATR	ACS

GRADUATE RECORD EXAMINATIONS® - GRE® - GENERAL TEST

SIDE 1

DO NOT USE INK

Use only a pencil with soft, black lead (No. 2 or HB) to complete this answer sheet.
Be sure to fill in completely the space that corresponds to your answer choice.
Completely erase any errors or stray marks.

1. NAME Enter your last name, first name initial (given name), and middle initial if you have one.
Omit spaces, apostrophes, Jr., II., etc.

Last Name (Family Name or Surname) - First 15 Letters

First Name Initial | Middle Initial

● BE SURE EACH MARK IS DARK AND COMPLETELY FILLS THE INTENDED SPACE AS ILLUSTRATED HERE.
YOU MAY FIND MORE RESPONSE SPACES THAN YOU NEED. IF SO, PLEASE LEAVE THEM BLANK.

SECTION 1
(questions 1–38, answer choices A B C D E)

SECTION 2
(questions 1–38, answer choices A B C D E)

SECTION 3
(questions 1–38, answer choices A B C D E)

2.

YOUR NAME: _____
(Print)
Last Name (Family or Surname)   First Name (Given)   M.I.

MAILING ADDRESS: _____
(Print)
P.O. Box or Street Address

City _____ State or Province

Country _____ Zip or Postal Code

CENTER: _____
City _____ State or Province

Country   Center Number   Room Number

SIGNATURE: _____

3. DATE OF BIRTH

Month	Day	Year
Jan.		
Feb.		
Mar.		
April		
May		
June		
July		
Aug.		
Sept.		
Oct.		
Nov.		
Dec.		

4. SOCIAL SECURITY NUMBER (U.S.A. only)

5. REGISTRATION NUMBER (from your admission ticket)

6. TITLE CODE (on back cover of your test book)

7. TEST NAME (on back cover of your test book)

FORM CODE (on back cover of your test book)

8. TEST BOOK SERIAL NUMBER (red number in upper right corner of front cover of your test book)

SHADED AREA FOR ETS USE ONLY

2986-06,07   54074 • 011644 • CV82R200   MH/CHW02162   I.N. 994464

(ETS)

SIDE 2

GENERAL TEST

DO NOT WRITE IN THIS AREA.

0

BE SURE EACH MARK IS DARK AND COMPLETELY FILLS THE INTENDED SPACE AS ILLUSTRATED HERE: ● .

YOU MAY FIND MORE RESPONSE SPACES THAN YOU NEED. IF SO, PLEASE LEAVE THEM BLANK.

SECTION 4

1 (A) (B) (C) (D) (E)
2 (A) (B) (C) (D) (E)
3 (A) (B) (C) (D) (E)
4 (A) (B) (C) (D) (E)
5 (A) (B) (C) (D) (E)
6 (A) (B) (C) (D) (E)
7 (A) (B) (C) (D) (E)
8 (A) (B) (C) (D) (E)
9 (A) (B) (C) (D) (E)
10 (A) (B) (C) (D) (E)
11 (A) (B) (C) (D) (E)
12 (A) (B) (C) (D) (E)
13 (A) (B) (C) (D) (E)
14 (A) (B) (C) (D) (E)
15 (A) (B) (C) (D) (E)
16 (A) (B) (C) (D) (E)
17 (A) (B) (C) (D) (E)
18 (A) (B) (C) (D) (E)
19 (A) (B) (C) (D) (E)
20 (A) (B) (C) (D) (E)
21 (A) (B) (C) (D) (E)
22 (A) (B) (C) (D) (E)
23 (A) (B) (C) (D) (E)
24 (A) (B) (C) (D) (E)
25 (A) (B) (C) (D) (E)
26 (A) (B) (C) (D) (E)
27 (A) (B) (C) (D) (E)
28 (A) (B) (C) (D) (E)
29 (A) (B) (C) (D) (E)
30 (A) (B) (C) (D) (E)
31 (A) (B) (C) (D) (E)
32 (A) (B) (C) (D) (E)
33 (A) (B) (C) (D) (E)
34 (A) (B) (C) (D) (E)
35 (A) (B) (C) (D) (E)
36 (A) (B) (C) (D) (E)
37 (A) (B) (C) (D) (E)
38 (A) (B) (C) (D) (E)

SECTION 5

1 (A) (B) (C) (D) (E)
2 (A) (B) (C) (D) (E)
3 (A) (B) (C) (D) (E)
4 (A) (B) (C) (D) (E)
5 (A) (B) (C) (D) (E)
6 (A) (B) (C) (D) (E)
7 (A) (B) (C) (D) (E)
8 (A) (B) (C) (D) (E)
9 (A) (B) (C) (D) (E)
10 (A) (B) (C) (D) (E)
11 (A) (B) (C) (D) (E)
12 (A) (B) (C) (D) (E)
13 (A) (B) (C) (D) (E)
14 (A) (B) (C) (D) (E)
15 (A) (B) (C) (D) (E)
16 (A) (B) (C) (D) (E)
17 (A) (B) (C) (D) (E)
18 (A) (B) (C) (D) (E)
19 (A) (B) (C) (D) (E)
20 (A) (B) (C) (D) (E)
21 (A) (B) (C) (D) (E)
22 (A) (B) (C) (D) (E)
23 (A) (B) (C) (D) (E)
24 (A) (B) (C) (D) (E)
25 (A) (B) (C) (D) (E)
26 (A) (B) (C) (D) (E)
27 (A) (B) (C) (D) (E)
28 (A) (B) (C) (D) (E)
29 (A) (B) (C) (D) (E)
30 (A) (B) (C) (D) (E)
31 (A) (B) (C) (D) (E)
32 (A) (B) (C) (D) (E)
33 (A) (B) (C) (D) (E)
34 (A) (B) (C) (D) (E)
35 (A) (B) (C) (D) (E)
36 (A) (B) (C) (D) (E)
37 (A) (B) (C) (D) (E)
38 (A) (B) (C) (D) (E)

CERTIFICATION STATEMENT

Please write the following statement below, DO NOT PRINT.

"I certify that I am the person whose name appears on this answer sheet. I also agree not to disclose the contents of the test I am taking today to anyone."

Sign and date where indicated.

SIGNATURE: _____

DATE: _____ / _____ / _____
Month   Day   Year

IF YOU DO NOT WANT THIS TEST TO BE SCORED

If you want to cancel your scores from this test administration, complete A and B below. You will not receive scores for this test; however, you will receive confirmation of this cancellation. No record of this test or the cancellation will be sent to the recipients you indicated, and there will be no scores for this test on your GRE file. Once a score is canceled, it cannot be reinstated.

To cancel your scores from this test administration, you must:

FOR ETS USE ONLY	V1R	V2R	VTR	VCS	Q1R	Q2R	QTR	QCS	A1R	A2R	ATR	ACS